# RESEARCH IN SOCIAL MOVEMENTS, CONFLICTS AND CHANGE

*Volume* 5 • 1983

# RESEARCH IN SOCIAL MOVEMENTS, CONFLICTS AND CHANGE

*A Research Annual*

*Editor*: LOUIS KRIESBERG
Department of Sociology
Syracuse University

VOLUME 5 • 1983

 JAI PRESS INC.

*Greenwich, Connecticut*                    *London, England*

# CONTENTS

# LIST OF CONTRIBUTORS

*Szymon Chodak*

Department of Sociology
Concordia University
Canada

*James A. Geschwender*

Department of Sociology
State University of New York at
Binghamton

*William Harris*

Department of Sociology
Wesleyan University

*Irving Louis Horowitz*

Department of Sociology
Livingston College
Rutgers University

*Alfred McClung Lee*

Professor Emeritus
Drew University and Brooklyn
College of the City University of
New York

*Ronald M. McCarthy*

Department of Sociology
Merrimack College

*Paul Meadows*

Department of Sociology
State University of New York at
Albany

*Pamela Oliver*

Department of Sociology
University of Wisconsin at Madison

*Karl Pillemer*

Department of Sociology
Brandis University

*C. A. Rootes*

Faculty of Social Sciences
The University of Kent at Canterbury
England

*David R. Segal*

Department of Sociology
University of Maryland

*Mady Wechsler Segal*

Department of Sociology
University of Maryland

*David Horton Smith*

Department of Sociology
Boston College

*George Thomas*

Department of Sociology
Arizona State University

*Henry Walker*

Department of Sociology
Stanford University

*Morris Zelditch, Jr.*

Department of Sociology
Stanford University

# INTRODUCTION

In the Introduction to Volume 4 of this series, I discussed what appeared to be an emerging paradigm in the contemporary analysis of conflicts, social movements, and change. The general framework or orientation was called the multiple interaction paradigm. Four ideas are particularly important in this framework. First, many actors are involved in all social conflicts, movements, and change and these actors are not all mutually exclusive, clearly bounded entities. Second, members of these entities are purposive and give meaning to their actions and the actions of others as they seek to advance what they regard as their interests. As Meadows points out in his contribution in this volume, recent theories of revolution see it as drama, as intentional action of actors. Third, the actors interact with each other in many processes; they conflict, exchange, collaborate, assimilate, compete and so on. Finally, as a resultant of these processes of interaction among the many actors, patterns are established which are experienced as constraints for future interactions. Although the actors are unequal in their abilities to shape developments, none of them is able to fully determine them. Consequently, there is a problematic quality to the outcome of any course of action as well as important regularities.

In this introduction, I will discuss three inter-connected topics, relevant to this paradigm, which will serve to link together the contributions in this volume. The topics are one set of themes among others that the reader may discover. The varied topics, approaches, and methods are brought together here in part to stimulate comparisons and reveal similarities and differences that otherwise might not be noticed and yet which are revealing and helpful to our understanding of each contribution. After discussing the themes, I will make a few observations about each article in the volume.

The topics to be discussed are: (1) that multiple actors and processes converge to produce particular events, (2) that patterns of thought emerge and guide collective conduct, and (3) that structure results from and channels interaction. The discussion of these topics and their relationship to the contributions will not only link the contributions, but will also serve to test the usefulness of the core ideas of the multiple interaction approach and to elaborate and specify it.

A fundamental emphasis in the multiple interaction approach is that many actors are engaged in every social movement, conflict, or change. These actors are not mutually exclusive, but they cross-cut each other and they enclose or are enclosed by others. For example, as Lee writes in his contribution in this volume, the current troubles in Northern Ireland involve people who think of themselves and act collectively as Nationalists, Loyalists, or British and as United Kingdom government representatives, Roman Catholics, Protestants, the Protestant Orange Order, the Provisional Irish Republican Army and many other entities.

For critical events to occur, many processes of interaction among the many actors must coincide. Social conflicts, movements and changes escalate or deescalate as forces converge in the same direction. Coalitions among several actors are formed, dissolved, and reformed. Those changes are crucial to conflict escalation and deescalation. Similarly, change within many different actors together in interaction produce social changes. For example, in analyzing the increased utilization of women in the U.S. military forces, Segal and Segal trace the interconnected changes in the military institution, population composition, and women's roles in society.

One implication of giving weight to the importance of the convergence of many factors is that such convergence indicates that every time period is historically unique. For many issues that is a valid and fundamental truth. It sets limits on our ability to generalize about social phenomena. For example, McCarthy, in this volume, examines the American movement for independence in the late 1700s and Polish Solidarity movement in the late 1900s. The difference in their development and outcomes must be understood in terms of the many differences in the world context in which the movements occurred. For example, although rivalry between superpowers in the 1970s also gave challenger to a superpower more leverage than they would otherwise have, societal autonomy was in many ways more feasible in the 1700s than in the 1900s. The similarities, given the vast differences in historical context are nevertheless striking.

The second topic pertains to collective conduct and patterns of thought. The actors and their spokespersons interpret their own actions as well as that of their adversaries, allies, and audiences. They explain and justify their conduct to themselves and others. These interpretations and justifications are also a kind of constraint since constituency rivals and followers use them as guides. The interpretations are part of general understandings and patterns of thought which are to some degree shared by many within a collectivity acting as a unit. Consequently, the shared patterns of thought are important in channeling conduct. They help shape goals—immediate and long-term. They also help in forming and selecting the means to attain the goals. Thus, the self help groups examined by Smith and Pillemer in this volume have grown in the U.S. as traditional American ways of dealing with personal problems have been modified by the movements and ideologies of the 1960s.

The patterns of thinking themselves, we must also observe, are molded by the experience of the people involved in conflicts, movements, and change. Although shared ways of thinking are collectively developed and passed on and serve as lenses through which experiences are perceived, ways of thinking are also the product of those experiences. Thus, persons differently located in the social structure will have their own experiences which modify the understandings they bring to the experience. Rootes, in his contribution in this volume, analyzes these issues and notes the different experiences and therefore views of students and faculty in universities.

Given the richness of experience and the range of thought which is shared by any large collectivity, there is room for much selectivity in interpretating events. People draw from their past experiences in order to understand and cope with the present. Sometimes this is the case in continuities in people's immediate experience. Thus, Oliver found, in her analysis reported in this volume, that neighborhood paid and volunteer movement activists of the 1970s tended to have been activists in the 1960s. The use of past experience to understand and guide conduct in the present is found more generally in the uses made of history. Interpretations of the past, why wars broke out or victories were won, are certainly selective. The interpretations then become justifications for seeking one end rather than another, or using one means rather than another. Lee's examination of the struggle in Northern Ireland documents the use of history to justify a strategy of violence rather than nonviolence.

Differently located people develop varied interpretations of the same phenomena, based upon their different experiences and interests. This is the basis for competition, contention, and collaboration among groups within every collectivity to define that collectivity and its adversaries and allies. Some of the factions within a collectivity may form a coalition and negotiate from a position of strength so that its interpretation of social phenomena is dominant. In a large collectivity, the many smaller entities within it may contend, compete, and collaborate in hidden and indirect ways. The parties in interaction develop patterns of thought about how they should relate to each other. Typically, in democratic societies, political parties compete for electoral support and for money to wage electoral campaigns. But, as Geschwender discusses in his contribution to this volume, some parties follow other strategies. One such strategy is that of the vanguard party—a party that regards itself as a combat organization providing leadership in a struggle to bring about the socialist transformation of a capitalist society. Obviously, that strategy is related to the party members' characterization of a capitalist society, their desired goals, and their expectations of the likely response of opponents to those goals.

The third topic is the relation between social structure and multiple process of interaction. There are four inter-related questions that significantly pertain to that relationship: what are the important units constituting the social structure? What is their structural relationship? How do those structures constrain and channel the processes of interaction? How is the structure of relations generated by the processes of interaction?

The multiple interaction approach does not posit particular units or social cleavages as always being the most fundamental. Which ones are particularly important shift from issue to issue and time to time. That statement unfortunately does not give any guidance about the relative importance of some social cleavages compared to others. We want to know which cleavages will become important to people and serve to organize their lives. We want to know the likelihood of different cleavages emerging into social awareness and being used in mobilizing people for conflicts, movements, or change. Two qualities are particularly important in these regards: the primordial and pervasive character of the cleavages.

By primordial, I mean those identities and qualities which are learned early in socialization and are deeply inculcated. These include gender, ethnicity, religion, and perhaps other status attributes. Pervasiveness refers to the extent to which a particular cleavage affects other possible cleavages or aspects of social life. Thus, class and power differences affect so many aspects of life that it is hard to imagine that people would be indifferent to their places in class or power hierarchies.

For entities based on certain kinds of cleavages, their relationship is inherent in the cleavage. Thus, entities based upon power differences are related in a superordinate and subordinate fashion. Even if this is not inherent, however such hierarchical relations are a fundamental characteristic of the relationship among entities, for example, ones based upon ethnicity. The ordering of entities in terms of power and their relative control of resources is undoubtedly a widespread and important aspect of social structure within and between collectivities. This ordering is relevant for decisions and actions of each such collectivity in so far as its conduct is directed by another in two ways. First, the actions of members of one collectivity may be dominated by another in an adversarial sense as when one group struggles with another over resources which are to be divided between them. Second, the two or more entities may be engaged in making decisions which affect them jointly; such collective decisions may have some allocative dimensions, but they can also be viewed as entailing mutually shared losses or gains.

In any hierarchical relationship, the ability of the dominant group to gain relatively in allocative decisions or to influence collective decisions is significantly affected by the legitimacy of that relationship in the minds of the parties involved. With legitimacy well entrenched, many issues may not even be considered to require decisions. Such nondecisions are a reflection of and sustain the legitimate order. Zelditch and his associates, in their contribution, conclude that "the acceptance of a normative order by some suffices to mobilize collective resources behind its enforcement on those who do not accept it."

In large-scale collectivities, such as societies, social structures are embodied in organizations. The existence of organizations, with their internal means of control and division of labor, enable those in leading organizational positions to wield great power *over* others or *with* others in making collective decisions. It is the existence of such organizations in societies that give persons in government and in the military so much ability to influence the course of developments in their societies. The organizations themselves, however, are constraining and channeling of change as the members have diverse interests and views which they seek to advance. Chodak in his contributions about etatization in advanced industrial societies discusses shared trends in the working out of state activities.

Organizations and power relations, like many other aspects of the social structure, are in many ways the residue of past struggles, developments, and movements. Thus, the social structure may be seen as generated by the multiple interactions of many entities. Thus, in Oliver's contribution we can see some of the ways the neighborhood movements of the 1970s follow from the movements of the 1960s. Horowitz's analysis, also in this volume, examines the importance of the military organizations in third world countries. That importance is a resultant of the struggles of some of those countries for independence and the location of those countries in a world characterized by military rivalry between world superpowers.

The discussion of multiple actors, patterns of thought, and social structures illustrate one way in which the diverse papers in this volume can be linked together. The discussion also indicates that the multiple interaction paradigm as outlined in the outset is broad enough to be relevant to at least some aspects of a wide variety of contemporary work in social movements, conflicts, and change. Hopefully it also indicates that it is focussed enough to illuminate important issues and to suggest critical avenues for further exploration. I will now introduce each contribution, in sequence, with less regard to commonalities.

Zelditch, Harris, Thomas, and Walker have created a laboratory experiment that has enabled them to test hypotheses derived from Bachrach and Baratz's theorizing about nondecisions. In doing so, they have contributed to our understanding about the existence of unrecognized issues, the sources of legitimacy, and the way in which a power structure can result in not deciding about an issue. These are fundamental questions in the study of social conflicts and social change. Does an underlying conflict exist, aside from the awareness of adversaries? Does the existence of a power structure result in the nonconsideration of issues about changing the power structure? What are the sources of legitimacy for a power structure? The laboratory experiment, by changing some conditions and not others allows the experimentors to disentangle properties of situations in ways that are not possible in the full complexity of more natural settings. For example, the authors were able to conclude that change was prevented or delayed "if the existing system of inequality was justified by a legitimate source, if an issue would clearly damage legitimate objectives, if change was politically impossible, if peers endorsed the existing system, if authorized powers preferred it, or even if the preferences of such powers were uncertain, but they could do serious damage."

Rootes, too discusses the relationship between objective or underlying conflict conditions and subjective awareness of the conflict by the adversaries. His approach, however, is different. He draws on the theories of Marx and Mannheim to consider how it is that variously situated categories of people develop diverse views of their situation. He points out that not only are there differences in interest related to people being variously located, but the resulting diversity in perspectives and orientations exacerbate the conflicts of interest. These points are illustrated by considering the diverse perspectives of various categories of people within a university organization.

Meadows provides us with a taxonomy, not of revolutions, but of theories about revolutions. In doing so he broadens our range of fundamental assumptions. His taxonomy is based on the dimension of time in relationship to revolutions. He discusses the changes from an ontological perspective prior to the French Revolution to theories oriented to history in the 19th Century and then to the instrumental or dramatistic perspective of the 20th Century. He argues that contemporary writers view the actors in revolutions as independent makers of history. He makes clear how this perspective, natural as it seems to us, is not the only possible one.

McCarthy explores the conditions under which social movements attempting to prevent undesired changes may be transformed into agents for the development of new and renewed institutions. He examines and compares two non-violent resistance movements: the American Independence Movement of 1765–1775 and the Polish resistance movements of 1956–1981. He concentrates his discussion around two propositions. First, that continuing inability to repress the resistance movement leads to its institutional development. Second, that the resistance movements' response to the repression leads to high priority to defense of their continued existence. The analysis reveals the importance of the social structure in channeling interaction and outcomes and also the indeterminacy of contentious interaction.

Lee provides us with an analysis of a particular case of struggle—the current troubles in Northern Ireland. He examines the interaction of many actors, illuminating how violence generates violence. He usefully examines the efforts of nonviolent struggle and how those efforts broke down. Violence, however, has not been any more effective for the partisans than was nonviolent means. Lee locates the current struggle in history. But his interest in history is different from Meadows'. Lee points out how history is selectively drawn upon to give meaning and significance to the roles of the current actors.

Oliver presents a systematic comparison of paid and volunteer activists in neighborhood movement organizations. Her study integrates commitment and collective action models, with their differing suggestions about the extent of similarities between paid and volunteer activists. Oliver found no evidence that salary was an alternative or supplemental motivation for social movement action; the paid activists are especially committed and experienced. Such detailed studies of particular movements reveal that each is not isolated from others or from history. Movements, like conflicts, interlock in a continuing chain. The neighborhood movements of the 1970s are linked to the movements of the 1960s. Such linkages are significant for the mobilization of people and in the justifications for the strategies to be followed. This is illustrated, too in the analyses of the struggles in Northern Ireland, Poland, and the American Independence Movement.

Geschwender's analysis of a vangard party suggests how ideology shapes and is shaped by organizations and how historical experience instructs organizational leaders by revealing what has not succeeded. Geschwender provides a case study of a vanguard party, the Revolutionary Communist Party and the struggle over land use in the Waiahole and Waikane valleys in Hawaii. After discussing the characteristics of vanguard parties and the Waiahole-Waikane struggles, Geschwender argues that much of the success of the struggles were attributable to the vanguard characteristics of the RCP.

Smith and Pillemer provide a survey of the literature about the increasingly important self-help groups. They define a self-help group as "a voluntary group valuing personal interaction and mutual aid as a means of altering or ameliorating problems perceived as alterable, pressing, and personal by most of its participants." They discuss how the internal processes of such groups are presumed to be related to personal change, e.g. how the person giving help benefits from playing that role. The emphasis is upon experiential knowledge among members, rather than professional expertise, and sometimes this constitutes a challenge to professional providers of service. Furthermore, to some extent the organizations are even part of a social movement helping to create informal social support systems. They discuss, too, variations in the social change orientation of self-help groups.

Segal and Segal analyse the increase in women's representation in the U.S. military forces in the 1970s. They account for this in terms of the convergence of three sets of factors: first, changes in the military institution—its technology, mission, and reliance on volunteers; second, the bursting of the baby-boom bubble, and third, the changing roles of women in the society. Their discussion makes us aware that a change is not undirectional, as they point out the opposition and limits to women's representation. The variations over time and among different branches of the military forces makes it possible to consider the relative role of the many factors effecting women's representation in the military forces.

Chodak describes what he regards to be a pervasive contemporary trend: the increase in etatization. Etatization refers the emergence of societal systems that are highly controlled and regulated by the state. He argues that "the state is evolving towards a new type of existence. It is in the process of superceding society." One might see the self-help groups described by Smith and Pillemer as a kind of reaction, at the interpersonal level, to such a development. Some of the other contributions in this volume, by attending to revolutions, point out other kinds of reactions to and variations in etatization. Chodak also examines variations in the degree of etatization among societies of Europe, but he stresses the commonalities indicating that this is an inevitable developmental change.

Finally, Horowitz discusses Third World countries, arguing that they are moving toward broad-based democratization. He sees this democratization emerging although other observers contend that it is constrained by the generally dominant military forces in Third World countries. He applies the paradigm of C. Wright Mills, stressing the importance of large-scale factors: economic, political, and military, analyzing their relative importance in developed capitalist, Communist-dominated, and Third World countries, respectively. He stresses the military origin of Third World social structures and that the very definition and nature of their independence is symbolized by their own militarization.

Clearly, the contributors in this volume, whatever the degree to which they share the multiple interaction orientation, do not share substantive questions. Nor do they share beliefs about the directions of major changes of the effective ways to bring about change or waging conflicts. Perhaps relatedly, they do not seem to share the same value priorities. The relationship between questions, beliefs, values, and policy are important to consider in comparing analyses of social movements, conflicts and change. There are different policy implications of the contributions by Geschwender, McCarthy, and Lee and of Horowitz and Chodak. Consideration of issues relating to values and policy, however, go beyond the bounds of this introduction.

As for past volumes, many persons have helped in the editing by reviewing the contributions. For this volume, I want to thank the following persons for their thoughtful critiques of manuscripts: Michael Barkun, Lewis Coser, Peter Dreier, James Fendrich, Kurt Lang, Allan Mazur, John Nagle, Richard Ratcliff, Gunter Remmling, Roger Sharp, Gary Spencer, Neil Smelser, Dale Tussing, Paul Wehr, and George Zito.

# DECISIONS, NONDECISIONS, AND METADECISIONS

Morris Zelditch, Jr., William Harris,

George M. Thomas and Henry A. Walker

## I. INTRODUCTION

The controversy over community power was wearing thin in the early sixties when Bachrach and Baratz seemed to breathe new life into the subject with two classic papers on "nondecisionmaking" (1962; 1963). Like Dahl (1958), Bachrach and Baratz objected to "the sociological method" of studying community power—making inferences from positions, resources, or reputations; but they also objected to any alternative founded on the observations of contested decisions. They based their objection on the fact that making a decision is only one stage in the process by which policy is formed. Observing decisions, they conceded that one discovers a pluralist politics. But, they argued, no theory of power is com-

Research in Social Movements, Conflicts and Change, Vol. 5, pages 1–32.

1

plete that does not study predecision politics in which issues are identified, alternative courses of action defined, and agendas decided. Many factors that are not problematic at the decision stage are of fundamental importance in predecision politics, such as the legitimacy of issues, actors, and tactics. They did not argue that predecision politics were in any way theoretically distinct: their argument rested, in fact, on the unity of the policy process. It is this unity that gives significance to the central "fact" that in their view called for explanation: by the time an agenda is decided only "safe" issues remain, issues that do not challenge a society's existing system of inequalities, the mechanisms through which unequal benefits and burdens are allocated, or the values, beliefs, rules, practices, and procedures on which these inequalities are based. "Important" issues, meaning redistributive issues, are not observed at the decision stage of the process because predecision politics operate to suppress them. Observing the predecision process, what one finds, they insisted, is that the politics of "important" issues is elitist. It was the process that operates to suppress "important" issues to which they referred by the term "nondecisionmaking." The mechanisms of this process were basically two: One founded on (a largely potential) power that, though not visibly exercised, operated to suppress issues through a "law of anticipated reactions" (Friedrich, 1963); the other founded on the "mobilization of bias" (Schattschneider, 1960), that is, the operation of the legitimating values, beliefs, rules, practices and procedures of a society, which they assumed to be indissolubly linked with power. The combined effect of these two mechanisms gave to the basic institutional and social structure of a society a central part to play in shaping its political agenda.

On the main points, Bachrach and Baratz seemed unrebuttable: That decisionmaking was only one stage of the policy process, that no theory of power is complete that does not take into account predecision politics, that many questions that had not seemed problematic for a theory of decisionmaking were important, such as the legitimacy of issues, actors, and tactics. But "nondecisions" posed a nasty problem of method: they are the undecided issues of a polity but there are an infinite number of things a polity does not decide, only some of which are suppressed issues. The others were never issues to begin with. The problem was to distinguish the nonissue from the suppressed issue. Bachrach and Baratz provided no independent test of issueness, that is, of the intensity and/or scope of a population's preferences for change, hence could not empirically identify nondecisions. (See Frey, 1971; McFarland, 1969; Merelman, 1968; Wolfinger, 1971). There the subject seemed to stick: Frey (1971) and Bachrach and Bartz themselves (1970) tried solving the problem, without much success. McFarland (1969) recognized fairly quickly that comparison provided an independent criterion of issueness and his solution was quickly and brilliantly applied by Crenson (1971). But the complexity and multicolinearity of the variables correlated with the "objective" causes of issueness, together with problems of cross—level inferences about issueness from aggregate measures and about dynamics of the process from cross–sectional analysis left serious problems of internal validity unsolved. (Cf. Polsby, 1980, ch. 11).

The new vitality that nondecisionmaking had seemed to breathe into the study of power quickly began to flag as tedious, tiresome controversy over Bachrach and Baratz's methods displaced the earlier controversy over "sociological" methods. The study of agendas, as a matter of fact, flourished—but at the expense of the framework and the problem to which Bachrach and Baratz had directed it. Behaviorists, the dominating force in empirically–oriented political science, made up for their earlier neglect of the subject by vigorous and systematic investigation of agendas (for example, see Braybrooke, 1974; Jones 1977, chs. 3–4; the first three papers in May and Wildavsky, 1978; Polsby, 1971; Walker, 1977). Important books on the subject, like Cobb and Elder's *Participation in American Politics* (1972), were widely read, cited, and discussed. Agendas had a major impact on the study of international relations (see Keohane and Nye, 1977, who apply them brilliantly). They even became the centerpiece of a new "paradigm" of global politics (Mansbach and Vasquez, 1981). But the study of agendas, however fruitful, is not the study of the politics of the suppression of issues. The controversy over the "suppression" of issues itself quickly took on the irreconcilable character of a quarrel over foundation questions—over logics of observation and inference, the empirical status of theoretical unobservables, and basic conceptualizations of the nature of man and society. Like most such quarrels it generated a great deal of heat but very little light. By 1975 it seemed to achieve stalemate: Debnam (1975) insisted not only that propositions about nondecisions were untestable but that the concepts and methods of the theory were obscure and superfluous. Bachrach and Baratz (1975) replied that their theory was being assessed by the wrong kinds of criteria and came close to saying that it was good in itself, testable or not. Lukes (1975), from a quite different perspective, argued that Bachrach and Baratz had not gone far enough in exploiting false consciousness, having yielded too much to the behaviorists. Reviewing Lukes' book, Baratz (1977) turned over much the same ground already thoroughly plowed in the early sixties. Meanwhile, very little research was being done. One can count four not very compelling case studies—Bachrach and Baratz, 1970; Bachrach and Bergman, 1973; Molotch, 1970, and an earlier precursor, Vidich and Bensman, 1958—and only two serious, systematic investigations (Crenson, 1971; Smith, 1979).

As a result, it came to be fairly widely agreed that although Bachrach and Baratz had had some insights of permanent value, their theory fell far short of its original promise. But this was not due to any overwhelming evidence against it, or in favor of some alternative. It was due partly to criticism of their value–laden, imprecise, and circular language, partly to criticism of their methods of observation and inference, but most importantly to criticism of the strategy that lay behind their theory. It was felt in some quarters at least that even if their difficulties in theory construction and method were remedied, their hypotheses would still be untestable because they rested on assumptions about materialism, individual self–interest, and the nature (and objectivity) of conflict that were *irremediably* untestable.

In one sense this was true: One cannot test assumptions about the universality of two–person, 0–sum conflict unless one is willing to give up false consciousness as a convenient escape; one cannot test assumptions about the objectivity of conflict without begging the question; one cannot test highly general axioms about individual self–interest—they are purely tautological, asserting no more than "people prefer to do what they prefer to do." At this level, conflict theory is irremediably untestable. But the same is true of every alternative strategy with which one might replace it. It is as true of behaviorism (or functionalism, or phenomenology, or ecology), for example, as "conflict theory." What must be shown is not only that Bachrach and Baratz rest their theory on an irremediably untestable strategy but that they offer nothing else. But this seems to us too strong a claim. All the criticisms of Bachrach and Baratz could be true—as a matter of fact, in our view they are—and it could still be argued that they are remediable, and if remedied that Bachrach and Baratz have some testable hypotheses. It is this view that we take in the present paper. This does not mean that we claim their theory is true; what we claim, rather, is that the theory is corrigible.

Accordingly, our purpose in the present paper is to isolate a core of testable theory in Bachrach and Baratz's several works. To accomplish this purpose, in Part II we explicate the terms of their theory, rendering them more precise and removing the causal assumptions built into them that make them circular, and provide a method of observation and inference that makes the propositions built up from these terms testable. In Part III, we construct a specific technique based on this method of observation and inference that meets the strictest possible standards of internal validity and employ it to test a number of hypotheses implied in the theory.

## II.  AN EXPLICATION OF BACHRACH AND BARATZ

The objectives of Part II are to render the terms of Bachrach and Baratz's theory more precise and provide an independent test of issueness that will render a theory using them testable. Section A describes their theory and the strategy underlying it; Section B briefly describes the most common objections to it; Section C explicates the central terms of the theory and a criterion of issueness that permits their operationalization.

### A.  *Bachrach and Baratz's Theory*

The strategy that underlies Bachrach and Baratz's theory is founded on two–person, constant–sum conflict. All actors in the theory are rational and driven solely by self–interest. All benefits (all resources and rewards) are "biased", that is, unequally distributed; all structures of domination are "biased", that is, participation in them is unequally distributed; and the two kinds of bias are perfectly correlated. Because of the conflict assumption, any system can be completely described by the relations between two actors: we will call them A (who benefits) and B (who does not). The theory characterizes A and B by their location in the system of bias. Because actors are rationally self–interested and the distribution of benefits is biased, the only question to be settled is why B does not attempt to challenge the existing system of inequalities. One can assume the motives of the have–nots. Challenge can, therefore, be taken for granted whether actually observed or not. All questions addressed by their theory are therefore framed in terms of what delays or prevents change. The principal focus of the theory is on the behavior of A. However, because A obviously never challenges his own position, the behavior of A on which the theory focuses is entirely reactive. B, on the other hand, is both proactor and reactor. B initiates; A reacts, B then reacts to A's reactions.

The society of which A and B are the (only) two parts is characterized by the distribution of benefits among members, the manner (the mechanisms) in which such benefits are allocated, and the values, beliefs, rules, practices and procedures that create and maintain these mechanisms. The polity of this society consists of some authoritative procedure by which collective decisions are made and one or more interests with legitimate access to this authoritative procedure (hence "members" of the polity). This polity is both small and unrepresentative, hence also "biased" (from Schattschneider, 1960), and the bias of the polity correlates perfectly with the biased distribution of benefits. All members of the polity are A's; no B's are members.

The policy made by this polity is the outcome of a complex formative process. A simplification of Bachrach and Baratz's conception of this process is shown in Figure 1a. The omitted details are largely irrelevant and this simplification is in much the same spirit as theirs (cf. 1970, ch. 4, particularly their Figure 2). The crux of this process is still the decision stage, at which a collective choice is made among alternative possible joint policies. But it is extended both backwards and forwards: there is a *predecision* stage, in which actors are deciding just what it is that they will decide, and a *postdecision* stage in which policy is implemented. At any stage, a polity may either do something or nothing with any particular issue. At the predecision stage, for example, the polity may decide that an issue must be decided and formulate possible policies, say x, or y, between which it will decide; or it may *not* recognize an issue, or not consider it political, or not consider x or y among its policies. If it decides to decide between x and y, the policies x and y are the polity's *agenda*. If some policy, say x, is a challenge, and can reasonably be said to exist whether it is on the polity's agenda or not, it is assumed by the theory to be suppressed if it is not on the agenda. Such suppressed issues are called *nondecisions*.

At different times, Bachrach and Baratz have defined nondecisions as the

*Figure 1.*  The Policy Process, Showing Nondecision Outcomes

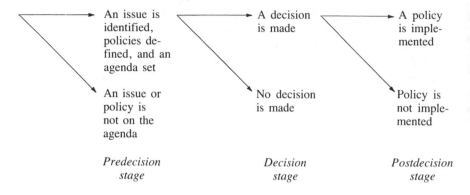

| | | |
|---|---|---|
| An issue is identified, policies defined, and an agenda set | A decision is made | A policy is implemented |
| An issue or policy is not on the agenda | No decision is made | Policy is not implemented |
| *Predecision stage* | *Decision stage* | *Postdecision stage* |

*Figure 1a.*  The Principal Stages of the Policy Process

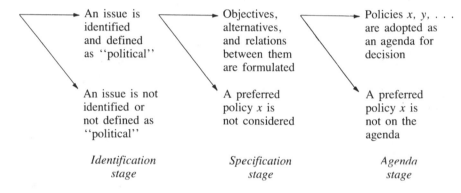

| | | |
|---|---|---|
| An issue is identified and defined as "political" | Objectives, alternatives, and relations between them are formulated | Policies *x, y, . . .* are adopted as an agenda for decision |
| An issue is not identified or not defined as "political" | A preferred policy *x* is not considered | A preferred policy *x* is not on the agenda |
| *Identification stage* | *Specification stage* | *Agenda stage* |

*Figure 1b.*  The Stages of Predecision Politics

"mobilization of bias" in the interest of suppressing issues that threaten the status quo (1962), as keeping issues covert through the mobilization of bias, or the use of force or power (1963), or as a decision by A that thwarts challenge by B (1970).[1] They can occur at any stage of the process: Issues are most easily suppressed before they reach the decision stage, but they can be suppressed at the decision stage by tabling them, referring to committee, or prioritizing them into legislative oblivion; and they can be suppressed at the postdecision stage either by not implementing policy at all, or by using the discretionary powers of the public bureaucracy to reshape intended policy in A's interests.

Bachrach and Baratz give their greatest attention to predecision politics. Figure 1b shows this process in more detail. They distinguish (as many others do) a recognition or identification stage, in which some feature of a society or its situation is recognized as a "problem" that is defined as "political", that is, something about which the polity can and should do something; a stage in which this "issue" is specified, that is, alternative courses of action defined, objectives of such action identified, and the relation between alternatives and objectives established; and finally, a stage in which some of these possible policies are made part of the formal agenda of the polity. An alternative preferred by none is not, in Bachrach and Baratz's view, a nondecision. But any alternative preferred by B to any on the agenda has obviously been nondecided. Again, this can occur at any stage of predecision politics: It can mean not recognizing a problem that exists, or defining it as private; not identifying an alternative that is actually preferred, or not making an issue (or a preferred alternative) part of the polity's agenda for decision.

Thus, at any stage of a rather complex policy process an issue can be either suppressed or reshaped. In accounting for the fate of an issue, Bachrach and Baratz throughout think of predecision politics as an interactive outcome of the dual mobilization of actors A and B. The principal behavior of A is the "mobilization of bias." The mobilization of bias consists of three kinds of behavior: making rules, reinforcing rules, and invoking rules. It is assumed that rules made by the polity are biased, in fact that *all* rules are biased, benefiting some more than others. Rules are, in fact, assumed to be purely instruments of power and it is purely power that makes them. Because "power" in this particular sense means membership in the polity, and it is in the interests of the polity's members that the rules are made, the bias of the rules is perfectly correlated with the bias of the larger system of stratification. A, therefore, finds it always in his interest to reinforce the existing values, beliefs, rules, practices, and procedures of society which create and maintain this system and the "mobilization of bias" is in fact the normal routine behavior of any society. Although A thus acts to reinforce the rules at all times, whether or not there is any immediate and concrete reason for doing so, the making and invoking of rules depends on what kinds of issues arise in the policy process.

Issues are characterized by Bachrach and Baratz in terms of their consequences for the existing system of bias. It is redistributive issues, that is, challenges to the existing system of bias that precipitate the mobilization of the values, beliefs, rules, practices, and procedures of the society so as to delay or prevent such challenges from ever reaching the polity's agenda. In particular, emergence of a new kind of actor claiming legitimate access to the polity is a challenge resisted by the mobilization of bias—one of the most important properties of the polity is its proficiency in maintaining its boundaries against encroachment by nonmembers.

The principal behavior of B, of course, is challenge. At each stage of the policy process, B either does or does not recognize an issue, does or does not express his views if he does recognize it, and is or is not mobilized—in the resource–mobilization sense—to accomplish his objectives. Three factors determine B's behavior: first, the level of resources available to B; second, the extent of B's dependence on A and vulnerability to sanctions controlled by him; and third, the legitimacy of B as a political actor and of the tactics available to B. In particular, what the mobilization of bias does from B's point of view is to define B's issue as criminal or subversive, delegitimate B as a political actor, and make the tactics available to him illegitimate.

The aggregate outcome of the A and the B processes is a self–maintaining system of bias. At the aggregate level, the principal variable is simply the likelihood that an issue or policy is in fact decided. One factor in this is issueness—the intensity and scope of preferences for some alternative to the existing policy of a polity. Issueness arises out of the existing bias of the distribution of benefits. But both the existence and the mobilization of bias operate to counteract the effect that the issueness of bias causes. Bias in the distribution of resources decreases the likelihood of mobilization for collective action and increases B's dependence on, and vulnerability to sanctions controlled by, A. Hence, challenge does not arise in the first instance because B does not have the resources required to mount it and even if he did the power–dependence relation between A and B would operate to produce compliance by B with easily anticipated negative reactions by A. If a challenge does emerge, A possesses the authority to invoke (or if necessary make) values, beliefs, rules, practices and procedures that define the challenge as crime or subversion, the challenger as an outsider, the challenger's tactics as unwarranted; and, if necessary, they justify forceful oppression.

The concrete details of the nondecisionmaking process depend on the particular stage of the policy process at which it operates. At the identification stage of the process, the myths and institutional practices of the society make most challenges (literally) unthinkable. The status quo, in a Berger–Luckmann–like world, acquires a facticity that removes it from the world of human creations and hence from a world of things which a polity can or should change. If B does come to recognize an issue, he is still not likely to voice his preferences because existing procedural rules and institutional practices deprive him of access to the polity; he is vulnerable to the negative reactions he anticipates from A, and lacks resources to make protest effective. The same, of course, is true for any B: Hence, any one B must also be uncertain of support by others in the same position as he is, and therefore view the prospects for collective action as at best uncertain, at worst poor. If B does voice his views, the fact that B lacks legitimate access to the polity makes him vulnerable to mobilization of bias by A, which in turn makes it legitimate for the state, in A's interests, to oppress B by force if he persists in doing so. At the specification stage of the process, an issue may be recognized, but all the same factors operate to suppress the most threatening possible solutions, or reshape the issue so that only "safe" solutions are considered. At the agenda stage of the process, the chief importance of the mobilization of bias lies in the decisive control it gives to A of the agenda procedure itself. A has the legitimate right to use this power to decide that an issue is not to be decided. B, who has no such powers, has no redress; or, more exactly, can seek redress only from A. (There are no disinterested agents of authority in Bachrach and Baratz's world.) Thus, the process is hermetically sealed unless some exogenous force disrupts it: The values, beliefs, rules, practices and procedures of society create and maintain the mechanisms through which benefits are allocated; these mechanisms create, and subsequently operate to reproduce, the existing distribution of benefits; the existing distribution of benefits creates the interests that motivate the making, reinforcing, and invoking of rules that operate to maintain the existing mechanisms of allocation, hence the existing distribution of benefits.

## B. Criticisms of Bachrach and Baratz's Theory

Criticisms of Bachrach and Baratz's theory are of three kinds: criticisms of the way it defines its central terms, of the conflict assumptions underlying them, and their operationalization, hence testability.

The criticisms of its central terms, and particularly of "nondecisions," are legion: they are value–loaded, imprecise, ambiguous, circular. Bachrach and Baratz define words after the fashion of Samuel Johnson, whose dictionary, for example, defined an excise tax as a "hateful tax . . . levied by wretches." They have a predilection for rich, evocative language that not only stretches the word "bias" to cover virtually every feature of institutional and social structure, but also uses "nondecision" ambiguously to refer sometimes to an event (a decision intended to suppress an issue), sometimes to an outcome (the issue suppressed), and sometimes to a process (nondecisionmaking as distinct from nondecision). (See particularly Bachrach and Baratz, 1970 and their discussion of Debnam's "errors of interpretation" in Bachrach and Baratz, 1975.) The confusion of meaning is exaggerated by the kind of primitive terms used to define nondecisions: it is defined by other terms, like "the mobilization of bias," or the "importance" of issues that are as much in need of explication as nondecision itself. (Frey, 1971; McFarland, 1969; Wolfinger, 1971). They also have a predilection for condensing whole theories in a word. To *define* nondecision as the mobilization of bias in the interest of suppressing issues that threaten the status quo, or as keeping an issue covert by using bias, power, or force, or as a decision that suppresses issues that threaten the interests of decision–makers makes any theory using the term circular. In two cases the effect is defined by its causes; in one the cause is defined by its effects. (The same difficulty afflicts Frey's otherwise very intelligent defense and reformulation of Bachrach and Baratz— see Frey, 1971. He ends with a definition in terms of power both as cause and criterion of suppressed issues.)

Many objections to the terms of the theory have been not so much to circularity itself, however, as to the kind of theory implicit in the causes (or effects) condensed in them: that all conflicts are two–person, constant–sum conflicts, that group decisionmaking can be thought of as dyadic interpersonal power, that the behavior of any polity is completely driven by pure self–interest. There are no disinterested parties, no group interest, and the interests of the parties at conflict are always diametrically opposed. To the extent that one takes these claims not as tautological axioms of a strategy but as matters of empirical fact, critics have not been willing to accept them as realistic depictions of communities, objecting that there may be more than two interests and some people may be indifferent (Merelman, 1968). Nor have they been willing to accept the assumption that the mobilization of bias depends purely on self–interest (Merelman, 1968; Wolfinger, 1971). And objections to dyadic conceptions of the polity have of course been common (cf. Lehman, 1969 or Nagel, 1975). It would be equally unrealistic to assume there is *no* conflict in a community. But the two extremes are not the only possibilities: a conflict with n parties (n > 2) and a mixture of competitive and cooperative motives is probably more realistic than either perfect conflict or perfect consensus.

But the most serious objections to the concept of "nondecisions" have had to do with testability. Because there are an infinite number of things a polity does not decide, a testable theory of nondecisions must provide some line of demarcation between the suppressed issue and the nonissue—the matter in which no one has an interest. This requires a definition of "issue" that is independent both of the position of an issue in the decision process and its eventual fate. Neither of Bachrach and Baratz's methods of observation and inference satisfy this requirement. They rely on inferring the interests of members of a polity either from its distribution of benefits, or from its system of values, beliefs, rules, practices, and procedures. The first method relies heavily on the ability of an outside, objective observer to validly infer the value of benefits to members. Use of the method has led, in Frey's view for example, to the foundering of the whole subject on conflicts over implicit and contestable value judgments (Frey, 1971). The second method is problematic because it is no simple matter to assess the norms and values of a society, and in any case it begs the question to assume they are equivalent to the interests of members. The strongest objections of all have been to the assumption that if these methods do not yield conclusions consistent with the behavior of the members of a polity this is explained by false consciousness, itself a form of nondecision. Except for Lukes (1975), who thinks Bachrach and Baratz do not rely on it enough, false consciousness has been rejected by almost everyone as untestable in principle.

## C. *Explication of the central terms in Bachrach and Baratz's Theory*

Our purpose is to render the terms in Bachrach and Baratz's theory more precise, and to rid them of pejorative evaluations and the appeal to causes and effects that makes them circular. To accomplish the required definitions, we assume quite conventional concepts of what a *decision* is, that is, *a choice among alternatives,* and what a *collective* decision is, that is an *authoritative* decision, however arrived at, that binds all members of a group, independent of their individual preferences. (Collective decisions, for our purposes, can be made by any kind of mechanism whatever—dictatorship, committee, majority vote, unanimous consensus, or any other binding procedure.) The set of all issues to be decided by this procedure is the group's political *agenda*. The simplest agenda consists of one issue, and the simplest issue consists of one set of mutually exclusive, independent alternatives. Thus simple agendas can be completely described by the set of alternatives, or *policies,* among which the group will decide. A more complex issue is a composite of several independently decidable simple issues. In this case, the idea of an agenda requires the additional notion that some order is imposed on the several subissues, that is, they are to be taken up in some predetermined sequence. However, this idea, which is central in studies of the effects the agenda has on the outcomes of collective decisionmaking (Cohen, et al., 1978; Fiorina and Plott, 1978; Levine and Plott, 1977; Plott and Levine, 1978; Plott and Rogerson, 1979) plays no role in our attempt to explicate Bachrach and Baratz. Actual agendas, of course, will often consist of more than one issue, again in some order that is irrelevant for present purposes.

The agenda is merely one stage in the process by which a group decides on a policy. We take the simplified variant of Bachrach and Baratz's model of the policy process in Figures 1a and 1b to adequately describe the stages in the process as a whole. The "stages" of this model are not necessarily temporally distinct. They are simply analytic distinctions referring to various aspects of the process and arranged in logical order—logical in the sense that one cannot specify an issue one has not recognized, cannot decide an issue one has not decided to decide, and so on. But all of them could occur almost instantaneously, from a temporal point of view, and any stage can be retraced any number of times once the process begins. All that part of the process that ends in an agenda we will refer to as the *metadecision* stage of the process, that is, the stage in which decisions are made about decisions; deciding what to decide is what predecision politics is essentially about.

The progress of an issue to decision, described by Figure 1, begins with the recognition that something is a "problem" about which the group, as a group, should do something. To decide what might be done requires specification of the issue, that is, conceiving alternative solutions, their possible outcomes, and the relations between these two. The agenda selects some (at least) of the possible policies as the "issue" that must be decided, and it is this issue as defined by the agenda that is in fact the framework for collective decision. The elements that survive at each stage of the process form, in a sense, its positive outcomes. At this point, like Bachrach and Baratz, we require some idea of issueness if we are to define the meaning of its negative outcomes. We take the liberty of presuming a solution exists to the question of what makes some state of affairs an issue, a question dealt with (at length) below. If we assume we have something we know to be an issue, obviously the simplest way to define a nondecision is to recognize that at any stage of the process (including the decision stage) there is always the possibility of doing nothing (cf. Dahl, 1957, p. 209). At the identification stage an issue may simply not be recognized, or it may be seen as only a private matter. At the specification stage some alternative may simply not be considered. At the agenda stage agenda gatekeepers may decide not to decide an issue, or what comes to the same thing, may simply not decide to decide it. Thus:

*Definition 1.* A *nondecision* is any outcome of a metadecision process such that
1.   there is an issue in the polity, that
2.   the polity has not decided to decide.

We call attention again to the fact that there are two ways that a nondecision can occur. A group can actually decide not to decide an issue. Or it can simply not decide to decide it. In the latter case, there may be no visible decision to point to as a nondecision, but providing the first part of the definition is satisfied, that is, the issue meets some standard (to be provided below) of issueness, then it makes no difference whether or not an explicit decision is made to not consider the issue. Most of the special features of the metadecisionmaking process arise from this fact.

The definition of a nondecision obviously depends for its usefulness on a definition of the term "issue." The definition of "issue" is complicated by shifts that tend to occur in the sense of the term at different stages of the policy process. At the earliest stage of the process, when what is in question is recognition of the issue, the term will often be used to mean that someone has identified a "problem" that they feel calls for group decision. The word "problem," in turn, will usually mean that there is some disparity between an existing state of affairs and some person's preferences. The problem may be quite vaguely defined, the person recognizing it having little idea what might be done about it, hence what alternatives an agenda might consider. As the "problem" comes to be defined, that is, the issue comes to be specified further, it will acquire much greater definition: Alternative courses of action will be conceived, their outcomes identified, information will be sought (and some will be provided) about the relation between each alternative and the various possible outcomes of a decision. Possibly, though not necessarily, people will acquire some goals or objectives in terms of which they can decide which alternatives are preferred; in any case, they will form preferences for the various alternatives based on preferences for the outcomes to which they are relevant. In this stage, the word "issue" tends to mean "controversy," that is, a matter with respect to which different people have different preference orders for different possible policies. In both senses of the word, it is usually assumed that the issue has not yet been authoritatively decided; even if one disagrees with the outcome of a collective decision, one does not refer to it as still an "issue" unless one does not accept the decision as authoritative. To create an "issue," it will also be necessary that policies ordered by the members are mutually exclusive. If they are not, obviously no choice is required.

In order to define an "issue," therefore, one must be able to characterize people by their preference–ordering for different policies. One can think of such preference orders in more or less the usual way: the outcomes of each possible policy must have some kind of value for people affected by them that induces a preference order on the outcomes; the preference order on the outcomes, in turn, induces one on the alternatives linked to them. (We can neglect the probabilistic case because it affects only the kind of decision rule employed, which is irrelevant to defining an issue for present purposes.) To define the difference between two such preference orders we obviously require some notion of their similarity. We will say that two preference orders are the same if and only if they are made up of the same policies in the same order. This implies, for example, not only that $x > y > z$ is different from $x < y < z$, it is also different from $x > y$. Thus, it is sufficient to make nuclear arms policy an issue if one segment of the community prefers unilateral nuclear disarmament while another does not even consider the alternative a possibility to be debated. Indifference among alternatives we will count as a preference order that is consistent with every other preference order—hence, raises no issue. However, this way of thinking about the difference between two preference orders does not require that every alternative be well–defined. For example, $x > \bar{x}$ is a different preference order from $x < \bar{x}$, without $\bar{x}$ having to be a well–defined policy in the minds of the actor. Thus, the desire for something, anything different from present policy is a meaningfully different preference order. This will be true even if every member of the polity shares the same preference order. The difference that makes an "issue" is, in this case, the difference between $x > \bar{x}$, implicit in the existing policy $x$, and the order $\bar{x} > x$ preferred by dissenting members of the polity. We will therefore define an issue as:[2]

*Definition 2.* A present (or prospective) state of affairs is an *issue* in a polity if and only if
1.  there are two or more distinct preference orders for the outcomes of a collective decision,
2.  the outcomes ordered by these preferences are mutually exclusive,
3.  and policy has not been authoritatively decided in the minds of those who have a stake in the outcome.

Note, of course, that covert issues are still issues by this definition. It also implies that the reshaping of issues in the course of debate is nondecisionmaking just as much as complete suppression of an issue is. (This, of course, is consistent with Bachrach and Baratz, as it is intended to be.) The "shape" of an issue can be described in terms of (1) how "political" it is seen to be (as opposed to how "private" it is); (2) the set of alternatives considered; and (3) the set of outcomes perceived as the consequences of these alternatives. Thus, one individual may see health care as a technical issue and think of it in terms of costs, efficiencies, and effectiveness. Another may define it in terms of changes in the relations between the private and public sector, hence define the issue in terms of private versus social medicine. Still others may not even consider national health insurance among the possible alternatives. We will use the term "issue" throughout to mean a *specific* ordering of specific alternatives and outcomes, hence modifying in any way the alternatives or the outcomes considered counts as a redefinition or reshaping of the issue.

One can describe positions on an issue by describing the distribution and intensity of these preferences in a population. Its "issueness" is a question of the scope and intensity of these preferences. But preferences are purely subjective and subjective preferences are unobservables. Thus, definitions 1 and 2 may make the concept of a nondecision more precise, but unless an independent test of issueness is found it is still incapable of figuring in testable theories. If an issue is not on a polity's agenda, what ground is there for inferring that it is an issue?

Definitions 1 and 2 imply that nondecisions are essentially counterfactual agendas—issues that, in the absence of some countervailing factor *would* have been on the polity's agenda. What has to be shown is that, other things being equal, the issue *would* have emerged. The comparative method is the conventional solution to such problems (and is used in the nondecision literature, for example, by Crenson, 1971 and Smith, 1979). Comparing otherwise similar polities, a variable $X$ can be said to cause a nondecision if and only if the issue is present when $X$ is absent. It may be difficult to accomplish the comparison: Polities have to be equated both for factors relevant to the creation and formulation of issues and for otherwise extraneous factors correlated with the behavior of the polity. But in principle there is nothing mystical about the inference that needs to be made. The operational definition of a nondecision depends on:

*Criterion 1:* An issue not on a polity's agenda is a nondecision if and only if, in the absence of some identifiable factor $X$, the issue is on the agenda of otherwise similar polities.

The syntax of the rule is slightly tortured because it provides a rule identifying a state (nondecision) rather than the factor that causes it ($X$). A deceptive consequence is that the syntax emphasizes a negative test (the absence of $X$). Its most important implication is in fact more positive: What one is really looking at is not something called the "nondecisionmaking process" but rather the metadecision-making process as a whole. To refer to the process one is studying as the "nondecision" process, as Bachrach and Baratz often do, means one is not looking at positive outcomes—an error the mirror opposite of the one Bachrach and Baratz criticized in formulating the concept in the first place. Just as Bachrach and Baratz underlined the unity of the entire policy process, Criterion 1 underlines the unity of the metadecision process. The positive outcomes (agendas) and the negative outcomes (nondecisions) cannot be studied as two separate kinds of process, they are inseparably part of the one process. Thus, research on "nondecisionmaking" cannot focus solely on factors suppressing an issue and cannot be concerned with nondecisions *per se*.

If "nondecisions" were ambiguous, circular, and value–loaded, "mobilization of bias" is more so. The solution, however, is simpler to arrive at. Going back to its origins in Schattschneider, the term "bias" referred to inequalities in the allocation of values and in participation in making policy and rules. It gradually acquired the meaning, in addition, of a "bias" in the mechanisms that operated to allocate these values, hence, in the end, also of the values, rules, practices, and procedures that operated to create and maintain these mechanisms. Only if one assumes, as Bachrach and Baratz do, that all these form a single monolithic structure can one refer to all this by the one concept. But what is at work, clearly, is the legitimation process, and what Bachrach and Baratz (and Schattschneider) think is the key to that process is the system of values, beliefs, rules, practices, and procedures to be found in a society. Hence, without attempting a formal definition of the expression (despite our frequent use of it in Part III), we will simply use the term to refer to "legitimacy," and follow Bachrach and Baratz in thinking of legitimacy as created by the existing values, beliefs, norms, and practices of a society.

## III. TESTING BACHRACH AND BARATZ'S THEORY: THE POLITICS OF THE SUPPRESSION OF ISSUES

Our purpose in part III is to construct a specific technique, based on the method of observation and inference proposed in Part II, that meets the strictest possible standard of internal validity and to employ it to test seven hypotheses implied by Bachrach and Baratz's theory.

### A. Scope of This Investigation

Throughout, we test this theory under the following conditions: First, the groups we study are engaged in collective, interdependent tasks and have a procedure capable of making authoritative, collective decisions. Second, we focus throughout on the agenda stage of the policy process. In some sense we are concerned with the mobilization of resources; what the agendas are about is a change in the costs that are to be borne by members of the group. But the focus is on the point at which a member of the group initiates an agenda. Third, all the agendas we study are member–initiated. In this we follow Bachrach and Baratz, but it should be emphasized that the agenda of any group can arise in a number of other ways. Some issues arise exogenously—not only in the sense that they are *about* the external environment of the group, but also in the sense that the external environment establishes a group's agenda. (Meyer, for example, emphasizes how many features of educational and political systems arise not because they serve any purpose from the point of view of the group itself but because external sources of support and resources think a group legitimate only if it has such features. See, particularly, Meyer, 1977.) Some issues arise endogenously, but out of the routines evolved by the group for accomplishing its purposes and sustaining its existence. Thus, Polsby (1971) distinguishes inside from outside initiatives on the basis of a distinction between governmental versus nongovernmental sources of an issue, and Cobb and others, (1976) make this distinction the basis for three distinct models of agenda–setting. In Polsby's language, we are concerned in the present investigation only with "outside" initiatives. However, "outside" is slightly ambiguous: From the perspective of the literature on social movements, we are entirely concerned with "insiders'" politics. Although we study challenges, there are no "outsiders" in our groups in the sense of persons without legitimate access to the polity. Fourth, we study n–person, mixed–motive conflicts. In this respect, we depart sharply from Bachrach and Baratz, whose definition of a nondecision commits them to a dyadic conflict model. The way in which we have redefined the term makes no such *a priori* commitment. This is not because we think such conflicts never occur. But as a starting point they neglect too much. The principal application Bachrach and Baratz make of their theory is to the politics of communities. In effect what their assumption does is focus entirely on the distributive aspects of a community's politics. They treat polities as if they either had no corporate existence or all agents of that corporate existence were coopted by economic elites. Possibly some communities have no corporate existence and possibly some polities are coopted by economic elites, but both characteristics vary across polities. Furthermore, with respect specifically to the distributive aspects of politics, they also assume that every single individual is in some way affected by every redistributive issue, which seems to us much too strong. Only in the limit would one expect to find *no* disinterested parties to a conflict. Thus, the redistributive issue that we create in the laboratory makes room for a mixture of cooperative as well as competitive, and disinterested as well as interested, motives.

## B. Techniques of Investigation

Any weight given to "realism" may seem odd in an investigation that creates redistributive issues in the laboratory. But one purpose of our method is to achieve the highest possible standard of internal validity. Nonexperimental comparisons such as Crenson (1971), or Smith (1979) obviously satisfy the criterion laid down in Part II. But even comparative studies have been plagued by serious difficulties of internal validity. These difficulties are essentially the same as those pointed out by Snyder (1979) in studies of collective violence. Polsby (1980, Ch. 11), for example, has criticized Crenson, the exemplar for this kind of study, because he arbitrarily assumes that objective conditions can have only one subjective meaning—which is exactly like trying to infer relative deprivation from changes in GNP. Snyder (1979) identifies the problems of such inferences as due partly to inferring cross–level effects from measures at only the aggregate level, partly to inferring process from cross–sectional causal models, and partly to the numerous factors incorporated into aggregated indicators besides the concepts they are taken to indicate. Crenson, for example, was in the fortunate position of having an objective measure of pollution. Holding other relevant factors constant, he found that as the particulate level in the air increased, the issueness of pollution increased. But holding the particulate level constant, as concentration of economic power increased, the issueness of pollution decreased. Crenson inferred that the issue had been suppressed. Polsby objected that Crenson was in no position to rule out the rival hypothesis that the population of such communities did not *want* pollution ordinances because they traded off clean air for employment and commercial opportunities. However objective the measure of air pollution is, issueness is a subjective state of mind. There is no warrant for directly inferring issueness from any objective indicator; other factors, correlated with, but distinct from both the objective measure and the hypothetical suppressant, may also determine the meaning of the indicator.

A method by which a stricter standard of internal validity can be achieved is experimentation. Our objective in using this method is to create an unambiguous instance of a redistributive issue that no one can claim is not "really" an issue. To accomplish this requires the capacity to manipulate the conditions that create an issue, to control (or to randomize) the effects of factors that might confound its interpretation, and to almost completely control the conditions of its observation.

To create a redistributive issue in a laboratory setting, rewards are distributed inequitably to groups having the capacity to change the structure that creates the inequity: Five–member teams are required to solve ten (independent) problems; the solution to each depends on coordinating information distributed to members at the beginning of the problem such that each has some, but no one has all the information required to solve it. Subjects (S's) work in separate rooms, communicating by written messages only. Messages can pass only to those other members of the team linked to S by "open" channels of communication (from Bavelas, 1950). All teams start in the most highly centralized network possible, called the "wheel." (See Figure 2a.)

This structure has one central and four peripheral positions. The central position can communicate directly with all the others, but all the others communicate

*Figure 2.* Most and Least Centralized Communication Networks Possible in the Experiment

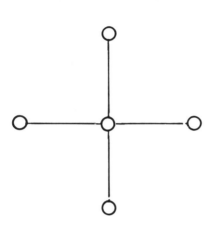

*Figure 2a.* Bavelas's "Wheel".
All communication is controlled by
the central position.

*Figure 2b.* An "All-to-All" Network. All positions have equal access
to all information.

only with (or through) the center. The central position is also materially advantaged: although each S gets some share of the team's total earnings, which
depend on the number of correct solutions to each problem, there is also a bonus
paid on each problem to the member who first reports the correct solution to the
experimenter (E). (The value of this bonus equals the value of the team's earnings on one problem if all its solutions are correct.) It will of course always be
earned by the central position. To underline the inequity of this, S's are told early
in their instructions that all of them are alike and were allocated to their positions
by chance. But a team is allowed to add more channels of communication if it is
willing to pay a small cost, to be shared by all members (Mackenzie, 1976). An
all–to–all network, for example, (shown in figure 2b), would equalize opportunity to win a bonus. To add more channels, a majority of the group must agree.
An "election," to decide the issue, is held by E if a member of the group (1)
proposes a specific agenda and (2) obtains a second by one other member. Thus,
from the point of view of any given disadvantaged (peripheral) member, the
problem is to mobilize the resources of his peers to accomplish a change that
restores equity. From the point of view of any given advantaged (central) member, the problem is to suppress the issue—a capacity within his powers because
he controls communication. No election is actually held: each S is stopped and
interviewed at the point at which a proposal to change the structure is first made
or endorsed. Where required, S is placed in E's "office" where, in addition to

responsibility for calculating team earnings and allocating the bonus, S is asked to function as an agenda gatekeeper. In any one experiment, S's are placed in only one position in this structure; all other positions play roles pre–programmed by E, so that each of the roles in the process can be studied for given conditions of their joint relationship. Hence, we have two kinds of studies to report, one concerned with how powerful beneficiaries behave (Section C below) and the other with how less powerful and deprived actors behave (Section D below).

In all experiments using these methods, a "baseline" condition measures the magnitude of the pressure created by the inequitable allocation of the bonus to change the structure of the communication network. Other things being equal, almost half the S's in the "peripheral" positions of the wheel have tried to get another member of the group to endorse a proposal to change the structure of the communication network by the end of the third problem (or "trial" of the experiment). By the end of the tenth trial, 80% of S's have responded in this way, which is referred to as a "change-," or simply "C-" response. (Figure 3 shows the distribution of such responses in the form of a *survival curve*, that is, the percentage surviving at the end of each trial of the experiment.) A disinterested agenda gatekeeper placed in the "office" of the experiment will endorse such an agenda 95% of the time. (See Table 1 below.)

But what is the cost to external validity of this kind of method? In general, an answer to this kind of question depends on the purpose to which an experiment is addressed. The purpose of an experiment is to test an abstract, general, explanatory hypothesis (cf. Zelditch, 1969); it should be understood that that is the purpose of the present investigation—it is *not* our purpose to say anything descriptive about metadecisionmaking in particular concrete communities. Given our purpose, standards of external validity applied to experiments are the same as those applied to generalizing from *nonexperimental* investigations. Generalization from any instance to any other depends on successfully abstracting the relevant variables common to both. There are two ways in which external valid-

*Table 1.* Proportion of Change–Responses Made By Agenda Gatekeepers Under Various Conditions of Interest and Legitimacy

| Condition | N | Proportion of Change-Responses | Statistics of the Logit Analysis | | | | |
|---|---|---|---|---|---|---|---|
| | | | Effect | Parameter* | Chi Square | df | Probability |
| Baseline | 20 | .95 | Grand Mean | 0.29 | 0.75 | 1 | n.s. |
| Interest | 20 | .60 | Interest | −0.96 | 8.00 | 1 | p < .005 |
| Legitimacy | 23 | .35 | Legitimacy | −1.38 | 16.64 | 1 | p < .001 |
| Interaction | 20 | .15 | Interaction | 0.31 | 0.85 | 1 | n.s. |

*Note:*
*These estimates are the logs of the ratio of the proportion endorsing to the proportion not endorsing change.
*Source:* Zelditch, et al., 1981.

*Figure 3.*    Mean Survival Curve, Showing the Baseline Rate of Change For S's in the Peripheral Positions of Centralized Communication Networks, for 111 Subjects in 5 Experiments.[3]

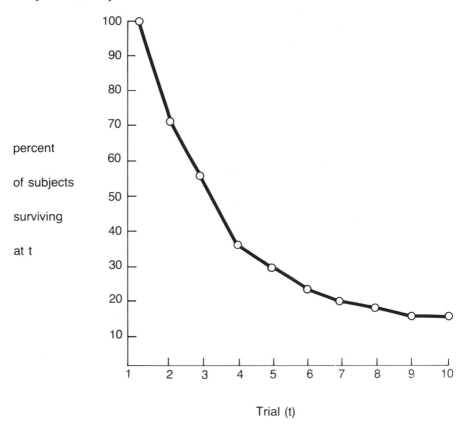

ity in this sense can fail: the theory employed can fail because of specification errors, that is, it may omit some relevant variable; or one (or both) of the instances may not be valid instances of the theory. In the case of experiments, specification errors may themselves be of two kinds. The theory tested may omit an important factor that is not incorporated into the experimental setting employed to test it. Or the theory fails to recognize the significance of an important factor that *is* incorporated into the setting used to test it, treating as theoretically irrelevant factors that actually determine the outcome. Of particular importance in guiding the construction of an experimental setting is the precise theoretical specification of the nature of the relations between variables. Since very often the effects produced by experiments in the laboratory occur during short periods of time, at low levels of involvement, and through small ranges of the theoretically relevant variables, one's theory must assure one that the process is merely magnified, but not changed in form, over longer periods, in more involving conditions, at more extreme values of the same variables. This is, of course, the standard kind of objection to experiments in sociology. But it is important to understand that what does *not* matter is the fact that an experiment will not match the descriptive generalizations made about natural settings. That is precisely what they are created *not* to do. Generalizing the result of any experiment (or, for that matter, any *non* experiment) is conditional. Extrapolating it to a natural setting is possible if and only if precisely the same initial and scope conditions are reproduced by the natural setting. The experiment guarantees only the relation "if x, then y," never the *fact* of *x* in a natural setting. It is because of this that one should not, except for occasional and unpredictable accidents, directly extrapolate the results of any one experiment to any concrete natural setting. The function of the experiment is to inform the experimenter about an aspect of a theory. It will never test the whole theoretical formulation, because its entire function is to isolate and manipulate particular parts of the theory while controlling other parts of it. The proper way to relate an experiment to a natural setting, therefore, is to apply the theory to which it is relevant to the natural setting. Failures of external validity are therefore as often failures of theory as they are failures of validity. In assessing the external validity of the present experiments, what one wants to look for, first of all, is the success with which the experiment creates the variables abstracted by the theory. In case the obvious needs explicit statement, note that application of the theory to natural settings is both an important criterion of its utility and one not guaranteed by experiment.

## C. Studies in the Causes of the Mobilization of Bias

In Bachrach and Baratz's theory, the principal behavior of the "haves" is the mobilization of bias to delay or prevent challenges from reaching the agenda for decision. This behavior includes two kinds of events, making new rules and invoking existing ones. The theory treats the invoking of existing rules as a multiplicative interaction between interest and legitimacy (given power). Failing an interest, there is nothing impelling an actor to use the rules. Failing legitimacy, there are no rules to invoke. In the latter case, assuming the power of the actor to make rules, a different model of the mobilization of bias predicts his behavior: The mobilization of bias will lead to the elaboration of the given system of rules for the purpose of justifying the interests of the powerful. In either case, given a vested interest, there are strong pressures to prevent change by making it counternormative. Lacking such an interest, there are not pressures either to use or to make rules.

To test this model, 83 male undergraduate paid volunteers were seated in a room labelled "office," where they were instructed to tabulate the number of correct solutions, team earnings, and bonuses for a team at work in the setting described in Section B. They were also given responsibility for deciding whether to hold an election or not if members wished to rent more channels of communication. Thus, the office held veto power over any agenda for change. A confederate sent a proposal for change (to an all–to–all network) on the third trial of the experiment. A "change-response" in this experiment consists of endorsement of this proposal by the agenda gatekeeper.

In the baseline condition of the experiment, S was paid a flat fee for his participation. Under this condition, 95% of S's made a C-response (see the first row of Table 1). A vested interest in the existing structure was created in a second condition, by making S's rewards depend on how much the central position earned. More exactly, S's were told that introducing a bonus complicated the problem of paying the office, but they would be paid an amount equal to the highest individual earnings in the work team. This substantially decreased C-responses; only 60% of S's endorsed the confederate's proposal to change to an all–to–all network in this condition. Legitimacy was created in a third condition, by allowing S to hear instructions given by E to the work team explaining that it would damage the objectives of the experiment if members changed the existing structure before the eighth problem because it took that long before the behavior being studied in the experiment could be reliably measured. Like S's in the baseline condition, these S's were paid a flat fee for participation and had no vested interest in the kind of communication system used by the work team. Under these conditions, only 35% of S's made a C-response. That the legitimacy effect is stronger than the interest effect is not informative, because the two manipulations are arbitrarily sampled points from two multi–valued variables; other values of these variables, had they been sampled instead, would have produced stronger (or weaker) effects. What *is* significant is that legitimacy has an effect that does not depend on interest. An even more clear evidence of the independence of legitimacy from interest is shown by the fourth condition of the experiment, in which interest and legitimacy combine to reduce the level of C-responses to 15% (see the last row of Table 1). Legitimacy and interest are evidently additive, not interactive. The rate of change is the lowest of the four conditions, of course, but is no lower than one would predict simply by adding the effect of legitimacy to that of interest.

Justification for this conclusion rests on the "logit analysis" shown in the right–hand columns of Table 1. Logit analysis is basically linear regression with a dichotomous dependent variable. The "parameters" shown in column 5 are logs of the ratio of the proportion of change–responses to the proportion resisting change. The parameter for the interaction effect is not significantly different from zero.[4]

What these results imply is that legitimacy has an effect on the behavior of the agenda gatekeepers whether or not there is any self-interested motive for "mobilizing" it, and the effect it has is the same whether there is an interest or not— that is, the existence of a vested interest does not multiply the legitimacy effect. This is not the kind of proposition that one accepts or rejects on the basis of a single experiment; but the experiment does give one reason to doubt Bachrach and Baratz's reduction of legitimacy to a purely material basis.

## D. Studies in the Effects of The Mobilization of Bias

In this section we consider six hypotheses deriving from Bachrach and Baratz that have to do with the effects, as distinct from the causes, of the mobilization of bias. These effects are of three kinds: direct effects of legitimacy on the acceptance of, and hence voluntary compliance with, a normative order; indirect effects of the acceptance by others of a normative order as legitimate; and direct effects of the authority conferred by legitimacy, which, by justifying the collective mobilization of members' resources, concentrates the power required to enforce unwilling compliance with a normative order on those who do not accept it.

To study these effects, S's were put in the peripheral positions of the centralized network shown in Figure 2a. The results of six experiments with various ways of manipulating the legitimacy of a normative order or its authority are displayed in Table 2. The first line in the body of this table shows the result of a

*Table 2.* Percent of the Baseline Rate of Change Initiated by Peripheral Positions That is Delayed or Prevented by Various Manipulations of Legitimacy and Power[a]

| *Experimental Condition* | N | *Percent of Baseline Rate of Change Delayed or Prevented*[b] |
|---|---|---|
| Inequality is justified by differences in relative contributions to the task | 21 | 63%** |
| Change would damage the objectives of the experiment | 31 | 67%** |
| Collective change is politically impossible | 20 | 43% |
| Peers believe that the existing structure of the communication system is appropriate | 40[c] | 49%** |
| A power legitimated by E prefers the existing communication system | 24 | 60%* |
| A power legitimated by E *could* sanction S *if* he preferred the existing system | 24 | 58%** |

*Notes:*

[a]The rate of change includes both individualistic and collective change-responses in all experiments. See Note 5 for the method by which the "per cent of change delayed or prevented" is computed.

[b]There are small changes in procedure from experiment to experiment, but each comparison is made to an exactly similar baseline.

[c]Pooled data from two experiments. After being run with males, the same condition was replicated on females. There were no differences by sex.

*P < .05
**P < .01

*Sources:* Line 1 is from Lineweber, et al., 1980; line 2 from Thomas, et al., 1980; line 3 from Thomas, et al., 1981; line 4 from Walker and Smith-Donals, 1981; line 5 from Ford, 1981; and line 6 is from Zelditch and Ford, 1980.

direct attempt to make inequality appear legitimate, that is, equitable. To accomplish this, E informed S's that all of them had been randomly allocated to positions in the network except for the central person, who had been specially chosen (on the basis of previous experiment) for superior ability at the task. In the baseline condition of this experiment, 95% of S's made a C-response some time during the experiment. In the equity condition, only 62% did. Thus, one might say that a third of the change observed in the baseline condition was suppressed by legitimating inequality. The observed proportion of C-responses, however, is a seriously misleading statistic. It does not distinguish faster from slower rates of change, differences that are observable only by displaying entire survival curves (as in Figure 3). The same is true of the mean or median of these curves. What Table 2 shows, therefore, is a statistic that more precisely reflects the differences in shape of the two survival curves being compared. It is based on the ratio of the relative rates of change in the equity treatment compared to its baseline condition,[5] and can be read "the percent of change in the baseline condition that is delayed or prevented by the treatment in the experimental condition." It is adapted from a statistic used to evaluate clinical trials in medical experiments. By this measure, the justification of inequality by E delayed or prevented 63% of the change found in the baseline condition (Lineweber, and others, 1980).

An even stronger effect was produced simply by labelling the issue illegitimate. This was done by making S's believe that it would damage the objectives of the experiment if a change were actually made. S's were told that E was interested in the "detailed pattern of information flow" in communication networks of various kinds, that this pattern did not stabilize, and therefore could not be reliably measured before the eighth problem, and that E would return at the end of the eighth problem in order to measure this flow. This delayed or prevented 67% of the change observed in the baseline (Thomas, and others, 1980).

As one might expect, making change politically impossible eliminated it completely. What we were trying to create, in this case, is something like the *facticity* of a normative order that Bachrach and Baratz (like Berger and Luckmann) believe it acquires by being upheld by others. Whether or not any given individual accepts the legitimacy of an order, the fact that it comes to be embodied in everyone's conduct gives it an unquestioned reality that makes other possibilities vanish. Not only does "how it is done" become a fact of nature instead of a fallible human creation (hence unthinkable as a "political" issue) but it forms well-beaten paths that channel behavior as effectively as if the paths not there were actual barriers. To make change politically impossible, we eliminated the rental procedure. The only difficulty was to devise a dependent variable comparable to that in the baseline. For this purpose we observed individualistic as well as collective change-responses. Adding more channels of communication is a response to inequity that requires collective mobilization of resources. Some S's in all our experiments find this a "hassle," and instead, attempt directly to negotiate a share of the bonus on an individual basis, or withhold, or send false information. (The proportion of change-responses that is individualistic varies from experiment to experiment. We do not study it here because it does not bear on Bachrach and Baratz's theory.) However, to make the responses in all six experiments comparable, we include both individualistic and collective change–responses in all the results shown in Table 2. The political impossibility of change delayed or prevented 43% of changes (of all kinds) observed in the baseline. More important, no S in the experimental condition thought of the possibility of collectively changing the structure of the system of communication. All of the suppressed change was due to the difference in collective change–responses; the rate of individualistic change–responses was about the same in both conditions. Or, put another way, the political impossibility of change did not seem to substantially increase private grievances (Thomas, and others, 1981).

The effect of legitimacy in Bachrach and Baratz does not depend on S's own beliefs in the legitimacy of a normative order. The beliefs of others play a central role in delaying or preventing change. In fact, although they do not use the term or even the idea, what Dornbusch and Scott call the ''validity'' of a normative order is sufficient (Dornbusch and Scott, 1975). *Validity* means essentially the *existence* of a binding normative order, as opposed to S's personal belief that it is right (which Dornbusch and Scott refer to as the order's *propriety*). Validity has the effect of inducing others to support such an order and inducing any particular individual to *expect* that other others will support it. In the equity experiment referred to in the second paragraph of this section, for example, post–session interviews found that S's did not personally believe in the legitimacy of the inequality created by the experiment. They felt the task was too simple to require much ability, hence did not see how the central position's superior ability could matter. But they did not attempt to change the structure of the communication system because they felt that in an experiment rules made by and beliefs held by E were valid, hence binding on them. Furthermore, they felt that in some sense E's authority *backed* the normative order (Lineweber, and others, 1980). Borrowing again from Dornbusch and Scott, we have found it a useful elaboration of Bachrach and Baratz to be more specific about *who* supports an order, hence to distinguish between ''endorsement'' and ''authorization'' of the validity of an order. By *endorsement* is meant the support of a normative order by others like S. By *authorization* is meant the support of a normative order by others more powerful than S. Authorization, as we will see in a moment, has a stronger effect than endorsement but endorsement is a critical factor nevertheless in the mobilization of revolutionary coalitions (see Lawler, 1975; Michener and Burt, 1975; Michener and Lawler, 1971; Michener and Lyons, 1972). To study its effects, a short questionnaire was administered after one practice trial, the (fictitious) results of which were fed back to S's who were told that four of the five members of the group felt that the wheel was the most appropriate and most efficient way to organize the group for its task. This had the effect of delaying or preventing 49% of the change found in the baseline (Walker, 1979; Walker and Smith–Donals, 1981; Walker, and others, 1981).

To study the effects of authorized power, E gave the central position the power to decide, as it saw fit, how to divide team earnings. Although Bachrach and Baratz discuss power a good deal, and have what we believe to be one of the better analyses of its different forms (1963, 1970, ch. 2), it is important to keep in mind that what they are talking about is almost never pure power. They are almost always talking about power backed by legitimating values, rules, beliefs, practices, and procedures. The importance of this, in their analysis (as in many others), is that it confers the capacity to mobilize collective resources, which once assembled, concentrates sufficient power to back rules by sanctions. It is, therefore, not necessary that any particular individual accept the propriety of an order if he is aware that it is authorized, hence backed by the assembled resources of the community. What E did by delegating the right to divide team earnings to the center was therefore to authorize its power, in the Dornbusch–Scott sense. But, following Bachrach and Baratz, what we were concerned with was the more invisible ways in which this power might operate to delay or prevent change. Their analysis rests on two ideas: That potential power is as or more important than actual power and operates to produce its effects through the "law of anticipated reactions" (Friedrich, 1963). E therefore informed S that past experience showed that the person in the central position preferred centralized communication networks and almost always used his power to prevent change. The expected value of his sanction, had it been used, was greater than the expected value of the gain S would derive from a change, but the central position neither used nor threatened to use any actual sanctions. The reactions anticipated by S nevertheless delayed or prevented 60% of the change found in the baseline (Ford, 1981). Virtually the same effect, however, was found when S had no clear idea what the person in the central position preferred or how likely he was to deploy the sanctions he controlled. Uncertainty about the central position's preferences was created by informing S that based on past experiments one could not tell how the person in the central position would behave, because some factors led him to prefer the wheel (such as the responsibility), but some led him to prefer a change (such as the inequality). Uncertainty about the position's preferences delayed or prevented 58% of the change found in the baseline (Zelditch and Ford, 1980).[6]

## IV. CONCLUSIONS

The first conclusion to draw from these experiments is that legitimacy is not reducible to a purely material basis. No one experiment is sufficient evidence against a whole way of thought and we did not even *try* to test the theory of norm–formation that is at the heart of this way of thought, but we found no evidence to support the hypothesis that the "mobilization of bias" depends on a vested interest. The same "bias" was mobilized without such an interest and its effects was independent of the existence of such an interest.

But second, the evidence clearly supported all six of the hypotheses tested about the effects Bachrach and Baratz claim that the "mobilization of bias" has on the mobilization of discontent. If the existing system of inequality was justified by a legitimate source, if an issue would clearly damage legitimate objectives, if change was politically impossible, if peers endorsed the existing system, if authorized powers preferred it, or even if the preferences of such powers were uncertain, but they could do serious damage—all these conditions delayed or prevented change.

A third conclusion one can draw from these experiments is that Bachrach and Baratz seem if anything to have understated the features that make metadecisions and nondecisions special. What makes a metadecision different from a decision is that one of its alternatives is to do nothing. A decision is a choice among possible policies: if one chooses a policy *x*, one at the same time rejects a policy *y*, and whichever of the two one chooses, the outcome is a visible commitment to some policy. A metadecision is a choice between doing something and doing nothing, but to do nothing may or may not be a visible commitment. There are two distinct ways of doing nothing: one can decide not to decide something such as tabling a motion, or one can simply not decide to decide, evading the issue altogether. The significance of the difference between the two kinds of nondecision is that it makes nondecisions in an important sense beyond compliance. For the most part, Bachrach and Baratz reason from specifically anticipated reactions to specifically compliant actions. But compliance isn't required to nondecide an issue. Doing nothing is as likely to occur when the preferences of the powerful are uncertain. In this respect, the legitimacy of power works in much the same way as the legitimacy of a normative order. As Bachrach and Baratz would have predicted, we found that norms do not depend for their effect on their acceptance by any particular individual. "Acceptance" is a collective not an individual process, and the acceptance of a normative order by some suffices to mobilize collective resources behind its enforcement on those who do not accept it. In other words, it is sufficient that a normative order exist. In the same way, the sheer existence of a power structure, over and above any specifically anticipated reaction, is sufficient to nondecide an issue.

What emerges from these experiments is a somewhat more thoroughgoing structuralism than Bachrach and Baratz's. Bachrach and Baratz's theory is "structural" in the sense that issueness depends neither on the correlation between individual discontent and collective action, on the one hand, nor on the correlation between individual acceptance of rules and compliance with them on the other. It is the social distribution of resources (including access) operating through the dual mobilization of A and B (not discontent) that determines challenge and the existence of a normative order in the sytem as a whole, not the beliefs of particular actors that determines nondecisions. But their structural approach breaks down at two crucial points: They mean "mobilization of bias" quite literally, thinking throughout in terms of specific concrete acts by A that have a centrally coordinated intended outcome. And the effects of this bias are often thought of as event–specific, as motivated compliance by B with the specific wishes of A. What one sees in our experiments is somewhat different: Nothing in our research speaks to the question of how a structure emerges, but once it emerges its operation does not depend on concrete suppression by A nor concrete compliance by B. Nondecisions are as much the outcome of the structure of the AB relation as of A's intentions or B's anticipations. The mobilization of bias arises as much from the existence of a normative order as it does from any specific acts by A; its effects on B arise from the collective acceptance of that order, not acceptance by any particular B; and the effects of authorized power arise as much from the sheer existence of a structure of power as from the anticipation of concrete reactions by B. Hence, it does not require a conspiracy by A to mobilize bias and its effects do not depend on how the rules were made. Nondecisions are as much the outcome of the way a system is organized as of concrete actions by particular actors.

## ACKNOWLEDGMENT

This research was supported by NSF grant No. SOC-7817434. We wish to thank Terry Amburgey, Dorine Barr-Bryan, Joan Ford, Ed Gilliland, Jon Hooper, David Lineweber, and Louise Smith-Donals for their assistance in carrying out this research and their comments on an earlier version and Nancy Tuma for her assistance with methods of analyzing survival data.

## NOTES

1.   Bachrach and Baratz did not actually define "nondecisionmaking" explicitly until *Power and Poverty* and even then they gave two conflicting definitions of it. Hence, any discussion of the concept must reconstruct their meaning from the surrounding commentary and their methods of reasoning.

2.   We define "issueness" in terms of outcomes and do not try to clarify further the meaning of differences among alternative ways of achieving any given outcome although we recognize that "issues" arise with respect to procedure and/or strategy also. For the sake of simplicity, two strategies that yield the same outcome are formally equivalent. What often causes problems for such an analysis are multi–attribute outcomes, i.e., outcomes that can be ranked according to two or more dimensions. Hence, what creates issues are often different evaluations of various trade–offs possible among different policies. For our purposes, different orderings of the different aspects of an outcome create an issue.

3.   The baseline rate of change in a sixth baseline, part of an experiment in which change was made politically impossible, was significantly lower than the pooled average shown in Figure 3, reflecting the effects of inflation on the amount of money at stake in the experiment.

4.   A more detailed analysis shows that if anything, the interaction of interest and legitimacy produces *less* change than would be predicted by adding their independent effects, an important result that we do not pause to explain because it adds nothing to the test of Bachrach and Baratz's theory. See Zelditch, et al., 1981.

5. The essential feature of methods for treating survival curves is that observed change is compared to expected change at each trial (or period), which in turn depends only on the number exposed to risk at the beginning of each trial. If $m$ S's make a C-response at trial $t$ and a proportion $p$ of all S's were in condition $i$ when trial $t$ began, then the expected number of C-responses in condition $i$ should be $p_i m$ assuming there is no true difference between conditions. The quantity $r_i = O_i/E_i$, the ratio of the observed to the expected number of change–responses, gives the *relative* rate of change in the $i$th condition, i.e., the rate of change in the $i$th condition compared to that in the population as a whole. The quantity $R = r_i/r_j$ gives the ratio of the relative rate of change in the $i$th condition to that in the $j$th condition—reflecting the shape of the two curves because the expected values are computed trial by trial and are based on the numbers surviving up to the time each trial begins. The quantity $S = 1 - R$ provides essentially the same information, but has a more natural interpretation in the present case as the "suppression" rate, i.e., the rate at which change in the baseline is delayed or prevented by any given experimental treatment. The statistic $(O - E)^2/E$, furthermore, is distributed as chi square with (in this case) 1 df, which is the basis for the significance levels in the notes to Table 2. For a comprehensive survey of methods of analyzing survival curves, see Elandt–Johnson and Johnson, 1980. An especially clear and nontechnical treatment based on the (nonparametric) "logrank" statistic that is used here, can be found in Peto, et al., 1977.

6. Two explanations of this result seemed plausible: that the situation was so obviously to the center's advantage that many S's still believed he would prefer it, despite the instruction by E; or that under uncertainty S's minimize the worst that could happen by doing nothing. (Cf. any game-theoretic discussion of the minimax principle.) A survey of an independent sample drawn from the same population found that if the situation were stripped of all cues from which to infer preferences, but there was still a good deal at stake, over half the respondents predicted that anyone else (though not they themselves) would do nothing, playing it safe. (See Zelditch and Ford, 1980).

# REFERENCES

Bachrach, P., and M. S. Baratz
  1962   "Two faces of power." APSR 56: 947–952.
  1963   "Decisions and nondecisions: An analytical framework." APSR 57: 632–642.
  1970   Power and Poverty. Oxford: Oxford University Press.
  1975   "Power and its two faces revisited: A reply to Geoffrey Debnam." American Political Science Review 69: 900–904.
Bachrach, P., and E. Bergman
  1973   Power and Choice: The Formulation of American Population Policy. Lexington, Toronto and London: D. C. Heath & Co.
Baratz, M. S.
  1977   "Review of Nagel's, The Descriptive Analysis of Power and Lukes', Power: A Radical View."
Bavelas, A.
  1950   "Communication patterns in task-oriented groups." J. Acoustical Society of America 22: 725–730.
Braybrooke, D.
  1974   Traffic Congestion Goes Through the Issue-Machine. London and Boston: Routledge & Kegan Paul.
Cobb, R. W., and C. D. Elder
  1972   Participation in American Politics. Baltimore and London: Johns Hopkins University Press.
Cobb, R. W., J. Keith-Ross, and M. H. Ross
  1976   "Agenda-building as a comparative process." APSR 70: 126–138.

Cohen, L., M. E. Levine, and C. R. Plott
    1978   "Communication and agenda influence." Pp. 329–357 in H. Sauermann (Ed.), Coalition
           Forming Behavior. Tubingen, Germany: J. C. B. Mohr (Paul Siebeck).
Crenson, M.
    1971   The Unpolitics of Air Pollution. Baltimore and London: Johns Hopkins University Press.
Dahl, R. A.
    1957   "The concept of power." Behavioral Science 2: 201–215.
    1958   "A critique of the ruling-elite model." American Political Science Review 52: 463–469.
Debnam, C.
    1975   "Nondecisions and power: The two faces of Bachrach and Baratz." American Political
           Science Review 69: 889–898.
Dornbusch, S. M., and W. R. Scott
    1975   Evaluation and the Exercise of Authority. San Francisco: Jossey-Bass, Inc.
Elandt-Johnson, R.C., and N. L. Johnson
    1980   Survival Models and Data Analysis. New York: Wiley.
Fiorina, M. P., and C. R. Plott
    1978   "Committee decisions under majority rule: An experimental study." American Political
           Science Review 72: 575–598.
Ford, J.
    1981   "The law of anticipated reactions." Unpublished manuscript. Laboratory for Social Re-
           search, Stanford University.
Frey, F. W.
    1971   "Comment: On issues and nonissues in the study of power." American Political Science
           Review 65: 1081–1101.
Friedrich, C.
    1963   Man and His Government. New Jersey: McGraw Hill Book Co.
Jones, C. O.
    1977   An Introduction to the Study of Public Policy. (Second edition). North Scituate, MA:
           Duxbury Press.
Keohane, R. O., and J. S. Nye
    1977   Power and Interdependence. Boston and Toronto: Little, Brown & Co.
Lawler, E. J.
    1975   "An experimental study of factors affecting the mobilization of revolutionary coalitions."
           Sociometry 38: 163–179.
Lineweber, D., D. Barr-Bryan, and M. Zelditch, Jr.
    1980   "Effects of a legitimate authority's justification of inequality on the mobilization of revolu-
           tionary coalitions." Unpublished manuscript. Laboratory for Social Research, Stanford
           University.
Lehman, E. W.
    1969   "Toward a macrosociology of power." American Sociological Review 34: 453–465.
Levine, M. E., and C. R. Plott
    1977   "Agenda influence and its implications." Virginia Law Review 63: 561–604.
Lukes, S.
    1975   Power: A Radical View. London: Macmillan.
McFarland, A. S.
    1969   Power and Leadership in Pluralist Systems. Stanford, CA: Stanford University Press.
Mackenzie, K. D.
    1976   A Theory of Group Structures. New York: Gordon & Breach.
Mansbach, R. W., and J. A. Vasquez
    1981   In Search of Theory: A New Paradigm for Global Politics. New York: Columbia University
           Press.

May, J. V., and A. B. Wildavsky (eds.)
1978 The Policy Cycle. Beverly Hills and London: Sage Publications.
Merelman, R. M.
1968 "On the neo-elitist critique of community power." American Political Science Review 62: 451–460.
Meyer, J. W.
1977 "Education as an institution." AJS 83: 55–77.
Michener, H. A., and M. R. Burt
1974 "Legitimacy as a base of social influence." Pp. 310–348 in J. T. Tedeschi (ed.), Perspectives on Social Power. Hawthorne, NY: Aldine Publishing Co.
Michener, H. A., and E. J. Lawler
1971 "Revolutionary coalition strength and collective failure as determinants of status reallocation." Journal of Experimental Social Psychology 7: 448–460.
Michener, H. A., and M. Lyons
1972 "Perceived support and upward mobility as determinants of revolutionary coalition behavior." Journal of Experimental Social Psychology 8: 180–195.
Molotch, H.
1970 "Oil in Santa Barbara and power in America." Sociological Inquiry 40: 131–144.
Nagel, J. H.
1975 The Descriptive Analysis of Power. New Haven: Yale University Press.
Peto, R., M. C. Pike, P. Armitage, N. E. Breslow, D. R. Cox, S. V. Howard, N. Mantel, K. McPherson, J. Peto, and P. G. Smith
1977 "Design and analysis of randomized clinical trials requiring prolonged observation of each patient." British Journal of Cancer 35: 1–39.
Plott, C. R., and W. P. Rogerson
1979 "Committee decisions under majority rule: Dynamic theories and experimental results." Social Science Working Paper No. 280. California Institute of Technology.
Plott, C. R., and M. E. Levine
1978 "A model of agenda influence on committee decisions." American Economic Review 68: 146–160.
Polsby, N. W.
1971 "Policy initiation in the American political system." Pp. 55–67 in I. L. Horowitz (ed.), The Use and Abuse of Social Science. New Brunswick, NJ: Transaction Books.
1980 Community Power and Political Theory (Second enlarged edition). New Haven and London: Yale University Press.
Schattschneider, E. E.
1960 The Semi-Sovereign People. New York: Holt, Rinehart and Winston.
Smith, R. A.
1979 "Decision making and non-decision making in cities." ASR 44: 147–161.
Snyder, D.
1979 "Collective violence processes: Implications for disaggregated theory and research." Pp. 35–61 in Vol. 2 of L. Kriesberg (ed.), Research in Social Movements, Conflicts and Change. Greenwich, CT: JAI Press.
Thomas, G. M., J. Hooper, and M. Zelditch, Jr.
1981 "An experimental study of the pressure to change when change is politically impossible." Unpublished manuscript. Laboratory for Social Research, Stanford University.
Thomas, G. M., H. A. Walker, and M. Zelditch, Jr.
1980 "Nondeciding Inequity: An experimental study of some effects of the mobilization of bias." Unpublished manuscript. Laboratory for Social Research, Stanford University.
Vidich, A. H., and J. Bensman
1958 Small Town in Mass Society. Princeton, NJ: Princeton University Press.

Walker, H. A.
    1979    The Effects of Legitimacy on the Inhibition of Structural Change. Unpublished PhD
            dissertation. Stanford University.
Walker, H. A., and L. Smith-Donals
    1981    ''Gender or status? The effects of differences in sex on behavior under certain conditions of
            disadvantage.'' Paper presented at the annual meeting of the American Sociological Asso-
            ciation, Toronto, Canada.
Walker, H. A., G. M. Thomas, and M. Zelditch, Jr.
    1980    ''Endorsement, legitimacy, and the mobilization of revolutionary coalitions.'' Un-
            published manuscript. Laboratory for Social Research, Stanford University.
Walker, J.
    1977    ''Setting the agenda in the U.S. Senate: A theory of problem selection.'' British Journal of
            Political Science 7: 423–445.
Wolfinger, R. E.
    1971    ''Nondecisions and the study of local politics.'' American Political Science Review 65:
            1063–1080.
Zelditch, M., Jr.
    1969    ''Can you really study an army in the laboratory?'' Pp. 528–539 in Etzioni, A. (ed.), A
            Sociological Reader on Complex Organizations. (Second edition). New York: Holt,
            Rinehart and Winston.
Zelditch, M., Jr., and J. Ford
    1980    ''Potential power.'' Unpublished manuscript. Laboratory for Social Research, Stanford
            University.
Zelditch, M., Jr., E. Gilliland, and G. T. Thomas
    1981    ''An experimental study of the mobilization of bias.'' Unpublished manuscript. Laboratory
            for Social Research, Stanford University.

# ON THE SOCIAL STRUCTURAL
# SOURCES OF POLITICAL CONFLICT:
## AN APPROACH FROM THE SOCIOLOGY OF
## KNOWLEDGE

C. A. Rootes

## ABSTRACT

The often violent and apparently irreconcilable conflicts that characterize relations between such macro–social aggregates as classes and generations as well as those between smaller, concrete groups engaged in face–to–face relations, may be better understood if an attempt is made to illuminate the ways in which conflict situations are shaped by the perceptions of the protagonists, perceptions that are themselves socially structured, in particular, by the social distribution of knowledge.

The approach to explanation that the consideration of such factors suggests is not, however, a psychological one such as is so often adopted in the political science literature on political conflict, but is a nonreductionist sociological one.

Research in Social Movements, Conflicts and Change, Vol. 5, pages 33–54.
Copyright © 1983 by JAI Press Inc.
All rights of reproduction in any form reserved.
ISBN: 0-89232-301-9

That the perspectives and methods of the sociology of knowledge should have been so little utilized in the social-scientific explanation of political conflict is surprising in view of the fact that the analysis and the resolution of conflict was the principal motivation of Karl Mannheim's pioneering efforts in the sociology of knowledge.

The advantages and some of the limitations of Mannheim's approach are discussed, but the main burden of the paper is to demonstrate by reference to some recent instances of social conflict the utility of an approach that stresses the socially constructed nature of political knowledge. Such an approach helps to explain the nature of the conflict itself, the value positions of the protagonists, and the typifications of the motivations of their opponents that are adopted by the protagonists. It has the advantage of supplementing existing structural approaches and, in particular, it helps to fill the lacunae in such approaches that have rendered them susceptible to the charge of mechanistic determinism.

# I. IDEOLOGY: MARXISM AND MANNHEIM

Not the least of the puzzles in the literature that discusses the relationship between ideology and political conflict is the fact that the two most prevalent strains in that literature should reach conclusions that are apparently opposed. On the one hand, the view which has become most general in western Marxism holds that ideology, insofar as it conceals from the proletariat the true nature of its subordination and prevents it from transforming itself from a 'class–in–itself' into a 'class–for–itself' conscious of its revolutionary mission and organized for political action, mitigates conflict and so conduces to the maintenance of a form of political order that serves the interests of the existing dominant class. On the other hand, there is a well–established school of thought that includes Karl Mannheim as well as writers more explicitly functionalist than he, including the authors of the 'end of ideology' thesis, which holds that ideology generates or exacerbates conflict and must be transcended or expunged if political and social order is to be secured.

Nor is the contradiction simply a product of the employment of definitions of ideology which are at variance one with another: whatever their other differences, the two schools share a conception of ideology as an idea, or more usually a set of ideas, which is in some degree false or partial, and belief in which serves the (generally concealed) interests of a group or class.[1] Between these shared elements of definition and the contending theoretical propositions themselves there lies a range of conceptual and theoretical differences and it is these I briefly want to explore.

One immediate difference between the theories consists in their location of the *source* of the distortion that ideology embodies. For the 'end of ideology' school and most functionalist writers, the source of the distortion is psychological. Ideology is for them a product of the improper investment into politics of passion, especially the idealist passion that comes of intellectual speculation.[2] Ideology is the result of a failure to recognize the proper limits of politics, to fail to see it as a matter of the 'administration of things' (Lipset), of 'who gets what, when, why and how' (Lasswell). It is, moreover, a product of the failure to employ the proper rational criteria of evidence in the discrimination between political alternatives, namely (and herein lies not the least paradoxically ideological element of the 'end of ideology' thesis) the criteria of academic social science (Parsons, 1959: 25).

Mannheim, on the other hand, distinguishes between ideological distortions whose source is psychological—the 'particular' conception of ideology—and those whose source is sociological—the 'total' conception of ideology. The particular conception of ideology includes:

> . . . all those utterances the "falsity" of which is due to an intentional or unintentional conscious, semi–conscious or unconscious, deluding of one's self or of others, taking place on a psychological level and structurally resembling lies. (Mannheim, 1936 :238)

It involves 'more or less conscious disguises of the real nature of a situation, the true recognition of which would not be in accord with [the speaker's] interests.' (Mannheim, 1936 :49)

The 'total' conception, on the other hand, refers to the 'total structure of mind' of a group or an historical epoch:

> Whereas the particular conception of ideology designates only a part of the opponent's assertions as ideologies—and this only with reference to their content, the total conception calls into question the opponent's total *Weltanschauung* (including his conceptual apparatus), and attempts to understand these concepts as an outgrowth of the collective life of which he partakes. (Mannheim, 1936 :50)

In consequence, with the particular conception of ideology:

> If it is claimed . . . that an adversary is lying, or that he is concealing or distorting a given factual situation, it is still nevertheless assumed that both parties share common criteria of validity—it is assumed that it is possible to refute lies and eradicate sources of error by referring to accepted criteria of objective validity common to both sides. The suspicion that one's opponent is the victim of an ideology does not go so far as to exclude him from discussion on the basis of a common theoretical frame of reference. (Mannheim, 1936, :50–51)

The total conception of ideology, on the other hand, refers not merely to the content of thought or utterance, but to its form, to the 'fundamentally divergent thought–systems and . . . widely differing modes of experience and interpretation' that separate the intellectual worlds of one historical epoch from another and the categories of thought of one 'historically determined social stratum' from another. The total conception of ideology, then, considers 'the conceptual framework of a mode of thought as a function of the life situation of a thinker

(Mannheim, 1936: 51) not merely as an individual but as a member of a social group, stratum, or class that may be considered the bearer of the ideological thought–system as a whole. The analysis of ideology at this level therefore refers not to the discrete experience of individuals but to the (reconstructed) thought–system of a class of epoch as a whole.

It should be clear that this latter conception is very close to that most commonly employed by Marxists. In fact, Mannheim, in introducing the total conception of ideology, cites Marx's *The Poverty of Philosophy:*

> The economic categories are only the theoretical expressions, the abstractions, of the social relations of production . . . The same men who establish social relations conformably with their material productivity, produce also the principles, the ideas, the categories, conformably with their social relations. (Mannheim, 1936: 51)

For Marx, ideology was a product of the social relations in which men engage. In its most general form ideology under conditions of capitalism consisted chiefly in the 'fetishism of commodities,' which was the manifestation at the intellectual level of the alienation of man from his species being, from his true human nature, which capitalist relations of production necessarily entailed.[3] If commodity fetishism is bourgeois ideology at its most general, subsequent Marxists have concerned themselves with the elaboration of the understanding of bourgeois ideology and the means of its transmission, particularly with reference to the ideological incorporation of the proletariat to which they attribute the failure of the western working classes to develop in the direction of revolutionary action or consciousness. Most such writers have, like Marx, clearly maintained that the sources of ideology were social rather than psychological. The Marxist conception of ideology is, then, substantially coterminous with Mannheim's 'total' conception of ideology.

Mannheim sees the 'total' conception of ideology as having developed out of the 'particular' conception. (Mannheim, 1936: 57–62). This process of development is historical: it is only with the disintegration and fragmentation of the unified world–view of the medieval order that it becomes possible to move beyond naive distrust of an opponent to the conviction that the fundamental intellectual categories by which he orders the world are different from one's own and, indeed, inimical to one's own interests.

The key to the fragmentation of the intellectual unity of the medieval world–order is the ascendency of a bourgeoisie that could not be contained within the severely circumscribed place reserved to it under the feudal order. A first stage in the development of the total conception of ideology is the subjectivism of Enlightenment philosophy, a philosophy of consciousness. The second stage in that process was the achievement of Hegel and the Historical School: the emergent 'total but super–temporal' conception of ideology was placed in historical perspective. Specifically, it was recognized that the unity of the world and of consciousness existed in a process of continual historical transformation and tended to repeated restorations of equilibrium at successively higher levels. The next and most important step in the development of the total conception of ideology came with the shift from the conception of nation or *volk* as the bearer of historically evolving consciousness to the attribution of a similar status to class. The shift of perspective, which occurs with the materialist critique of Hegel's idealism, yields the insight that the structure of society and its corresponding intellectual forms vary with the relations between social classes.

The paradox of this final stage is that, on the one hand, consciousness reaches an unprecedented pinnacle of development—the possibilities of comprehending the unity of the world, of relating the formerly incoherent elements of experience, have never been greater. At the same time, with the emergence of the total conception of ideology and its progressive subsumption of the particular conception, the conception of the sources of the contradiction between contending viewpoints is shifted ever more resolutely from the psychological level of the personal and individual roots of intellectual bias and to the level of the very structure of thought itself, with the result that disputes that might formerly have been resolveable by appeal to evidence or impartial adjudication now appear as total and irreconcilable conflicts of world view. No longer is dialogue or even comprehension possible: the disputants are, as it were, speaking different and mutually incomprehensible languages. Thus just as the possibilities of universal consciousness are most highly developed, so conflict, too, approaches an unprededented degree of totality because for the first time it is possible not merely to disagree with an opponent, to challenge the details of his thought, but possible to claim totally to annihilate his position by demonstrating the determinative connection between his arguments, his forms of thought and his social–historical situation.

## A. Ideology and Conflict: Marxism

If so many elements of the sociological conception of ideology are common to Mannheim and the Marxists, how then is it that theories that appear to share basic concepts should nevertheless arrive at such opposed conclusions?

Part of the answer lies in their conception of the nature, or more precisely, the *levels* of conflict. Marxists do not in general contend that ideology suppresses conflict entirely[4] so much as that it displaces and diverts conflict away from the line of the fundamental contradiction of capitalist society—the objective antagonism between capital on the one hand and wage labour on the other—and onto relations *within* classes, most particularly, within the proletariat, with the result that what are in reality conflicts between classes are manifested as status conflicts within classes. In the words of Lukács (1970: 58), 'status consciousness masks class consciousness; in fact it prevents it from emerging at all.' The argument has been made repeatedly in response to the question, 'Why is there no socialism in the United States?' that the status and ethnic particularisms introduced by successive waves of immigration served to fragment the unity of the working class with the result that conflict when it inevitably occurred, followed lines of ethnicity rather than class.[5] The pattern of conflict and invidious distinctions of status this reinforced continues even after the great waves of immigration are past; indeed, it is perpetuated by a mode of production that continually degrades humanity and drives even its least fortunate victims to desperate attempts to retain some shred of dignity and personal worth.[6]

The intercommunal conflict in Northern Ireland is another case in which such arguments have frequently been applied. Marxists have long argued that this conflict, which is along ostensibly religious lines, is in reality a manifestation of class conflict. The tensions and resentments that fuel the intercommunal violence are generated by objective class conflicts, but through the operation of sectarian ideology perpetuated by the province's quasi–colonial status, are displaced onto the line of greatest cleavage within the working class, which is religion and ethnicity. In the words of one recent analyst:

> Ideological social relations have as a principal function the task of appropriating distinctions within the division of labour and displacing and refashioning these distinctions within other areas of the social formation . . . Northern Ireland sectarianism is the ideological manifestation of a society characterized by a Protestant working–class 'labour aristocracy' and a Unionist cross–class political alliance. (Burton, 1979: 61)

Similar arguments are advanced in the more general case of nationalism. In the first place, the conditions of international capitalist competition turn the socially fragmented international proletariat into a mass of sectional alliances with national capitals, and secondly, the international division of labour itself generates in the capitalist metropoles a 'labour aristocracy' that comes to identify its own interests as opposed to those of the proletariats of less developed states.

If the general tenor of the Marxist argument is that in capitalist societies the phenomenal forms of conflict frequently follow lines other than the real fundamental antagonism that is their ultimate source, it is by no means the case that the conception of class conflict as involving clashes between monolithic and more or less homogeneous classes divided along the capital–wage labour axis has gone unquestioned even by Marxists. Witness, for instance, the recent argument over the correct location of the class position of that increasingly numerous stratum of technically qualified and educated labour that has variously been referred to as a 'new working class,' a 'new mass intelligentsia,' and a 'new petit bourgeoisie,' and Erik Olin Wright's (1978) conclusion that the position of this class is intermediate and its politics correspondingly indeterminate.

It has, however, principally been left to sociologists to investigate the divisions internal to the proletariat. A particularly pertinent example is David Lockwood's (1958) study of the class position and class consciousness of clerical workers. Lockwood argued persuasively that to regard the lack of disposition of clerks to identify themselves with other sections of wage labour and to join trades unions was to fail to appreciate that the consciousness of clerks in fact reflected material and social conditions that were, in important respects, different from those endured by other sections of the proletariat. Secondary divisions within the primary division of the labour–capital relation these might be, but they were real divisions nonetheless and nothing about the attitudes or behaviour of clerks controverted the proposition that consciousness reflects social position.

There is, however, good reason to decline to concede even this much to the more familiar forms of Marxist argument. As Parkin (1979) has argued, there is in general nothing secondary, transitional, or residual about the particularisms of status, race, gender, and ethnicity: all may form the bases for processes of social exclusion and appear to do so no less frequently than does class.[7]

## B. Ideology and Conflict: Mannheim

Lockwood's work is as we shall see, in many respects a vindication of the perspective Mannheim recommended.[8] For Mannheim although he shared much of the Marxist analysis of the sources of conflict,[9] the question of the ultimate source of such conflicts was less important, both because it was clear that the lines of social division capable of sustaining consequential social conflict were more numerous and more complex than the highly simplified dichotomous model of class–conflict allowed, and because Mannheim's own analysis of the means of transcendence of social conflict was so different from that of the Marxists.

Whereas the Marxists believed that the conflicts of capitalism would be transcended only by the development of a revolutionary proletariat and its inevitable accession to dominance as a universal class, Mannheim was altogether more skeptical. The grounds for his skepticism are not clearly laid out, but he appears to have doubted that a class that was itself directly locked into the confines of a particular form of economic activity and which displayed the ideological distortions of consciousness appropriate to those conditions could transform itself into a universal class or develop the consciousness necessary to transcend its immediate circumstances.[10] For Mannheim, after all, Marxism was itself partly ideological and he regarded it as a failure on the part of Marxists that they did not apply the critique of ideology to themselves: instead they had fused the total and the particular conceptions of ideology in order to wield ideology as a political weapon.

Furthermore, Mannheim wrote as one schooled in European high culture at a time when that culture appeared to be under the most imminent threat of being overwhelmed by barbarism. Indeed he had, in true idealist fashion, first identified the crisis that beset Europe as a cultural one. The catastrophe theory then so prevalent in Marxist circles must have seemed all too plausible, but Mannheim could not share the optimism of those other partisans of high culture, the Marxists of the Frankfurt School that anything good could survive the ashes of capitalism's self–immolation.[11] For Mannheim the actual conflict—the social, political and cultural crisis that was ultimately to lead to the rise of Nazism—was proximate enough to demand confrontation. Nor could Mannheim believe that the factors which had produced the cataclysm of the collapse of the Weimar Republic would simply disappear in the aftermath of war. Both to achieve rational postwar reconstruction and to counter at its source the problem of ideology, Mannheim placed his faith in an elite of planners and educators who, removed from the direct constraints of conventional economic activity (and so enjoying the status of a 'relatively free floating intelligentsia') and schooled in the sociology of knowledge, would see beyond the particularisms of class interest and effect reconciliation between groups more directly bound.[12]

For Mannheim, the development which moves political conflict onto an ever more total plane requires a corresponding commitment at the level of sociological analysis. It is not enough for sociology to concern itself with the collection of discrete and particular fragments of information, of data, to challenge or correct the particular factual misstatements of an opponent. For one thing, such evidence will fail to convince since it is itself the product of a particular theoretical–conceptual structure of whose ramifications social scientists themselves, so long as they proceed in this manner, are evidently unaware or wilfully negligent. Sociological analysis, if it is to come to grips with the problem of ideology, if it is to develop any genuine understanding of the processes of ideological distortion, must embrace the sociology of knowledge and apply its methods and insights even to itself.[13] It is not that the sociology of knowledge should *replace* a more familiar form of empirical sociology so much as that all social scientific analysis, all collection of social scientific data, should be thoroughly informed by its insights. This is especially essential if social science pretends to any practical relevance, and particularly if it is to be applied to the understanding of political conflict or to the determination of its outcome.

Mannheim's perspective upon the transcendence of social conflict differs from the Marxian one in that it is sceptical of the transcendental claims made by Marxists on behalf of the proletariat (most notably by Lukács), and in any case declines to wait upon the proletariat's accession of the consciousness of its historical mission before addressing the problem of conflict. Moreover, it is sufficiently sceptical of millenarian claims in general to believe that piecemeal social reforms are necessary if an improvement of the human condition is ever to be achieved, and it is sufficiently imbued with the rationalism of the Enlightenment to believe that the employment of an appropriately trained intellect is more likely to encompass adequate proposals for the solution of social problems than is the half–blind striving of the directly oppressed in behalf of their particular interests.

One of Mannheim's central propositions was that ideology represented a consciousness that was not so much false as one that was partial.[14] Indeed, he conceived of 'truth,' or rather, the nearest approximation to truth that was available in a particular historical situation, as a 'dynamic synthesis of all partial viewpoints.' The production of such a synthesis would be the task of the intelligentsia, Mannheim envisaged, a task achievable by them because of their own status as an 'interstitial stratum' and because of the synthesizing skills Mannheim expected them to acquire from their sociological education.[15]

Whatever the plausibility of this solution, the conception of the problem of ideology as one of the non–identity of cognitive perspectives is clearly of utility for the sociological analysis of intergroup conflicts. Insofar as it is possible to demonstrate that groups, however much they see the problem in the same way (and that they do is the inescapable if contentious implication of Marxist and neo-Marxist arguments about the universalization of 'bourgeois ideology'[16]), nevertheless see different *aspects* of it simply because their social and material circumstances expose them only to particular parts of the whole. Then the precise identification of the social locations of individuals and groups will be a first and necessary step to the comprehension of the way they see the situations in which they find themselves and the situationally–determined differences between different parties to any particular instance of social conflict.

The sociology of knowledge is as yet little developed beyond, on the one hand, the quite abstract and quasi–theoretical analysis of historical *Weltanschauungen,* and on the other, the rather crude identification of the social situations with which particular beliefs are associated. In particular, there have been rather few attempts systematically to link the two levels. Marxists have, unfortunately, been too little concerned with careful empirical analysis at the grassroots level, and too much given to the formularistic and frequently mechanical application of abstract models to concrete situations conceived in general terms.[17] Sociologists, even in the rare cases when they have undertaken empirical research in the sociology of knowledge, have too frequently been content to rely upon the correlation of a particular form of social consciousness with an occupational milieu. The recent spate of research in Britain into 'working class images of society' is a case in point.[18] As Davis (1979: 182) has pointed out, the problem with seeing work and community as the basis of interpretations of class and society as a whole is that to do so presupposes that the formation of social consciousness is a one-way process in which one begins with the concrete daily experiences of work and moves towards increasingly abstract experiences and relationships, whereas in fact dominant social institutions are powerful sources of ideas and vicarious experiences. As Burton (1978: 7) puts it, accounts often:

. . . seek to specify the socio–structural determinants of meaning and consciousness but largely neglect how material reality is mediated in context. The ideological representations of any material reality can never be given im–mediately. States of consciousness in any society will differ for a variety of reasons, not least because of a class or group's structural position in that society. Moreover, there will always be lags before shifts in material relationships become registered in the social consciousness. Consequently to restrict analysis to one level, that of the socio–structural determinants of meaning, is to neglect the whole theoretical arena of the relative autonomy of mediation.

Again:

> Precisely because ideological and political social relations are conjuncturally determined, to
> restrict theoretical investigation to the level of the structural determinants of a world–view is
> to neglect the whole arena of mediated reality. (Burton, 1978: 157)

The unsatisfactoriness of the attempt, so common in Marxist and sociological literature, to reduce what are evidently collisions of world views to the social structural locations of their holders is well exemplified by Cotgrove and Duff's (1980, 1981) accounts of the clash between environmentalists and industrialists. Cotgrove and Duff, in their first article (1980), see the clash as one of 'competing cultures and meaning systems' rooted in the protagonists' respective social positions. As though recognising the arbitrariness of so crude a reduction of values to structurally determined interests, in their second article (1981), Cotgrove and Duff restore to values such autonomy as permits people actually to choose their occupations on the basis of their values.

Unfortunately, the failure to distinguish properly cognitive aspects of ideological conflict from the more frequently examined normative aspects is quite general in the literature. This is a pity since although there do indeed appear to be ideological disputes that are clashes of irreconcilable values, and which cannot satisfactorily be reduced or even perhaps traced to social structural sources, there are ideological disputes that are primarily cognitive, rather than simply normative, and which may be illuminated by examination of the constraints social structural situations impose upon the stocks of knowledge of their protagonists.

W. I. Thomas's dictum that 'what men believe to be real is real in its consequences' has long been a commonplace of sociological lore. Yet in the social scientific analysis of political conflict its point has been little appreciated. Innumerable studies, abstractly theoretical and narrowly empirical, have examined the significance of the values and normative orientations of groups and individuals for conflict or order. But if the normative element has been much studied, the cognitive aspect of conflict situations has been relatively neglected. This is all the more odd since the cognitive process might reasonably be considered to be logically prior to the normative: only if one perceives the existence of a condition is one in any position to make a moral evaluation of it.[19] Cognitive processes are, like those of moral reasoning, socially structured,[20] and an aspect of that process is the social structuring of the perspectives by which the cognitive faculties are focussed upon the objects of cognition.

I can best demonstrate the utility for the analysis of conflict of considering the 'partial perspectives' of socially structured viewpoints by reference to a form of social conflict with which we are probably all, at first hand, familiar—that which occurs from time to time between students, administrators, and faculty in universities and colleges.

# II. THE SOCIAL STRUCTURAL BASES
# OF CONFLICTS IN UNIVERSITIES

Although the social scientific literature on student activism amply demonstrates the importance of processes of political socialization for the development of radical values among students, and some of that literature has addressed itself to the social structuring of the relevant socialization experiences,[21] less attention has been paid to the direct constraints and opportunities imposed by the student condition itself upon the development of student politics.

The forms of political action that students adopted in the course of development of the student movements of the 1960s appeared to many observers, and to more than a few academic social scientists among them, as bizarre and even irrational. A careful examination of the opportunities and constraints that their situation imposed upon students, however, reveals that much of this apparently bizarre and irrational behaviour was in fact quite rationally motivated, and that its unconventionality was in large part the product of the particular circumstances in which students were obliged to work out their political commitment. (Rootes, 1978)

Why then should that action have appeared irrational to so many? The simple answer was that the political and social situations of these observers were different from those of the protestors: the set of obstacles and opportunities with which their situation confronted *them* in the staking of any political claim that they might envisage was quite different from that confronting protesting students. The result was that actions they could not imagine themselves taking appeared to differently situated observers as pathological.

It is not difficult to see why for social elites the behaviour of subordinate groups should always display something barbaric and pathological. It is not merely that elite groups, in making such moral evaluations, are simply making ideological statements that have the function, whether or not intended, of concealing their real interests (that is, the 'particular' conception of ideology). Whether or not that may be the case, such moral evaluations rest upon a basis of cognition, of a perception that is itself socially constrained. The stock of knowledge that elite actors bring to political situations is quite different from that brought by the members of subordinate groups.

Nor is this simply a question of expert knowledge, although sociologists are by now well aware that in all areas of life there are hierarchies of knowledge, technical knowledge, expert knowledge, in relation to which the socially privileged enjoy relatively privileged access and from which the least socially privileged are, in general, effectively excluded. At the level of common–sense knowledge, too, knowledge and its distribution are socially structured.

A member of a social elite 'knows' that if one wants to seek redress for a political grievance, one telephones or writes to one's M.P., or Congressman, or to some other political 'influential.' He 'knows' that if one objects sufficiently strongly, one has recourse to legal action. A member of a socially subordinate group 'knows' none of these things. If he has even formal access to M.P.s, congressmen, or political influentials at all, he 'knows' that they are unlikely to act effectively on his behalf. He 'knows' too that recourse to legal action to redress a grievance is out of the question, not least because it is prohibitively expensive, and because he is in no position to judge the quality of any advice he might be given.

In short, the members of social elites perceive situations and the courses of action appropriate to them from the perspective of their particular vantage point, a position of power that stems in large part from their privileged access, both formal and informal, to information and to decision–makers. Political procedures that appear rational and effective to members of an elite group may well appear remote, arbitrary, dilatory, and ineffective to members of groups more remote from access, both formal and informal, to the centres of power. Lack of appreciation of the special circumstances of the less well–connected alone suffices to render the protest politics of the politically marginal unintelligible to the elite.

The gulf that separates the socially privileged from the socially disadvantaged or marginal is not then simply a question of 'interests' or values, nor even of the resources for successful conventional political action–it is a manifestation of the socially structured distribution of practical knowledge.

It is clear that such a distribution of knowledge exists within universities as in other institutions. Students, administrators, academics, and other university employees each occupy, both within the university and in society, quite different structural positions, positions which have profound ramifications upon their perspectives of the university's institutional arrangements and of the actions of other sections of the university population.

Administrators and senior academic staff with administrative responsibilities occupy the most central position within both the formal and informal structures of the university. They are typically permanent members with long experience of such institutions, much of it gained in the particular university in which they presently work. The advantages in terms of access to information and to decision–makers that this long tenure confers are reinforced by the whole bureaucratic apparatus of files and specialist personnel that the university employs. Such individuals are, as a result, in an especially privileged position in which to draw upon the 'collective memory' of the institution. Other academic staff are typically less centrally located in the web of information and decision, but nevertheless, by virtue of their relative permanence as members of the institution, develop the resources of informal networks and participate to varying degrees in the transmission and augmentation of a collective memory.

The situation of students is quite different. In the first place they are, in the university's eyes (if not always in their own[22]) transients; secondly, they approach the university as clients, subject to rules that they are typically disabled from playing any part in framing. As a result they are marginal, both in relation to the formal and informal procedures and stocks of knowledge that the university as an institution embodies, and for a large part of the time, even to the official student organizations. Nor can student organizations, even if they do successfully integrate the annual influx of new members, hope completely to fill the gap. The high turnover of office bearers that is inflicted upon student organizations by the transience of their members and the other exigencies of the student life prohibits them ever from developing the degree of expertise, or the collective memory of which organizations and stable elites characteristically dispose.

The structural location of academics and administrators in universities necessarily conduces to what, to other members of the university not charged with the responsibility for decision–making and day to day administration, appears as unnecessary bureaucracy and legalism. To students, whose circumstances propel them to dramatic mobilizations and short, sharp campaigns as the tactics most likely to be effective in prosecuting the claims of a group whose time is fragmented and brief and whose resources, other than numbers and relative freedom from direct constraint, are slender, the apparatus of committees by which universities are run often appears positively byzantine. This structure itself is often sufficient to generate conflict: the perspectives of administrators are necessarily focussed upon the medium and long-term; but for students, there is with regard to the university no long–term.

When conflict does occur, it is usually exacerbated by the failure of the parties to understand the ramifications of each other's perspectives. For students, especially in the circumstances of mobilizations about specific issues, whatever knowledge of normal procedures and arrangements and even points of fact that were privy at least to the few student 'leaders' (who may have held office or sat on committees) is overwhelmed by the tensions between formal and informal organization that emerge in the course of virtually any campaign.[23] Staff, more stably tied into networks and specific processes of decision–making which, however slow, are seen by them as legitimate, have better and surer access to information.[24] Thus it is that elite groups so frequently make the claim that proper procedures have not been observed, and protest that they or their efforts have been misrepresented by student activists. As a strict matter of fact, such claims and protests are usually correct but those who make them have very often failed to appreciate that the students of whose actions they complain are seldom merely evil or willful, but are more usually subject to a wholly different range of constraints upon knowledge and action from those to which administrators and academic staff are liable.[25]

The way in which universities are structured means that the potential for conflict is built–in. There are structural asymmetries that cannot be eliminated without utterly transforming the very basis of our conceptions of education.

Some of the worst effects of these conflicts might be mitigated, however, if the parties concerned were to make more concerted efforts to understand the positions of their antagonists. Inevitably, given the way power, information, and access are structured in the university, the responsibility for such efforts must bear most heavily on the administration and academic staff. Yet given the extent to which they themselves are enmeshed in the day to day processes that the operation of the institution involves, their perspectives are bound always to be limited. For this reason, the work of reconciliation, of the interpretation of the perspectives of one party to another, is most likely to be achieved by an intermediary whose own status is relatively detached from the area of conflict and whose training especially equips him for the conceptual tasks of interpretation and negotiation that conflict resolution involves.[26]

My purpose here has not been to propose an explanation of the variable incidence of student protest, and the fact that conflicts in universities have over the past decade diminished in frequency and intensity in no way vitiates this analysis. Whether conflicts within universities become manifest depends upon a great many factors, and not least upon the degree to which extra–university factors have stimulated a high degree of politicization among students, especially where university authorities feel obliged or are called upon by external authority either to regulate student political activity or to administer procedures dictated by the matters of public policy against which students protest. I have not been concerned to offer a general explanation of students' satisfactions and discontents, but to explain why, when they do become dissatisfied, their complaints often take forms which appear bizarre to observers not similarly situated, and why official attempts to resolve the conflict are so frequently misunderstood. What I have sought to demonstrate by this analysis is that Mannheim's diagnosis of the sources of social conflict and his proposals for its resolution are relevant both to our analytical and to our practical concerns.

## III. TOWARDS THE (PARTIAL) RESOLUTION OF CONFLICT

Mannheim has often been accused, particularly by Marxists, of being naive about the nature and sources of social conflict. But there is nothing in the sociology of knowledge approach to conflict resolution that necessarily conflicts with a theory that sees the roots of conflict as lying deep in structural contradiction which no well–intentioned meliorism can hope to resolve. We might regard social conflict as existing at two levels:

1.    deeply structurally embedded conflicts (for example, as between capitalist and wage labourer), which themselves can be identified as the source of a variety of subsidiary conflicts and which are in this limited sense 'primary,' and

2. conflicts arising from the way in which knowledge is socially structured, but not necessarily coincidental with 'primary' conflicts, and often in fact serving to conceal the true nature of 'primary' conflicts.

The distinction is important because insofar as 'secondary' conflicts obscure the nature of more deeply embedded 'primary' ones, they may well obstruct the process of the resolution of particular conflicts on the basis of optimal compromise. The approach suggested here may help to clear away some of the clutter of the secondary features of conflict in order that the contest may be about the fundamental issues and may, for instance, avoid bogging–down in a welter of acrimonious bloody-mindedness that can serve nobody's interests. Moreover, such an approach may do something to counteract the tendency to conspiracy theories such as flourish on both sides where the conflicting parties are socially isolated from one another.[27]

The aim of this process is less one of permanent and final reconciliation than that of laying the bases for optimal (and inevitably provisional) compromise as the basis of escape from stalemated conflict situations. Deep–seated structural conflicts are not resolved by attempts at reconciliation; but nor are they merely papered over. Eisenstadt has recently remarked that, "While institutionalization of ground rules of interaction copes with the problems of social order, it does not solve them. It only transposes them to another level." (Eisenstadt with Curelaru, 1979: 369). Perhaps so, but the level to which they are transposed may be one at which more effective negotiation may be possible, not least because it may require all parties to a dispute to distance themselves from the ordinary language and consciousness of their particular situations; at least to the extent of transacting their communications in an unfamiliar medium. Insofar as institutionalized ground rules facilitate interaction on the basis of trust and stable expectation they constitute an indispensable basis for the de–escalation of conflict and for the opening of a dialogue such as might lead to a more permanent harmonization of relations.

Nor is it necessary or legitimate to regard all political conflicts, including class conflicts, as taking the form of a zero–sum game.[28] The resolution of particular instances of political conflict depends precisely upon arriving at an agreed perspective, a compromise, which enables the parties to see their conflict as a *non*–zero–sum game.

This is not necessarily merely a matter of ideological imposition by the (hegemonically) stronger party. Even the familiar conservative rejoinder to proposals for the redistribution of wealth—that the important thing is to be less concerned about the size of the respective portions of the cake allotted to the various sections of society than about increasing the total size of the cake, so that *all* shares may be larger—is not unmitigatedly ideological. There is enough truth in the argument that energy may be expended on attempts at the more equal distribution of existing wealth, to the detriment of efforts to increase the total wealth available for distribution, for a negotiated compromise between the two contending positions to produce a result that benefits both parties. Indeed, there is every evidence that the decline in overall economic performance greatly exacerbates economic conflicts precisely because it shapes the conflict situation so that it increasingly resembles a zero–sum game. In times of declining, or relatively declining, total wealth the margins of calculation of gain and loss are so fine that it becomes increasingly difficult to persuade the contenders that they are both able to gain by any negotiated compromise.

Clearly external factors (among them those generated by the primary structural features of a society) establish constraints both upon the ability of arbitrators actually to propose non–zero sum solutions, and upon their ability to persuade disputants that a compromise is indeed in both their interests. One result is that just as compromise becomes more urgent (if protracted dispute is not seriously to interfere, for example, with the generation of new wealth), so it becomes more difficult to reach.[29]

How one regards this prospect will depend upon how sanguine one is about the prospects of improvement issuing fairly directly from breakdown, and since there are no clear grounds for believing that the fruits of the collapse of liberal democratic institutions would be less bitter now than they were in Mannheim's time, it would seem reasonable to take the steps necessary to avert such a crisis. Mannheim's own suggestions about the infusion of the sociological perspective into the education of *all* members of society, but especially of those who will perform the higher technical and administrative functions, seems no less relevant now than it did in 1940.[30]

The obstacles to even so modest a measure of reconciliation as is promised by the approach I have outlined are formidable. If ideology is, as Habermas puts it, "distorted communication," then the problem of unscrambling that distortion is nothing less than that of "translating the meanings attached to an event in one social world into the medium of another social world" (Burton, 1978: 132). The problems confronting attempts at fundamental reconciliation of parties in conflict exceed even those of producing a general explanation of the conflict. As Burton (1978: 162–3) observes, any such general explanation is necessarily an outsider account and it must be able to locate the level of the mediated realities of the protagonists into its framework since it is that level—the 'mediated realities' of ordinary social consciousness—at which ideological and political struggle is ordinarily conducted. The burden shouldered by the ambitious conciliator entails both the construction of such a general explanation *and* selling it to the conflicting parties.

It would be pointless to minimize the obstacles confronting such an approach, but in the absence of any plausible or palatable alternative, the onus is upon those who would emphasize the difficulties to demonstrate that they are greater than are the costs of the failure even to try.

# ACKNOWLEDGMENTS

For their helpful comments on earlier versions of this paper, first presented to the Workshop on Social Conflict at the Joint Sessions of the European Consortium for Political Research, Brussels, April 1979, I am indebted to John Jervis, Louis Kriesberg, Ray Pahl, Michael Stohl and Rupert Taylor.

I am grateful to Frank Burton and to Messrs Routledge & Kegan Paul Ltd. for permission to quote from *The Politics of Legitimacy* and to Routledge & Kegan Paul Ltd. for permission to quote from Karl Mannheim *Ideology and Utopia*.

# NOTES

1. See Miller (1972), Seliger (1977), Giddens (1979:166–168), Larrain (1979:210–211). The question of the nature and role of ideology has in recent years become a major point of contention within Marxism. Nowhere is the treatment of ideology as a means of social cohesion more pronounced than in the earlier writings of Althusser (1969, 1971) and Poulantzas (1973), each in turn influenced by Gramsci's (1971:328) description of ideology as a sort of 'social cement.' For a vigorous and persuasive argument that such a treatment finds no support in the writings of Marx and Engels themselves, for whom ideology was simply an idea or set of ideas that served class interests and that carried no implication of partiality or falsehood, see McCarney (1980).

2. See, e.g. Bell (1968:96). "What gives ideology its force is its passion . . . one might say, in fact, that the most important, latent, function of ideology is to tap emotion."

3. For a very cogent discussion of commodity fetishism see Geras (1972). It is beyond my purpose here to offer a detailed exegesis of Marx's writings on ideology or to enter into the argument about the extent to which Marx believed ideas were determined by social and economic conditions, but see Seliger (1977), especially Ch. 2.

4. Though some come close to doing so: see e.g. Althusser's (1971) remarks on ideology as the 'cement' which binds together society, any society, be it capitalist, socialist or communist. More orthodox is the view that ideology is a feature of class society, something which will be transcended by the success of the proletarian revolution. (Larrain, 1979:210).

5. See for empirical examination of the American experience, Wachtel (1974).

6. For an excellent discussion of this phenomenon see Sennett and Cobb (1977).

7. As recent research on Northern Ireland has also concluded. See, e.g., Thompson (1979) who, though he acknowledges the independent significance of class structure, emphasizes in the tradition of the analysis of plural societies that ethnic or racial cleavages cannot be reduced to aspects of economic structure.

8. Albeit *not* of the one he actually employed in his own analysis of 'proletarian thought,' which as Alan Swingewood (1975:76) points out, is 'abstract and speculative' and omits all consideration of 'specific mediations.'

9. Which is not to say that he was not vigorously criticized for not being Marxist enough. See Remmling (1975:57–63). The secondary literature on Mannheim has been much improved by the publication of works that reflect a sympathetic and constructive reading of what Mannheim wrote rather than the repetition of the dimissive remarks made about him by others. See, especially, House (1977), Seliger (1977) and Simonds (1978).

10. In this he was directly and deliberately rejecting the position adopted by Lukács in *History and Class Consciousness*. Scepticism about the capacities of the proletariat to achieve its self–emancipation was, of course, evinced by Lenin, and more trenchantly, Bottomore (1975:Ch. 7). See also Bon and Burnier (1971), and Kumar (1978).

11.   It is this lack of faith in the Marxian dialectic, or rather the Third International's version of it that contributes to the charge recently repeated by Swingewood that Mannheim possessed a merely mechanical rather than dynamic conception of the dialectic. It is ironical that Adorno and Horkheimer, the leading lights of the Frankfurt School, should so soon after their slighting of Mannheim have descended into a pessimism so total as to render them politically quiescent, whereas Mannheim continued, even in exile, to commit himself to the project of social reconstruction.

12.   My account here necessarily compresses and simplifies the development of Mannheim's thought over a period of more than twenty years, a period in which Mannheim moved from Hegelian idealism to the pragmatics of postwar planning. Remmling (1975:8–11) has identified four distinct phases in this progress, but I have preferred to follow Ackroyd (1972) in regarding it as a single, continuous process of development in which the later sociology of education is the fulfilment of the moral and political concerns of Mannheim's Budapest years.

13.   This I take to be the substance of Gouldner's (1970) plea for a 'reflexive sociology.'

14.   How far Mannheim's conception differs from that of Marx in this respect is not altogether clear because as Seliger observes, Marx never developed a systematic discussion of the problem. There is, however, some substance to Swingewood's (1975) charge that Mannheim's conception of the relationship between man, society and knowledge is, by comparison with that of Marx, mechanical rather than dialectical, though not, I think, for the reason Swingewood suggests: the conception of ideology as a 'partial' but not merely false 'viewpoint' sits somewhat uncomfortably with the total conception of ideology's focus upon the whole structure of thought, and Mannheim is disconcertingly vague about how the task of 'dynamic synthesis' is actually to be performed.

15.   It is important to recognize that Mannheim's conception of the intelligentsia was prescriptive rather than descriptive. The German intelligentsia of the 1920s could scarcely, as Remmling (1975:71–73) observes, have been a model. Löwy (1979: 85) follows Joseph Gabel in claiming that "whether consciously or not, Mannheim probably used the *szellemkek* [the *Geisteswissenschaften* circle of Budapest in 1918–19] as a model when he later formulated his well-known analysis of the *freischwebende Intelligenz.*".

16.   This tendency is most marked amongst those 'critical theorists' who conceive of ideological domination in the advanced societies in terms of the 'total domination' of technical rationality. For a recent critique of earlier versions of such theses, see Abercrombie, Hill and Turner (1980). The latter do, unfortunately, have a tendency to throw the baby out with the bath water (Rootes, 1981).

17.   A partial and salutary exception is the work of Antonio Gramsci.

18.   For a compendium of these studies, stimulated by Lockwood's (1966) essay, see Bulmer (1975).

19.   The importance of normative commitment, of interest, to the sharpening of perception is not, of course, to be denied. The revisionist philosophy of science, and more particularly, of the social sciences, has amply demonstrated the fruitfulness of commitment to the generation of insight.

20.   On cognitive processes see the work of Jean Piaget and his school; on moral development, Lawrence Kohlberg; and on the interrelation of the processes of cognitive and moral development during the college years, see the work of William Perry.

21.   See especially the work of Kenneth Keniston, Richard Flacks and Michael Miles for the United States, and for a study of the sources of student radicalism in an altogether different political culture—that of Franco's Spain—Maravall (1978). See also Maravall (1976).

22.   The relativity of the meaning of time itself is too little considered in the analysis of inter–generational conflicts. The time perspectives of the young are, inevitably, comparatively foreshortened. Three years has, after all, a very different meaning to someone aged eighteen than to someone aged forty–five or fifty.

23.   A similar situation obtains in industrial action: witness the contrast between (orderly) "official" strikes and (often disorderly) "unofficial" or "wildcat" strikes.

24.   The failure to appreciate the import of these constraints may lead to incomprehension even where it does not lead directly to conflict. Indeed the incident I have in mind that best reveals the

problem occurred in the course of a quite courageous attempt by a senior academic to effect some reconciliation between students and staff during a particularly divisive campus conflict. In the course of a speech to a mass meeting of students, the academic sought to remind his audience of the procedures that the university operated to ensure equitable treatment and cited the case of a recent *cause célèbre* to prove his point. He was greeted with a glum silence—he had forgotten that the case he had cited, which was still part of the stock of common room conversation, had occurred nearly four years previously, and so was quite unknown to more than 90% of the students in his audience. The Students Union has, however, since inscribed this same *cause célèbre* in the canon of its official history. It has thus entered the 'collective memory' of the student body with the result that students eight years after the event are, ironically, better informed about it than were those to whom its occurrence was closer in time.

25.   University employees, other than administrators and faculty, have been omitted from this account, just as they are typically left out of consideration by the major parties to conflict within universities. The small armies of generally poorly paid, frequently part–time and often female staff are typically left as they have always been, more acted upon than acting. The neglect of their interests and their perspectives is, of course, structurally generated—they, after all, merely perform the entirely routine and taken–for–granted activities that keep the basic facilities of the university going—until, of course, they strike, which again for structural reasons, they rarely do.

26.   This, after all, is essentially the role of the industrial relations arbiter in industrial disputes. On the possible role of mediators, see Mitchell (1981: 313): "The basic intermediary function becomes an educational one of bringing about a redefinition of the nature of the problem among the parties themselves. If they are able to re-conceptualise the conflict and their relationship, then an integrative solution, not involving sacrifices or compromise, can be envisaged. . ." See also Heirich (1971: 424) whose analysis of the development of the conflict at Berkeley in 1964 in certain respects anticipates my own. I regret that I did not have access to Heirich's work until the present article was in the proof stage.

27.   The approach that stresses the contribution of the social structuring of perspectives would seem to be clearly at odds with a currently prevalent view that social segmentation may in fact contribute to social harmony rather than detracting from it. An American historian and social critic has recently argued that 'what has held Americans together is their capacity for living apart.' (Wiebe, 1975). One might retort that the capacity for living apart is very much a product of the *possibility* of doing so—a luxury relatively less common in Europe and Asia than it is in North America. The point is surely, insofar as social segmentation exists it may indeed conduce to a low level of conflict on a routine, day–to–day level, but increases the possibility that conflict, when it does occur, will be more violent and more spectacular than it might have been had a higher level of routine social interaction built up the basis of a greater measure of inter–subjectivity—the greater mutual comprehension of alternative viewpoints.

28.   As, e.g., Kumar (1978: 373) appears to do.

29.   Paige's (1975) explanation of the conditions that produce pressures toward agrarian revolutions bears this out: when industrial and finance capital are the major sources of upper class wealth, concessions can always be made and rural social movements diverted before they reach revolutionary proportions; when, however, landed property is the only source of income, conflicts over the ownership of property and control of the state are inevitable, and as a result, revolutions begin not among the class–conscious proletariat of the industrial plantation, but among the proletarianized sharecroppers and migratory labourers of landed estates. It is in the latter case that the conflict is a zero–sum game. Schwartz's (1976) study of the protests of American tenant–farmers reaches a similar conclusion.

30.   The notion that *all* might benefit from such a reform does not seem utterly unrealistic notwithstanding the indisputable fact that the distribution of technical knowledge of all kinds is powerful skewed to the advantage of the socially and economically privileged. As for the notion that reform is, *per se*, inimical to the real interests of the less privileged, as Marxists no less eminent than

Habermas (1971) and Miliband (1977) have recently reminded us, the antinomy between reformism and revolution is a thoroughly false one.

# REFERENCES

Abercrombie, Nicholas, Stephen Hill, and Bryan Turner
   1980   The Dominant Ideology Thesis. London: Allen & Unwin.
Ackroyd, Stephen
   1972   "The development of Karl Mannheim's sociology: An alternative view." Sociological Analysis (Sheffield) 2 (3): 69–73.
Althusser, Louis
   1969   For Marx. Harmondsworth, England: Penguin.
   1971   Lenin and Philosophy and Other Essays. London: New Left Books.
Bell, Daniel
   1968   "The end of ideology in the West." In Chaim I. Waxman (ed.), The End of Ideology Debate. New York: Funk & Wagnalls.
Bon, Frederic, and Michel-Antoine Burnier
   1971   Classe Ouvriere et Revolution. Paris: Editions de Seuil.
Bottomore, T. B.
   1975   Sociology as Social Criticism. London: Allen & Unwin.
Bulmer, Martin (ed.),
   1975   Working Class Images of Society. London: Routledge.
Burton, Frank
   1978   The Politics of Legitimacy: Struggles in a Belfast Community. London: Routledge.
   1979   "Ideological social relations in Northern Ireland." British Journal of Sociology 30 (1).
Cotgrove, Stephen, and Andrew Duff
   1980   "Environmentalism, middle-class radicalism and politics." Sociological Review 28 (2): 333–351.
   1981   "Environmentalism, values and social change." British Journal of Sociology 32 (1): 92–110.
Davis, Howard H.
   1979   Beyond Class Images. London: Croom Helm.
Eisenstadt, S. N. with M. Curelaru
   1976   The Form of Sociology: Paradigms and Crisies. New York: Wiley.
Geras, Norman
   1972   "Marx and the critique of political economy." In Robin Blackburn (ed.), Ideology in Social Science. London: Fontana.
Giddens, Anthony
   1979   Central Problems in Social Theory. London: Macmillan.
Gouldner, Alvin
   1970   The Coming Crisis of Western Sociology. New York: Basic Books.
Gramsci, Antonio
   1971   Selections from the Prison Notebooks. London: Lawrence & Wishart.
Habermas, Jurgen
   1971   Towards a Rational Society. London: Heinemann.
Heirich, Max
   1971   The Spiral of Conflict: Berkeley, 1964. New York: Columbia University Press.
House, J. Douglas
   1977   "In defense of Karl Mannheim." Sociological Analysis and Theory 7 (3): 207–225.

Kumar, Krishna
  1978   "Can the workers be revolutionary?" European Journal of Political Research 6 (4).
Larrain, Jorge
  1979   The Concept of Ideology. London: Hutchinson.
Lockwood, David
  1958   The Blackcoated Worker. London: Allen & Unwin.
  1966   "Sources of variation in working-class images of society." Sociological Review 14.
Löwy, Michael
  1979   Georg Lukács: From Romanticism to Bolshevism. London: New Left Books.
Lukacs, Georg
  1970   History and Class Consciousness. London: Merlin.
McCarney, Joe
  1980   The Real World of Ideology. Brighton, England: Harvester.
Mannheim, Karl
  1936   Ideology and Utopia. London: Routledge.
Maravall, Jose M.
  1976   "Subjective conditions and revolutionary conflict: Some remarks." British Journal of
         Sociology 27 (1).
  1978   Dictatorship and Political Dissent: Workers and Students in Franco's Spain. London:
         Tavistock.
Miliband, Ralph
  1977   Marxism and Politics. Oxford: Oxford University Press.
Miller, David
  1972   "Ideology and the problem of false consciousness." Political Studies 20 (4): 432–447.
Mitchell, Christopher R.
  1981   The Structure of International Conflict. London: Macmillan.
Paige, Jeffery M.
  1975   Agrarian Revolution: Social Movements and Export Agriculture in the Underdeveloped
         World. New York: Free Press.
Parkin, Frank
  1979   Marxism and Class Theory: A Bourgeois Critique. London: Tavistock.
Parsons, Talcott
  1959   "An approach to the sociology of knowledge." Transactions of the Fourth World Congress
         of Sociology.
Poulantzas, Nicos
  1973   Political Power and Social Classes. London: New Left Books.
Remmling, Gunter W.
  1975   The Sociology of Karl Mannheim. London: Routledge.
Rootes, C. A.
  1978   "The rationality of student radicalism." Australian & New Zealand Journal of Sociology
         14 (3) (Part one): 251–258.
  1981   "The dominant ideology thesis and its critics." Sociology 15 (3): 436–444.
Schwartz, Michael
  1976   Radical Protest and Social Structure: The Southern Farmers' Alliance and Cotton Tenancy
         1880–1890. New York: Academic Press.
Seliger, Martin
  1977   The Marxist Conception of Ideology. Cambridge, England: Cambridge University Press.
Sennett, Richard, and Jonathon Cobb
  1977   The Hidden Injuries of Class. Cambridge, England: Cambridge University Press.
Simonds, A. P.
  1978   Karl Mannheim's Sociology of Knowledge. Oxford: Oxford University Press.

Swingewood, Alan
  1975   Marx and Modern Social Theory. London: Macmillan.
Thompson, John Patrick Lawrence
  1979   Dual Incorporation in Northern Ireland: A Theory of Social and Political Structure. Un-
         published Ph.D. dissertation, University of California, Los Angeles.
Wachtel, H.
  1974   "Class consciousness and stratification in the labor process." Review of Radical Political
         Economy 6 (1): 1–31.
Wiebe, Robert H.
  1975   The Segmented Society: An Introduction to the Meaning of America. New York: Oxford
         University Press.
Wright, Erik Olin
  1978   Class, Crisis and the State. London: New Left Books.

# POLITICAL REVOLUTION:

## A TAXONOMIC REVIEW OF PROCESS
## THEORIES


Paul Meadows

---

## I. INTRODUCTION

In this discussion I shall try to develop a taxonomic perspective on theories of revolutionary process. Following Mannheim's concept of perspective orientation, theories may be said to be perspective organizations of data. In this instance the various theories of political revolution as a process constitute the data. Taxonomy is necessarily an initial perspective orientation, a preliminary sorting out of theories according to some significant perspective of the taxonomist, who may indeed be a partisan, or an uninvolved observer.

There has, of course, been no scarcity of theories of political revolution. Some have emphasized stages.[1] Others, causes.[2] Still others, analytical modes.[3] And a number have dwelt on the role significance of revolution itself as the most dramatic and consequential form of collective behavior.[4] The present discussion

Research in Social Movements, Conflicts and Change, Vol. 5, pages 55–74.
Copyright © 1983 by JAI Press Inc.
All rights of reproduction in any form reserved.
ISBN: 0-89232-301-9

limits the taxonomist's task to those theories that are concerned with revolution as process of collective behavior within the framework of history. It is by now conventional in sociological literature to distinguish change and process: the latter specifies a designated and directional pattern of change over time. Theories of revolutionary process may organize data in terms of patterned change over a long–term period, and they may focus only on those data of revolution during the limited period of historic onset and apparent termination of the process. This discussion deals exclusively with theoretical perspectives, which are concerned with political revolution as limited process within the framework of history.

The key to the sense of revolution as process lies in the theorist's conception of revolution as a form of collective behavior. It should be noted in this connection that this collective behavior orientation does not include the work of a growing number of cross-sectional comparative structural theories of revolution, whose writings require a separate treatment. Within this collective behavior framework I shall be concerned with those theories that reflect the dimension of time in relationship to revolution. Thus, by way of anticipation, I shall discuss (1) those theories of revolutionary process in which the conception of time itself is the major determinant of the theory: the *ontological* perspective; (2) those theories that view revolution as a set of events *in* time: the *historistic* perspective; and (3) those theories that see revolution as a set of collective behaviors of persons— actors—engaged in a great drama of collective action: the *instrumental* or *dramatistic* perspective.[5] In all three theoretical perspectives history as the time dimension of revolution is the central frame of reference, but one which, as we shall see, has been differentially defined.

This set of historical perspective orientations on revolutionary process enables us to understand more fully the difficulties that beset any effort at that most elementary task in theorizing about revolution, that is, the problem of definition. Both "revolution" and "history" have a stratified formation of historic meanings that not only reflect the theorist's period as well as his purpose, but also the conglomerate of meanings that these words share with other strategic constructs to which they have been related over a period of time. Their meanings are context and time bound.

Thus, the nucleus of meaning of revolution bears on the notion of revolving. That nucleus, as may be seen in Hatto's masterful article,[6] which has put us all in his debt, suggests not only the influence of the wheel as master metaphor, but also astrology, and before that, cosmology. These images, however, express the dominant ontology of early (and still persisting) views of revolution: the captive condition of archaic and classical societies as they saw history as embedded in eternity. It was not until the post–Renaissance times, when history began to be freed of the burden of ancient cosmology and became the record of unique and novel encounters of men with their special environments that a teleological and deliberate conception of revolution was possible. Even then there was a prolonged, tortured, and often tortuous struggle with inherent necessity before the arrival of open and liberative conceptions of revolutionary process.

It is in this context that Jacques Ellul's appraisal of modern revolutions takes on a startling significance: they represent "a fresh start from zero."[7] He quotes Michelet who in his *Histoire de la Révolution* declared: "On that day everything was possible. . . . The future was present . . . that is, time no longer existed. . . ." But it is a beginning that so reconstructs the past that a new future is possible. Said Camus: "To kill a God and build a Church is the unremitting and conflicting pattern of revolt." It is in this context of liberation from time that the modern conceptions of revolution are able to envision it as transformation, sudden perhaps, but not necessarily violent, often total, primarily political, but in its primitivistic redemption from the bondage of time generally liberational and inventive.

But it is also in this context that we can understand more clearly the abundance of contemporary theories of political revolution, which building on the conception of openness of history as well as reflecting the pluri–bondedness of contemporary societies, provide us with a multiplicity of behavioral and systemic conceptualizations of revolution.

To appreciate fully the significance of these conceptualizations, it is important to see how theories of political revolution as process have themselves undergone an historical process of development. The historic gradient of theories of revolutionary process proceeds from the bondage to cosmology, through the intermediate struggle with the role of history in revolutionary events, to the functions of personality in revolutionary action; from "Eternal Return" of nature, to determined pattern of human events, and to discernible behavioral patterns of deliberate action; from cycled events, through deterministic events, to freely meaningful action.

A word of warning is in order: this historic sequence is, of course, not so neatly compartmentalized as the preceding description may suggest. It never is. An analogy may be useful: change in definition is a succession of geological faults in which new meanings upthrust through prevailing layers of meanings— giant faults of historic perspectives, which despite their novelty, depend on previous ones and which may through erosions of experience mingle with older and later strata of problems and significance. In more familiar terms, theories of revolutionary process were, prior to the French Revolution, largely oriented to ontology. Beginning with the late 18th century and throughout the 19th they were largely oriented to history. The revolutionary theory of the 20th century is largely dramatistic, oriented to action.

## II. THE ONTOLOGICAL PERSPECTIVE ON REVOLUTIONARY PROCESS

Contemporary social theory seems to be fascinated with the problem of change. But change is the other side of the coin of social reality—order. Historically, as Helmut Kuhn has pointed out,[8] there have been two images of order: *orde ordinans*—"order ordering": order as an active force in creating novel patterns;

and *ordo ordinatus*—"order ordered": order as an already existent pattern. Theories of revolutionary process historically started with the latter, particularly with the latter as it eventuated in some *principium ordinis ordinatus*—"principle of the order that orders."

Elsewhere I have discussed this as "the eschatological eschaton."[9] An extension of *mythos* via myth, the eschatological eschaton expressed the belief, in Eliade's words, that it is "the first manifestation of a thing that is significant and valid, but not its successive epiphanies."[10] Essential here is the idea of "the perfection of the beginning . . . projected into a timeless future."[11] Progressive degeneration from perfection is followed by destruction and re–creation, the myth of the "Eternal Return": what took place *ab origine* predicts what will take place; cosmology thus "fixes" ontology—of man and the universe jointly. The timeless is separated from time; change is non–historical because it is transcendent. The *principium* here is substantialist, as Collingwood understood: "the historical agent is regarded as an unchanging substance in relation to which his actions are accident." The agent from which the actions flow, "being a substance, is eternal, and unchanging and consequently stands outside history."[12] Human actions are only events in a cosmic order of cycling change, a revolving.

In revolutionary theory, as elsewhere, the concept of the periodicity of the course of worldly events has had decisive importance. This fact is mirrored in the etymology of the word revolution itself.[13] Plato's linear disintegration of the ideal state into a timocracy and oligarchy and so on through democracy and tyranny was an early formulation of cycle, a conception that was completed later by Polybius, who spoke of the slowly turning wheel powered by Fortune. "Such," he wrote in his *History,* "is the cycle of political revolution, the course appointed by nature in which constitutions change, disappear and finally return to the point from which they started."[14] Although Aristotle rejected Plato's cyclic theory, he did detail how the various types of constitutions turn from one to the other. Later the Romans, like the Greeks, who rooted revolutionary process in observations of general change, spoke of *res novare* and noted—Cicero, for example—a pattern of natural cyclical process. This theme, to the 17th century, emphasized a return to a starting point, an imagery employed by the 15th and 16th century Italians, no less than the 17th century English.

It is important to stress here, as does Peter Calvert, that the cyclical pattern of revolutionary process was linked by the classical observers to both political and social change, the latter inextricably intertwined with the former. The imagery is organic, like the cosmology itself, as when Thucydides described the dissolution of the state (*stasis*) leading to a complete reformulation of basic social relationships, and when Aristotle itemized physical and social causes of revolution. His balance of social power theme expressed it well. "Revolutions," he said in *The Politics,* "break out when opposed parties, e.g., the rich and the poor, are equally balanced, and there is little or nothing between them; for, if either party were manifestly superior, the other would not rise to an attack on them."[15]

Collapse of the social order, as Calvert has noted, was for him a stage in the course of a familiar sequence. Throughout ancient and medieval theory the historic was patterned by the cosmic.

The shift in the imagery of the dominant ontology from nature to history, achieved finally in 18th and 19th century theory, was mediated by the Judaic–Christian eschatology. The Judaic tradition for which the unity of history is controlled by its meaning—the guidance and education of the people of God— was transformed in the Pauline eschatology to an apocalypse, in which the central reference is not that of a nation but the individual, whose redemption is in preparation during the present for eternity. The present, in Bultmann's beautiful phrase, is that time that lies between "the no longer" and "the not yet."[16] The delay in the coming of the *parousia* encouraged a preoccupation with history; and in time the organicity of the older eschatology was replaced by the teleology of apocalypse: literally, tragedy by justice. The new understanding of time, adumbrated by St. Paul, is fully illuminated by St. Augustine. Time and history are not an eternal cyclical movement; there is a beginning and an end, set by God. History is that testing ground between *Civitas terrena* and *Civitas dei:* history is a field of decision. Eschatological consummation becomes the necessary end of history. The redemptive task of history, a theme that burdened the Reformationists, awaits only the secularization processes of the 17th and 18th centuries for its conversion into a revolutionary organon, in which the *telos* of the process, now finalistically viewed, is situated within, not outside, history.

The transition, heated by the polemicists of Church and Throne in the political struggles of the pre–Reformation period,[17] was only heralded by Machiavelli, for whom the *mutazioni, variazoni* and *alterazioni* of political life must be seen in terms of the underlying search for the permanent and enduring.[18] Machiavelli was not a man of the modern revolution, for he understood the foundation of a united nation–state, *lo Stato,* as a *rinovazione.* In the same manner, the 17th century English "Glorious Revolution" was still a restoration, "freedom by God's blessing restored," as the inscription on the Great Seal of 1651 reads. Even the American revolutionist Tom Paine rejected the role of novelty; like Burke, he felt, as Arendt has observed, that novelty "would be an argument against, not for, the authority and legitimacy" of rights.[19]

The emergence of the idea of revolution as an irresistible process, denoted by novelty and beginning with violence in the institution of a new state system, occurred among the 18th century French revolutionists. It was an idea that transferred the classical ontological perspective of nature to history. Said Louis XVI to his messenger, Liancourt: "C'est une révolte." "Non, Sire, c'est une révolution." Subsequent language was more substantial and graphic: Desmoulins described it as *torrent révolutionnaire;* Robespierre as *tempôte révolutionnaire* and as *le marche de la Révolution.* The sudden, sweeping torrent became by Proudhon's time *révolution en permanence.* The ontological perspective of history had become an ontological imperative. The lawfulness of revolution, shorn of its cyclical periodicity, became historical inevitability; the actors of revolution agents of history, as in the Hegelian philosophy of history, agents of the "cunning of reason."

It is in this sense that one must understand Camus' famous discussion of "metaphysical rebellion."[20] Its backgrounds lie in destiny, affirmation always counterbalanced by negation. Among the ancients, he wrote, "to rebel against nature amounted to rebelling against oneself. . . . Therefore, the only coherent act of rebellion was to commit suicide."[21] Revolution is set in the framework of Greek tragedy. Between this imagery and that of man free to establish a new beginning—literally, free *from* history—lies the intervening hurdle of theory, which holds that man is only free *within* history. The slow shifting of the eschaton of revolutionary process from inevitable torrent of immanent *telos* to the open plains of existential choice—from historicism to dramatism—is the story of the ferment of revolutionary theorizing of the 19th century.

## III. THE HISTORISTIC PERSPECTIVE ON REVOLUTIONARY PROCESS

The resources for this task of intellectual reconstruction of the ontological status of man were already abundantly available in the older cosmological eschatons: the concept of nature and history as unitary; cosmogonic myths of perfection; the shift from cosmogony to cosmology, from *mythos* to *logos;* the concept of sacred history having for the believer education–corrective value (as in the Judaic tradition); the "sacrality" of the cosmos and the redemptiveness of history. These aspects of the theme of permanence–in–change are supplemented by yet others equally significant for the re–definition of the nature and role of the revolutionary process. Thus, the Judiac–Christian concept of history as memory generates a variable imagery of the past, in Niebuhr's words, "varying degrees of revocable tentativity and irrevocable finality."[22] As a memory clothed with faith, history thus contrasts with a meaningfulness derived from the world of natural recurrences.

Above all, the new historistic perspective on revolutionary process is linked to the prestigious "Great Chain of Being" doctrine: "no genuine potentiality of being can remain unfulfilled, that the extent and abundance of the creation must be so great as the possibility of existence and commensurate with the productive capacity of a 'perfect' and inexhaustible Source. . . ."[23] There are no gaps in creation; *la scala naturae* is a gradient of being in which each higher order possesses all of the powers of those below it in the scale: literally, the metaphysics of Progress.

Moreover, the earlier metaphysical propositions had an unmistakable human-istic quality: humans perceiving, participating, realizing themselves in nature; the identification of permanence–in–change with the nature of humans them-selves; the just and optimistic value–orientation of redemptive eschatology;

change as the realization of potentiality; and even the apocalyptic imagery of decline. The latter itself gives a special warrant to the "arguments for design," popular in post–Renaissance Europe, and in the age of European expansion. For increasingly appalled by the pointlessness of such apocalypse, European writers turned to the possibility of transcendence of nature *in* history. The first, identified with rationalism, sought an epistemic, the second an axiological transcendence. The Augustinian "New Jerusalem," a transcendence *of* history, became in progress theory, a transcendence *within* history.[24] Millenium is the work of saints, not of a savior. This adaptation of apocalyptical theology moved along two avenues of intellectual invention: the reinterpretation of the Providential view of history and the resurgence of ancient gnosticism. The teleology of Providence became the immanent *telos* of history; and the gnostic divinization of history established the unity of nature and history self–endowed with symbol–determined meaningfulness. With secularization the gnostic view became, as Eric Voegelin has demonstrated,[25] metaphorically and philosophically the new basis of politics in the Western world.

The second route to transcendence of nature, value oriented, turned to a universal uniformism, which was viewed as immanent in nature and symbolized in that magisterial metaphor, the machine, produced a single, unifying principle underlying all reality, a new *principium ordinis ordinatus,* substantial for nature and history alike. Initially located in the cosmos, as the Great Machine, it was subsequently situated in nature and in human society.[26] In terms of revolutionary theory, the transcendence lay in a humanistic value–orientation: symbolization of reality—of nature and of history—by humans, for humans, and of humans as agents and actors in an all–encompassing process. The accent came to be placed, in the name of progress, on reversible process—the formation of a counter–existential dream—which in time became utopian when the wish–image assumed a revolutionary function.[27] The revolutionary act becomes an affirmation in the name of justice, and is stripped of its tragic overtones, of counter–existential possibility (the realization of the inner meaning of history), of the underlying (and therefore real) drifts of history, of the inherently optimistic temporalization of *la scala naturae.* It was counter–existentialism fused with *possibilism* ("that eternal logical order which contains the Ideal of all things possible"), with *dualism* (the intereference with possibility by a species of extraneous "anti–God"), and with *perfectionism* (in the Aristotelian sense). Thus there was provided a new vision of *telos,* an epiphany of nature and history ruled by abstract, conceptual patterns. The full flowering of this new *mythos* at the hands of Hegel and the neo–Hegelians is a familiar story.

The ingenuity of these new model–makers of transcendence is truly amazing.[28] Holding on to the ancient concern with the discovery of underlying patterns common to nature and history, the historistic theorists of process constructed a magnificient overlapping network of bridges between nature and history: (1) the doctrine of a universal *substance,* a universal system–in–reality:

God, matter, energy, and other constructs; (2) the doctrine of a universal *process,* entropy, evolution, interactional processes (for example, conflict); and (3) the doctrine of a universal *dynamic,* structure–function, organization, event–structuralization, ideas–in–realization, and so on. Taxonomically, these historistic eschatons provided a unity of nature and history, either in terms of a meta–theory of events or in terms of a meta–theory of action. The separation of the latter from the former awaited the advent of a later generation of theorists oriented to science, especially to social psychology and secondarily to historical sociology. The nineteenth century historicisms of revolutionary process—Marxists, anti–Marxists, Social Darwinists, among others—wrestled with the problems of an ongoing event–structured historicism, or with the problems of the relationships of "action" to "event" in some theory of revolution as a facilitation of history.

At the heart of any theory of revolutionary process through transcendence of nature in history is some species of gnosticism. That is, the belief–controlled *mythos* that a reality lies behind and beyond appearance, a reality that can be shared only by true believers who by less than readily public routes have come through special and sacred symbolization to know, thus creating a community of paracletic elite having by virtue of this personal knowledge a very special mission.[29] Gnosis comes by many routes of personal knowledge: intellectually, through speculative grasp of the mysteries of existence; emotionally, through ecstatic divine indwelling; volitionally, through revolutionary activism.[30] Through gnosis, reality is re–divinized, a self–endowment of history with privatized meanings.

The revolutionary carriers of gnosis have varied with period and culture: the band of Saints of the Puritan revolution, the proletarian party of Marxism, the communitarians of the 19th century. Gnostic counter–existentialism may, at one extreme, be private escapes from the horror of universal human experience; intermediately, a nihilism as celebrated in the literature on problematic humanity, and at the other extreme, some specific form of utopian change that projects an imagery of existence freed of such horrors. At either pole an ordered society is envisioned, one that primitivistically recovers the true order of things. Reality, as Voegelin says, is blurred in the gnostic dream: dangers and difficulties are met by "magic operations in the dream world, such as moral disapproval, moral condemnation, declarations of intentions, resolutions, appeals to the opinion of mankind, branding of enemies as aggressors, outlawry of war, propaganda. . . ."[31]

Gnosticism, committed to immanence, proceeds in the political realm to a radical immanency of history,[32] that is, to a claim which identifies a discerned and proclaimed logic of history with an imperative of future process. In such forms it eventuates in a total critique of existence, one which is a–historical if not anti–historical, is value–oriented to abstract ideal propositions, is legitimized by appeals to an ultimate social harmony beyond good and evil, and is given credentials by secret and sacrosanct personal knowledge. Reality is fixed final-istically, as in the Aristotelian sense, by a *telos* of the future, that "Archemedian point."[33] The present is an extreme antithesis of the future, whose goal is in Turgot's famous phrase, "the total march of humanity." The participation of Hegelianism and post-Hegelianisms of all varieties in this *mythos* is over-whelmingly obvious.

In the gnostic dream hope is proclaimed in an epiphany of history, in the belief in a divine irruption, which having happened once, can and will happen again. Time is thus not "morally neutral," but is the ground of "intra-mundane salvation," in Gellner's words.[34] On the one hand, episodically inclined gnosti-cists enlarge on the redemptive role of facilitating human actions (as in fervent revolutionary elitism, or even in philosophically oriented activism pursuing a Sorelian myth of violence). On the other hand, processual gnosticists locate the prospect of intra-mundane salvation in the inevitable progression of patterns of change whose a-historicism is obscured if not in fact disguised by a facile use of empirical labels (for example the increasingly popular Saint-Simonian view of world industrialism as envisioned in current congruence theory).

A variant of the gnostic interpretation of revolutionary process, which passes muster as empirical research, has tied revolutionary process to an unfolding pattern of change that proceeds through typical natural history stages to some *dénouèment.*[35] Essentially a dramatistic version of immanent historical process, it achieves its greatest clarity and cogency in portrayals of the "Great Revolu-tions" of the eighteenth, nineteenth and twentieth centuries, whose eventual terminus provides the necessary final element of Greek drama, that is, the unity of beginning, time, place and end. The literature on sequence patterns has evolved a familiar if not definitive pattern of stages, suggesting that the inev-itability of historic process on the grand and global scale is equally matched by the inexorable process of limited historic revolutions.

In the same family of gnostic endeavors at discerning underlying historical patterns to which revolutionary process is irretrievably bound are more recent studies, which center on the interrelationships between revolutionary process and contextual or systemic variables. Some, echoing the Aristotelian forms of causa-tion, isolate antecedent and consequent factors.[36] Others, employing general social science models—those of conflict theory, communication theory, social action theory—are also cases in point.[37]

Indeed, traditional structuralism with its selection of still-shots from the film of process echo a familiar universal uniformism—that happy hunting ground of gnostic symbol-searchers.[38] Seeking to remove time and space marks from experience, it has proved to be one of the more attractive spin-offs from philoso-phy of history. In some of its many varieties—from economic or other determin-isms through the post-Kantian uncovering of constants in human nature, and of cross-cultural invariances in social change to the phenomenological pursuits of the ultimate constants of solipsism—it suggests that the inevitability of time in traditional historicisms has been replaced by the inevitability of culture: the ontic character of time replaced by the equally ontic character of nature, in this case, of course, of human nature.

The most celebrated version of these traditional structuralist theories, certainly one having sweeping revolutionary impact of its own, is that of 19th century Marxism. In the present context it may be summarily described in terms of its social logic and its social methodology.[39] The social logic of Marxism sought to formulate a theory of social change by means of a scientifically couched interpretation of natural law and of the relations between nature and history, being and thought, theory and practice. The Marxian predictive assumption was that the elimination of these conceptual dualities through revolution would clarify the nature of social organization. The prevalence of these antinomies spells a rigid perpetuation of historic dichotomies. Pre–Marxian social thought—for example, Hegelianism—had established that social change is a unitary process; hence, a just and social unity, the goal of revolutionary thought is processual. The process is basically dialectical: the permeation of opposites and thus development through opposition. A just social unity is achieved through social definition, differentiation, opposition, and interaction, categories that were for Marx existential, not merely ideational as they had been for Hegel. The Marxian dialectic is a social logic that treats social action as a *social* process characterized by opposition and interaction, and as a social *process* having succession of new meaning and objective reference, its constituent units maintaining internal not external relationships (in the organic sense). The process is realistic, deterministic, emergent, temporal, and interactive. "History" is no less causal in the process than "nature." Declared Marx: "So long as men exist the history of nature and human history will condition one another." Repudiating the ancient concept of tragedy, he held: "necessity is blind only in so far as it is not understood."

Marxian understanding of necessity is grounded in both dialectical and historical materialism. The first is the logical pattern of social change; the latter, the historical pattern of change conceived of as dialectical. Culture is an inter related developing whole with an independent variable shaping its course. This variable, a union of culture and nature in the form of the mode of economic production, is expressed by the interactional unity of *Produktvergältnisse* (productive relations), *Produktkräfte* (technology, inherited traditions, ideology), and *Produktbedingungen* (conditions of production—natural supply of raw materials, climate, and so on). An organic unit, it forms along with social structures necessarily following from it, according to Engels, "the basis upon which is built, and from which alone can be explained, the political and intellectual history" of an epoch. The "inevitable" development of the mode of production brings (despite the prospective ascendancy of one class and the displacement of another), the relations of production—that is, the class relations—into antagonism. Thus antagonized, classes turn to "the political process": history as political is a record of class struggle. The opposition of classes means "an epoch of social revolution."

Marxian social methodology was a deliberate derivation of the social logic. To theorize is indeed to act: subjective practice (theory) is an operation performed on data through objective practice (action); and from this interaction comes social invention (synthesis). Social action as revolutionary is both secular and cyclical; it is characterized by a long–time and a short–time process. It arises out of cultural *stasis*. Marx wrote in *Revolution and Counter-Revolution:* "Everyone knows nowadays that where there is a revolutionary convulsion, there must be some social want in the background, which is prevented by outworn institutions from satisfying itself. The want may not yet be felt as strong, as general, as might ensure immediate success; but every attempt at forcible repression will only bring it forth stronger, until it bursts its fetters." The structure of revolutionary action is thus seen as the functional product of institutionally blocked human wants.

The Marxian social methodology is characterized by a two–fold pattern of analysis: one stresses the "substratic" phases of social change, the onward motion of productive forces; the other emphasizes the "aspectual" phases, the delayed motion of social forces, of human wants and needs. When human wants are viewed as class needs and ends, they thus account for the shift from the unitary approach of Marxist social logic to the hierarchical approach of Marxist social methodology. His observed substratic pattern of historic change is regarded as inevitable. His pattern of future change realistically concedes that telic change must be instrumented institutionally: change is volitional and thus problematical.

Given then, the economic (substratic) basis of social change as portrayed in historical materialism, the problem becomes: what are the phases of social change as telic (that is, as revolutionary)? The Marxist thesis may be described in the following phases: (1) psycho–structural; (2) political: "seizure of power" and "dictatorship of the proletariat"; and (3) societal: "withering away of the state" and the establishment of the classless society. The first phase is one of preparation for the revolution; it is characterized by the development of an "oppression psychosis" within one class, the sub–dominant class. A definition of action emerges: the dominant class must be displaced—the conquest of power, the second phase. "The main question of every revolution," said Lenin, "is undoubtedly the question of state power." The state, being an organ of class domination, must be captured, its economic machinery replaced through the action of the proletariat as a collectivity, led by the proletarian party, the third phase.

Marxist social methodology, from the short–time standpoint, then, becomes a matter of seizure and policy of power. The essential Marxist doctrine as to the former is the "permanent revolution"; given this *sub specie tempore*, the extra–legality, or illegality of tactics is irrelevant. "Force," said Marx, "is the midwife of every old society pregnant with a new one.'' But force must not be diffused, it must be focussed. Orthodox Marxist tactics, thus, call for (1) propaganda, (2) organization, both class and party, and (3) insurrection. The purpose is the realization of a political apparatus for the control of strategic social institutions.[40] Understanding this necessity leads to revolutionary freedom within history.

## IV. THE DRAMATISTIC PERSPECTIVE ON REVOLUTIONARY PROCESS

Unlike historistic versions of revolutionary process, contemporary theories dwell in T. S. Eliot's language, on the present as an interpenetration of the past and the future. The significant difference lies in the sense of the degree of freedom from either one or the other. Hegelian chialism had sketched out a new world: the mold of past inevitability being broken, rationality and practicality would be reconciled in an immanent transfiguration of human existence.[41] In a letter to Arnold Ruge in 1843 Marx put it this way: ''What we must accomplish is the ruthless critique of everything that exists. . . . Out of the principles of the world we develop new principles for the world.'' The recovery of human freedom lies in the *via negativa* of a new creation.

Having de–divinized history, it was necessary to humanize it: to introduce ''design'' as a human variable into the system of change itself; nature and history as designed or intentional action. This is the underlying motif of the dramatistic eschatons. The source of this new vision lay in the emerging machine technology of the 19th century, as Arendt has pointed out.[42] Technology as system–in–process is not only the interpenetration of nature and history, it is a humanly designed system–in–process: the modern triumph of the human image, not its annihilation. Machine fabrication of meaningfulness is itself a revolution in human consciousness. This is nowhere more startlingly clear than in the technology of contemporary control engineering whose ''automata'' are modelled after the human physiological process. They exist, as Norbert Weiner says, ''in the same sort of Bergsonian time as the living organism. . . .''[43] In more general philosophical language Marx described this human transmogrification when he wrote in *The 18th Brumaire:* ''Man makes his own history, but does not make it out of whole cloth; he does not make it out of conditions chosen by himself but out of such as he finds close at hand.''

The shift from revolution as myth—as part of determinate history—to revolution as drama occurs with the sense of intentional freedom to invent purposed novelty. This theme lies in the background of Marx's comment on the *Brumaire:* ''The social revolution of the 19th century must draw its poetry not from the past, but only from the future. . . . Earlier revolutions required recollections of past world history in order to drug themselves concerning their own content. In order to arrive at its own content, the revolutions of the 19th century must let the dead bury the dead.'' History—memory clothed with faith, as in the Hebraic-Christian tradition—becomes prompted by injustice, inspired and influenced by imagination. The re–orientation is not only dramatistic; it is, initially at least, romantic drama; revolution is the heroic, romantic deed, man as the supreme master of history.[44]

However, the collapse of the Paris Commune heralded another dramatic form, a realistic version of revolutionary drama. Situated in objective conditions, revolutions come when time is ripe for them, that is, they occur only in revolutionary situations. A whole generation of *fin-de-siècle* writers—for example, Ward, Ellwood, Pareto, Brooks Adams, de Tocqueville—like Marx viewed political revolution as the sundering of institutional bonds by repressed forces of development. ''Nations,'' observed de Tocqueville, ''that have endured patiently and almost unconsciously the most overwhelming oppression often burst into rebellion against the yoke the moment it grows lighter. The regime which is destroyed by a revolution is almost always an improvement on its immediate predecessors.''[45]

This realistic dramatism of revolutionary process is oriented to a synchronic perspective with its delineation of social structures and to speculations regarding their function.[46] Its accent, thus, is on a systematic sociology of revolutionary action, embracing behavioral patterns and institutional processes as variables in the emergence and operation of revolutionary process. Illustrations are abundant, chiefly because this is the perspective of contemporary functionalist theory. The following citations, taken from Israel Kramnick's comprehensive review, will suffice.[47] Thus, Samuel Huntington, concerned with revolution as a political change through violent means, observes: ''Revolution is the extreme case of the explosion of political participation. . . . A full–scale revolution involves the destruction of the old political institutions and patterns of legitimacy, the mobilization of new groups into politics, the redefinition of the political community, the acceptance of new political values and new concepts of political legitimacy, the conquest of power by a new, more dynamic political elite, and the creation of new and stronger political institutions.''[48] Another *dramaturgie* of revolution enlarges on the role of economic conditions, either their improvement or immiseration, as part of the emergence of the revolutionary situation. The actors in this version of revolutionary drama are sometimes billed as the *nouveaux riches,* sometimes as the *nouveaux pauvres,* and both are seen as products of rapid growth serving as a destabilizing force. The whole society, observes Kramnick, ''seems to be the actor that brings about the revolution.''[49]

In like manner, the sociological interpretation of revolution, true to the conservative matrix of the sociological discipline itself, locates the drama of revolution structurally in the action of macro–social units—groups, affiliations, societal roles, division of labor, hierarchy and value structure. Typical is Chalmer Johnson's thesis that ties revolutions to ''dysfunctional social systems which have experienced a failure of societal integration processes, failure arising out of the impact of sources foreign or domestic of new ideas or new natural and technological features of life. There emerges "value–environmental dissynchronization."[50] In a not too dissimilar vein Smelser identifies revolution with a "closing off" of the means of reconstituting the social order: "Alternative means . . . are perceived as unavailable."[51] This unavailability, he observes, has three aspects: "(a) The aggrieved group in question does not possess facilities whereby they may reconstitute the social situation; such a group ranks low on wealth, power, prestige, or access to means of communication. (b) The aggrieved group is prevented from expressing hostility that will punish some person or group considered responsible for the disturbing state of affairs. (c) The aggrieved group cannot modify the normative structure, or cannot influence those who have the power to do so."[52] Smelser acknowledges that there is an "indeterminate" relationship between the strains and their resolution. Revolution, it seems, is only one of the many kinds of novel value–creations emerging in such a resolution, though it is by all measures the most far–reaching.

The dramatistic perspective is by no means committed to historical determinism; the systemic necessity that generates revolution is seen as efficient, not as finalistic. Revolutions, far from being (as Trotsky averred in his *My Life*) the "mad" inspirations of history, are one of the many creative inspirations of collective behavior, which in the dramatistic frame is regarded as a process of resolving problems beyond the capacity of institutional behavior. Certainly the dramatistic view has moved a great distance from the Kantian theodicy of nature: "the history of mankind," observed Kant, "can be seen, in the large, as the realization of Nature's secret plan to bring forth a perfectly constituted state. . . ."[53] Dramatistically, they represent a collective intervention in the institutional order in the name of some theory of social justice in order to control the processes of the State, which is held with great realism to be far from being perfectly constituted.

Inevitably, many contemporary discussions of modern revolution, like discussions of any modern social phenomenon, express the reductionist tendency of current social theory. Indeed, even systemic analysis in its most deliberate form—Parsonian sociology, for example—grapples with the problems of solipsism inherent in any analysis of social behavior. Thus, Johnson observes: "the idea of personal 'internal tension' opens up an entirely new range of problems for social systems analysis and for the analysis of revolution because the individual human being constitutes a system that is not identical with the social system."[54] At this point, therefore, we tend to be, in the theory of revolutionary process, at the mercy of the individual writer's own personal paradigm. This circumstance should not be regarded as especially unusual or strange, for one of the most revolutionary changes in this age of revolutions has been the generation of a great variety of selective behavioral models of social action.

One way out of the conceptual maze which this prolixity of model–making has produced is to utilize some variant of the ancient dualism of body–mind doctrine:

to substitute micro–macro behavioral parallelism for the venerable psycho–physical parallelism. Following Simmel, institutional change may be regarded as externalization, even as projection, of "the revolutionary personality."[55] Another simplifying strategy, which like the preceding one is also often a "discount downward" in Kenneth Burke's words (like utilizing parallelism), is a psycho–culturalism that finds in both micro–and macro–social units the same behavioral properties. Institutions, associations and persons react to the same stimulation field with the same patterns of response mechanisms. One thinks here of the many cybernetic models, for example, Etzioni's *Active Society,* or much earlier, of the impulse patterns and reflex mechanisms of Sorokin's *Sociology of Revolution.*[56]

One of the most persuasive paradigms has been the selection of some analytical property of the human personality—sexual repression, anxiety, motivation–sets, expectations, cognitive dissonance, to cite a few—as a means of illuminating the dramatistic interpretation of revolutionary process.[57] Hardly less persuasive has been the utilization of role theory—of leadership, followership, membership, functional types, exigency patterns, to name only some topics—in an explicit *dramaturgie* of revolution, revolution as theater.[58] It is interesting, however, that nobody—except for a passing comment by Marx—has sought to explicate revolution as theater by developing the many revolutions of modern times in terms of a modern conception of tragedy, or tragi–farce, or romantic comedy.[59] The materials, incidentally, for such a portrayal can be found in abundance in the writings of Kenneth Burke or H. J. Mueller.

Finally, and by no means the most highly regarded, there is the social psychological depiction of revolutionary dramatism that resorts to the construct of "collective consciousness." The literature here extends from the "planes and currents" psychology of LeBon and Tarde and Ross to the current evocations of "revolution by consciousness" by Charles Reich, Herbert Marcuse, Norman Brown, Abbie Hoffman and the latest though hardly the last writer on feminine liberation. The collective behavior approach to resolution as process can hardly be made more explicit than it has in this literature.

The personality paradigms are especially meaningful in this period of history, which has not only witnessed the establishment of highly productive social science models of the human being but has also undergone a sea–change in prevailing attitudes toward history. The latter is associated with the dominant existentialist mood, which going beyond the interactions of self and society, gives voice to the confrontations and commitments of the transactions between self and the world.[60] Camus captured a great part of this mood, which seems to be at the heart of much contemporary theory of revolutionary process, a mood that seeks transcendence of all reality in the very priority of existence. "Who is a rebel? A man who says no, but whose refusal does not imply a renunciation. He is also a man who says yes, from the moment he makes his first gesture of rebellion. . . . What was at first the man's obstinate resistance now becomes a whole man, who is identified with the summed up in this resistance. The part of himself that he wanted to be respected he proceeds to place above everything else and proclaims it preferable to everything, even to life itself. It becomes for him the supreme good.''[61]

## V. A RETROSPECTIVE ON THE THREE PERSPECTIVES

This discussion started with the theme that any theory is a perspective organization of data, a perspective that the theorist brings to his data, which helps in the selection, organization and interpretation of his data. Political revolutions, being old, hugely varied and multi–dimensional (like all human actions) have been the occasion for a parallel variety of perspectives. Political revolutions are also historical phenomena, so that the data of revolutions are perforce historical data. It is this fact, aside from their intrinsic and instrumental significance, that has been primarily responsible for so many perspective approaches to the interpretation of revolutions.

Being historical phenomena, political revolutions have invited, so to speak, the development of theoretical perspectives that have dealt with, in some selective way, their historical character. At first, theories of political revolutions were attracted to their historicity: their embeddedness in and embodiment of the history of peoples. Here some conception of history has dominated completely the conception of revolution. Subsequent theorists of political revolution were attracted to the historicality of revolutions: that is, to the fact that patterns of many sorts could be discerned in their rise, operation and conclusion, and thus to the fact that they may be discerned to have identifiable causes, stages, form, dynamics, and consequences. Here some conception of history is constructed alongside some conception of collective action. Later theorists of political revolution dwelt on the highly visible and variable dimensions of social action before, during and following the revolution. Here the conception of history has been subordinated to some conception of human action. In all of these instances the accent has been placed on pattern, both in history and in revolution, with pattern as well as revolution being variously conceived and conceptualized.

In general, we may say that the identification and discussion of pattern is a function of the problematics of the theorist. The earlier problematics reflected a concern with causes, form, stages, consequences—an evocation of the four modalities of causation of Aristotle. Later theories have reflected a concern with the contextual character of both history and revolution. Thus, in the first perspective discussed in these pages, revolutions were conceptualized as a function of history as context; later versions emphasized the history of society as context; and still later versions focussed on the history of the actors themselves in the collective drama of revolution within the context of the revolutionary situation.

In this discussion we have sought to set forth two parallel sets of conceptions of revolution, one set is that of history, the other set is that of human action. The conceptualizations in each case have been viewed not as conceptual enclaves firmly separated from one another but as forming a palimpset, such that the revolution is seen through the successive overlays of historical and action theories. The main thrust of the argument in this discussion has been that revolutionary action is seen as occurring in terms of theoretical perspectives, such that revolutionary action is viewed as having happened with increasing degrees of freedom from history. The argument has been presented basically in terms of three functional propositions:

- action =f (history);
- history =f (action);
- action =f (personality).

This gradient is the basis for the designation of the third theoretical perspective as dramatistic. Theories of revolution represent varieties of scenarios in which history supplies the plot, place, theme, characters and passion of the revolutionary action. Both participants in and observers of revolution may be regarded as in fact scenario writers. Both have drawn on history as repertoire, but increasingly on the history of human beings as the main source of the scenario: people themselves as the new magisterial metaphor of the collective action.

Moreover, both the history theme and the action theme have been presented in terms of the idea of process. This idea, reaching back, as Nisbet has shown, to the conception of *physis*, considers action as a sequence over time, having a beginning, growth and end, therefore as a series of changes over time. Literally, thus, when "direction" is added to "change," the product is "process." The key term, thus, becomes the idea of directionality. Early theorists of revolutionary process saw directionality as supplied by history itself (*telos*). Later theorists found directionality in the discernment of patterns of history (historicality/historicism). And still others found directionality in human action itself (dramatistic metaphor). If theories of revolutionary process can be thought of as scenario writing, the first perspective viewed process as linear and inevitable; later theorists regarded it as multilinear and immanent; and still later theorists conceived of process as multi–dimensional and stochastic.

In any process approach to any reality, time is essential. In the first perspective on revolutionary process time was literally and ontologically "of the essence." In the second, place was added to time: historical time. In the third, place drops out and time becomes the social time of the actors themselves. This sequence suggests a fourth possibility, now being vigorously pursued in contemporary cross–cultural and comparative structural studies, one in which both time and place have been dropped out in favor of timeless and spaceless invariances in relationships among constituent or systemic parts. At such a point, the theory of political revolution as process formally crosses the threshold from interpretation to explanation. As this effort matures, the theory of revolutionary process, like the phenomenon of revolutionary process itself, will have indeed experienced all the possible encounters with time.

# NOTES AND REFERENCES

1.   Cf. Brinton, C., *The Anatomy of Revolution* (New York: W. W. Norton, 1938); Edwards, L. P., *The Natural History of Revolution* (Chicago: University of Chicago Press, 1967); Gorrow, B. J., "The Comparative Study of Revolution," *The Midwest Sociologist,* Spring, 1955, pp. 54–60; Hertzler, J. O., "The Typical Life Cycle of Dictatorships," *Social Forces,* XVII (March 1, 1933), pp. 303–309; Hopper, R. D., "The Revolutionary Process: A Frame of Reference for the Study of Social Movements," *Social Forces,* XXV (March, 1950), pp. 270–279; Meadows, P., "Sequence in Revolution," *American Sociological Review,* XXV (May–June, 1944), pp. 702 ff; Yoder, D., "Process in Revolution," *Sociology and Social Research,* XII (1927–1928), pp. 263 ff.

2.   Ellwood, C. A., "Psychological Theory of Revolution," *American Journal of Sociology,* XI (1905), pp. 49 ff; Gottschalk, L., "Causes of Revolution," *American Journal of Sociology,* XL, No. 1 (July, 1944), pp. 1–8; Johnson, C., *Revolutionary Change* (Boston: Little, Brown, 1966); Kuttner, A. B., "The Cycle of Revolution," *New Republic,* XX (1919), pp. 86–88; Reeves, S. A., *The Natural Laws* of Social Convulsion (New York: E. P. Dutton, 1939); Schwartz, D. C., "A Theory of Revolutionary Behavior," in J. C. Davies, ed., *When Men Revolt and Why* (New York: Free Press, 1971; Sorokin, P. A., *The Sociology of Revolution* (Philadelphia: J. B. Lippincott, 1920).

3.   Davies, J. C., "Toward a Theory of Revolution," *American Sociological Review,* XXVII, No. 1 (1962), pp. 5–19; Friedrich, C. J., "An Introductory Note on Revolution," in Friedrich, ed., *Revolution* (New York: Atherton, 1967); Gerschenken, A., "Reflections on the Economic Aspects of Revolution," in H. Eckstein, ed., *Internal War* (New York: Free Press, 1964); Halpern, M., "A Redefinition of the Revolutionary Situation," in Miller, N. and Aya, R., eds., *National Liberation: Revolution in the Third World* (New York: Free Press, 1971); Kamenka, E., "The Concept of a Political Revolution," Chapter VI in Friedrich, *op. cit.;* Kramnick, I., "Reflections on Revolution: Definition and Explanation in Recent Scholarship." *History and Theory,* XI, No. 1 (1972), pp. 26–57; Lichtheim, G., *The Concept of Ideology* (New York: Random House, 1967); Martin W. C., "Toward a Theory of Revolution: A Social Structural Strategy," unpub. mss.; American Sociological Association Convention, 1972); Meadows, Paul, *The Many Faces of Change* (Cambridge: Schenkman, 1971), Chapter IV: "Patterns of Revolutionary Thought."

4.   Arendt, H., "The Meaning of Revolution," Chapter I in Arendt, *On Revolution* (New York: Viking Press, 1961); Blanksten, G., "Revolutions," in Davis, H. E., ed., *Government and Politics in Latin America* (New York: Ronald Press, 1957); pp. 119–146; Ellul, J., *Autopsy of Revolution* (New York: A. A. Knopf, 1971); Johnson, C., *Revolution and the Social System* (Palo Alto: Hoover Institution Studies, Stanford University Press, 1964); Lederer, E. "On Revolutions," *Social Research,* III (1936), pp. 1–18; Marcuse, H., *Reason and Revolution: Hegel and the Rise of Social Theory* (Boston: Beacon, 1960); Selden M., "Revolution and Third World Development," in Miller and Aya, *op. cit.,* pp. 214–248; Voegelin, E., *The New Science of Politics* (Chicago: University of Chicago Press).

5.   This typology is adapted from the present writer's "Eschatons of Change: Philosophical Backgrounds of Development Theory," *International Journal of Comparative Sociology,* IX, No. 1 (March, 1968), pp. 41–60; also *The Many Faces of Change, op. cit.,* Chapter II.

6.   Hatto, A., "'Revolution': An Enquiry into the Usefulness of an Historical Term." *Mind,* LVIII (1949), pp. 459–517.

7.   Ellul, *op. cit.,* p. 49.

8.   Kuhn, H., "The Case for Order in a Disordered Age," in Kuntz, P. G., ed., *The Concept of Order* (Seattle: University of Washington Press, 1968), pp. 442 ff.

9.   "Eschatons of Change . . . ," *op. cit.*

10.  Eliade, M., *Myth and Reality* (New York: Harper Torchbook, 1963), p. 34.

11.  *Ibid.,* p. 52.

12.  Collingwood, R. G., *Idea of History* (Oxford: Oxford University Press, 1946), p. 43.

13.  Hatto, *op. cit.,* cf. also, Calvert, P., *Revolution* (New York: Praeger, 1970).

14.  VI, 9, x; quoted by Hatto, *op. cit.*

15. *The Politics,* Book V. iv, 11.

16. Bultman, R., *History and Eschatology: The Presence of Eternity* (New York: Harper Torchbook, 1957).

17. It is important to note here that the modern debates concerning authority and liberty, person and State, conformity and dissent were anticipated in the struggles between Church and Throne in the emerging nation–states of Europe.

18. Arendt, *op. cit.,* p. 29.

19. Arendt, *op. cit.,* p. 38.

20. Camus, A., *The Rebel* (New York: Vintage Books, 1956).

21. Camus, *op. cit.,* p. 27.

22. Niebuhr, R., *Faith and History* (New York: Charles Scribner Sons, 1949), p. 20.

23. Lovejoy, A. O., *The Great Chain of Being: A Study in the History of Ideas* (New York: Harper Torchbook, 1936), p. 52.

24. Tuveson, E. L., *Millennium and Utopia: A Study in the Background of the Idea of Progress,* (1964), Chapter I: "The Apocalyptic Image of History.

25. Voegelin, *op. cit.*

26. Tuveson, *op. cit.,* Chapter III: "A Mechanist New Jerusalem."

27. Mannheim, K., *Ideology and Utopia* (New York: Harcourt, Brace, 1935), p. 192.

28. Cf. Foss, M., *The Idea of Perfection in the Western World* (Princeton: Princeton University Press, 1946); Lee, A. E. and Beck, R. N., "The Meaning of Historicism," *American Historical Review,* LIX, No. 3, pp. 568–577; Meadows, Paul, "The Metaphors of Order," in Gross, L., *Sociological Theory: Inquiries and Paradigms* (New York: Harper, 1967), Nisbet, R. A., *Social Change and History* (New York: Oxford University Press, 1969).

29. Cf. Gellner, E., *Thought and Change* (Chicago: University of Chicago Press, 1961); Niemeyer, G., *Between Nothingness and Paradise* (Baton Rouge: Louisiana State University Press, 1971).

30. Niemeyer, *op. cit.*

31. Voegelin, *op. cit.,* p. 170.

32. Cf. Mannheim, *op. cit.*

33. The phrase is Niemeyer's, *op. cit.*

34. Gellner, *op. cit.,* p. 3.

35. The reference here is to the studies of stages listed in footnote 1.

36. Cf. Gottschalk, *op. cit.;* also Tanter, R. and Midlarsky, M., "A Theory of Revolution," *Conflict Resolution,* XI (1967), pp. 264–271.

37. Cf. Willer, D. and Zollschan, G. K., "Prolegomena to a Theory of Revolution," in Zollschan and Hirsch, eds., *Explorations in Social Change* (Boston: Houghton, Mifflin, 1964); Kirchheimer, O., "Confining Conditions and Revolutionary Breakthroughs," *American Political Science Review,* LIX (1965), pp. 964–974; Meadows, P., "Theses on Social Movements," *Social Forces,* XXIV, No. 4 (May 1940), pp. 408–412; Smelser, N., *Theory of Collective Behavior* (New York: Free Press, 1962), Chapter X.

38. Cf. Runciman, W. G., "What Is Structuralism"? *British Journal of Sociology,* XX, No. 3 (September 1969), pp. 253–265.

39. Cf. Meadows, "Patterns of Revolutionary Thought," in *The Many Faces of Change, op. cit.*

40. Cf. Becker, F. B., "Lenin's Application of Revolutionary Tactics," *American Sociological Review,* II (June, 1937), pp. 353–362; Gottschalk, L., "Leon Trotsky and the Natural History of Revolution," *American Journal of Sociology,* XLIV (1938), pp. 339–354; Gross, F., *The Seizure of Power* (New York: Farrar and Rinehart, 1935).

41. Niemeyer, *op. cit.,* p. 81.

42. Arendt, *op. cit.,* p. 60.

43. Weiner, N., *Cybernetics or Control and Communication in the Animal and the Machine* (New York: John Wiley, 1948), p. 49.

44. Kamena, *op. cit.,* p. 125.

45. de Toqueville, A., *The Old Regime and the Revolution* (New York: 1856), p. 214.

46. Willer and Zollschan, *op. cit.*, p. 126.

47. Kramnick, *op. cit.*

48. Huntington, S., *Political Order in Changing Societies* (New Haven: Yale University Press, 1968), pp. 260, 268.

49. Kramnick, *op. cit.*, p. 45.

50. Johnson, *Revolutionary Change, op. cit.*

51. Smelser, *op. cit.*, p. 325.

52. *Ibid.*

53. Quoted by Beck, L. W., "Kant and the Right of Revolution," *Journal of the History of Ideas*, XXXII, No. 3 (July–September, 1971), p. 418.

54. Johnson, *op. cit.*, p. 73.

55. For example, cf. the important study, Wolfenstein, E., *The Revolutionary Personality: Lenin, Trotsky, Gandhi* (Princeton: Princeton University Press, 1967).

56. Sorokin, *op. cit.*

57. Cf., Johnson, *op. cit.*, for a review of these approaches; also Kramnick, *op. cit.* In addition, cf. Gamson W., *Power and Discontent* (Homewood: Dorsey Press, 1968); Reich, C. A., *The Greening of America* (New York: Random House, 1970), "Revolution by Consciousness," pp. 323–378; Riezler, K., "On the Psychology of Modern Revolution," *Social Research,* XI (1943), pp. 320–336; Scott, M. B. and Hyman, S. M., "Mass Society and the Ideology of Rebellion," Chapter II in their *The Revolt of the Students* (Columbus: C. E. Merrill, 1930); Wallin, S., "Violence and the Western Political Tradition, *American Journal of Orthopsychiatry,* XXXIII (June, 1963), pp. 15–28.

58. For example, cf. Lasswell, H. D. and Lerner, D., *World Revolutionary Elites* (Cambridge: M.I.T. Press, 1966); Stark, "Toward a Psychology of Charisma, I, II" *Psychological Reports,* XXIII (1968), pp. 1163–1166; XXIV (1969), pp. 88–90; Willer and Zollschan, *op. cit.*

59. Cf. Mazlish, B., "The Tragic Farce of Marx, Hegel and Engels: A Note," *History and Theory,* XI, no. 1 (1972), pp. 335–337.

60. Cf. Meadows, "Eschatons of Change . . ." *op. cit.,* pp. 54–60.

61. Camus, *op. cit.,* pp. 13, 15.

# INSTITUTIONAL DEVELOPMENT AND NONVIOLENT RESISTANCE

Ronald M. McCarthy

## I. INTRODUCTION

Many social movements rise and decline leaving scarcely anything to show that they ever existed. Others reach some of their goals and a measure of success. Still others are movements whose experience is marked by long years in which no lasting changes result from their actions. For them, success is temporary, at best, or their sporadic turns to direct action are suppressed before lasting gains are made. Yet some of these movements, in the end, mark the society in which they arise for years to come. Not only do the organizations that carried the movement's challenge outlive the conflict, but law comes to recognize new rights and new standards of justice, people's beliefs about their place in the world change, and the political decision–making process goes on differently. Some movements, in short, leave a legacy of new and transformed social, economic, political, and cultural institutions, developed as an outcome of the movement.

Research in Social Movements, Conflicts and Change, Vol. 5, pages 75–98.
Copyright © 1983 by JAI Press Inc.
All rights of reproduction in any form reserved.
ISBN: 0-89232-301-9

The purpose of this paper is to present two propositions explaining the circumstances under which nonviolent resistance movement organizations, their ideas and methods, and changes in political structure that they bring about become permanent parts of the society in which they take place. The propositions will be expanded upon and explored with comparative data from two resistance movements. This leads to review of the ways in which movement responses to typical organizational tasks result in the development of movement organizations and movement ideology into lasting social institutions.

It has long been recognized that social movement organizations change their structure and goals in response to changes in the political environment as well as to internal, organizational tasks and problems (Zald and Ash, 1966; Rudwick and Meier, 1970; Messinger, 1955). There has also been much concern with the circumstances under which social movements bring about change in the institutional structure of the society. Recently, researchers have challenged many long–held assumptions about how social movements operate and how they bring about change (Gamson, 1975; Gamson, 1980; Piven and Cloward, 1979; Goldstone, 1980; Olson, 1971). In the process, it has become clear that one measure of a movement's ''success'' is not simply that its program be adopted but that movement organizations and outlooks be broadly accepted, outlasting the struggles that brought them to life (Gamson, 1975; Abel, 1937).

Researchers studying the use of nonviolent action in social movements have long been interested in a similar problem, the problem of empowerment. How, they ask, can social movements act to gain power and autonomy for their constituents? The interest of these researchers is not just a wish to make movement organizations permanent, but an interest in finding ways in which people could act, under a variety of circumstances, to gain power for themselves (Sharp, 1973; Sharp, 1980; Lakey, 1973; Bruyn, 1979).

One important measure of social change brought about by social movements is change in institutions. When social movement goals are adopted, even though the organizations themselves are not accepted, the policies and sometimes the personnel of existing institutions may be changed in turn. Social movement organizations themselves may be transformed over the period of the struggle into institutions that legitimately continue to represent a constituency. Of course, such institutions or organizations may have been ''co–opted,'' gutted of their significance, and only representing a source of legitimation for established structures, or transformed into something rather less change-oriented than they had been (Weber, 1978:1121–23, 1146–48; Zald and Ash, 1966). On the other hand, organizations arising out of social movements may carve out a lasting place of influence in the society, possessing legally recognized rights and powers. This, it could be argued, has been the case with the labor movement in the United States, which has long since gained the right to organize, strike, and conduct boycotts, free from the damaging interference of injunctions and other anti–union measures.

Social movements also make their contribution to political culture. The more radical the movement, the more its ideology will be a rejection of the accepted world view (Bittner, 1963:931–34). Movement outlooks may also bring about the questioning of values and incorporation of new values into members' world view and ideology (Carden, 1978:184–85). On the other hand, not all social movements are pledged to bring about change in social and political practices or ideologies, many attempt to resist change and preserve current institutions (Vander Zanden, 1959). This paper will explore the conditions under which such movements, which have their origins in attempts to prevent undesirable changes, may be transformed into agents for the development of new and renewed institutions.

## II. CHARACTERISTICS OF RESISTANCE MOVEMENTS

Here, the term *resistance movement* will be used to encompass those mass movements that utilize direct action to protest, counter, and oppose the actions or policies of others. These actions or policies are perceived by the resisters as being either illegitimate or harmful, and include institutional "decline" as well as overt actions (Vander Zanden, 1959; Walzer, 1960; Hirschman, 1970). As government or other social movements, either within the resisters' society or affecting it from outside, move to make concrete changes in social, economic, or political life and relationships, resistance movements work to block, minimize, or at least express their opposition to those changes. At other times, resistance movements may act to oppose existing social arrangements which were accepted in the past but now are seen as unacceptable (for example, Vander Zanden, 1963).

It is not simply a matter of a group believing that others are acting illegitimately, but that it take collective measures to protest or prevent this from occurring. Consequently, the problem of how to conduct mass action successfully, of what means would make the group's opposition most effective, is central to such a movement. When collective action employs means that attempt to resist change or to channel change into acceptable forms and these means attempt to manipulate the social, economic, and political relations that the parties share, while refraining from violence toward persons and the destruction of property, the actors are utilizing nonviolent resistance. This kind of movement will be called a nonviolent resistance movement. (See Sharp, 1973: 63–74, 451–642; Sharp, 1980:91–112, 209–32; Sternstein, 1969; Skodvin, 1969; Liddell Hart, 1969; Ebert, 1970; Stiehm, 1972.)

Nonviolent action is essentially the generic term for the enormous number of actions comprising nonviolent protest and persuasion; social, economic, and political noncooperation; and nonviolent intervention, as characterized by Sharp (1973). For resistance movements choosing to avoid violence, terror, or destruction, yet refusing either to remain passive or limit themselves to making use of constitutionally available channels, these methods constitute a kind of tool kit of possible actions. Groups need not choose nonviolent action on the basis of principle. Rather, in choosing nonviolent means, resisters are seeking individual means of action suited to reaching their perceived goals, and often choose nonviolent means piecemeal.[1]

It is important to recognize, in this context, the growing body of literature rejecting the theory that social movements are an anomic reaction to social strain (Smelser, 1962) whose actions are consequently irrational. Rather, recent research into crowd actions from early modern times to the present, as well as the ability of collective action to achieve "success" and bring about change has stressed the conscious goal orientation and "rationality" of collective action (Rudé, 1964; Griessinger, 1981; Thompson, 1971; Gamson, 1975). Like all social action by collectivities, the actions chosen by resistance movements must solve problems posed by their social, economic, and political environments. A particular problem for resistance movements, however, is that many of these problems are posed by an opponent capable of responding with repression. Since the main goal of a resistance movement is to induce the opponent to alter objectionable behavior, this always has to be taken into account (Ebert, 1970:46–63).

## III. FROM ORGANIZATION TO INSTITUTIONAL DEVELOPMENT: TWO PROPOSITIONS

The following sections of this paper will present and explain two propositions on the conditions under which institutional development during resistance movements may take place. They will not be concerned primarily with organization–building or attempts to preserve organizations after their issues have been resolved, which have been considered elsewhere (Zald and Ash, 1966; Messinger, 1955). Comparative case material drawn from the primarily nonviolent phase of the American Independence Movement, 1765–1775, and the contemporary movement in Poland, from 1956 through the fall of 1981, will be drawn on in support of the propositions.

Both of the cases considered here involved quarrels over a broad range of issues between sectors of the population and governmental and economic institutions. In both cases, the legitimacy of the existing system was challenged by the resistance movements: the legitimacy of specific acts, and ultimately the legitimacy of the system itself. Resisters pushed to make the continued legitimacy of the system contingent upon its conforming to their developing definition of the situation and their needs, not simply upon official definitions and practices.

In these and similar cases, the repression that the government or other opponents were able to bring to bear was not effective enough to ensure a permanent solution to these crises of legitimacy. Although short–lived individual challenges could be brought to an end, sometimes through repression and sometimes through concessions, the conditions that had led to resistance in the first place recurred, and fresh movement action arose. Just as importantly, the movements grew, in a sense, both during and in between campaigns as links were made in action, ideology, and continuity among movement sectors. The challenge raised by the resistance movements did not restrict itself to details of the system, but went to very basic questions.

## A. Proposition One: Ineffective Repression Leads to Institutional Development

Continued or repeated crises of legitimacy raise several essential questions. First, who rules and by what authority? Second, can new organizations and institutions representing constituencies of the resistance movement take an autonomous place in the social and political order? Third, will the existing dominant sectors continue to define the accepted world view or will movement actions and the thought developed by adherents be able to challenge or possibly replace the dominant ideology? A decision favoring the resistance movement may mean that the repression that the existing structure had available was not sufficient to resolve these questions. This leads to the first proposition.

Proposition One: the first contributing factor leading to institutional development of resistance movement sectors is the continuing inability of the opponent to repress movement organizations and actions, opinion–making representatives, and ideologies. At the same time, the opponent refuses an accommodation that would bring the challenge to an end.

## B. Proposition Two: Organizational Response to Repression

In the face of continued or even sporadic attempts at repression, resistance movements find that defense of their continued existence and autonomy becomes a priority. Where movement organizations have arisen, they will attempt to continue to be effective even though repression is occurring. Also, movement organizations generally take some steps to defend the lives and freedom of those who take part. Where repression is violent, leaders often attempt to reduce the number of casualties, or to keep movement members out of prison if possible. This is a task for nonviolent resistance movements as well as for movements using other means, and nonviolent means may be chosen partly in response to these tasks (see below and Sharp, 1973:583–86). Likewise, the movement's constituency often claims certain rights, which may have to be defended, and gains made must often be defended against erosion as well.

Beyond this, lines of authority within movement organizations or between organizations must be clarified as organizations become more permanent. As the struggle proceeds, organizations may claim that they have certain rights and authority over parts of the population, much in the way a labor union claims the right to organize a craft, and work to solidify those claims. Not all changes in the direction of greater institutionalization are concrete organizational changes. Procedures found to be effective for mobilizing adherents or making appeals, for example, may be utilized by many groups. Methods of opposition which resisters can turn to on an *ad hoc* basis, as a kind of regularized opposition procedure, arise in many circumstances. There is a cultural aspect to this process as well. What Useem has called "domestic protest traditions," (1975:40) fleshed out with popular ideologies justifying resistance in specific cases—or even requiring it—arise. In some political cultures, including that of the American colonies as discussed below, these traditions may be passed down for generations, as a thorough institutionalization of movement–originated culture. These observations lead to the second proposition.

Proposition Two: actions taken by resistance movements and resistance movement organizations to defend autonomy, claimed rights, and gains achieved, and to clarify developing lines of authority are the actions that most contribute to the institutional development of resistance movements.

# IV. EXPLORATION OF THE PROPOSITIONS

## A. *Methods and Data*

The larger question of institutional development could profitably be broken down so as to explore the circumstances under which new institutions are developed, existing institutions transformed, and ideological and cultural contributions made by resistance movements. However, it is seldom the express intention of resistance movements to bring about these changes. Rather, as movements develop, the kinds of tasks the second proposition mentions force organizations to make unintended contributions to change. Consequently, the propositions already made will be explored by looking comparatively at several basic tasks of resistance movements as they were approached by two movements that achieved a measure of institutional transformation.

The movement tasks that will be looked at in testing the propositions are, first, defending the autonomy of movement organizations and existing institutions; second, defining the operation of existing institutions through resistance; and third, creating lasting institutions that supplement or replace those already in existence. Following this, the significance of institution formation by social movements for political culture will be reviewed briefly.

One source of case material is the first and primarily nonviolent phase of the American Independence Movement, from 1765 to 1775. Opening with the resistance against the Stamp Act in 1765 and early 1766, this phase of the Independence Movement included major campaigns against the Townshend Acts, from 1768 through 1770, and the Coercive Acts, in 1774 and 1775. In addition to these, several other resistance campaigns occurred, some in only a single colony, and others such as the protests against the Currency Act of 1764 and resistance against the Tea Act in 1773, involving several colonies. (See Conser et al., forthcoming, for evidence establishing that the movements of these years were a series of nonviolent resistance campaigns.)

The second source of case material is the Polish experience since 1956, including the rise of the Solidarity trade union and its activities through the fall of 1981. The Polish movement began with major strike waves in 1956 and 1970, each of which brought about the fall of the then-current premier. In 1976, less widely spread strikes occurred that were followed by the organization of committees of dissidents who worked toward a renewal of Polish socialism and free labor organizations. In the course of a major wave of strikes in 1980 the autonomous labor union Solidarity was organized, which was the major focus of the movement at the time this was written.

## V. THE CASES COMPARED

These cases were chosen because of the role of nonviolent action in each. They are also similar because both were in part responses to economic crises within their respective countries and contributed to ongoing crises of legitimacy.

It has become well accepted that the American Independence Movement took place during a series of trade depressions in the colonial economy, particularly affecting the cities. During the same time, attempts were made by successive British ministries to tax American commerce, keep it within bounds set by British law, and strengthen administrative control. Beyond this, the ministries tried to alter the administration of the American colonies, whether at Whitehall or in America, to make it more responsive to policies the ministries set. (See Schlesinger, 1968; Sachs and Hoogenboom, 1965:152–72; Egnal and Ernst, 1972; Nash, 1979; Maier, 1972).

What is less well recognized is the extent to which active resistance was carried on and the role of violence in the campaigns consciously limited. During the first weeks of the Stamp Act resistance, starting in August 1765 and going into the first week of November, street crowds threatened the tax collectors and military officers who tried to protect the stamps, and houses of those identified as supporters of the Stamp Act were destroyed in several places. Thereafter, the leaders of the movement consciously sought means that would be effective in reaching their goals, but which were nonviolent (Maier, 1972:27–48). While discipline was not always maintained and activists did on occasion threaten or intimidate opponents, crowd actions were almost invariably nonviolent. In place of violence, the colonists developed a wide range of uses for crowd actions and mass meetings as well as the commercial boycott (called nonimportation) as an "economic club" to influence British officials (Sachs and Hoogenboom, 1965:162; Maier, 1972:27–48, 61–76, 117–34; Schlesinger, 1968).

These ten years saw the development of an institutional basis for American independence. A transformed political ideology was developed out of earlier Whig sources. This ideology was used to justify both the resistance and eventual separation from Britain (Bailyn, 1967). Organizations capable of actively carrying on resistance and of renewing themselves after a period of quiet in between campaigns were created. By the beginning of the War of Independence, organizations and institutions were in existence in nearly every colony which carried on the struggle as it shifted to a military campaign.[2]

The recent movements in Poland have also been, in part, responses to economic crises. These crises, marked by the inability of the government to deliver assured supplies of food to the cities, and by corruption and the misuse of foreign loans (Szafar, 1981:289–92; Spiegel, 1981b:109, 111; Singer, 1981:187–90), have come to include the "trigger" that releases strike waves—steep increases, put into effect overnight, in the prices of basic foodstuffs.

When strikes responding to these economic crises began in October 1956 and in the Gdansk and Szczecin shipyards in 1970, angry strikers streamed into the center of the cities. There they demonstrated, broke into party headquarters buildings and damaged them, and were fired upon by police. Then and after the 1976 strikes, security forces carried out many arrests and beatings after the strikes were settled. In these actions many lives were lost, and many workers lost their jobs. Those students involved were also expelled from the universities (Singer, 1981:164–70, 182–84; Spiegel, 1980a:98; Association of Polish Students, 1977:50–69, 96–102).

After the strikes in 1976, dissident intellectuals organized the Committee for the Defense of the Workers (KOR). This organization prompted workers to reconsider the use of actions that made repressive violence legitimate. Articles in the KOR–sponsored newspaper *Robotnik* (Worker) took a cue from the 1971 occupation of the Warski shipyard in Szczecin. Several workers had previously been killed or beaten in the streets and the strikers decided upon occupying the yards rather than leaving themselves open to this treatment. The nonviolent occupation forced party secretary Edward Gierek to come to the yards and negotiate in person while police kept their distance (Singer, 1981:170–78).

KOR cautioned the workers at the beginning of the major strike movement in July 1980 to avoid violence. Instead, KOR called for "forms of protest," which would not allow the state to use the protests as a provocation to violence (Spiegel, 1980a:98–99; 1980b:90). The Polish workers, in other words, chose to utilize nonviolent methods; in particular, their "occupation strike;" after recognizing that their strength lay in the factories where they worked, and was most effectively utilized if they avoided violence (Singer, 1981:214, 216, 217–24; Spiegel, 1981a:111).

These comparisons are not meant to obscure the significant differences between the cases. Besides being on either side of the historical gulf of industrialization, they differ in that colonial America's history was one of decades of near autonomy, while Poland has been under the domination of powerful neighbors for centuries. There is no comparison in the American experience either to Poland's thirty years under socialism, including the hope for a new socialism aroused in parts of the populace. In addition, there was little in the American colonial experience that could fall under the rubric of repression before 1775, while Poland's government has used violent force on several occasions. On the other hand, the Polish government has also restrained its use of open repressive violence since 1980. The two most important comparisons between the cases are: first, each included a long period of intermittent resistance struggle in which nonviolent action made a contribution; second, both are cases in which neither repression nor temporary settlements led to an end to resistance.

## A. Autonomy and Defense

The first task of resistance movements whose contribution to institutional development will be explored is that of defending either the autonomy of existing institutions, especially when attempts to change them are made, or the organizations and supporters who are carrying on the resistance. The term ''defense'' is used in part because it corresponds to the terminology of the contemporary movement in Poland, where organizations such as KOR have looked for ways of making strikers less vulnerable to repression.

In several of the American colonies, there were lengthy struggles over the autonomy of colonial institutions. In particular, the struggle involved whether they could be controlled by Parliament and the ministry, or whether colonial politics would decide how institutions conducted themselves. In some colonies, these included open resistance following attempts by the British government to define the authority of colonial legislatures or courts.

In colonial Massachusetts, a controversy took place between the years 1772 and 1774 over the British government's attempt to pay the salaries of some colonial officials and judges of the Superior Court directly from revenues collected by British customs officers. The legislature, which had always paid the officials, protested to the governor, but he supported the plan. Beginning with Boston, many of the colony's towns elected committees of correspondence charged with expressing the colony's grievances, consulting with other committees, and advising the towns on further action. Over the course of two years, a network of these committees grew to span the colony (Brown, 1970).

This conflict climaxed in 1774 when the provincial government moved to enforce the provisions of the Coercive Acts. These were passed by Parliament to punish Massachusetts for the Boston Tea Party and to alter local government in hopes of destroying the basis of support for further defiance. One of these acts which rendered the courts largely independent of local government and was totally unacceptable to the organized political resistance. The higher courts, however, were under the domination of the powerful, loyalist, Hutchinson–Oliver faction, so little could be done from within. To the resisters, under the leadership of the committees of correspondence, the judges would be acting unconstitutionally if they continued to hold sessions under the new statutes.

Rather than have this happen, the courts were prevented from sitting. In several rural counties, large and well–organized crowds blocked up the court houses and the roads leading to them so that the justices could not attend. The committee of correspondence in Worcester voted to instruct the town's jurymen to refuse to be sworn if Chief Justice Peter Oliver should be present. Oliver had accepted the royal grant, and was also being impeached by the legislature. Oliver stayed away, however, and the court sittings were not held (Patterson, 1973:98–100; Lincoln, 1862:774–75).

When the August court was held at Boston, crowd actions were out of the question because of the presence of the occupying troops. In a coordinated move, the panels of jurors chosen to serve drew up statements in which they explained that they refused to take the oath. They protested that their consciences would not allow them to take part in breaching their country's constitution. This act of civil disobedience, in which Paul Revere joined, prevented the Superior Court from hearing cases and it was adjourned the next day. The long campaign to prevent changes in the operation of the courts was sufficiently successful that the courts, although closed during this stage of the resistance, were later revived practically unchanged under the independent provincial government (Patterson, 1973:99–100; Boston Evening–Post, 1774; Nelson, 1975).

In South Carolina, the lower house of the legislature found itself forced to defend its privileges by extraconstitutional means in a struggle lasting several years. After the Commons House of Assembly sent a gift of money to John Wilkes for his legal defense in 1769, the Privy Council of England instructed the acting governor, and each succeeding administration, not to allow the House to pass any more money bills without the concurrence of the governor and council. Stripped of a privilege it had long enjoyed, the Commons House refused for several years to pass any bills at all unless its budgets were again accepted without the governor's consent. Since it could not act legally, the legislature devised extra-legal ways of operating effectively. In particular, it developed a thoroughly revised committee structure. Standing committees whose life continued after the legislative session, which had not existed in the province before, took up much of the public business. A system of certificates of public indebtedness was devised, guaranteed by the legislature on its own authority. Although the royal government did not recognize the authority of these measures, their legitimacy was accepted by the people of South Carolina, and they prepared the groundwork for an early and effective provisional government (Greene, 1963; Frakes, 1970: 112–14).

In Poland, where the government and government–run firms have been the opponents, resisters have tried to insure the actual physical protection of workers, students, and intellectuals involved in the movement there. As was mentioned, the Polish workers achieved their "veto" over steep price rises and altered production standards (Singer, 1981:180–81) at the cost of many killed, jailed, or removed from jobs and schools. Although opposition intellectuals were concerned and had written theses demanding political reform in Poland (for example, Kuron and Modzelewski, [1964]), there was little contact between workers and intellectuals until 1976. When KOR was founded in September 1976, its initial tasks were to raise funds for the legal defense of arrested and fired workers, aid their families, and investigate undercover actions by police and prosecutors (Staar, 1981:149; Szafar, 1981: 293–94; Singer, 1981:176).

Between 1976 and 1980, KOR increased contacts between workers and intellectuals. It proposed both a form of autonomous labor organization based on the ILO Charter and the development of ''institutional guarantees of civil rights and freedoms'' (Staar, 1981:151). In connection with this program, an expanding KOR added the name Committee for Social Self–Defense (KSS) to its organizational name (Singer, 1981:186). At the prompting of KOR members, a small number of committees were formed, especially in the coastal region, to work for the formation of future trade unions (Mertens, 1981:529–31).

When the strikes of July and August 1980 came, with accompanying demands for sweeping changes in Poland's political and economic institutions, the workers who organized the strikes did not forget either KOR's lessons or its members. Eighteen KOR activists were arrested in August 1980 and taken into custody several times thereafter without charges. Among the twenty-one demands of the interfactory strike committee (MKS) at Gdansk were the freeing of all political arrestees, reinstatement of released workers and students, and lifting of repression against those with dissenting convictions (Singer, 1981:226; 21 Forderungen der Streikenden in Danzig, 1981:A2–A3; Spiegel, 1980C:93).

As Singer points out, the KOR members were not specifically mentioned in the text of the final agreement, although it was assumed that the agreement meant that they and others would be released. The final protocol, however, did promise to rehire all workers fired in 1970 and 1976 and promptly to investigate all other cases. Gdansk MKS chairman Lech Walesa pledged more strikes if KOR colleagues were not released (Singer, 1981:229; Abkommen von Danzig, 1981:A5). Since 1980, the strike weapon has also been used on occasion to gain the release of arrested Solidarity members, for example, at the Szczyglowice coal mine in September 1981 (Spiegel, 1981b:159).

## B. Action to Define Terms of Institutional Operation

When political and economic controversies break out, a major part of the dispute often involves the classic political and economic questions of who gets what, when, and on what terms, and who decides these things. Resistance movements among those with little institutionalized voice in the making of decisions may have as one of their tasks the attempt to force institutions to be more responsive to their interests.

The unresponsiveness of imperial political institutions was a major, if indirectly stated, issue in the American colonial resistance. Unrepresented in Parliament, the colonies had no direct voice in the decisions made by the British government. Instead, the colonies maintained agents to lobby for them. As political positions hardened in the aftermath of the Stamp Act resistance, Parliament began more and more to restrict the amount and kinds of access the agents had and refused to hear American petitions, closing off one of the few avenues of expression open to the colonies (Kammen, 1968).

Consequently, the only way in which the colonies could influence decisions of Parliament, many felt, was by means of resistance. The commercial boycott (nonimportation) was suggested as such a means (Schlesinger, 1968). Pennsylvania political leader John Dickinson, for example, wrote in a widely–read series of newspaper essays that when the colonies found their petitions for relief unanswered, they ought to turn to depriving Britain of the "advantages" it received in American trade. Then, he argued, "experience will teach them what reason did not" (Dickinson, [1768], 1903:31, 35).

Colonial resistance was not successful in forcing the British government to be more attentive to American interests. However, the resistance campaigns did reduce the effectiveness of government policy in America by nullifying important acts of Parliament. The Stamp Act was repealed in 1766 in the face of American resistance to it (Langford, 1973). In 1770, the bulk of the Townshend Act duties were also repealed, although the most remunerative, the tea duty, was retained. During the repeal debate, the prime minister made specific reference to American resistance, and his desire to bring it to an end, in supporting partial repeal of the Townshend Acts (Barrow, 1967:243). In the long run, however, the ministry refused to consult colonial interests or recognize their claim of rights, which would have limited Parliament's authority.

Until the recent trade union movement began, the resistance movement in Poland has had analogous outcomes. Alterations in prices or policies could be blocked when they were made, but the process by which they were made was little, if at all, changed.

The demands of Polish strikers since 1956 have often been economic, but not restricted to bread–and–butter issues. Rather, it was increasingly perceived that the state maintained the privileges of a few while the many paid for them, creating a new privileged stratum of functionaries, that it attempted to manipulate the workers through misrepresentation (see the Szczecin complaints of 1970; Singer, 1981:172–78), and that the party was out of touch with the populace.

According to Singer (1981:180), the 1970 strikes achieved "the power to say no" to economic policy, a power used again in 1976 and 1980. When food prices and work norms were raised by the government in July 1980, the first demands were indeed for wage raises to compensate, lowered prices, and guaranteed food supplies (Singer, 1981:211–15). By the time the strikes spread to the Baltic shipyards in August, however, matters were different. There, many workers were familiar with KOR's position through the newspaper *Robotnik*. With the strikers led by members of a committee for autonomous trade unions, which had existed since 1978, demands quickly went beyond strictly economic issues. Indeed, Singer (1981:219) reports that the initial decision of the Gdansk MKS to accept a large raise and settle the strike there on 16 August was rejected by workers conscious of the larger issues, who rekindled the strike around wider demands.

The twenty-one demands of the Gdansk interfactory strike committee (MKS) show the changes in institutions of government and factory management that the strikers sought (21 Forderungen der Streikenden in Danzig, 1981:A1–A2). These included independent trade unions, guarantees of the right to strike, freedom of access to mass media as well as the right to establish independent newspapers, and the freeing of political arrestees. There were, of course, many economic demands, but several had political significance as well. These included demands that markets accessible to everyone be fully stocked with foodstuffs, the ending of the "commercial" and "internal export" shops, and abolition of other privileges for party members and security personnel.

After the Gdansk protocol was signed by representatives of the government and of Solidarity, the agreement had to be further authorized by the courts to insure that it was in compliance with Polish law. Initially, the regional court attempted to change the language of the protocol, which was challenged by Solidarity. In early November 1980, the highest court accepted the agreement without alteration, encouraged by government officials and by the threat of a general strike (Mertens, 1981:531). This gave Solidarity the legally recognized right to organize and to strike. One year later, however, the party was continuing efforts to declare the strike weapon illegal once again (Boston Globe, 1981c:12).

## C. Formation of New Institutions

One possible outcome of social movement activity is the development of new institutions. In some cases, especially when a struggle is lengthy, resisters deliberately try to set up institutions to replace existing ones. When both old and new institutions struggle for legitimacy and authority at once, it has been called "dual power," or parallel government, or parallel institutions (Sharp, 1973:423–33; Lakey, 1973; 147–50). Just as importantly, social movements may be institutionalized into the society's basis through wide adoption of movement ideology, by the populace learning to use tested means of resistance over again, and by "role innovation" (Ebert, 1970:194–97).

The Sons of Liberty in colonial America are an example of this second form of institutionalization. The Sons of Liberty were first organized during the Stamp Act resistance. As Maier (1972) has shown, most of the Sons of Liberty organizations were dissolved at the end of that campaign. In some places, an organization, or more accurately, an organizing committee of activists calling themselves Sons of Liberty were active in the Townshend Acts resistance as well. The real significance of the Sons of Liberty was broader than what was contained in any organization, though. People came to think of themselves and call themselves Sons of Liberty when they supported the cause of the resistance movement and its goals, regardless of whether they joined any formal group.

The attitudes fostered by being a Son or Daughter of Liberty spread widely in the population. One example of this was the continued support in some cities for a part of the campaign of commercial resistance even after the nonimportation movement of 1769 and 1770 had collapsed. This was expressed by using as many American–made goods as possible and by spinning yarn to supply American weavers. Largely symbolic, of course, it allowed people a sense that they continued to be united. A young woman living in Boston in 1772, for example, wrote that as "a daughter of liberty" she was careful to wear American–made clothing whenever she could (Earle, 1970:32).

More striking was the reconstruction of institutions that went on in almost every colony during the resistance against the Coercive Acts in 1774 and 1775. Passed to punish Massachusetts for the Boston Tea Party and to strike at the institutional basis of that colony's continued defiance, the Coercive Acts united the colonies against Britain. By threatening the long–established rights of one colony, the acts "focused attention on the basic issue of legislative power within the Empire and its limitations, if any" (Christie and Labaree, 1976:204).

The First Continental Congress was convened in Philadelphia in the late summer of 1774 so that delegations could consult on a response to the Coercive Acts. Although Georgia sent no delegation, representatives of the other colonies agreed on a common plan of resistance. This plan revived the commercial boycott as a weapon against Britain. Experience had shown that this was unlikely to be effective without coordination. As a result, the resistance plan, called the Continental Association, was an attempt at the "standardization and nationalization" of a coordinated effort by all the colonies (Schlesinger, 1968:423). Since the Continental Congress would dissolve when it completed its work and leave no central organization behind, the crucial provision of the Continental Association was that committees be established in every town, county, and city in the country. These committees were to watch over the commerce of their areas to ensure that the resistance plan was followed and were empowered to punish their opponents by turning the boycott against them as well (Schlesinger, 1968:427–28; Maier, 1972:281–84).

These committees were established in most towns and counties in nearly every colony during 1774 and early 1775 (Ammerman, 1974). In most places, these were the first regular committees organized during the ten years of resistance. In other places, especially the major ports, the enforcement committees descended from those that had carried on earlier campaigns, as occurred in Philadelphia (Ryerson, 1974). In Massachusetts, the committees of correspondence that had been active since 1772 were expanded and formed the basis for the transformation of the colony's political institutions (Brown, 1970).

The committees' quest to define the bounds of their authority was essential to their transformation into autonomous institutions with real public functions. Maier (1972:118) has pointed out that the public meetings regularly called in Charleston, South Carolina to discuss enforcement of the nonimportation resolutions in 1769 broadened their scope to become a "surrogate" for a local government, which the city did not yet have.

An important task for the committees organized in 1774 and 1775 was to establish their authority as sole interpreters of the Continental Association. When the voters of Falmouth, Virginia elected a committee made up of known conservatives in early 1775, the county committee called a meeting of all the committees in the area to investigate. The Falmouth members were interrogated, and it was found that they had been chosen in violation of the resolutions of the county committee. The real concern, however, was that the Falmouth committee would not be strict in enforcing the Association, and it was instructed to disband. The meeting restrained spectators who threatened the Falmouth committeemen, but told them that their names would be published in the newspapers and they would be boycotted if they did not resign. In the face of this, the Falmouth committee decided to disband (Anderson, 1917:162–64).

Another case was one in which local committees refused to take on authority they considered unnecessary. The Continental Association included several trade regulations that were to be enforced by economic boycotts of persons who broke them. In early 1775, the committees in the ports of Essex County, Massachusetts were approached by shipowners who wanted to carry certificates, signed by the committees, saying that they were "friends to the liberties of America." This would prove to potential customers in other colonies, they thought, that the mariners were not violating the Association. At first, the committees considered granting the certificates, but later decided that they were unnecessary and might even disadvantage traders who had sailed without them.[3]

The Solidarity labor union in Poland carefully renounced any intent of becoming a political opposition party and set its energies instead on building the new labor organization. In October 1980, the leadership that emerged from the strike committees, in accordance with the theory that democracy required decentralization, moved to establish some fifty autonomous regional branches as the core of the organization. Solidarity's structure, then, is a federation of these regional organizations, containing some two–thirds of the members, plus several allied craft organizations (Mertens, 1981:532–33). Although the regional organizations are autonomous, pressure to control unrestricted strike activity has come from the center, and Solidarity chair Lech Walesa made it clear during the first Solidarity congress, in September 1981, that "a little bit dictatorial" control from the center was needed (New York Times, 1981c:1).

Early KOR activist Stanislaw Baranczak stresses that Solidarity is not simply a labor organization but an expression of the "whole nation" searching for "basic rights and freedoms" (Boston Globe, 1981a:2). The traditions of dissent in the post–war years, the hope for a reformed Socialism, which was not simply a restatement of the Soviet model, as well as the nation's discontent with the economic and political crises of the past years have all devolved upon Solidarity. The movement cannot limit its sphere of action as long as it is perceived not merely as a union but, as an observer sees it, the holder of a mandate "from the people to be the improvement of Poland's institutions" (Valkenier, 1981:4).

One outcome of this is Solidarity's support for other organizations. Some, such as the Committee for the Defense of Prisoners of Conscience, a human rights organization, have political goals (Boston Globe, 1981b:12). Other unions have also grown up under Solidarity's wing, such as the farmers' union Rural Solidarity and the film workers' union. In the case of university students, an official student organization had been founded during the early post–war years (Goldfarb, 1980), and lengthy student strikes were held early in 1981 to gain recognition of an autonomous student union (Boston Globe, 1981b:12).

An event occurring in the summer of 1981, although atypical, suggests the extent to which Solidarity has been viewed as a universal guardian of civil rights. Prisoners in the city of Bydgoszcz, after a brief revolt in which some escaped, occupied the prison and enlisted the local Solidarity branch to mediate their dispute with the prison administration. Solidarity became involved by sending teams of "volunteer hostages" into the prison as well as arranging negotiations. Outside the prison, groups of marshalls calling themselves "worker guards" controlled a crowd of some 1000 onlookers and at one point interposed themselves, arms linked, between the crowd and riot police (New York Times, 1981b:27).

Beyond the construction of a permanent, autonomous labor organization, should that succeed, Solidarity's main opportunity for effecting change in Poland's institutional structure lies in the demand for worker self–management. The August 1980 Gdansk protocol included a clause requiring the government to propose a plan of economic reform. Although the government's own experts were agreed on the failure of economic planning to date (v. Delhaes and Peterhoff, 1981), the plan presented in July 1981 was not one Solidarity would accept. In the union's view, the proposals for worker control were a front for changes intended only to increase production. In response, the "network" of local unions from the largest industrial firms drew up a counterproposal (Valkenier, 1981:4). This proposal concentrated on a plan for erecting workers' councils with real powers within each factory. This would change not only the formal structure but, in Valkenier's words (1981:4), "the nature of the system" as well. In August 1981, the Parliament refused its approval of the government's self–administration plan (Walc, 1981:140), but no further action had been taken as of the end of November.

Two trends in the direction of greater institutionalization of the Solidarity organization and of a lasting impact on the country's institutions can be seen. One lies in the increasing regularity of the organization's methods and its negotiations with the government and plant administration. This corresponds to Simmel's well–known observations on the centralization and increasing cohesion of groups in conflict (1955). It also suggests a learning process, by which the movement and its members have become more specific, over the course of the year between August 1980 and the first Solidarity congress, about the significance of the demands contained in the Gdansk protocol.

The second trend toward institutionalization lies in the extent to which much of the energies and ideology of the movements occurring since 1956 have devolved onto Solidarity. Solidarity has combined the efforts of Polish nationalists, Catholic intellectuals who first organized in 1956 (Valkenier, 1981:5), and the socialists of KOR. Many view it as a political as well as a trade union organization. Indeed, the official report presented to the delegates at Solidarity's September 1981 congress recognized these strivings explicitly, stating that the movement had grown into a "powerful liberation movement involving human and civil rights" (New York Times, 1981a:1).

Although Solidarity has also avoided stating the depth of the crisis of legitimacy in Poland, the recognition is there. Walc (1981:140) wrote during the Solidarity congress that "the delegates see the way out of the crisis only in a step–by–step takeover of control over production by the union." At the end of November, Jacek Kuron carried the argument somewhat further. After KOR was disbanded in September 1981, in recognition that its program now belonged to the union (Spiegel, 1981b:155), Kuron took steps to found political clubs dedicated to founding new political parties. Kuron claimed that the current ruling structure was based solely on the power of the Soviet Union, not on its own legitimacy, and proposed the formation of a republic in its place (Boston Globe, 1981b:12; 1981c:4).

## D. Culture, Commitment, and Change: Enculturation of Movement Sectors

Restrictions of space preclude more than the briefest discussion of what may be, in the long term, one of the most significant aspects of the institutionalization of social movements, their inclusion within culture. Ultimately, institutionalization of resistance movements involves the institutionalization of an altered world view. This requires incorporation of attitudes arising within the movement into the political culture of the population; in short, the development of opposition "traditions."

A fine example of this point is made in Goldfarb's (1980) study of Polish student theater. Itself a relatively autonomous institution, Polish student theater utilizes, incorporates, and extends earlier traditions of dissent (Goldfarb, 1980:87–99). Goldfarb reports on the 1968 suppression in Warsaw of performances of *Dziady,* a play by the nineteenth century writer Adam Mickiewicz. The audience responded warmly to the line, "We Poles have sold our souls for a couple of silver rubles" (Goldfarb, 1980:138–39). In context, the line referred to Russia's domination of Poland in the pre–Soviet period. Part of this idea, settling for too little, continues to inform the movement of today. Singer (1981:214) records that after the workers of Lublin settled their first strikes in 1980 for wage increases, they came to perceive that "they had sold their rights 'for twenty groshy,'" and demanded political reforms as well.

Symbols first used by resistance movements are also incorporated into the culture. In late–colonial America, Liberty Trees that were found throughout the colonies were a popular and common symbol of the struggle. Following independence, Liberty Trees were for several decades a symbolic part of United States political culture (Schlesinger, 1952). Celebrations, like theater and symbolism, may not act directly against the opponents of the movement but help to create the climate of opinion which is one of the many supports of the ongoing movement. The Boston Sons of Liberty held one such celebration, an open–air dinner for over three hundred supporters, in August 1769. The celebration, which included carriage parades, the singing of liberty songs, and the presence of honored guests from other colonies, was approved of by John Adams, who was there. The leaders were wise to hold these "festivals," Adams wrote in his dairy (1964:341), for "they tinge the Minds of the People, they impregnate them with the sentiments of Liberty. They render the People fond of their Leaders in the Cause, and averse and bitter to all opposers."

# VI.  DISCUSSION AND CONCLUSION

A small portion only of the complexity of the cases could be discussed here. They do, however, lend support to the propositions. Proposition One suggests that long–term social movements that neither bow permanently to repression nor are able to achieve their goals are the most likely to contribute to institutional development. This is in part because continued innovation of effective means as well as continued development of ideology and techniques for mobilizing adherents are needed. This in turn lends support to Proposition Two, which suggests that certain activities of resistance movements are more significant than others for institutional development. One of these activities is the task of finding ways to defend the participants, organizations, and associations arising out of the movement. When this is successfully done, it insures that the movement can persist. Just as importantly, however, it is these "defensive" actions that provide the greatest opportunity for the development of the movement's distinctive understanding of the situation.

Both cases were ones in which countermeasures by the opponent were far from being sufficient to stop the movement from developing, even though police in Poland in both 1970 and 1976 were very brutal. Indeed, it has been suggested that repression of the movement, in conditions where resisters feel able to act, may increase cohesion (Sharp, 1973:636–89). Likewise, neither movement was able for several years to gain enough power to force some lasting settlement. In America, the continuing refusal of the British government even to discuss the merit of American demands led to the belief that the ministry was corrupt and essentially opposed to their interests. Soon, even the king, whom the Americans continued to revere from some time after resistance began, was indicted as well.

In the process, the colonial Americans were forced to think not only of the basis on which they could reject colonial institutions but what could replace them (Maier, 1972).

As has been seen, this did not involve wholesale replacement of existing institutions with "revolutionary" courts or legislatures. Rather, colonial resistance served to maintain some of these institutions. In Massachusetts, such a "conservative" institution as the royal council, the institutional voice of the colonial elite, was "transformed" into one of the bodies that supported the resistance, opposing the governors whom it was expected to advise (Walett, 1949). In fact, several of the colonies, especially in New England, preserved their colonial institutions practically intact into independence, including their law, court structure, and legislatures. In the process of resistance, the people of the colonies defended the autonomy they claimed, but also had to decide how autonomous government was to be structured and run. In Carl Becker's (1968:22) classic characterization, said of New York, there were two questions, "the question of home rule" and that "of who shall rule at home."

The lack of an effective voice in making law and policy, in political parties, and in the governmental process, is part of the reason extralegal means are chosen in the first place. Continued lack of success in gaining a voice or in making the opponent recognize the rights and interests of the resisters, when accompanied by organizations, associations, and a developing ideology based in the movement sector, contributes to the reevaluation of the unresponsive institutions, the transformation of some into movement–oriented institutions, and the creation of others.

While the broad outlines of Poland's situation are not analogous to that of colonial America, there are important similarities. This study has not been able to do justice to the role of Polish nationalism, of antagonism toward the Soviet Union and toward the existing government, of continued membership of the mass of the Polish people in the Catholic Church, and to the Eastern European resistance tradition of attempting to create a renewed, more humane socialism. In addition, a shift to military struggle as took place in America is unlikely if Solidarity wishes to survive. Lastly, the Polish government's decision of 1980 that it would not make the attempt, perhaps ineffective, to repress the movement is open to revision, a revision that would test the movement's resolve to use only those weapons it has learned to use the best.[4]

Analogous to colonial America and other resistance struggles, however, is the gradual growth in the country of the movement that has brought about the decisive crisis. Organizations and associations have grown from a few members to ten million, as Solidarity and related bodies have taken shape. These autonomous organizations, parallel to but opposed to the official bodies, are similar to what has elsewhere been called "counter–institutions" (Baumgartner, Burns, and Deville, 1978:133). These groups are proceeding toward a possibly lasting transformation of Poland's "numbed institutions" (Gross, 1980:9). As importantly as any of the rest is that the habit of obedience, rarely broken in the past and never with lasting determination, seems to be at an end.

In conclusion, it has been shown that institutional development resulting from a nonviolent resistance movement is not simply the conversion of movement organizations into more or less permanent structures. Rather, the actions that movements take and the ideology they develop to inform them contribute to the defense of some existing institutions in forms the resisters can accept. In addition, some institutions may be renewed and transformed, and thereby permanently changed. Newly created institutions, ideologies, and an expanded political culture complete this vital part of the movement's contribution to lasting social change.

## NOTES

1. See, for example, the discussion of the choice of "protest tactics" in Useem (1975:32–38, 41). Although Useem's concept is not devoted to nonviolent action as a category, the methods mentioned are primarily nonviolent ones.

2. In later years, John Adams often expressed the opinion that the significance of the movement was that it had accomplished the break with England, factually as well as ideologically, before the war began. Adams wrote to chronicler Hezekiah Niles in 1818 that a "radical change in the principles, opinions, sentiments and affections of the people was the real American Revolution." Quoted in Bailyn (1967:160).

3. Beverly Committee of Correspondence to Salem Committee of Correspondence, 25 November 1774; Marblehead Committee of Correspondence to Salem Committee of Correspondence, 25 November 1774; Gloucester Committee of Correspondence to Salem Committee of Correspondence, 28 November 1774; draft reply, Salem Committee of Correspondence, 30 November 1774; draft certificate, 28 November 1774. Timothy Pickering Papers, Massachusetts Historical Society, Boston.

4. This paper was completed before the events of December 1981 took place. Solidarity's suspension and the imposition of martial law have themselves been the objects of resistance.

## REFERENCES

Abel, Theodore
    1937    "The pattern of a successful political movement." American Sociological Review 3:347–52.
Das Abkommen von Danzig (31 August 1980)
    1981    Osteuropa Archiv, Osteuropa 31:A3–7.
Adams, John
    1964    Diary and Autobiography of John Adams. L. H. Butterfield (ed.), New York: Atheneum.
Ammerman, David
    1974    In the Common Cause: American Response to the Coercive Acts. Charlottesville: University Press of Virginia.
Anderson, D. R.
    1917    "The letters of William Allason, merchant, of Falmouth, Virginia." Richmond College Historical Papers 2:118–75.

Association of Polish Students and Graduates in Exile
   1977   Dissent in Poland: Reports and Documents in Translation, December 1975–January 1977.
          London: Association of Polish Students and Graduates in Exile.
Bailyn, Bernard
   1967   The Ideological Origins of the American Revolution. Cambridge, MA: Belknap Press.
Barrow, Thomas C.
   1967   Trade and Empire: The British Customs Service in Colonial America, 1660–1775.
          Cambridge: Harvard University Press.
Baumgartner, Tom, Tom R. Burns, and Philippe DeVille
   1978   "Conflict resolution and conflict development: A theory of game transformation with an
          application to the Lip Factory conflict." Research in Social Movements, Conflicts and
          Change 1:105–52.
Becker, Carl L.
   1968   The History of Political Parties in the Province of New York. Madison: University of
          Wisconsin Press.
Bittner, Egon
   1963   "Radicalism and the organization of radical movements." American Sociological Review
          28:928–40.
Boston Evening-Post
   1774   5 September, supplement. Worcester: Micro Research, n. d.
Boston Globe
   1981a  23 April:2.
   1981b  23 November:12.
   1981c  24 November:4.
   1981d  28 November:12.
Brown, Richard D.
   1970   Revolutionary Politics in Massachusetts: The Boston Committee of Correspondence and
          the Towns. Cambridge: Harvard University Press.
Bruyn, Severyn T.
   1979   "Social theory of nonviolent action: A framework for research in creative conflict." Pp.
          13–63 in S. T. Bruyn and P. Rayman (eds.), Nonviolent Action and Social Change. New
          York: Irvington.
Carden, Maren Lockwood
   1978   "The proliferation of a social movement: Ideology and individual incentives in the contem-
          porary feminist movement." Research in Social Movements, Conflicts and Change
          1:179–96.
Christie, Ian R., and Benjamin W. Labaree
   1976   Empire or Independence, 1760–1776. New York: Norton.
Conser, Walter H., Jr., Ronald M. McCarthy, David J. Toscano, Kenneth W. Wadoski, and Gene
Sharp (eds.)
   forth-   To Bid Defiance to Tyranny: Nonviolent Action in the Movement for American Indepen-
   coming   dence, 1765–1775. Boston: Porter Sargent.
von Delhaes, K., and R. Peterhoff (eds.)
   1981   "Polen: Kritik am bestehenden Wirtschaftssystem. Ein Dokument zur Wirtschaftreform."
          Osteuropa Archiv, Osteuropa 31:A460–72.
Dickinson, John
   [1768] Letters from a Farmer in Pennsylvania to the Inhabitants of 1903 the British Colonies. New
          York: Outlook.
Earle, Agnes Morse (ed.)
   1970   Diary of Anna Green Winslow: A Boston School Girl of 1771. Boston: Houghton-Mifflin.

Ebert, Theodore
    1970   Gewaltfreier Aufstand: Alternative zum Bürgerkrieg. Frankfurt/M: Ger.: Fischer.
Egnal, Marc and Joseph Albert Ernst
    1972   "An economic interpretation of the American revolution." William and Mary Quarterly
           (Third series), 29:3–32.
Die 21 Forderungen der Streikenden in Danzig (August 1980)
    1981   Osteuropa Archiv, Osteuropa 31:A1–2.
Frakes, George E.
    1970   Laboratory for Liberty: The South Carolina Committee System, 1719–1776. Lexington:
           University of Kentucky Press.
Gamson, William A.
    1975   The Strategy of Social Protest. Homewood, Ill.: Dorsey.
    1980   "Understanding the careers of challenging groups: A commentary on Goldstone." Ameri-
           can Journal of Sociology 85:1043–60.
Goldfarb, Jeffrey C.
    1980   The Persistence of Freedom: Sociological Implications of Polish Student Theater. Boulder:
           Westview.
Goldstone, Jack A.
    1980   "The weakness of organization: A new look at Gamson's The Strategy of Social Protest."
           American Journal of Sociology 85:1017–42.
Griessinger, Andreas
    1981   Das symbolische Kapital der Ehre: Streikbewegungen und kollektives Bewusstsein deu-
           tscher Handwerkgesellen im 18. Jahrhundert. Frankfurt/M., Ger.: Ullstein.
Greene, Jack P.
    1963   "Bridge to revolution: The Wilkes fund controversy in South Carolina, 1769–1775."
           Journal of Southern History 29:19–52.
Gross, Jan T.
    1981   "Creative politics in Poland." New Leader 64, 20 April:9–10.
Hart, Liddell B. H.
    1969   "Lessons from resistance movements: Guerilla and non-violent." Pp. 228–46 in A.
           Roberts (ed.), Civilian Resistance as a National Defense. Baltimore: Penguin.
Hirschman, Albert O.
    1970   Exit, Voice, and Loyalty: Response to Decline in Firms, Organizations, and States.
           Cambridge: Harvard University Press.
Kammen, Michael G.
    1968   A Rope of Sand: The Colonial Agents, British Politics, and the American Revolution.
           Ithaca: Cornell University Press.
Kuron, Jacek, and Karol Modzelewski
    [1964] An Open Letter to the Party. Published as: A Revolutionary Socialist Manifesto. London:
           Pluto Press, n.d.
Lakey, George
    1973   Strategy for a Living Revolution. New York: Grossman.
Langford, Paul
    1973   The First Rockingham Administration, 1765–1766. London: Oxford University Press.
Lincoln, William
    1862   History of Worcester, Massachusetts. Worcester: Charles Henry.
Maier, Pauline
    1972   From Resistance to Revolution: Colonial Radicals and the Development of American
           Opposition to Britain, 1765–1776. New York: Knopf.

Mertens, Anna
  1981  "Die 'Solidarität.' Zum Charakter der neuen Gewerkschaften in Polen." Osteuropa
        31:529–47.
Messinger, Sheldon
  1955  "Organizational transformation: A case study of a declining social movement." American
        Sociological Review 20:3–10.
Nash, Gary B.
  1979  The Urban Crucible: Social Change, Political Consciousness, and the Origins of the Ameri-
        can Revolution. Cambridge: Harvard University Press.
New York Times
  1981a  7 September:20.
  1981b  8 September:25
  1981c  10 September:1.
Olson, Mancur, Jr.
  1971  The Logic of Collective Action: Public Goods and the Theory of Groups. Cambridge:
        Harvard University Press.
Patterson, Stephen E.
  1973  Political Parties in Revolutionary Massachusetts. Madison: University of Wisconsin Press.
Pickering, Timothy, Papers Boston, MA: Massachusetts Historical Society.
  unpublished
Piven, Frances Fox, and Richard A. Cloward
  1979  Poor People's Movements: Why They Succeed, How They Fail. New York: Vintage.
Rudé, George
  1964  The Crowd in History, 1730–1848. New York: Wiley.
Rudwick, Elliott, and August Meier
  1970  "Organizational structure and goal succession: A comparative analysis of the NAACP and
        CORE, 1964–1968." Social Science Quarterly 51:9–24.
Ryerson, R. A.
  1974  "Political mobilization and the American Revolution: The resistance movement in Phila-
        delphia, 1765 to 1775." William and Mary Quarterly (third series), 31:565–588.
Sachs, William S., and Ari Hoogenboom
  1965  The Enterprising Colonials: Society on the Eve of the Revolution. Chicago: Argonaut.
Schlesinger, Arthur M.
  1952  "Liberty Tree: A genealogy." New England Quarterly 25:435–58.
  1968  The Colonial Merchants and the American Revolution. New York: Atheneum.
Sharp, Gene
  1973  The Politics of Nonviolent Action. Boston: Porter Sargent.
  1980  Social Power and Political Freedom. Boston: Porter Sargent.
Simmel, Georg
  1955  Conflict and the Web of Group-Affiliations. K. H. Wolff and R. Bendix (trans.), New
        York: Free Press.
Singer, Daniel
  1981  The Road to Gdansk. New York: Monthly Review Press.
Skodvin, Magne
  1969  "Norwegian non-violent resistance during the German occupation." Pp. 162–81 in A.
        Roberts (ed.), Civilian Resistance as a National Defense. Baltimore: Penguin.
Smelser, Neil J.
  1962  Theory of Collective Behavior. New York: Free Press.

Der Spiegel
    1980a  "'Die Führung hat total versagt': Spiegel-Interview mit dem polnischen Regimekritiker
           Jacek Kuron über die Welle von illegaler Streiks." Der Spiegel 34, 4 (August):98–100.
    1980b  "Streiks in Polen—gegen die Partei." Der Spiegel 34, 18 (August): 90–97.
    1980c  "'Segne, Herr, das freie Vaterland Polens.'" Der Spiegel 34, 25 (August):80–94.
    1981a  "'Die Fabrik ist unsere Festung': Wie Polens unabhängige Gewerkschaft 'Solidarität' an
           der Basis arbeitet." Der Spiegel 35, 1 (June):109–13.
    1981b  Polens Revolution: Eine 'finnische Lösung'?" Der Spiegel 35, 5 (October):136–59.
Staar, Richard F.
    1981   "The opposition movement in Poland." Current History 80 (April):149–81.
Sternstein, Wolfgang
    1969   "The Ruhrkampf of 1923: Economic problems of civilian defense." Pp. 128–61 in A.
           Roberts (ed.), Civilian Resistance as a National Defense. Baltimore: Penguin.
Stiehm, Judith
    1972   Nonviolent Power: Active and Passive Resistance in America. Lexington: D. C. Heath.
Szafar, Tadeusz
    1981   "Die Dekade Gierek." Osteuropa 31:277–96.
Thompson, E. P.
    1971   "The moral economy of the English crowd in the 18th century." Past and Present
           50:76–136.
Useem, Michael
    1975   Protest Movements in America. Indianapolis: Bobbs-Merrill.
Valkenier, Elizabeth K.
    1981   "The road from Gdansk." New Leader 64, 21 (September):3–6.
Vander Zanden, James W.
    1959   "Resistance and social movements." Social Forces 37:312–15.
    1963   "The nonviolent resistance movement against of segregation." American Journal of So-
           ciology 68:544–50.
Walc, Jan
    1981   "'Weil es mit ihnen zu Ende geht': 'Solidarnosc'-Journalist Jan Walc über den Danziger
           Kongress." Der Spiegel 35, 5 (October):140.
Walett, Francis G.
    1949   "The Massachusetts Council, 1766–1774: The transformation of a conservative institu-
           tion." William and Mary Quarterly (third series), 6:605–27.
Walzer, Michael
    1960   "The idea of resistance." Dissent 7:369–73.
Weber Max
    1978   Economy and Society: An Outline of Interpretive Sociology, G. Roth and C. Wittich
           (eds.). Berkeley: University of California Press.
Zald, Mayer N., and Roberta Ash
    1966   "Social movement organizations: Growth, decay and change." Social Forces 44:327–42.

# TERRORISM'S SOCIAL-HISTORICAL CONTEXTS IN NORTHERN IRELAND

Alfred McClung Lee

## I. INTRODUCTION

Sensational acts that appear to threaten "law and order" seize the attention of government policymakers and administrators. Theft, arson, murder, and terrorism—even nonviolent but substantial representations of dissent—demand of them immediate attention to the events as such. Considerations of the contexts of such events and especially of their multiple causes is usually laid aside for some future agenda or merely ignored. As that apologist for the radical right, William F. Buckley, Jr. (1977) states, ". . . to spend one's time in probing the *cause* of our social maladies . . . distracts us from coping with crime." In this paper, consideration is given to contexts and causes overlooked in such a view. Repre-

Research in Social Movements, Conflicts and Change, Vol. 5, pages 99–131.
Copyright © 1983 by JAI Press Inc.
All rights of reproduction in any form reserved.
ISBN: 0-89232-301-9

sentative government works to obviate causes before politically explosive tensions become threatening.

The causes of terrorist events are complex. What they might be is often a controversial issue. To try to cope with those causes rather than only with the perpetrators of the current and symptomatic events would make political and economic leaders attempt to face crime–producing characteristics of their society. It is far less complicating to rely on punitive and "corrective" measures aimed at those taken to be criminals. Such measures may do little or nothing to reduce the frequency of such threats to the status quo. As usually conceived and carried into practice, they are often actually counterproductive—as they can currently be seen to be in the case of Northern Ireland's civil conflict.

Even though terrorism is acceptably defined as a means of coercion that exploits fear or fright and the dread of violence to persons and property, the mass media employ the term selectively. They ordinarily use it only to designate anti–establishment efforts. Terrorism by governmental functionaries is translated into accounts of measures to "restore peace," "maintain law and order," or "restabilize society." That those protective labelings have class and other sectarian biases is habitually ignored. The social contexts of rebel terrorism and reasons for the failure of nonviolent alternatives are rarely set forth in adequate detail in the mass media. Even whether or not the actions of dissidents are or are not potentially or actually "violent" does not keep the establishment–oriented media from indiscriminately calling many of them "terrorist." (CIA, 1981: ii; Hinkle, 1981; Lee, 1981a)

Sensational offenses that are considered "political" are, if anything, more confusing to policymakers and to administrators than are other types of "crime." Democracy presumably assures the right of dissent, but what forms of dissent should be deemed "legal" and what forms "criminal"? As Max Lerner (1934: 203) notes, "Political offenses have been the despair of jurists because of their relativist character." With such persons as George Washington and Eamon de Valera in mind, he adds that "political attempts cease to be crimes as soon as they have succeeded in overthrowing the regime." The tendency of governmental agents to increase and expand the categories of political events called "criminal" reflects a rigidifying tendency in social structure, a greater unwillingness to face social needs and to accept the costs of social change. (Blumenthal et al., 1971)

The present paper is an effort to suggest as briefly as possible the complicated social–historical contexts of political terrorism in the current Northern Ireland struggle. What do terrorists draw from the historical backgrounds of the groups involved? How do such backgrounds color motivations, conceptions of obstacles and opportunities for individuals and groups? What acts of terrorism are symptomatic in the province's evolving class and ethnic structure? From what sources come the rhetoric, myths, and fantasies employed in terrorizing actions and counteractions? For what purposes are mass media instruments employed? How do sought for, possible, and actual consequences of action efforts contrast?

## II. THE CURRENT "TROUBLES"

Before trying to set Northern Ireland's current terrorism in its broader contexts, let us look quite briefly at evidences of what has been happening there since 1968.

The three principal sides of the struggle—to simplify the picture—are the British, the Loyalist (or Unionist, or Orange), and the Nationalist (or Republican, or Green). The "British" include representatives of the United Kingdom government and of English and multinational corporations, some of their employees, and soldiers. Like the other two, the "British" represent a quasi-ethnic category, but one more mixed, especially because of the inclusion within it of soldiers, as we shall see. The Loyalists are overwhelmingly Northern Irish natives identified with Scottish and English traditions, with their own Northern Irish customs, and with the Protestant and dissenting churches, especially the Episcopalian (Church of Ireland), Presbyterian, and Methodist. The Nationalists identify with Irish traditions, with their own rather different Northern Irish customs, and with the Roman Catholic Church.

The religious tag on contemporary Loyalists and Nationalists does not mean that this is basically a "religious" struggle. So far as all three of these groups are concerned, one does not have to dig far into the records to conclude that the conflict is a politico–economic one. The religious tags label ethnoid divisions, sometimes linked to alleged "racial" differences. (Lee, 1972–73, 1974, 1977, 1979) They provide a rationale for splitting the population and especially the lower class against itself. As the noted labor leader James Connolly (1913: 263) pointed out, "According to all Socialist theories North–East Ulster, being the most developed industrially, ought to be the quarter in which class lines of cleavage, politically and industrially, should be the most pronounced and class rebellion the most common. As a cold matter of fact, it is the happy hunting ground of the slave–driver and the home of the least rebellious slaves in the industrial world." Thus, quite accurately, most church leaders and the radical activists insist that the current conflict there is not basically religious even though its propagandists in part use religious themes as alleged justifications for their violent actions. (Daly & Gallagher, 1977; PIRA, 1973; in contrast, see Paisley, 1972)

In 1970–80 in this small statelet of one and one-half millions, warfare among the army, police, and paramilitaries has cost the lives of 139 police, 441 soldiers, and 1,478 civilians. Of the civilians, perhaps one–third were "terrorists," and the rest were so–called "innocent bystanders." In that period, 9,151 persons were arrested and charged with terrorist offenses. Violent incidents included 10,130 bombings, 27,738 shootings, and 12,424 civilian injuries. (N.I.I.S., 1981: 24) These official figures, as such, are only roughly accurate.

Statistics on the forced moving of families as a result of intimidation are inadequate, but some are available. As a result of the violence in August and September 1969, 1,820 families in Belfast (80.5 percent Roman Catholic) changed their homes. (Poole, 1971) For the same period, more generally, the figure was estimated to be 3,500 (85 percent Roman Catholic). During three difficult weeks, two years later, in August 1971, the Northern Ireland Community Relations Commission discovered that 2,069 families had to leave their homes. The social scientist John Darby (1976: 43) notes, "Between and after these two periods of exceptional violence, a less spectacular but steady flow of families abandoned their homes from fear or intimidation." He placed the number in Greater Belfast at some 8,000 to 15,000. As Darby points out: "Apart from the suffering of the victims, who were forced by general pressure or personal threat to seek more secure living areas, the main result of the process has been to increase greatly housing segregation in the Belfast area."

An indication of ethnoid involvement comes from a careful study (McKeown, 1980: 4–5) of the first 2,000 fatalities in the struggle. Only two of the 182 Republican and all of the 43 Loyalist paramilitaries were Protestants. Deaths among the locally recruited security forces—the Royal Ulster Constabulary, the Royal Ulster Constabulary Reserve, and the Ulster Defense Regiment—came to 215 Protestants and only 13 Roman Catholics, a suggestion of the ethnoid bias of those bodies. Of the 2,000 toll, 1,631 were Northern Ireland natives. Of these natives, even though one–third of the province's population is Green, 916 of the dead were local Roman Catholics and only 715 Protestants. Because of misdirected efforts, the balance among the groups responsible for fatalities is different. The same study reports that of the first 2,000, security forces killed 220 or 11.0 percent; Republicans, 1,024 or 51.2 percent; and Loyalists, 574 or 28.7 percent; 182 or 9.1 percent could not be classified.

## III. THE STRUGGLE'S SOCIAL-HISTORICAL CONTEXTS

Elsewhere I have discussed many ways in which terror enters the lives of these people. (Lee, 1980a,b, and 1981b) I have also outlined the confusingly interrelated character of the many aspects of the Northern Ireland conflict. (Lee, 1980a,b, 1981a) Let me now illustrate how terrorist acts and threats are class–stratified in terms of those immediately responsible and indicate their social–historical contexts. Within each ethnoid segment of the population, social class identities have formed the basis for offensive and defensive strategies. The strategies are crudely automatic adaptations based upon class–cultural patterns, not carefully worked out conspiracies.

In the Northern Ireland conflict since 1968 (as I have perceived it through observation, interviews,[1] and documents) terrorist acts and threats of such acts reflect a definite class–stratification in their patterning, a stratification that has ancient Irish, Scottish, and English roots. The acts have included (1) terrorizing decisions and indecisiveness by upperclass people, (2) terrorizing "law and order" activities by (a) middle–class and (b) lower–class governmental functionaries guided by their own interpretations of official policies, (3) terrorizing threats by other middle–class "respectables" on the three principal sides of the conflict, and (4) terrorizing operations by the predominantly lower–class insurgents. These acts and threats have been directed against (i) symbolic prestige persons, (ii) symbolic groups, (iii) rank and file members of the three sides, (iv) random members of the three quasi–ethnic populations, and (v) property, chiefly symbolic structures, business buildings, and lower–class ghetto dwellings. Let us look first at the general historical background.

## A. The Abrasive Theme of Superiority/Inferiority

In a comprehensive review of the many books published in 1969–71 dealing with the Northern Ireland conflict, J. Bowyer Bell (1972: 148) concluded: "History seemingly in the case of Northern Ireland is destiny. Just exactly what history is and means then becomes the very stuff of the conflict."

Just what is the core of this historical stuff? To what extent is it embedded in the popular traditions, in the cultural patterns of thought that influence possible behavior among the opposing groups? To what extent has it been created and manipulated by scholars and by professional propagandists? How selectively is it remembered?

As the noted Protestant Irish historian W. E. H. Lecky (1892: I, 1, 4) concludes, Ireland's history reveals "with singular clearness the perverting and degrading influence of great legislative [and administrative] injustices, and the manner in which they affect in turn every element of national well–being." From the twelfth century, those who represented English power regarded "the Irish as later colonists looked upon Red Indians—as being, like wild beasts, beyond the pale of the moral law."

Irish and English historical "stuff"—symbolic events and ethnic myths— pervade political propagandas in all of Ireland. They are especially made to elaborate the basic theme of ethnoid superiority/inferiority constantly exemplified in all its ramifications in the daily lives of the people. Myths, traditions, and events provide materials for ritualistic rehearsals and actual conflicts that exacerbate that basic inequality theme on all three sides. The events, personages, and sayings of many yesterdays make a lethal mixture in today's struggles. Let us look at some of that background, especially in Northern Ireland.

During the reign of Elizabeth I (1558–1603), a series of wars against the Irish "broke the force of the semi-independent chieftains, crushed the native population to the dust, and established the complete ascendency of English law." Systematic slaughter and starvation of men, women, and children and the destruction of houses were carried so far that Elizabeth was told that she "had little left to reign over but ashes and carcases" in much of Ireland. "It is easy to imagine what feelings it must have planted in the minds of the survivors." (Lecky, 1892: I, 5, 7, 10) This holocaust and the ones in subsequent centuries rankle in Irish traditions much as do the Russian pogroms and the Nazi holocaust among the Jews.

The separation of the Anglican church (including the Church of Ireland) from Rome under Elizabeth's father, Henry VIII, strengthened the hold of the suppressed Roman Catholic Church upon the Irish as their ethnic defense body. It became even more crucial to the Irish than the dissenting churches were to the lower–class English. As Lecky (1865: II, 64–65) asserts: "Anglicanism was from the beginning at once the most servile and the most efficient agent of tyranny." With "the assistance of temporal authority and by the display of worldly pomp" that church "naturally flung herself on every occasion into the arms of the civil power." Thus the utilization of the established Church of Ireland by the British as an instrument of domination had primarily political and class rather than religious significance. Lecky (1892: I, 11) adds, "the English cared much more for the suppression of the Irish race than for the suppression of its religion." They did not even have the Anglican *Book of Common Prayer* translated into Irish. On the contrary, they did what they could to discourage the use of the Irish language and of other Irish customs. The evident purpose was genocide, the absorption of the Irish into the British lower class.

With the seventeenth century, the Tudors systematically confiscated land from the native Roman Catholics in the northern province of Ulster and gave control of it to Scottish and English Protestants (Anglicans) and dissenters (Presbyterians and Methodists). As the Irish historian F. S. L. Lyons (1978: 19) notes: "Because it [Ulster] was the last part of Ireland to be colonised, and because the previous population were not wiped out when they lost their land and their status, and because the newcomers included both Episcopalians and Presbyterians, the triangular friction with which we are familiar became an integral part of Ulster history." Thus was laid the general basis for the threefold—West English, Orange, and Green—ethnoid siege mentality, a kind of frontier insecurity, now to be found especially in the six of the nine Ulster counties making up Northern Ireland. As a joint Irish Council of Churches (Protestant) and Roman Catholic Working Party (Daly & Gallagher, 1977: 13) stated: "Britain, like most imperial powers, whether Protestant or Catholic, frequently used religious division as an instrument of imperial policy. Down to the middle of the nineteenth century, there was religious discrimination and denial of political rights and economic opportunities to Roman Catholics and to dissenters."

The intergroup terrorism stimulated by the Ulster plantation continued. In 1641–49, Roman Catholic peasants tried to regain their lands and in the process slaughtered thousands of Protestant settlers. In August 1649, an English Puritan army won a victory near Dublin, and two weeks later Oliver Cromwell landed with more Protestant troops. His visit of a little more than nine months is especially remembered for the general massacres he directed of the inhabitants following his successful siege of Drogheda and his storming of Wexford. As a historian (Costigan, 1969: 78) notes, "what shocks the modern conscience nearly as much as the actual details of the carnage is the complacency and sanctimoniousness with which Cromwell contemplated the massacres and sought to justify them in the sight of God and man."

All in all, it is estimated that in 1641–52, more than one–half of the Irish—some three–quarters of a million—either died or emigrated. Those not slaughtered by Roman Catholics or Protestants died of starvation or disease. Other thousands were forced to go to the Continent. Then in 1689 came the unsuccessful Roman Catholic siege of Protestant Derry in which the storied Apprentice Boys helped save the city, and in 1690, at the Boyne river, troops of the deposed Roman Catholic King of England, James II, were defeated by those of his Protestant successor, William of Orange. These are events constantly recalled in Orange propaganda. Their rehearsal helps maintain their siege mentality.

In brief compass, one cannot more than suggest the complicated, continuing, and all–pervasive ramifications of the bitter theme of inequality. From 1795, it fostered the Orange Order, controlled by upper–class Protestants and populated principally by lower–class dissenters and Protestants. That order "simply channelled a vast flow of fervent feeling which already existed into one enormous reservoir of partisan and religious ardour (or bigotry, according to how you view it)." (Gray, 1972: 57) As an inter–class, anti–Roman Catholic conspiracy, it was "productive of class peace." At the same time, to help keep the lower–class Protestants quiet, it also permitted that "certain forms of class conflict could be expressed." (Patterson, 1980: xi)

The holocausts of the later sixteenth century and of the 1640s had their parallels in the 1740s and 1840s, events that similarly arose from the bitter theme of inequality and that exacerbated the deeply felt siege mentality of both Protestants and Roman Catholics. The dependency of the Irish peasantry upon the potato grew steadily after its introduction late in the sixteenth century. Notable failures of that crop, attended by famine, disease, and emigration, occurred in 1726–29, 1739–41, 1756–57, 1800, 1807, 1816–17, 1822, 1839, 1845–48, 1863, and 1879. The failure of 1739–41 sent thousands to England and the Continent and, especially from Ulster, to the American colonies; that emigration, largely of middle–class farmers and artisans, is said to have provided much of the backbone for Washington's army. That disaster took about one–third of the island's population. (Salaman, 1949: 604–607) Then, the outflow of the poor "apparently began after the potato failure and typhus epidemic of 1817 and increased after the 1822 famine." (Kennedy, 1973: 27) The failure of 1845–48 is most often recounted. (Woodham-Smith, 1962) As in the case of the other disasters, the problem was not a food shortage in the British Isles or even in Ireland; it was inequitable food distribution. In speaking of the 1845–48 famine, an English historian (Shearman, 1952: 99) asserts that it was a problem "of destitution rather than food shortage. There was sufficient food in Ireland to feed the population, if they had been able to buy it." Each year, Irish grain was being shipped to England. In that disaster, Ireland lost more than two millions of its some eight and one–half millions and began a century of population decline, a decline due chiefly to emigration.

The egalitarian doctrines of the American and French Revolutions and especially the writings of Thomas Paine helped to stimulate an effort at a joint

Protestant and Roman Catholic revolt in 1796–98 led by Wolfe Tone. According to the historian J. C. Beckett (1966: 266–267), Tone's "plans were foiled not so much by the strength of England and the hesitation of France [to help] as by the deep–seated division among the people of Ireland." The revolt had middle–class Protestant and Roman Catholic support, but it lacked lower class backing. Nevertheless, although defeated, Tone "established, and later came almost to personify, a tradition of revolutionary violence that has never wholly died out of Irish politics."

Two leaders in particular characterize political struggles of the nineteenth century: Daniel O'Connell and Charles Stewart Parnell, a Roman Catholic and a Protestant, both often referred to popularly as "uncrowned kings of Ireland." O'Connell (1775–1847), also called the "Liberator," utilized the Roman Catholic clergy to organize a successful nonviolent struggle for the emancipation of the Roman Catholics and also, incidentally, of the dissenters. With similar tactics, climaxed by "monster meetings" of as many as several hundred thousand people, he tried to go on and gain a re–establishment of a separate Irish legislature, but in that he failed. Parnell (1846–91) also used nonviolent tactics of a spectacular sort—especially the boycott—to achieve land reforms that brought about more widespread land ownership. His efforts also gave a powerful impetus to Irish efforts eventually to obtain self–government. (Kee, 1972: parts 3–4)

James Connolly (1868–1916), an outstanding socialist labor leader and theoretician, similarly characterizes the struggles of the early part of the twentieth century. After extensive labor organizing, he joined in the planning of the 1916 rising against English rule and became military commander of the Republican forces in Dublin. Like other leaders of that crushed but significant rebellion, he became one of those executed by the English. An unanticipated consequence of that series of executions was the manner in which it publicized to the world the Anglo–Irish struggle and dramatized to the Irish of all social classes possibly attainable aspirations. (Levenson, 1973; Greaves, 1961; Beckett, 1966:441)

The four Irish holocausts and the reputations and sayings of Tone, O'Connell, Parnell, and Connolly still live in the struggles of the Northern Irish. Selectively and appropriately interpreted, they persist in the folklore, annual celebrations, and paranoid distrusts and hatreds of both Orange and Green people. They also help to account for the "racial" rejection of the Irish by the English and for the lack of empathy for Irish people and their problems.

## IV. RELATIONSHIP OF VIOLENCE TO SOCIAL CONTEXTS AND ASPIRATIONS

In the following, an effort is made to relate acts and threats of violence by members of various classes and groups to their social contexts and to current social aspirations.

## A. Terrorizing Upper-Class Decisions and Indecisiveness

Agitation for separation by Irish nationalists and against it by Protestants, especially in the northeastern counties, climaxed in the civil war of 1919–21 and the separation of the 26 counties of the "free state" from the six counties of the United Kingdom province of Northern Ireland.

When the first six–county government was announced in 1921 by Sir James Craig, the Prime Minister, it consisted entirely of wealthy Protestant landowners, merchants, and manufacturers. The overwhelming majority of the members of the provincial Senate and House of Commons were also Protestants. (Farrell, 1980: 67–69) Similar people continued to rule with the help of the Unionist Party, the Protestant Orange Order, repressive "emergency" legislation, and carefully cultivated anti–Roman Catholic prejudices. They gave substance to the latter through providing invidious privileges in employment, housing, education, and personal safety to the thus less underprivileged but still oppressed lower–class Protestants.

This provincial upper class gradually changed from the traditional land–based aristocracy to a class of enterpreneurial plutocrats at first centered in Northern Ireland and then more and more in England. The provincial upper class hold persisted until it was destabilized by increasing popular political sophistication, modern violence technology, and the shrinking of the world under the influence of the mass media and of politico–economic imperialism. In consequence, the United Kingdom government in 1972 "dismantled [the Northern Ireland provincial government at] Stormont because it had ceased to deliver ruling class dominance and the subordination of the masses." (Bew et al., 1979: 162)

The British and the multinational corporations that influence British policies apparently hope to continue to control Northern Ireland as a useful military outpost and as a profitable colony. (Lindsay, 1980: chap. 20; *Sunday Tribune*, 1981a,b,c) The province's low wages, low industrial absenteeism, few strikes, and high unemployment are notorious and continuing. (Wallace, 1971: chap. 5; Barritt & Carter, 1972: chap. 6; B.I.S., 1978: 26–27; Black et al., 1980; Hadden, 1980; Wall, 1980; N.I.I.S., 1981: 8) Partly in spite of and partly because of these considerations, the British appear to lack a willingness and probably also an ability to make realistic social changes. They fear any threats to the stability of their social control. Thus they persevere in the maintenance of a bitter stalemate carefully insulated by the major political parties—to the extent that they find possible—from inter–party struggles in Great Britain. For example, only one member of the British House of Commons in 1981 publicly condemned Prime Minister Margaret Thatcher's rigid attitude toward the dying Irish hunger strikers. She even went to Belfast during a 1981 local election campaign and sharply dramatized her inflexibility. (Cf. B.I.S., 1981a) As a journalist (McBride, 1981: 4) points out, that visit helped to drive "one part of the community into the eager arms of Paisley [the clergyman who leads the extreme Loyalists], another part into the equally eager arms of the Provos [the Provisional Irish Republican Army].'' Thus, people ''will die, because of Mrs. Thatcher's inability to accept that the British Government, no more than any other faction in Northern Ireland, cannot have everything its own way.''

Let us look at major steps of terrorizing by the dominant upper–class groups that did so much to bring Northern Ireland to its present situation:

Arising out of England's wartime struggle from 1914 to hold Ireland and, at least, Northern Ireland, a series of laws were applied, enacted, and implemented for the purpose of striking fear into the minds of dissidents. They granted unusual powers to the military, the police, and the judiciary. These laws began especially with the United Kingdom Defence of the Realm Act of 1914 as applied to Ireland. They were made even more sweepingly repressive by the Restoration of Order in Ireland Act of 1920. The latter authorized the military to imprison any Irish man or woman without charge or trial for an indefinite period of time. Through secret courts, ''political offenders were to be tried by their opponents . . . while prisoners of war could be tried by their enemy captors and sentenced on the charge of 'murder' to be hanged.'' (Macardle, 1951: 381)

In order to localize such terrorizing powers, the Northern Ireland government in 1922 adopted a ''temporary,'' ''emergency'' Special Powers Act that was then re–adopted with some strengthening until it was made continuing in 1933 and then replaced by the Emergency Provisions Act of 1938. In general, as the British National Council for Civil Liberties concluded in 1936, this legislation meant that ''individual liberty is no longer protected by law, but is at the arbitrary disposition of the Executive'' and ''that the Northern Ireland Government has used Special Powers towards securing the domination of one particular faction and, at the same time, towards curtailing the lawful activities of its opponents.'' (N.C.C.L., 1936: 39)

When nonviolent civil rights agitation became prevalent in the late 1960s, administrative policy permitted Loyalist paramilitary harassment notoriously facilitated by part-time and regular police. This terrorizing encouraged the violent among Nationalist dissenters. Thus officially permitted violence begot defensive and retaliatory violence. (Egan & McCormack, 1969; Jackson & Ashworth, 1979: 8)

Successive Northern Ireland and, from 1972, United Kingdom governments authorized ever more wide–ranging and repressive ''emergency'' powers and procedures. The emphasis of these measures was persistently on attacking unsettling symptoms, upon stifling the dissent of the deprived, rather than upon dealing with causes.

The legislation became so permissive, as enacted and interpreted at Stormont, that it precipitated a decision by Northern Ireland's highest court in February 1972 questioning the legality of a part of the Special Powers Acts. The court contended that Stormont's parliament had gone beyond the authorizations contained in the province's basic constitutional document, the British Government of Ireland Act of 1920. Under that act, only Westminster can control Crown armed forces; with the Special Powers Acts of Northern Ireland, the provincial government had assumed such control. Faced with this embarrassing ruling, the Westminster parliament rushed through an enactment that nullified the court's decision. (H. Kelly, 1972; Downey, 1972) Shortly thereafter, on March 24, the British government, in effect, lost its patience with the law and order procedures of the provincial government and took over its control. Little wonder that the ethnic minority and organized labor have little faith in recourse to the courts to defend their rights!

As a bulletin of the British Information Services (1978: 11) candidly admits, such British and provincial legislation and actions sanctioned "detention; the power to search, arrest and question suspects on suspicion of being involved in terrorism; the proscription of organisations; the abolition of trial by jury for terrorist offenses (because of the intimidation of jurymen and witnesses); and the making of exclusion orders [of people from the province]." The detention of suspects without charge for more than a few days ceased in 1975, but the holding of charged prisoners for long periods presumably awaiting trial continues.

A prison hunger strike and the growing volume of prisoners led the British administration in June, 1972 to try to cope with terrorist symptoms, in their limited facilities, by granting paramilitary prisoners "special category" status. While this was a matter of administrative expediency, it was taken by dissidents to be, in effect, a recognition of the "political" status of such persons. This category helped to justify the use of "Diplock" courts from 1973. These courts, recommended by an official Diplock Commission in 1972, are presided over by a single judge with no jury and a relaxation of the rules on the use of confessions. That "a very high proportion of cases in Diplock trials are wholly dependent on confessions obtained during interrogation, can only increase the general concern that the risk of innocent persons being convicted in Diplock courts is substantially greater than in jury trials." (Boyle et al., 1980: 62; v. Diplock, 1972)

"Special category" prisoners—men and women from the various organizations—wear their own clothes, do no prison work, socialize with their fellow paramilitaries, and have such other privileges as extra visits from outsiders and extra food parcels.

The British stopped granting this special status to prisoners convicted of an offense committed after March 1, 1976. Loyalist and Nationalist participants in the struggle called this a "criminalisation program" because it placed their convicts in the same category as the non–political, or "common criminals." It ceased to give any possible suggestion of "political" status.

This change led directly to noncooperation, to the "on the blanket" or "dirty" protest in the H–Blocks of the Maze (Long Kesh) Prison and later among the women in the Armagh jail. Those "on the blanket" refuse to accept "criminal status," with its requirement of prison garb and prison work. They wear nothing but a blanket. In retaliation, especially in the H–Blocks, the wardens—among other actions—confine the men to their cells and refuse to let them empty their slop containers. When prisoners broke windows to have an outlet for their urine and stools, wardens boarded up the windows and often upset slop containers in the cells. The prisoners were placed on half rations, and evidence has been produced of the extent to which prisoners are abused by the wardens. (Faul & Murray, 1979) As Cardinal Tomás O'Fiaich (1979: 93–94) contends after visits with these prisoners, "one would hardly allow an animal to remain in such conditions, let alone a human being." He adds: "The authorities refuse to admit that these prisoners are in a different category from the ordinary, yet everything in their trials and family background indicates that they are different." On the contrary, the British Northern Ireland Office (N.I.O., 1980) asserts:

"They foul their cells. They have smashed furniture. They have refused to wear prison clothing, or its substitute, civilian–type clothing. They refuse to work.

"This is done to try to force the Government to grant them 'special status'; in other words to establish that their murders, their bombings are in some way special and that they should be treated more favorably. . . .

"As part of the propaganda campaign the prisoners have sought to claim that the Government is responsible for the conditions in which these prisoners live; that normal facilities and basic needs are being denied them.

"The fact is that the prisoners have imposed the conditions upon themselves."

The statement contains no reference to the continuing existence of "special category" prisoners. At the end of 1976, there were more than 1,500 of that type; by May 1981, after many had been "phased out," there continued to be 332; at the same time, 416 were "on the blanket" in protest. (N.I.I.S., 1981: 23; cf. Coogan, 1980a) The differences between these categories and the intolerableness of treatment of prisoners on the "no wash, no toilet" protest led to the hunger strikes of 1980–81.

Similar on–again off–again indecisiveness is further illustrated by the hunger strike late in 1980. To end that strike, the government's representatives agreed to more tolerable prison conditions, and then they reneged. Thus the hunger strike tactic was resumed in 1981 and led to the deaths of IRA and British Parliament member Bobby Sands and a series of others, as discussed below.

The suspension of ordinary civil rights and a protective definition of terms make it quite easy for the British to claim that "there are no political prisoners in Northern Ireland." (B. I. S., 1978:11) As Secretary of State for Northern Ireland Humphrey Atkins asserted April 15, 1981 at Westminister: "The Government will not accord 'political' status to men convicted by the courts of acts which they claim were committed for political motives." (N.I.I.S., 1981: 23) Many other countries, including the Soviet Union, take a similar position. But, except in political terms, it is difficult to explain the jump in prison population from about 500 to as many as 3,000 during this period. (O'Fiaich, 1979: 94)

The picture that emerges from these and other data is one of stumbling efforts by upper–class groups in the province and in England to shore up their control through the use of short–range terrorizing procedures. Rather than facing and adapting to the changing social scene through negotiating nonviolently with deprived dissidents, they attempt to erase symptoms without examining and then dealing with causes. They rigidify their stance and the social structure more and more by sweeping aside many of the libertarian provisions that presumably gave plausibility to their claims to benign and legitimate control. It is part of a gradual stripping away of the pretentions of liberal democracy by an increasingly authoritarian and inflexible regime.

## B. Terrorizing "Law and Order" Activities by (a) Middle-Class and (b) Lower-Class Government Functionaries

The terrorizing policies adopted by the upper class in Northern Ireland are short–sighted enough. Their interpretation and implementation by their rank–and–file functionaries alerted social concern organizations internationally to the gravity of the situation.

Amnesty International, after investigation in 1977, focused attention on the brutality of police interrogation procedures for eliciting "confessions." As part of this, it expressed concern at trial of all persons charged under "emergency" legislation by non–jury courts sitting with single judges. As it concluded, "The majority of all persons convicted in this court are convicted solely on the basis of a confession made during their detention in police custody." The organization condemned the "maltreatment of suspects by the Royal Ulster Constabulary" and criticized the inadequacy of "the machinery for investigating complaints against the police." (Amnesty International, 1979: 1, 6; cf. Boyle et al., 1975: 6–26, 48–52; Taylor, 1980)

The United Kingdom Committee of Inquiry inspired by the Amnesty International findings admitted that private interrogation "creates the opportunity for unfair and violent means and methods to be used." It also noted that such interrogation in Northern Ireland was "mostly conducted by sergeants and constables" rather than by better trained officers. (Bennett, 1979: 135)

The government of the Irish Republic submitted to the European Commission on Human Rights (1976) written evidence concerning 228 cases of the ill–treatment of prisoners in 1971–74 in Northern Ireland, 154 of which had to do with interrogation abuses. The Commission dealt with eleven of the latter in detail and unanimously labeled as "torture" the interrogation practices to which the prisoners had been subjected. Upon appeal, the European Court of Human Rights (1978: 56–57, 82) refused to go that far, but it did decide with only one negative vote that the interrogation techniques complained of "constituted a practice of inhuman and degrading treatment." (Cf. Bennett, 1979: 50–51)

A statement by a Northern Ireland police surgeon broadcast from London Sunday, March 11, 1979 dramatized the class–stratified patterning of roles in the implementation of official interrogation procedures. Dr. Robert Irwin broke the middle–class functionaries' code of silence when he reported that 150 to 160 suspected IRA terrorists he had "examined in police custody during the past three years were beaten and otherwise 'physically illtreated' while being interrogated by police in Belfast." The official response was a shocked denunciation of Irwin. (Downie, 1979; Taylor, 1980: chap. 17)

Such middle–class functionaries in that tense society, whether they be physicians, judges, or administrators, were habitually expected to ignore violations of rules protective of the rights of subversives so long as the putative ends of "security" appeared to be served by such "practical expedients." As a theorist of repressive measures for the British (Kitson, 1977: 301) asserts, "From the start [of a struggle] insurgents, their supporters, and sympathizers, constantly try to limit the soldier's [and he could have added, the policeman's] ability to carry out his functions and to force him bit by bit into a state of uselessness." Thus this middle–class rationalist for social rigidification contends that physicians, judges, and administrators are in effect justified and even required to cover lower–class operatives' excesses that restore their "usefulness." (Cf. Evelegh, 1978: 6–90)

Among other middle–class complications in terrorizing is the recruitment of professional people for secret service jobs that "could hardly be advertised." They are employed "via the ramifications of personal introduction." In consequence also of their lack of "either civilian or military self-discipline, it was easy for the upper echelons of the secret departments to become havens of mediocrity or vapid eccentricity." (Page et al., 1977: 137–38) Reference is especially to leaders in the British DI5 and DI6 secret services, but the generalizations have wider application in Northern Ireland. Such individuals provide what guidance and permissive assistance there is to the largely lower–class counter–guerrilla guerrillas, "dirty trick" operatives, and agents provocateurs who infiltrate insurgent groups. (Kitson, 1971: chaps. 6–7; Lindsay, 1980: 274–288)

The chief governmental instruments in inter–sectarian strife are made up predominantly of lower–class Loyalists plus similar people recruited in Great Britain. They are the Royal Ulster Constabulary (RUC), the RUC Reserve (RUCR), until 1970 the Ulster Special Constabulary (USC) or "B Specials," and since 1970 the Ulster Defence Regiment (UDR). Unofficially, the RUC actually succeeded the private army organized in 1912 to oppose home rule for Ireland, the Protestant Ulster Volunteer Force (UVF). Many UVF members joined the RUC, and others came over from the disbanded Royal Irish Constabulary (RIC). These groups gave the RUC a strong Loyalist, anti–Nationalist, anti–Green, paramilitary character from its establishment in 1922. The RUC under centralized control includes 7,100 of whom one–tenth are women; the RUCR has 4,700 mostly part–time members of whom about one–sixth are women. Of the total in the RUC and RUCR, no more than one–tenth are Roman Catholics even though that ethnoid group constitutes one–third of the province's population. (N.I.I.S., 1981: 20; Flackes, 1980: 198–200) As the writer Jack

Holland (1981: 3) recalls from his own Belfast youth: "The state of which we were citizens . . . was set up to ensure privileges would be accorded to 'loyalists.' And loyalists were Protestants. By definition, a Catholic was a rebel."

The total number of complaints recorded against RUC members rose from 1,366 in 1975 to 2,331 in 1978, but the complaints procedure is notoriously ineffective. (Bennett, 1979: 143)

The B Specials had an especially flagrant record of Loyalist partisanship when they were finally disbanded in 1970. They then had 8,000 mostly part–time members who often drilled in Orange Lodge halls and frequently were seen to be active in conflicts with civil rights and Nationalist demonstrators. (Scarman, 1972: 17–19)

The UDR is part of the British Army. When organized in 1970 as presumably a more objective replacement for the B Specials, it enrolled 1,800 members, about one–fifth of whom were Roman Catholics. It then quickly became infiltrated by Loyalists. By 1979–81, it included about 2,700 full–time and 5,300 part–time soldiers, only two percent of whom were Roman Catholics. (N.I.I.S., 1981: 22; Tomlinson, 1980: 185)

The lower–class rank–and–file soldiers whom the British send to Northern Ireland are a mixed lot. As a British journalist (Barzilay, 1973: intro.) reported: "By the middle of 1973 there were virtually no British Army infantry units who had not seen service in Northern Ireland during the previous four years." Prior to his arrival there, "the ordinary soldier knew little of Northern Ireland and its developing problems." They are "briefed" as it were for the duties they will have there chiefly by the anti–Irish accounts in the sensational popular media of Great Britain and by the typically anti–Irish gossip of their social circles. (Curtis, 1971; Dummett, 1973; Chibnall, 1977: 17–18, 120–121, and so on) Thus, to them, all Irish regardless of religious label are "Paddies" and problems! This is shocking to Loyalists who also look down upon Nationalists as "Paddies"! (Insight Team, 1972: 152–153; Leach, 1979; Evelegh, 1978: 1)

The roles of these lower–class security forces in interrogation have been mentioned. Here are a few examples of their terrorizing behavior in the streets and in "lifting" people from their homes:

On October 5, 1968, the RUC stopped a peaceful but forbidden civil rights protest march in Derry. According to an official commission report (Cameron, 1969: 31), "One of the consequences of the break up of the demonstration . . . was . . . that some very damaging pictures of police violence were seen throughout the United Kingdom and abroad."

On August 12, 1969, in reaction against the annual Loyalist Apprentice Boys' march in Derry (celebrating the role of 13 apprentice boys in closing the gates of Derry against the army of King James II at the beginning of the siege of 1689), extensive rioting took place and continued for several days. (Stetler, 1970) With the failure of 1,000 police with armored cars, water cannon, and tear gas to cope, 300 British troops for the first time in the province were used for riot duty. An official tribunal (Scarman, 1972: I, 84) reported that the arrival of the soldiers "was welcomed. The city was tired and the army presence afforded a sound reason for going home." After a similar failure of the police in Belfast, soldiers were also called in there with the same initially pacifying response. During this five–day period of rioting throughout the province, eight persons were killed; 514 civilians, 226 police, and one soldier were injured; 161 were arrested.

At roughly 4:30 a.m. on August 9, 1971, on the basis of a compilation prepared by the RUC, soldiers "lifted" from their homes and arrested 342 men. The lists were defective; within 48 hours, 116 were released. With this sweep internment was reinstituted without trial. By November 10, some 980 had been arrested, and 508 had been released. The rest were either interned or held for disposition. (Compton, 1971: iv) Of those interned, many were "political opponents of the Unionists—like the PD [People's Democracy] and NICRA [Northern Ireland Civil Rights Association] members, old retired IRA ex–internees, militant trade unionists, public speakers, and, in some cases, people held on mistaken identity." (McGuffin, 1973: 87) One of the responses to this development was the call by the Northern Ireland Civil Rights Association (Keesing, 1971: 24913) for "all people to engage in a united massive campaign of resistance to internment through demonstrations and civil disobedience, including the withholding of rents and rates." A spokesman for the Irish Army revealed that 4,339 refugees from Northern Ireland were now camping in the 26–county Republic.

On January 30, 1972, "Bloody Sunday," British soldiers fired on a non-violent civil rights protest march in Derry and killed thirteen unarmed civilians and mortally wounded another. An official tribunal (Widgery, 1972: 38) later decided: "If the Army had persisted in its 'low key' attitude and had not launched a large scale operation to arrest hooligans the day might have passed off without serious incident. . . . None of the deceased or wounded is proved to have been shot handling a firearm or bomb." Violence swept the province. The Provos were further strengthened.

By July 31, 1972, 21,000 regular troops together with 9,000 mobilized UDR and 6,000 RUC were available in the province. At 4 a.m. on that day, they were used to take control of "no go" or citizen–erected barricaded areas in Derry and Belfast. To penetrate Derry's Nationalist ghetto, soldiers used 50–ton tanks and 100 other armored vehicles. The Green enclaves in Belfast and the Orange areas were more easily dismantled. Orange spokespeople welcomed this "operation motorman" as a victory.

These macro–events help to characterize the roles of the lower–class "security forces," but people of the province are more constantly and intimately touched by the frequent groups on patrol, the armed and armored cars, the body–searches before being permitted to enter public buildings, the barriers to be passed at key street points, the harassment of not–at–all–gentle house searches, and the brutalizing involvement of children and teen-agers in the spirit of the struggle. The so—called "Ulsterisation" of security forces through the use of fewer soldiers from Great Britain and more members of the RUC and RUCR has done little to change this ambience; the ethnicity of the RUC members is known.

What do security people think of their work under such conditions? Brian Moran, a Royal Marine Commando who deserted to Sweden, states: "We were supposed to be there to keep the peace, but I found a lot of prejudice in the Marines against ordinary Catholics. They gave a lot of public abuse in the streets. It was always covert—when there weren't any newspaper reporters about." (*Guardian,* Feb. 28, 1978) Ian Phillips, another Marine Commando, reports: "The amount of desertion is incredible, the numbers applying for discharges is increasing and this is very much connected with Northern Ireland as well as with pay and conditions." (*Information on Ireland,* No. 1, 1979: 25) Colonel Robin Evelegh (1978: 21), a former Royal Green Jackets commander, looks at the matter from a different standpoint when he criticizes the "unpredictability" of British law enforcement: "Flexible law has many synonyms. It is variously called 'showing political sensitivity,' or 'restraint,' or 'winning hearts and minds,' or 'low profile.' But whatever it is called, it always has the characteristic that the extent to which the published law will be enforced is uncertain to both the law breakers and the law enforcers. . . . One illegal procession would be permitted and another, apparently similar to it, would be stopped. One week vigilantes would be allowed, and the next week fimly suppressed."

These random quotations from participants in the Northern Ireland conflict suggest the contradictory complications that face policy makers and security forces. As Evelegh (1978: 3) points out, "to counter terrorism successfully, the Government must conduct a coordinated campaign bringing into harmony its economic, political, social, legal, military, police and public relations efforts against terrorism and insurrection so that each reinforces the others." He did not point to one wholly successful example of such a campaign.

## C. *Terrorizing Threats by Other Middle-Class "Respectables"*

These threats sometimes involve direct efforts to coerce, and sometimes indirect ones, through raising the possibility of lower—class violence as an alternative to compliance. They reflect the deep middle—class embedment in the three Northern Ireland ethnoid conspiracies. They find expression in policy statements, actions, and agreements relating to employment, housing, and social services including public safety. They contribute to all types of segregation and of efforts to aid members of the in—group at the expense of, or at least in preference to, members of other groups.

Middle—class dedication to compromise, a dedication that more often serves upper—class establishment interests than those of society more generally, finds many sophisticated forms of expression. For example, middle—class people devote themselves to so—called "peace" organizations connected with religious denominations and to voluntary social work, demonstration, and protest societies of a "respectable" or discreet sort. The net effect of these efforts has been largely either cosmetic at best or the promotion of a kind of social anesthesia that looks to the restoration of the pre–existing exploitative social order with no appreciable modification. (Lee, 1980b) These allegedly benign efforts terrorize the lower class because of the hopeless realization they give that lower–class needs are not to be met.[2]

Generally, terrorizing threats from the Roman Catholic middle class were not actually intended to be carried out. They mostly wanted "to reassure Protestants that Catholics were prepared to work within Northern Ireland to achieve a more democratic state." (Holland, 1981: 31) That ethnoid section of the middle class had expanded after World War II under the stimulation of an education act of 1947 as well as other changes. The act "threw open the door for Grammar school education for all those who by 'age, aptitude and ability' were suited for it." It also called for the provision of "scholarships to institutions of Further Education, which of course included Universities." (McNeilly, 1973: 112)

One of the relatively effective products of this ethnoid class was the civil rights movement of the 1960s that had much in common with the movement in the United States led by Martin Luther King, Jr. When those involved in the Northern Ireland Civil Rights Association joined in a protest march in August 1968, few appeared to realize that they would terrify the Loyalists, that the Loyalists would oppose them, and that that opposition would "set off a sectarian chain reaction." These Roman Catholics "were mostly moderate, middle-class people, with a sprinkling of earnest, radical young students and some republicans who were eager to get away from the failed politics of violence." (Holland, 1981: 31) That NICRA included some members of the Irish Republican Army, and later of its Official offshoot, has been used to denigrate its program, but that organization's effective dedication to nonviolent confrontations can scarcely be doubted. (NICRA, 1978)

Relatively effective nonviolent middle–class leadership of actionist efforts continued. It is expressed especially in the work of NICRA, of the lawyers in the Association for Legal Justice, and of such social investigators as Father Denis Faul and Father Raymond Murray. (Faul & Murray, 1976a,b, 1979; Brady et al., 1976) These groups worked not only through the United Kingdom courts but also through those of the 26 counties and of the European Commission and Court of Human Rights.

Roman Catholic—like other—middle–class involvements in cosmetic and social anesthesia initiatives were more prevalent than such actionist efforts. (Lee, 1980b)

### D. *Terrorizing Operations by the Predominantly Lower-Class Insurgents*

Orange, Loyalist, or Unionist terrorists are organized principally into the Ulster Volunteer Force (UVF) as reconstituted in 1966, the Ulster Defence Association (UDA) set up in 1971, and the Ulster Freedom Fighers (UFF) formed in 1973 apparently as a splinter from the UDA. The three attempted to bring together a variety of local defense bodies that had sprung up throughout the province. (Flackes, 1980: 138–141, 146–147)

Green, Nationalist, or Republican ranks are divided among the old Official Irish Republican Army (OIRA), the Provisional Irish Republican Army (PIRA) dating from a split within the OIRA in 1969–70, and the Irish National Liberation Army (INLA), a product of another OIRA division in 1972. (J. Bell, 1979: part 6; Coogan, 1980b: part 2)

The third principal collection of rank–and–file combatants consists, as we have seen, of largely lower–class security people, police and military, including undercover and plainclothes operatives who have, to a degree, infiltrated the above organizations.

The most active insurgent groups militarily have been the UVF, UDA and UFF and the PIRA and INLA, of which all but the UDA have been formally proscribed along with the OIRA for most of the period. At the same time, all have close ties with legal and open political parties.

The UVF claims a long history of Loyalist military efforts. When it was revived in 1966, it claimed descent from the organization of the same name that had been formed in 1912 to fight for the Unionist Protestants against Irish Home Rule then being sought. The old organization had even provided most of the members of the 36th (Ulster) Division of the British army in 1914, a unit that lost many in the Battle of the Somme in July 1916. Amidst a rash of petrol bombings of premises owned by Roman Catholics in the spring of 1966, coincident with the IRA's celebration of the 50th anniversary of the Easter Rising, the UVF again burst upon the Ulster scene. On May 21, Belfast newspapers carried a statement by a man said to be "Captain William Johnston, Adjutant, First Batallion, Belfast UVF," in part as follows:

> "From this day on we declare war against the IRA and its splinter groups. Known IRA men will be executed mercilessly and without hesitation. Less extreme measures will be taken against anyone sheltering or helping them. . . . [We] solemnly warn the authorities to make no more speeches of appeasement. We are heavily armed Protestants dedicated to this cause." (Dillon & Lehane, 1973: 28; Boulton, 1973: 40)

In response, Prime Minister Terence O'Neill at first announced that he would not invoke the Special Powers Act to proscribe any Protestant outfit, but after further atrocities, he stated June 28, 1966: "This organisation [the UVF] now takes its proper place alongside the IRA in the schedule of illegal bodies." (Dillon & Lehane, 1973: 29, 34)

From May 1974 to November 1975, the proscription was removed in order to try to turn the UVF from violence to political activity, but that recourse failed. Its paramilitary campaign continued.

By 1981, the UVF was taking a slightly more judicious view of compromise.

In *Combat: The Journal of the Ulster Volunteers* (vol. 4, issue 41, [1981] no date given), it states:

> "We support the granting of Special or Emergency Status for persons convicted for politically motivated offences. In return we have made it clear that we will use our influence to bring a stable democratic administration to Northern Ireland. . . . Special Category must be linked with a political settlement which in turn must be linked to discussions on a phased Amnesty. Once again we repeat:—
>
>> "1.  There must be a cessation of violence.
>> "2.  Troops should be withdrawn to barracks for a negotiating period.
>> "3.  The police should be accepted in all areas as a public service.
>> "4.  The British Government must convene an all–party conference and attempt to break the political deadlock."

Support for special category status and for the calling of an all–party conference resembles PIRA objectives, but in its next issue (42), *Combat* asserts: "Since 1968 every conceivable violent event has taken place in Northern Ireland. . . . So much has happened that people tend to forget what has happened, yet the only achievement of the I.R.A. is that they have achieved nothing." The UVF was actually finding itself in much the same position as the PIRA: Its "political" prisoners were being treated as "criminals." It was still proscribed. It, too, would like to look forward to a settlement in which its objectives might be gained and its prisoners amnestied.

Not at all hopeful of a British–sponsored compromise, the UVF joined in the reforming of the Ulster Army Council. This Council had originally been established in 1973 to be a united front of the UVF, UDA, Ulster Special Constabulary Association, Loyalist Defence Volunteers, Orange Volunteers, and Red Hand Commandos. It had been instrumental in supporting the Loyalist strike organized in 1974 by the Ulster Workers' Council that led to the collapse of a power–sharing administration set up January 1 that year at Stormont by the British government. When the Ulster Workers' Council planned another general strike in 1977 to achieve greater Orange control, it failed to gain sufficient support to succeed. In announcing the reforming of the Ulster Army Council in 1981, the UVF spoke of "the gravity of the situation" and said "it has been formed for the defence of Loyalist areas in Ulster. . . . If the need arises, it will have no hesitation in retaliation, even to the extent of taking the offensive." (*Combat,* vol. 4, issue 43)

Even though it is associated in the Ulster Army Council with illegal organizations and is understood to be related to the Ulster Freedom Fighters, the UDA maintains its legal status. Its uniformed members constitute the largest voluntary paramilitary organization. Advocating "Law before Violence," its membership reached a high point of 40,000 in 1972, but it claims to have limited itself to 10,000 to 12,000 members by 1978 in order to have a more controllable, more disciplined body. All along, the UDA like the UVF has sought to restore the

"Orange State" of 1921–72 or some dependent or independent approximation of that one–party Protestant setup. (Boulton, 1973; G. Bell, 1976; chaps. 9–10)

In 1981, UDA's chairperson since 1973, Andy Tyrie, still supports this presumably "legal" stance: "We are a counter-terrorist organisation. The only way we'll get peace here is to terrorise the terrorists." Since 1977, the UDA has also worked through a political wing, the New Ulster Political Research Group. The responsibility of UDA members for the killing of four prominent Republicans and for the wounding of Bernadette Devlin McAliskey (former British M.P.) brought on agitation again early in 1981 for the organization's proscription. As the London *Economist* noted on February 7, however, "The British government's opinion . . . is still that a ban [on the UDA] would not only be unenforceable, but also unhelpful to the security forces. It would tend to wipe out whatever influence the more moderate and more politically–minded elements in the UDA might have." UDA's legal status, the *Economist* realizes, "makes a mockery of the law" to many people.

Loyalist reactions against the civil rights marches and confrontations of 1968–69 found the IRA following a changed policy. The IRA's campaign of 1956–62 had been a violent one, and it had failed. This had led to a decision to infiltrate organizations that might forward its efforts to undermine the current provincial government. Thus, when the Cameron Commission reported to the Stormont Parliament in September 1969 on *Disturbances in Northern Ireland,* it spoke especially of the roles on the Green side of the Northern Ireland Civil Rights Association (NICRA), the People's Democracy (PD), and the Derry Citizens Action Committee (DCAC), but the IRA was there. As the commission concluded: "Because the Civil Rights movement and its published objects were (at the time) wholly rejected by the Government it was to be expected that the I.R.A. or members of it in Northern Ireland would seek to turn that situation to their advantage." At that stage, the commission found "no evidence . . . that such members either incited to riot or took part themselves in acts of violence." IRA members served especially as marchers or stewards in demonstrations and as organizers of street–by–street "Defence Committees" in the Green ghettos. (Cameron, 1969: 86)

NICRA, organized in 1967 as an affiliate of the English National Council for Civil Liberties, and related civil rights bodies shortly ceased to be the principal concerns of either the government or the Loyalists. Militants in the IRA had become restive with their own organization's political, Marxist–Leninist leanings. The PIRA break occurred in December 1969 when the IRA Army Council decided to give token recognition to the Westminster, Dublin, and Stormont Parliaments, a decided change from its traditional abstentionism and reliance on violence. Sinn Fein, the political party affiliated with the IRA, similarly split at its January 1970 convention. After the division, the Caretaker Executive for Provisional Sinn Fein asserted that the break occurred because of:

"the failure to provide adequate protection for Nationalist areas in the North in August [1969]; the adoption of an extreme Socialist policy leading to totalitarian dictatorship; favouring the retention of the Stormont Parliament as opposed to a takeover by Westminster; and the changes within the Movement since 1964, which saw the departure of many genuine Republicans and their replacement with people interested *in a more radical form of movement*." (J. Kelly, 1976: 23)

As a close observer (J. Kelly, 1976: 23) notes, "Both I.R.A.s, the Officials and the Provisionals, had the basis of an organisation in Northern Ireland when the British troops invaded the Falls [area of Belfast] in July 1970, but neither had the capability nor the backing necessary to be a credible fighting force. The British action changed all that, with the strength of the Provisionals, in particular, increasing rapidly." PIRA amalgamated many local defense groups that were springing up and that also would not accept OIRA's Marxist–Leninist orientation. PIRA's ideology is not too well defined. It has had financial support at times from well placed politicians and business men in the 26 counties. (Edmonds, 1971: 248; J. Kelly, 1971) But it aims at establishing an island–wide democratic and socialized state such as was envisioned by leaders of the Easter Rising of 1916. (PIRA, 1973: 94–96) An admirer (McCann, 1980: 176) nevertheless contends: "The Provos, despite all their imperfections and the heavy historical impedimenta they carry into political battle, are the vanguard of the anti–imperialist struggle in Ireland—this partly because of the failures of the left."

PIRA look upon their bombing methods and accomplishments as high points in their continuing terrorist campaign. Thus they were quite proud to publish in May 1979 British military Document 37 that they had captured. It spoke well especially of PIRA's ambush bombing techniques; it called them "discriminate" and "ingenious." PIRA then again illustrated this with what they called the "pinnacle of Republican achievement" in 1979 on August 27: "the I.R.A. executed war–monger [Admiral of the Fleet Earl] Mountbatten . . . and they mounted their most successful attack against British troops in 58 years, when 18, including 16 Paras, were wiped out in a double–bomb ambush." (PIRA, 1980: 5) PIRA called this a "discriminate operation to bring to the attention of the English people the continued occupation of our country." (Keesing, 1980: 30043) in view of the media–covered revulsion to these acts, it could be argued that this propaganda effort backfired.

The Irish National Liberation Army (INLA) is much smaller than the PIRA, but it "has been blamed by the British security forces for many murders and acts of violence in NI between 1976 and 1979." (Flackes, 1980: 72) Its activities are publicized in the periodical of its affiliate, the Irish Republican Socialist Party, called *An Camchéachta: The Starry Plough*. A high point of its terrorist program was the car–bomb "execution" of Airey Neave on March 30, 1979. He was British Shadow Government Spokesman on Northern Ireland. An official statement from the INLA Army Council the next day took responsibility for the killing with the assertion: "The INLA successfully breached intense security at the House of Commons [Westminster] to plant the device. . . . Neave was especially selected for assassination. He was well known for his rabid militarist calls for more repression against the Irish people and for strengthening of the SAS [Special Air Service] murder gang, a group which has no qualms about murdering Irish people." (Clancy, 1979)

INLA did not split from OIRA because of the latter's Marxist–Leninist ideology, but rather because of its willingness to try to work from within the Dublin and Belfast establishments. As the IRSP notes, "As early as 1972 the leadership of the Officials abandoned the struggle by declaring a cease fire at a time of escalating British repression." INLA is both Marxist–Leninist and terrorist. Its IRSP is amused that by 1979 the "existence of the Official I.R.A., despite public protestations that it is disbanded, is the most embarrassing contradiction that SF WP [OIRA's affiliated Sinn Fein the Workers Party] had to contend with." (IRSP, 1979)

Perhaps the most effective tactics that PIRA and INLA have had available for dramatizing to the world their struggle have been the hunger strikes of 1980–81. The impact of the publicity about the deaths of ten strikers in 1981 recalls that about the spaced out executions by the British of fifteen leaders of the 1916 Rising, May 3–12 in Dublin, and subsequent trials leading to suspended death sentences and to one further execution on August 3. (Kee, 1972: 572, 580) It also recalls the propaganda impact of the hunger strikes to death against the British in 1920 as part of the Irish independence war, especially that of the Lord Mayor of Cork Terence MacSwiney, which was well covered by the news media for 70 days. (Macardle, 1951: 391–92) MacSwiney wrote to his fellow hunger-strikers three weeks before his death: "Comrades, if we twelve go in glorious succession to the grave, the name of Ireland will flash in a tongue of flame through the world, and be a sign of hope for all time to every people struggling to be free." (Younger, 1968: 106)

The British reneged under extremist Protestant pressure on a December 18, 1980 agreement to improve prison conditions in Long Kesh (Maze). This agreement ended the 53–day hunger strike of seven Republicans before there were any deaths. Then Bobby Sands, as a leader among Provo prisoners, renewed the hunger protest on March 1, 1981. Sands was serving a 14–year term for the possession of a gun. The death of the British MP for Fermanagh–South-Tyrone, a strongly Nationalist area, provided an opportunity for Sands to run to succeed him. Sands won the contested by–election shortly before he died on May 5. His election, and that of his campaign manager to succeed him upon his death, demonstrated vividly a degree of popular support that governmental spokespeople had long denied. Two other Long Kesh prisoners (one on hunger strike) were elected to the Irish Parliament at about the same time. (PIRA, 1981b)

The media impact of Sands' protest, election, and death and of related incidents and deaths resembled that of the introduction of British troops in August

1969, the internment drive in August 1971, Derry's Bloody Sunday January 30, 1972, and the Loyalist strike that destroyed the power–sharing Northern Ireland executive in May 1974. (Foley, 1981: 14)

The 1981 hunger strike, supported by demonstrations both in Irish cities and abroad, continued until October 3 and cost ten lives. More than fifty other people were killed on the outside in clashes during the five months after Sands' death. PIRA claims that they "discouraged the prisoners on numerous occasions when they felt that a hunger–strike was the only logical means of bringing public attention to their plight and public pressure to bear on the British." (PIRA, 1981a) Like PIRA, INLA—three of whose members died in the strike—claims that the hunger strike decision was one made by the prisoners themselves, but that the effort is "the price to be paid for the winning of National Liberation." (IRSP, 1981)

Other Nationalist organizations, such as the Social Democratic and Labour Party, reacted negatively to the hunger strikes as well as to the "on the blanket" protest. In contrast, a political editor of *The Guardian* newspaper, Ian Aitken, stated August 13: "Many [British] Ministers have been distressed by the Provisional IRA's propaganda victory in Europe and America over the H–Block hunger–strikes. . . . A few of them . . . believe that the government should at least take steps to see that the procession of dying hunger–strikers is halted." Predictably, the UVF journal, *Combat* (vol. 4, issue 41), calls the hunger effort "this life–wasting tactic" and cites how "indirectly they have caused the deaths of others . . . not to mention the countless cost in injuries and damage to property." On the religious side, it presented a difficult ideological issue: Were the dead hunger–strikers murdered, as PIRA and INLA claimed, or were they suicides? Suicide is an ultimate sin, and thus to Roman Catholics, an unforgiven sin.

Prime Minister Margaret Thatcher made clear her government's position on the hunger strike in a letter July 28, 1981 to United States Senator Edward M. Kennedy. She said she shared his "deep concern about the deaths," but she added: "The responsibility for additional deaths rests firmly on the shoulders of those who are ordering these young men to commit suicide in the cause of subverting democratic institutions in Ireland North and South." (B.I.S., 1981b: 1–2)

When the strikers called off their effort on October 3, 1981, they stated: "We have been robbed of the hunger strike as an effective protest weapon principally because of the successful campaign waged against our distressed relatives by the Catholic hierarchy." As prisoners had lapsed into unconsciousness toward the end of their fast, their families had taken control and sanctioned forced feeding. A leading PIRA officer, Gerry Adams, asserted: "While we must adopt a compassionate and fraternal attitude to those families who intervened, one cannot underestimate the enormity of their action or the manner in which the defeatist and demoralising campaign by some clergymen influenced their decision." On the other hand, British Minister for Northern Ireland James Prior claimed that the "road to and search for peace so clearly and tragically set back by the hunger strike can now be resumed." (Borders, 1981)

All sorts of estimates are made of how many Orange and Green insurgents there might be and of the extent of their support. The Northern Ireland Attitude Survey (Moxon–Browne, 1979: 11–12, 21, 26) revealed that in 1978, 70.7 percent of the Northern Ireland Protestants rejected the establishment of a united Ireland even "by peaceful means." On the contrary, 82.8 percent of the Roman Catholics wished that solution. The Reverend Ian Paisley's extreme Protestant Democratic Unionist Party then claimed 11.8 percent backing, and the OIRA–affiliated Republican Clubs, 2.3 percent. At the same time, it is well to consider the point made by a careful sociological investigator (Burton, 1978: 128) that "the particular ideology of Provisional Republicanism has been able to fuse the social consciousness of Catholicism into a political practice . . . a politics of civil rights through national liberation." This strength does not necessarily show up in estimates of party membership.[3]

How are the paramilitaries financed? A perceptive reporter (Coogan, 1980b: 534–35) speaks of how " groups of young men uprooted by the troubles, roamed around the country pulling off robberies, either on behalf of some para–military organisation or for themselves—it was, and is, often very difficult to tell which—the skills and the guns required for such activities becoming all too easily available in the disorder of the times." Thus the robbing of banks and post offices north and south of the Irish border became a commonplace and involved millions of pounds. In addition, British Minister of State for Northern Ireland Adam Butler asserts: "By dint of a concentrated propaganda campaign within the United States, the Provisional IRA have succeeded in creating for themselves a supply of money and in some cases lethal equipment." (B.I.S., 1981c: 7)

And so the struggle still goes on. It has accurately been called a bitter stalemate. All three sides constantly see rays of hope that persist in remaining merely rays. Four prisons contain, as of May 1981, 2,291 men and 57 women; 229 more are in a young offenders' center. Of the men, as is pointed out above, 416 are "on the blanket" demanding "political status," and there are still 332 whose "special category" or quasi–political status has not yet been phased out. The corrective being implemented for this escalation of prison population is the usual one of attacking symptoms: Another prison is to open in 1982 that will accommodate 447 more males and 56 more females. (N.I.I.S., 1981: 23) The causes of the unrest continue to be neglected.

In a hauntingly accurate sense, there are no nonparticipants in this current conflict. The American social psychologist Rona M. Fields (1980: xii) concludes from her extensive field studies in the British Isles that all the people there share in being a composite of "villains, heroes, and victims" in the struggle. As she and others (for example, Fraser, 1973) have shown, the children are the most tragic victims, with so many of their lives distorted by violent experiences and an atmosphere of doom. As part of this, the Belfast psychiatrist H. A. Lyons (van der Vat, 1978) observes, ''The troubles have engendered a very powerful feeling of belonging.'' That ''feeling of belonging'' get translated into the obsessive ethnoid conspiracies for which middle–class people provide so much in the way of leadership and rationalization in the service both of upper–class desires and of lower–class dissatisfactions.

Can ''terrorism'' be regarded as a political resource? It stimulates police and military spending and enhances their importance and power. It justifies curtailment of civil liberties. It thus helps permit the short–sighted to simplify and tighten the existing control structure. It leads Secretary of State Alexander Haig in the United States to jump from a concern with causes to one with symptoms by asserting: ''International terrorism will take the place of human rights in our concern.'' (*Rights,* March 1981: 2) And, as the New York *Times* remarks editorially on May 6, 1981, British Prime Minister Thatcher similarly ''seems unable to address the grievances that make terrorists like [deceased hunger striker] Bobby Sands [M. P.] heroes to the Catholic minority'' in Northern Ireland.

From a Green standpoint, as viewed by the PIRA and INLA, terrorism and the melodrama of the hunger strikes offer the only ways available in which to destabilize British imperial control in the province. They hope it will make the six counties too expensive to retain. As part of this, they hope to embarrass Westminster with terrorizing events in Great Britain and even in British military installations on the continent of Europe. As the American Central Intelligence Agency reports, ''The PIRA has conducted more international terrorist attacks than any other single terrorist group. They routinely attack the British military in Europe.'' (CIA, 1981: 13) As time has gone on and as the paramilitary organizations have worked out tested procedures for financing themselves, for maintaining and protecting their membership, and for assaulting their selected enemy, members have settled into terrorism as a way of life. It is an exciting alternative to the scant labor market with its low wages.

The Orange terrorists of the UVF and UDA seek to destroy the leadership of the Green organizations, to discourage recruitment into them, and to make support for Green programs appear to be foolish, immoral, or futile gestures. As the American Central Intelligence Agency generalizes: ''Unlike publicity–seeking left–wing terrorist groups who tend to select targets that provide the greatest political impact, right–wing groups tend to be motivated by desire to terrorize or destroy specific enemies . . . they most often conduct assassinations and bombings.'' (CIA, 1981: 11) This is a reasonable summary of Orange operations. Orange leaders regard their procedures as the only ways available for them to stimulate the British government or to restore the ''Orange State'' as a protection for them from encroaching Green power from the south and from the more prolifically breeding northern Roman Catholics.

The British military deal principally with what are merely symptoms of discontent. Their service is dedicated to the provision of official terror as a force for "law and order." As a slogan in an Armagh army gym has it, "The strong shall live and the weak shall die!" What few soldiers' wives accompany them in Northern Ireland have problems: "Some of the wives have just given up and gone home. Some have had nervous breakdowns. A lot of them are very low." The chief entertainment for the men, other than watching the same TV newscasts that also preoccupy paramilitaries, consists of strip–tease shows and pornographic materials. Life is very restricted, especially by the closely surrounding and not easily identifiable enemies. (Walker, 1980: 148, 150)

It is tempting to compare or contrast the Northern Ireland struggle with that in other somewhat similar situations: ones having to do with American blacks, French Canadians, Sicilians, Bretons, Palestine Liberation Organization members, and so many other contemporary and historical groups. There are resemblances, but such comparisons tend to ignore significant differences. Uniformed UDA members do recall postures of the Ku Klux Klan and the Nazis, but such a comparison caricatures the UDA and obscures a more adequate understanding. The PIRA and INLA have points of similarity both to the Jews in their liberation struggle and to the current PLO, but there are also significant differences. The bitter sectarianism of Iran has something in common with extreme Protestant/Roman Catholic propaganda, but British involvement gives the Northern Ireland situation quite a different context.

That some sort of *modus vivendi* might well be found for the peoples of Northern Ireland is theoretically quite possible. It would require radical examinations of underlying factors and decisive political actions. These possibilities continue to be ignored, especially by so–called "responsible" leaders there. Such an approach might place at risk a party's ability to stay in power. Tried and true stances are much more attractive. At the same time, such a fundamental approach can scarcely interest Orange and Green insurgents for two reasons: They find themselves committed to a way of life, to procedures and ideology. They do not have the power or influence to implement such an approach in a police state.

To offset their most glaring dramatizations of social inequality, British political leaders have obvious lessons available in the two–century experiences of their country's former colony, the United States. They could learn from it the virtues of the separation of church and state, of a written constitution and bill of rights, of a judicial system more subject to law than to class and ethnic interests, of a type of federalism that assures some degree of "devolution" (as the English speak of local autonomy), and reasonably equal civil rights to citizens of each of fifty states.

In Northern Ireland and the United Kingdom as a whole, an effective initiative toward resolution must move the "haves," the "establishment" of the existing class–ridden and militarized state. More faith must be placed in politics and less in terrorist procedures by those dedicated to "law and order." Unfortunately, the "haves" in England feel that they must continue to fight to retain their exploitative position with as little modification as possible. They fear where any retreat from their privileged position might take them. In the center of a disintegrated empire, the English establishment does not wish to retrench itself any further.

## ACKNOWLEDGMENTS

This research was supported (in part) by grants from The City University of New York PSC–BHE Research Award Program. Helpful facilities were also provided by Drew University, Madison, New Jersey. In this, as in all my research, I am indebted to my wife and fellow social scientist, Dr. Elizabeth Briant Lee, for her aid and counsel. I have also benefited from discussions with Professors James M. O'Kane and David A. Cowell and from my repeated visits during the past 25 years to Northern Ireland and my continuing contacts with well–informed persons in Northern Ireland, Ireland, and England.

## NOTES

1. During my many field trips since 1956 to Ireland and especially to Northern Ireland, I have had opportunities generously provided to me to interview people from all segments of the population, and especially leaders of a variety of organizations. Although many sources are cited in this paper, my own personal on–site observations and interviews have helped me to fit such data into the perspective developed here.

2. Within the space available, detailed support for the generalizations offered in this and related paragraphs cannot be presented. The materials in the paper cited (Lee, 1980b) and extensive personal interviewing in Northern Ireland provided background.

3. A careful survey in the 26 counties (Davis & Sinnott, 1979) reveals that 41.8 percent are sympathetic with IRA motives. Only 33.5 percent reject them. Even with regard to IRA activities, 20.7 percent had supportive attitudes; 60.5 percent opposed them. Voting records there do not reveal as great support.

## REFERENCES

Amnesty International
   1979   Follow Up to the Report of an Amnesty International Mission to Northern Ireland (28 November–6 December 1977). AI Index: EUR 45/01/79, 26 February.
B.I.S.: British Information Services
   1978   Northern Ireland. New York.
   1981a  "Northern Ireland hunger strikes: Who is being flexible?" Policy Background 3/81, July 27, 3 pp.
   1981b  "Northern Ireland: Text of Prime Minister's letter to Senator Kennedy." Policy Statements 35/81, July 29, 3 pp.
   1981c  "Northern Ireland: The struggle against terrorism." Policy Statements 38/81, September 29, 10 pp.
Barritt, D. P., and C. F. Carter
   1972   The Northern Ireland Problem (second edition), London: Oxford University Press.
Barzilay, David
   1973   The British Army in Ulster. Belfast: Century Services.
Beckett, J. C.
   1966   The Making of Modern Ireland: 1603–1923. New York: Alfred A. Knopf.

Bell, Geoffrey
1976   The Protestants of Ulster. London: Pluto Press.
Bell, J. B.
1972   "The chronicles of violence in Northern Ireland: The first wave interpreted." The Review
       of Politics 34 (2) (April): 147–157.
1979   The Secret Army: The IRA 1916–1979 (revised edition). Dublin: Academy Press.
Bennett, H. G.
1979   Report of the Committee of Inquiry Into Police Interrogation Procedures in Northern
       Ireland. London: HMSO, March. Cmnd. 7497.
Bew, Paul, Peter Gibbon, and Henry Patterson
1979   The State in Northern Ireland: 1921–72. Manchester: University Press.
Black, Boyd, John Ditch, Mike Morrissey, and Richard Steele
1980   Low Pay in Northern Ireland. London: Low Pay Pamphlet 12.
Blumenthal, M. D., R. L. Kahn, F. M. Andrews, and K. B. Head
1971   Justifying Violence. Ann Arbor, Michigan: Institute of Social Relations.
Borders, William
1981   "Belfast prisoners end hunger strike that left 10 dead." New York Times (October 4): 1,
       17.
Boulton, David
1973   The UVF: 1966–73. Dublin: Torc Books.
Boyle, Kevin, Tom Hadden, and Paddy Hillyard
1975   Law and State: The Case of Northern Ireland. Amherst, MA: University of Massachusetts
       Press.
1980   Ten Years on in Northern Ireland: The Legal Control of Political Violence. London:
       Cobden Trust.
Brady, Brian, Denis Faul, and Raymond Murray
1976   British Army Terror: West Belfast. Pamphlet. October.
Buckley, W. F., Jr.
1977   "Attack the symptoms first in the crime epidemic." New York Post (August 11): 26.
Burton, Frank
1978   The Politics of Legitimacy: Struggles in a Belfast Community. London: Routledge and
       Kegan Paul.
Cameron, Lord, Commission Appointed by the Governor of Northern Ireland
1969   Disturbances in Northern Ireland. Belfast: HMSO, September. Cmd. 532.
CIA: Central Intelligence Agency, National Foreign Assessment Center
1981   Patterns of International Terrorism: A Research Paper. PA81-10163U, June.
Chibnall, Steve
1977   Law-and-Order News: An Analysis of Crime Reporting in the British Press. London:
       Tavistock Publications.
Clancy, Seamus
1979   "Airey Neave executed." Starry Plough (Dublin), April: 1.
Compton, Edmund
1971   Report of the Enquiry Into Allegations Against the Security Forces of Physical Brutality in
       Northern Ireland Arising out of Events on the 9th of August, 1971. London: HMSO,
       November. Cmnd. 4823.
Connolly, James
1913   "North-East Ulster." Forward, August 2, reprinted pp. 263–267 in P. B. Ellis, (ed.),
       James Connolly: Selected Writings. Harmondsworth, England: Penguin Books, 1973.
Coogan, T. P.
1980a  On the Blanket: The H-Block Story. Dublin: Ward River Press.
1980b  The I.R.A. (revised edition), London: Fontana Paperbacks.

Costigan, Giovanni
    1969    A History of Modern Ireland. New York: Pegasus.
Curtis, L. P., Jr.
    1971    Apes and Angels. Washington: Smithsonian.
Daly, C. B., and R. D. E. Gallagher
    1977    Violence in Ireland: A report to the Churches (revised edition), Dublin: Veritas
            Publications.
Darby, John
    1976    Conflict in Northern Ireland. New York: Barnes & Noble.
Davis, E. E., and R. Sinnott
    1979    Attitudes in the Republic of Ireland Relevant to the Northern Ireland Problem, vol. 1.
            Dublin: The Economic and Social Research Institute, September. Paper No. 97.
Dillon, Martin, and Denis Lehane
    1973    Political Murders in Northern Ireland. Harmondsworth, England: Penguin Books.
Diplock, Lord, chairman
    1972    Report of the Commission to Consider Legal Procedures to Deal With Terrorist Activities
            in Northern Ireland. London: HMSO, December. Cmnd. 5185.
Downey, James
    1972    "Troops get legal footing in North." Irish Times (Dublin), February 24: 1, 6.
Downie, Leonard, Jr.
    1979    "Ulster doctor says IRA suspects maimed in police custody." London dateline, Wash-
            ington (D.C.) Post, March 11.
Dummett, Ann
    1973    A Portrait of English Racism. Harmondsworth, England: Penguin Books.
Edmonds, Sean
    1971    The Gun, the Law, and the Irish People. Tralee, Co. Kerry: Anvil Books.
Egan, Bowes, and Vincent McCormack
    1969    Burntollet. London: LRS Publishers.
European Commission of Human Rights
    1976    Application No. 5310/71: Ireland Against the United Kingdom of Great Britain and North-
            ern Ireland. Report of the European Commission of Human Rights. Strasbourg, January
            25.
European Court of Human Rights
    1978    Case of Ireland Against the United Kingdom. Strasbourg, January 18.
Evelegh, Robin
    1978    Peace-Keeping in a Democratic Society: The Lessons of Northern Ireland. Montreal:
            McGill-Queen's University Press.
Farrell, Michael
    1980    Northern Ireland: The Orange State (second revised edition), London: Pluto Press.
Faul, Denis, and Raymond Murray
    1976a   SAS Terrorism: The Assassin's Glove. July.
    1976b   Majella O'Hare: Shot Dead. September.
    1979    H Blocks: British Jail for Irish Political Prisoners.
Fields, Rona M.
    1980    Northern Ireland: Society Under Siege (new edition), New Brunswick, New Jersey: Trans-
            action Books.
Flackes, W. D.
    1980    Northern Ireland: A Political Directory, 1968–79. New York: St. Martin's Press.
Foley, Gerry
    1981    "The making of a martyr." Magill (Dublin), 4, 8 (May): 11–14.
Fraser, Morris
    1973    Children in Conflict. London: Secker and Warburg.

Gray, Tony
    1972   The Orange Order. London: The Bodley Head.
Greaves, C. D.
    1961   The Life and Times of James Connolly. London: Lawrence & Wishart.
Hadden, Tom
    1980   "Poverty: Myths and facts." Fortnight (Belfast), 177 (July–August): 6–7.
Hinkle, Warren
    1981   "The Irish inquisition." Inquiry, 4, 5 (February 23).
Holland, Jack
    1981   Too Long a Sacrifice: Life and Death in Northern Ireland Since 1969. New York: Dodd
           Mead & Co.
IRSP: Irish Republican Socialist Party
    1979   "Officials accept partition." Starry Plough (Dublin) April: 8.
    1981   "The price of freedom." Starry Plough, June: 1.
Insight Team of London Sunday Times
    1972   Northern Ireland: A Report on the Conflict. New York: Vintage Books.
Jackson, Harold, and Georgina Ashworth
    1979   The Two Irelands. London: Minority Rights Group Report 2 (revised).
Kee, Robert
    1972   The Green Flag. New York: Delacorte Press.
Keesing
    1971   Keesing's Contemporary Archives.
    1980
Kelly, H.
    1972   "High court holds N.I. role of army unconstitutional." Irish Times (Dublin), February 24:
           1, 6.
Kelly, James
    1971   Orders for the Captain? Dublin: Kelly.
    1976   The Genesis of Revolution. Dublin: Kelly Kane.
Kennedy, R. E., Jr.
    1973   The Irish: Emigration, Marriage and Fertility. Berkeley: University of California Press.
Kitson, Frank
    1971   Low Intensity Operations: Subversion, Insurgency, Peacekeeping. London: Faber & Faber.
    1977   Bunch of Five. London: Faber & Faber.
Leach, Edmund
    1979   "The official Irish jokesters." New Society (London), December 20–27: vii–ix.
Lecky, W. E. H.
    1865   History of the Rise and Influence of the Spirit of Rationalism in Europe (re-issue), London:
           Watts & Co., 1910. 2 vols.
    1892   A History of Ireland in the Eighteenth Century (re-issue), London: Longmans, Green &
           Co., 1902. 5 vols.
Lee, A. McC.
    1972–  "Insurgent and 'peacekeeping' violence in Northern Ireland." Social Problems, 20,
      73   532–546.
    1974   "Efforts to control insurgency in Northern Ireland." International Journal of Group Ten-
           sions, 4, 346–358.
    1977   "Imperialism, class and Northern Ireland's civil war." Crime and Social Justice, 8 (Fall/
           Winter): 46–52.
    1979   "Interethnic conflict in the British Isles." Anthropology and Humanism Quarterly, 4, 2–3
           (June/September): 6–16.
    1980a  "Human rights in the Northern Ireland conflict: 1968–1980." International Journal of
           Politics, 10, 1 (Spring): 1–146.

1980b "Nonviolent agencies in the Northern Ireland struggle: 1968–1979." Sociology and Social Welfare, 7, 4 (July): 601–623.

1981a "Mass media mythmaking in the United Kingdom's interethnic struggles." Ethnicity, 8, 18–30.

1981b "The dynamics of terrorism in Northern Ireland, 1968–1980." Social Research, 48, 1 (Spring): 100–134.

Lerner, Max
1934 "Political offenders." Encyclopaedia of the Social Sciences, 12, 199–203.

Levenson, Samuel
1973 James Connolly, A Biography. London: Martin Brian & O'Keefe.

Lindsay, Kennedy
1980 The British Intelligence Services in Action. Newtown-abbey, Co. Antrim: Dunrod Press.

Lyons, F. S. L.
1978 The Burden of Our History. Belfast: Queen's University.

Macardle, Dorothy
1951 The Irish Republic (second revised edition), New York: Farrar, Straus and Giroux.

McBride, Steve
1981 "Maggie sweeps the boards." Peace by Peace (Belfast), 6, 11 (June 5): 4–5.

McCann, Eamonn
1980 War and an Irish Town (revised edition), London: Pluto Press.

McGuffin, John
1973 Internment! Tralee, Co. Kerry: Anvil Books.

McKeown, Michael
1980 "Chronicles: A register of Northern Ireland's casualties 1969–80." The Crane Bag (Holmsdale, Co. Wicklow), 4, 2, 1–5.

McNeilly, Norman
1973 Exactly Fifty Years: The Belfast Education Authority and Its Work (1923–73). Belfast: Blackstaff Press.

Moxon-Browne, E.
1979 The Northern Ireland Attitude Survey, ms. report. Belfast: Queen's University, May.

N.C.C.L.: National Council for Civil Liberties
1936 Report of a Commission Appointed to Examine the Purpose and Effect of the Civil Authorities (Special Powers) Acts (Northern Ireland) 1922 & 1933. London: N.C.C.L.

NICRA: Northern Ireland Civil Rights Association
1978 "We shall overcome": The History of the Struggle for Civil Rights in Northern Ireland 1968–1978. New York: District Council 37, AFSCME, AFL–CIO.

N.I.I.S.: Northern Ireland Information Service
1981 Facts at Your Finger Tips: Northern Ireland. Belfast: N.I.I.S., June.

N.I.O.: Northern Ireland Office
1980 H-Blocks: The Reality. Belfast: N.I.O., November.

O'Dowd, Liam, Bill Rolston, and Mike Tomlinson
1980 Northern Ireland: Between Civil Rights and Civil War. Atlantic Highlands, NJ: Humanities Press.

O'Fiaich, Cardinal Tomás
1979 "Statement on Long Kesh." Pp. 93–94 in U.S. Committee on the Judiciary, 1979.

Page, Bruce, David Leitch, and Philip Knightley
1977 Philby. London: Sphere.

Paisley, Ian
1972 The Dagger of Treachery. Belfast: Puritan Printing Co.

Patterson, Henry
1980 Class Conflict and Sectarianism: The Protestant Working Class and the Belfast Labour Movement 1868–1920. Belfast: Blackstaff Press.

Poole, Michael
    1971    "Riot displacement in 1969." Fortnight (Belfast), 22 (August 6): 9–11.
PIRA: Provisional Irish Republican Army
    1973    Freedom Struggle. (Irish edition confiscated; republished in the U.S.A.).
    1980    "1979 review: Resounding republican success." An Phoblacht: Republican News (Dublin), January 5: 5–7.
    1981a   "IRA attitude on H-Block." An Phoblacht: Republican News, September 5: 20.
    1981b   "8-strong fast." An Phoblacht: Republican News, September 26: 2.
Salaman, R. N.
    1949    The History and Social Influence of the Potato. Cambridge: University Press.
Scarman, Leslie, chairman
    1972    Report of Tribunal of Inquiry: Violence and Civil Disturbances in Northern Ireland in 1969. Belfast: HMSO, April. Cmd. 566. 2 vols.
Shearman, Hugh
    1952    Modern Ireland. London: George G. Harrap & Co.
Stetler, Russell
    1970    The Battle of the Bogside. London: Sheed and Ward.
Sunday Tribune (Dublin)
    1981a   "British want Irish bases." February 22: 1–2, 18–19.
    1981b   "Why NATO wants an Irish foothold." March 1: 8–9.
    1981c   "British have 50 agents in Ireland." April 5: 1–2, 8–9.
Taylor, Peter
    1980    Beating the Terrorists? Interrogation in Omagh, Gough and Castlereagh. Harmondsworth, England: Penguin Books.
Tomlinson, Mike
    1980    "Housing, the state and the politics of segregation." Pp. 119–147 in O'Dowd et al.
U.S. Committee on the Judiciary
    1979    Northern Ireland: A Role for the United States? Washington: U.S. Government Printing Office.
van der Vat, Dan
    1978    "Social focus: Ulster, a legacy of violence." London Times, August 15.
Walker, Ian
    1980    "Barrackroom ballads of Northern Ireland." New Society (London), April 24: 148–152.
Wall, Dave
    1980    "Administering the poor." Fortnight (Belfast), 177 (July–August): 7–8.
Wallace, Martin
    1971    Northern Ireland: 50 Years of Self Government. New York: Barnes & Noble.
Widgery, Lord
    1972    Report of the Tribunal Appointed to Inquire Into the Events on Sunday, 30th January 1972. London: HMSO, April. H.L. 101, H.C. 220.
Woodham-Smith, Cecil
    1962    The Great Hunger. New York: Harper & Row.
Younger, Calton
    1968    Ireland's Civil War. London: Frederick Muller.

# THE MOBILIZATION OF PAID AND VOLUNTEER ACTIVISTS IN THE NEIGHBORHOOD MOVEMENT

Pamela Oliver

## ABSTRACT

This paper compares the mobilization of paid social movement activists with the mobilization of volunteers, a topic mentioned but not treated systematically in previous work. Classic treatments of paid movement activists assume that they are the most dedicated and ideologically committed members of movement organizations, while collective action theory underlying the resource mobilization perspective suggests they may be less committed, that material incentives can compensate for lower ideological commitment. McCarthy and Zald's work documenting the rise in outside sources of support for movement activists furthers the idea that paid activists may be less committed to particular movements than volunteers. Their historical analysis of changes in resources in the 1960s raises the possibility of political generations affected by those changes; generations can also be analyzed in

Research in Social Movements, Conflicts and Change, Vol. 5, pages 133–170.
Copyright © 1983 by JAI Press Inc.
All rights of reproduction in any form reserved.
ISBN: 0-89232-301-9

either resource or commitment terms. Data collected at the 1979 convention of the National Association of Neighborhoods from paid and volunteer activists allows a comparison of alternate models of the mobilization of activists. There is definitely a commitment effect independent of resources: paid activists are just as politically and socially integrated as volunteers, but have significantly more leftist political orientations and longer histories of activism. There is a strong cohort effect, with the 60's generation being more likely to be paid activists than those older or younger. It is concluded that all activists are mobilized through commitment processes that are constrained but not determined by resources, and that the most committed will become paid activists if resources are available.

# I. INTRODUCTION

There have been paid activists in social movements for at least two hundred years[1] and probably longer. At the turn of the century, there was extensive debate in socialist circles about whether working–class movements should pay their leaders (Lenin, 1973:137–176; Michels, 1962:129–152). Nevertheless, collective behavior theorists writing about social movements generally devote a great deal of attention to the traits and activities of movement leaders without discussing whether they are provided livelihoods for their activism (Turner and Killian, 1972:388–405; Smelser, 1962:296–298, Lang and Lang, 1961:517–524; Killian, 1964:440–443). A few writers mention paid activists in passing, suggesting for example that they are more strongly committed to a movement because their livelihood depends upon it (Lang and Lang, 1961:526). Collective behavior theorists are doubtless well aware that some activists are paid, but have not considered the matter to be worthy of specific analytic attention, possibly because they assume that paid activists are supported by contributions from movement participants.

McCarthy and Zald (1973) changed the thinking of social movement theorists when they challenged this collective wisdom. They argued that the trend of the 1960s (which seemed to be continuing into the 1970s) was for more and more activists to be paid for their activism and for the source of that support to come from institutions or conscience contributors outside any membership base of potential beneficiaries; they argued that this trend has important consequences for social movements. McCarthy and Zald went on to argue that a new kind of social movement has emerged, a "professional social movement," characterized by a paid leadership cadre and the absence of any genuine participating membership. Interestingly, three other works published that same year commented on this phenomenon (Oberschall, 1973:161; John Wilson, 1973:182; James Q. Wilson, 1972:203); clearly an important historical trend was being noticed by many of the major theorists in the field.

In this paper I propose to address systematically one of the questions raised by McCarthy and Zald's work, but not pursued by them or subsequent writers: the mobilization of paid activists as compared to the mobilization of volunteer activists. I shall do this by laying out the two alternative theories of mobilization common in the social movement literature and showing the relation of these models to McCarthy and Zald's work as well as to other works which have addressed the problem. These models suggest empirical predictions about the differences or similarities between paid and volunteer activists; these predictions are developed in some detail, drawing on the relevant literature.

A partial test of these propositions is provided by data collected from a sample of paid and volunteer activists who attended the 1979 convention of the National Association of Neighborhoods. Despite some serious limitations in the sample (which are described in detail below), these data are important—perhaps unique—because there are sufficient numbers of similarly–situated paid and volunteer activists to permit statistical comparisons. Even though the data permit only cautious empirical generalizations, they provide strong support for a theoretical model that integrates resources and commitment in the process of mobilization.

## II. PAID ACTIVISTS AND THE NEIGHBORHOOD MOVEMENT

The neighborhood movement of the 1970s provides an excellent instance for testing theories of the mobilization of paid activists because it contains significant numbers of both paid and volunteer activists.

Although some writers used the term "neighborhood movement" in the 1960s, the movement's present configuration is very much a product of the 1970s.[2] As with all social movements, its boundaries are ill–defined (Gerlach and Hine, 1970:33–78). Speaking generally, this movement may be said to include the following elements: (1) A general ideology stressing local community control over local land use and services. (2) A proliferation of tens of thousands of block clubs and neighborhood associations in most urban areas of the country. These groups have arisen in both white and minority neighborhoods and span the economic spectrum from poor to middle class. Most are in central cities, although some are in suburbs or rural areas. The major growth period for these organizations was 1972–1979. (3) The creation in many urban areas of inter–neighborhood coalitions or coordinating bodies. (4) The creation of nearly a dozen national organizations, coalitions, and networks addressing "neighborhood issues" (Perlman, 1979). (5) Local strategies most commonly directed toward the physical and economic renovation of older urban areas as places of residence, or towards resisting the introduction of some noxious element into a neighborhood. (6) The use of a broad diversity of tactics, ranging from campaigning and block voting in elections through lobbying and petitioning, self–help projects, and participation in government-initiated programs to disruptive direct action projects.

The neighborhood movement is particularly appropriate as an arena for studying paid activists because it includes both paid and volunteer activists in leadership positions. The national organizations, coalitions, networks, lobbying groups, and organizers' schools are all staffed by paid professionals and may be thought of as "professional social movement" organizations in McCarthy and Zald's sense, except that some of them have real members who pay dues and attend conventions. With or without participating membership, all these organizations are dominated by their professional leaders. But the picture is more varied at the local level. Most movement organizations at the local level have at least some genuine voluntary participation in the leadership cadre, and some have only volunteers. Most block clubs or neighborhood associations have at least some active members, although these groups vary widely in the extent to which control is centralized in a few leaders, paid or unpaid. In city–wide coalitions, paid and volunteer leaders stand formally as peers, as representatives of their respective neighborhood organizations, although paid activists are more likely to be active in such coalitions than volunteers are.

The neighborhood movement has been heavily funded by what I call "external sponsors" (see the appendix): federal and local government agencies, private foundations, churches, and corporations. Progressive elites have long believed in and funded "community organization" in poor neighborhoods (Dillick, 1953). The modern burst of neighborhood organizing seems to have originated in the late 1950s and early 1960s: the Ford Foundation began funding a series of experimental projects to improve social life in American cities through community organization; the Kennedy/Johnson administration's "poverty program" drew heavily from Ford Foundation ideas (Moynihan, 1969). Throughout the 1960s, large numbers of people were paid to "organize" poor urban neighborhoods in the belief that this would contribute to an amelioration of urban poverty and urban violence. Almost all neighborhood organizing in the 1960s was directed toward urban minorities or Appalachian whites.

Many of these programs (or their successors) continued into the 1970s. But the 1970s saw a new development: increasing formation of neighborhood organizations by middle–class and working–class whites. I have research in progress trying to understand this development, and its causes are not central here. I can say that the evidence seems to be that it was due to a combination of a shift to block grant funding (which meant that neighborhoods could compete at the municipal level for federal monies) and various ideological and political tendencies, including "white backlash," the "revolt of the white ethnics" (both prominent topics of discussion in the early 1970s), and black separatism, which led white radicals to shift their attention towards organizing whites.

By the late 1970s, the neighborhood movement was variegated and multi-textured. In some cities there was bitter competition or racial antagonism between neighborhoods or organizations. In others a spirit of bi–racial or multi–racial cooperation prevailed. Some neighborhood organizations are made up of low–income people, some of middle–class people, and some are mixed; cities differ in the class composition of their neighborhood organizations. The neighborhood movement has to be seen in dialectic terms. On the one hand, an ideology of self–help has caught the imagination of many people and has evoked millions of hours of labor from dedicated volunteers; on the other, much of the movement is dominated by paid professionals subsidized by elite agencies. To focus on either aspect without considering the other is to distort the truth. It turns out that this dualism parallels what I have found in evaluating theories of the mobilization of activists.

## III. TWO THEORETICAL APPROACHES

This paper focuses on the mobilization of activists. By "activists" I mean those persons who commit a relatively large amount of time and effort to movement activities; they are generally part of the leadership cadre of movement organiza tions. The distinction between inner hard–working circles and outer circles of less involved participants is common in the literature (Lenin, 1973:137–176; John Wilson, 1973:306; Killian, 1964:443).

Activists may be paid or volunteer. McCarthy and Zald's concept of a "professional social movement" combines the presence of paid activists with the absence of a genuine membership base. These characteristics are, in fact, separable: Some movement organizations have both paid activists and genuine participating memberships, and some have neither (that is, may have only an all-volunteer cadre). Distinctions among kinds of paid activists are developed in the appendix.

By "mobilization of activists" I refer to the processes whereby people come to devote significant amounts of time and energy to a movement, that is, to the processes whereby they become activists rather than passive supporters or occasional participants.

Although the distinction between mobilizing activists and mobilizing less involved supporters has often been blurred, two traditions may be identified in explaining the mobilization of activists. These may be labeled commitment models and collective action models. These two traditions are not necessarily incompatible, although they have developed somewhat distinctly. Some theorists from each tradition have incorporated elements of the other into their theories. To foreshadow the conclusions of this paper, I believe the evidence indicates that a correct understanding of the mobilization of paid activists requires an integration of these two traditions.

Although not necessarily older in the history of ideas (see Oberschall, 1973:1–29), the commitment tradition is older in the sociological study of social movements. There are two key ideas in this tradition. The first is that people become involved in social movements because of changes in beliefs, values, and norms and that these involve emotional responses to events. The second is that commitment is a progressive process, with earlier experiences drawing the person into greater and greater involvement in and identification with the movement. Comprehensive treatments of commitment processes identify rituals and customs that tend to increase the recruit's dependence on the movement and to decrease his or her involvement outside of the movement (Turner and Killian, 1972:335–360; John Wilson, 1973:300–328; Gerlach and Hine, 1970:99–158; Kornhauser, 1962; Becker, 1960).

If they are mentioned by commitment theorists, paid activists are viewed as the most committed members of all, for they have cast their lot with the movement and they depend upon it for their very survival (John Wilson, 1973:306; Lang and Lang, 1961:526). It is nearly always either explicitly stated or implicitly assumed that paid activists rise through progressive commitment from the ranks of volunteers. Lenin explicitly argued that the professional revolutionary cadre should be chosen from the talented members of the mass base (1973:137–176), and most commitment theorists retain this image (e.g., John Wilson, 1973:306).

In contrast with the commitment tradition, the collection action tradition is based on the idea that people decide whether to participate in a social movement according to their expectations of benefits and costs. Most theoretical work is informed by Olson's *The Logic of Collective Action* (1965), which argues that pursuit of a group interest invokes the public goods problem from economics in which every actor prefers to share in the collective benefit without having to incur the costs of cooperating in the collective action; this implies that collective action requires private or selective incentives to reward those who cooperate with collective action or to punish those who do not. A subsequent critical literature has shown that Olson overstates the generality of his claims (Oliver, 1980; Frohlich and Oppenheimer, 1970; Frohlich et al., 1975; Chamberlin, 1974; Schofield, 1975; Bonacich et al., 1976; Smith, 1976), but the work remains important for calling attention to the problematic nature of mobilization. The resource mobilization perspective on social movements is based on collective action models of mobilization.

Paid activists are central to collective action theory, for a salary is an important private incentive for collective action. People who are paid for their actions in pursuit of a collective good do not experience the dilemma of the free rider problem. Completion of the logic of paid activism requires specifying who will pay the activist and under what conditions (Oliver, 1980). Entrepreneurial theorists argue that the activist absorbs the cost of creating a payment system in the expectation of making a profit by doing so (Frohlich et al., 1971; Frohlich and Oppenheimer, 1978:66–89). Alternately, persons or institutions who attach high value to the collective good and who have more money than time may prefer to hire an activist rather than be one themselves.

In its pure form, the collective action theory borrowed from economists assumes that activists are motivated by material gain, either from the collective good or their salaries as paid activists, or both. The assumption that people are motivated only by their own personal material gain is obviously incorrect, and a number of theorists within the collective action tradition modify the concepts of benefit and cost to take account of other motivations. James Q. Wilson argues that there are three basic kinds of incentives: *material incentives,* which are tangible rewards readily priced in monetary terms; *solidary incentives,* which are intangible rewards arising from the association with others; and *purposive incentives,* which are intangible rewards deriving from the sense of satisfaction of having contributed to the attainment of a worthwhile cause (1973:30–34). Fireman and Gamson (1979) construct an argument in a different way that arrives essentially at the same conclusion. Collective action models should include not only material self–interest but group solidarity that leads an actor to value group benefits and consciousness that leads an actor to want to contribute to a collective good. Much of Fireman and Gamson's article discusses the ways in which organizers and entrepreneurs (that is, paid activists) can induce others (that is, volunteers) to participate in collective action.

Both of these modifications to collective action models contain terms that interface with the commitment models, although the dynamic elements of commitment processes are only partially captured in Fireman and Gamson's work and hardly mentioned in James Q. Wilson's. Conversely, the classic discussions of commitment cited above interface with collective action models. They discuss such topics as turning resources over to the movement, bridge–burning rituals cutting off alternate actions, and shifts from extra–movement to intra–movement social ties, all of which can be recast as costs and benefits in collective action models.

## A. Mobilizing Paid Activists

The issue can now be posed simply. Are paid and volunteer activists mobilized through the same basic process, or are they mobilized in different ways? Are paid activists just activists who happened to be paid, or are they fundamentally different from volunteers? Do the factors which distinguish paid from volunteer activists arise in the larger society or within the internal processes of the movement?

The commitment tradition strongly suggests that paid and volunteer activists mobilize through the same processes, the paid only more so. Conversely, the collective action tradition implies that paid activists are mobilized, in ways different from volunteers, by the possibility of drawing a salary.

Even though the issue is not exactly isomorphic with the two theoretical traditions on mobilization, they are strongly related. Commitment theorists (if they mention paid activists explicitly at all) state that paid activists are the most committed activists and rise from the ranks of volunteers, implying that paid and volunteer activists are mobilized in the same general process.

On the other hand, collective action theory implies that paid and volunteer activists are often mobilized differently. Since paid activists are compensated by salaries, they require less interest in the public good and/or less concern with purposive incentives than do volunteers. McCarthy and Zald's articles imply that paid activists respond to different constraints in mobilizing than do volunteers (1973:18–25). James Q. Wilson speaks of an organization hiring staff in a way that implies that they would not necessarily come from the ranks of volunteers (1973:225–228). Oberschall analyzes the risks and rewards of mobilizing and argues that paid activists incur lower risks than other activists (1973:161), again implying that the two groups are affected by different factors in mobilizing.

Although commitment theories suggest similarities and collective action theories differences in the mobilization of paid and volunteer activists, there are ambiguities and contradictions in each stream of work. Commitment theories are strangely silent about the mobilization of leaders, particularly the kind that collective action theorists call entrepreneurs. A great deal of attention has been devoted to the motivations of the followers of charismatic and other leaders, and to the attributes of leaders that make people follow them (Turner and Killian, 1972:388–405; Lang and Lang, 1961:517–524; Killian, 1964:440–443, John Wilson, 1973:194–225; Heberle, 1951:286–290), but I know of none devoted to the question of what makes a leader want to be a leader. Such leaders are often supported by their followings—making them paid activists in the terms of this paper—and some treatments hint at financial exploitation of the following, but the suggestion of material gain as a motivation has not been pursued in this tradition.

For their part, collective action theorists are contradictory in their treatment of the obvious empirical phenomenon of intense ideological commitment among paid activists. Salaries are material incentives, and the main thrust of collective action theorists is to emphasize the importance of salaries in attracting activists. But James Q. Wilson (1973:227) and others suggest a salary might be a sacrifice if it is less than a person could earn in a non–movement job. McCarthy and Zald, especially in their 1973 article, talk about the dedication of young activists, the tone implying that committed activists look for ways to be paid for their activism rather than being attracted by the prospect of a paying job. A willingness to make a sacrifice or an active seeking support for activism sounds more like a result of a commitment process than a materially–oriented response to resource levels, but none of these authors sorts out these contradictions into a coherent model of the mobilization of paid activists.

## IV. PREDICTIONS FROM THE THEORIES

The data I have available do not contain direct information about activist careers or mobilization processes, but it is possible to derive a number of competing cross–sectional hypotheses from the theoretical traditions summarized above.

## A. Social Characteristics

A number of theorists provide predictions for the economic positions or backgrounds that are most likely to produce movement activists. Obviously, if paid and volunteer activists are mobilized by the same factors and processes, then they should appear to come from the same general population; if they are mobilized in different ways, they should come from different populations.

Pure commitment models make no particular predictions about the social characteristics of activists. Different ideologies will have appeal for different people depending upon their situation and experience, but no particular occupational group is treated as logically more predisposed to activism than any other.

By contrast, resource mobilization theorists make specific predictions about the occupations of volunteer activists. McCarthy and Zald put greatest emphasis on the convenience of action and predict that volunteer activists come from occupations with discretionary time (such as students and professionals), particularly when tactics require transitory teams (1973:9–11; 1977:1236).

Oberschall emphasizes the ratio of possible rewards to the risk of retaliation and argues that volunteer activists are persons for whom the risk of retaliation from the opposition is relatively low, either because they are in relatively secure occupations (such as free professionals or small business owners whose clientele are of the aggrieved population) or because their upward mobility is blocked and they have nothing to gain from refraining from movement activity (1973:159–171). Thus, Oberschall predicts that activists will be from the higher, secure strata, from groups whose income is independent of the opposition, and from the very lowest strata who have nothing to lose.

No theorist makes specific predictions about comparing paid and volunteer activists. McCarthy and Zald's notion of discretionary time as an explanation for the occupations of activists simply explains why paid activists are important, since they can devote all their time to the movement. But Oberschall's discussion of risks and rewards implies that the persons attracted to paid activism will be those for whom it is a relatively lucrative or secure position, that is, those whose occupational opportunities in the society in general are lower. These would be people who have blocked channels of access due to discriminatory social barriers, or those whose education or skills fit them poorly for high–paying jobs.

## B. Networks

There is strong evidence that persons mobilized for a social movement tend to be well integrated into social and organizational networks. Oberschall (1973:103–113) cites a great deal of evidence to support this position and to refute Kornhauser's mass society hypothesis; he also argues that those mobilized first are especially likely to be well–integrated (:135). Gerlach and Hine (1979:79–98) stress the importance of personal networks in recruiting and mobilizing converts to the Pentecostal and Black Power movements as does John

Wilson's review of the literature (1973:131–133). Snow and his colleagues (1980) review a number of different studies of movement recruitment and conclude that people are mobilized through personal influence networks.[3]

This evidence about networks applies to the mobilization of volunteer activists. Now if, as the commitment models predict, paid activists work their way up through the ranks of the volunteeers, they should be just as integrated—if not more integrated—into the social and organizational networks of their communities as the volunteers. By the same logic, paid activists would exhibit the same density of social connections to the movements' constituencies as volunteers would.

On the other hand, if paid activists are mobilized for the movement by the material incentive of a salary, they would not necessarily exhibit the same patterns of social integration as volunteers. Although I have found no author who makes an explicit prediction about social ties to the larger community, McCarthy and Zald argue that paid activists are more likely than volunteers to be divorced from their constituencies (1973:17–18), and that the true membership base of social movement organizations with paid leadership is smaller than the true membership base of organizations with volunteer leadership (1973:20–23). This difference between paid and volunteer would be predicted to hold true especially for those activists whose salaries are paid from sources external to the movement's membership base (which is true of virtually all paid neighborhood activists).

## C. Ideological Commitment and Involvement

Commitment models of paid activism imply the clear predictions that paid activists will, on the average, exhibit greater ideological connection to the movement and will have had longer histories of activism in that movement than volunteers. This follows necessarily from the assumption that paid activists work their way through the ranks of volunteers. As indicated above, commitment theorists generally assume that paid activists are leaders supported from sources internal to the movement; it is not clear if they would change these predictions for activists supported from external sources.

Pure collective action models ignore ideology and simply examine the balance of collective benefits and individual incentives versus costs; these pure models would predict no particular ideological differences between activists and nonactivists, or between paid and volunteer activists. However, the modified collective action models that admit intangibles such as purposive incentives do yield specific predictions about ideology and paid activists. Since tangible and intangible incentives are proposed to be additive, paid activists should be *less* ideologically motivated than volunteers at comparable levels of involvement. This is because volunteers would presumably be motivated solely by purposive incentives, while paid activists would have both. McCarthy and Zald's suggestion that paid activists are more responsive to ebbs and flows in resources than are volunteers is consistent with this analysis: They view all social movement organizations as responsive to resource levels (1977:1224–5), but imply that sensitivity to re-source flows is especially characteristic of movements controlled by professional activists (1973:18–25; 1977:12–4–5). Oberschall explicitly argues that being paid reduces the cost of activism (1973:161), which would seem to suggest that lower ideological motivation would be necessary. James Q. Wilson's discussion of organizations hiring staff implies that staff do not necessarily have the attach-ment to the movement of the volunteers who hire them (1973:225–230). His discussion of movement entrepreneurs argues that they are generally motivated by purposive incentives and willing to forego material gain (:196–197). En-trepreneurs foregoing material gain would show up as volunteers in a cross–sectional analysis, although persons who had foregone gain in the past and who were now being supported by the movement they created could be expected to show high ideological commitment as paid activists.

The suggestion proposed by Wilson (1973:226) that movement staff may view their paid activism as a sacrifice would make the generation of testable proposi-tions difficult. However, if paid activism is a sacrifice, it should be greater the better the activist's alternative occupations. Thus, paid activists with higher education or skill levels should be more ideologically motivated than those with lower education or skill levels. For similar reasons, better paid professional activists should be less ideologically motivated (on the average) than less paid movement activists.

Commitment theories imply that paid activists will have longer average histo-ries of movement activism than volunteers. Collective action theories do not yield clear predictions about the relative lengths of activist histories. The mobi-lization of paid activists may precede or follow the mobilization of volunteers, depending in part on whether their source of support is internal or external to the movement.

## D. History and Generations

McCarthy and Zald offer historical evidence that external support for social movements increased during the 1960s (1973:12–16). If this historical argument is correct (and I have seen nothing to dispute it), it must affect any empirical study of paid and volunteer activists in the recent period. For McCarthy and Zald, working in the collective action tradition, the important thing about the 1960s is the amount of resources available to support movement activists. But the commitment tradition calls our attention to the 1960s as a period in which many people, especially those who were of college age, became extremely involved in and committed to the civil rights and anti–war movements. Both theories require that attention be paid to the impact of the 1960s trends on people who came of age during the decade.

Building on the writings of Mentre, Mannheim, and Hellpach, Heberle defines a *political generation* as ''those individuals of approximately the same age who have shared, at the same age, certain politically relevant experiences'' (1951:119–120). He suggests that people are most affected by decisive experiences as young adults, that different sub–groups within an age cohort might have different decisive experiences and form different political generations, that traditions based on decisive experiences may or may not be transmitted across generations, and that political generations have been important in movements such as Nazism, whose leaders were all young adults when the Versailles treaty was signed (:118–127).

It is widely believed that the turmoil of the civil rights and anti–war movements in the 1960s created a political generation. Numerous articles and books written during the period and immediately after it focused on the question of generations and adduced various kinds of data to support the claim that the youth of this period were qualitatively different from their elders, although there is debate about whether these differences were disjunctive.[4] Comparisons of activist students with nonactivst students found that they were more likely to be politically radical; more likely to be liberal arts majors and especially social science majors; less likely to espouse "extrinsic reward values" such as money, prestige, and security; and more likely to plan to enter knowledge or social service careers (Braungart and Braungart, 1974; Demerath et al., 1971; Flacks, 1967, 1971; Kornberg and Brehm, 1971; Lipset, 1971; McFalls and Gallagher, 1975; Matthews and Prothro, 1966; Van Eschen et al., 1971).

The small accumulating literature on subsequent careers of movement activists suggests that they remain different from persons who were not student activists during their college days. The largest sample is Fendrich's, of male students who were in Tallahassee during the civil rights activities of 1960–1964; 95 white former Florida State University students were surveyed in late 1971, and 110 black Florida A & M students were surveyed in 1973. Men who had been arrested at civil rights demonstrations and student government leaders were disproportionately sampled. White civil rights activists were far more likely than nonactivists (including student government leaders) to have chosen academic professions or social service and creative occupations (a category that included paid activists), to claim to be politically radical, and to maintain a high level of political involvement as adults. Black activists were more likely to continue adult political activism, but student activism was not correlated with political radicalism or occupational choice among blacks.[5]

Other studies have found similar patterns for white 1960s activists: Isla Vista "Bank Burners" (Whalen & Flacks, 1980), student protesters at Berkeley (Maidenberg and Meyer, 1970; Green, 1970) and Kent State (Adamek and Lewis, 1973), civil rights workers (Demerath et al., 1971), youth movement activists (Weiner and Stillman, 1979), radical leaders (Braungart and Braungart, 1980), and OEO Legal Service lawyers (Erlanger, 1977) tend to be more radical, less likely to pursue financially lucrative careers, and more likely to pursue social service occupations than nonactivists. I know of no comparable follow–up studies of black activists.

These historical effects are relevant to both commitment and decision models of the mobilization of paid activists. If 1960s activists remain politically active in the 1970s, this supports the idea that the process of being committed to a social movement leads to permanent changes in one's ideological beliefs and actions. It is clear that part of the ideology of the time led to a rejection of ''establishment'' (that is, business) jobs and a preference for employment in academic or social service occupations, which would serve ideologically acceptable goals. In this context, paid movement activism would be viewed as the most extreme instance of this ideological tendency, as a willingness to dedicate one's life to ''the movement.''

But the historical features of the 1960s are also relevant to collective action models of paid activism, for this decade witnessed not only intense ideologies and political conversion experiences, but a tremendous expansion in the money available to pay people to be social movement activists (McCarthy and Zald, 1973). Career decisions are typically made when people are in their late teens and early twenties. The 60s generation is the first that could (in large numbers) rationally choose a career in movement activism. Thus the ideological and economic impacts of the decade are intertwined and cannot be separated; we will only be able to assemble indirect suggestive evidence as to the relative weights of these two kinds of effects.

# V. SOURCE OF DATA

Some of the observations I am able to make about the mobilization of paid and volunteer activists arise from my familiarity with published and verbal accounts of the neighborhood movement nationally and from my two and one-half years as a participant observer in the neighborhood movement in Louisville, Kentucky. Data uniquely relevant to the matter were obtained in a survey of the participants at the 1979 convention of the National Association of Neighborhoods (NAN). NAN was founded in 1976 by Milton Kotler, whose book *Neighborhood Government* (1970) articulates an ideology of extreme decentralization and local control. It is one of several national coalitions, including ACORN and National People's Action, each of which has a distinctive constituency and strategy, although they have significant overlaps and generally amicable inter–organizational relations. NAN puts more priority on providing services and obtaining governmental funding, while ACORN emphasizes confrontations with powerful persons and institutions (Rathke et al., 1979; Kotler, 1979). NAN is generally controlled by its paid staff, although it has a participating membership of individuals and organizations.

Many neighborhood activists who were not NAN members attended the 1979 convention. At the 1978 convention, NAN voted to launch a drive to promote neighborhood platform conventions in 50 cities; the goal was to broaden participation in NAN as well as to develop what was believed to be a useful political tool. NAN hired organizers to aid in promoting these local conventions. In

Louisville, the Louisville Inter–Neighborhood Coalition simply convened the convention through its pre–existing channels, although the publicity uncovered some new block clubs and mobilized some new activists to city–wide activity. But in some cities these conventions were the first major inter–neighborhood meetings, and they often pulled in local activists previously unconnected to national networks or organizations. Each local convention sent elected delegates who met along with regular delegates from NAN–affiliated organizations and individual NAN members at the national convention. This broader participation makes the sample less restrictive than it otherwise would have been, but it is still the case that people who attend a national meeting and take the time to fill out a questionnaire can represent only themselves, since they are in no sense a sample of any larger population. There were 179 questionnaires turned in, representing about 30% of the people who signed in at the registration desk. The respondents came from 52 cities in 26 states and represented something over 110 distinct organizations.

I have provided details about this sample to allow the reader to assess the limits that should be placed on empirical generalizations from the data. Compared with the quality of samples available in other fields of inquiry, this sample is quite limited. However, it is quite comparable to all other published samples of social movement participants, all of which couple relatively small sample sizes with limited populations such as students at a particular university, members of a particular group or attendees at a particular event (Snow et al., 1980; Fendrich, 1974, 1976, 1977; Fendrich and Tarleau, 1973, Fendrich and Krauss, 1978; McPhail, 1973; Haan, 1975; Demerath et al., 1971; Lofland, 1977; Lin, 1974–5). Although *attitudes* may be assessed in general population surveys, activist *behavior* generally cannot because the trait is too rare. Thus we are forced to piece together information from less than ideal specialized surveys.

Despite the limits on empirical generality, these data are uniquely suited to provide theoretical illumination on the mobilization of paid and volunteer activists, for they are the only data I am aware of that contain significant numbers of paid and volunteer activists in roughly comparable positions in a social movement. Many of the problems of self–selection in the sample affect paid and volunteer activists equally, so that comparisions of the two kinds of activists within the sample are subject to fewer distortions than arise when comparisons are made between activist samples and control groups of nonactivists.

# VI. RESULTS

## A. Characteristics of the Activists

*Occupations.* Information about the neighborhood activists' occupations was obtained in a standard open–ended occupation item on a page titled "background information"; the results are shown in Table 1. McCarthy and Zald's

*Table 1.* Occupations of Neighborhood Activists

|  | *n* | *Percent* |
|---|---|---|
| *All Activists* |  |  |
| No Paid Job | 32 | 19 |
| Paid Movement Activist | 75 | 43 |
| Non–Movement Paid Job | 66 | 38 |
|  | 173 | 100 |
| No Answer | 6 |  |
| *Paid Activists* |  |  |
| Paid by neighborhood movement organization | 57 | 76 |
| Paid by government agency | 18 | 24 |
|  | 75 | 100 |
| "Organizing" as part or all of job | 27 | 36 |
| Advocate, liaison, community education | 12 | 16 |
| Administrator, coordinator, director | 28 | 37 |
| Association officer (local leader) | 2 | 3 |
| Technical specialists | 2 | 3 |
| Consultant | 1 | 1 |
| City council member | 1 | 1 |
| Clerical workers | 2 | 3 |
|  | 75 | 100 |
| *Non–Movement Paid Jobs* |  |  |
| 1. Professor | 7 | 11 |
| 2. Minister, priest | 6 | 9 |
| 3. Other independent professionals | 4 | 6 |
| 4. Teacher | 4 | 6 |
| 5. Other professionals in organizations | 10 | 15 |
| 6. Independent creative occupations | 2 | 3 |
| 7. Small business owner | 4 | 6 |
| 8. Administrator, inspector | 3 | 4 |
| 9. Real estate sales | 5 | 7 |
| 10. Clerical and kindred workers | 7 | 11 |
| 11. Teachers' and nurses' aides | 7 | 11 |
| 12. Other blue collar workers | 7 | 11 |
|  | 66 | 100 |
| Professional, technical, kindred (#s 1–6) | 33 | 50 |
| Managers, proprietors (#s 7, 8) | 7 | 11 |
| Sales, clerical (#s 9, 10) | 12 | 18 |
| Blue collar (#s 11, 12) | 14 | 21 |
|  | 66 | 100 |
| Occupations with high independence and discretionary time (#s 1, 2, 3, 6, 9) | 24 | 36 |
| Occupations with some independence but also some constraints on discretionary time (#s 4, 5, 7, 8) | 21 | 32 |
| Occupations with little independence or discretionary time | 21 | 32 |
|  | 66 | 100 |

arguments about the importance of discretionary time receive strong support in this sample of activists: 43% are paid activists, and a total of 76% are in occupational situations with high discretionary time; only 12% are in occupations with little discretionary time. However, occupations with high discretionary time also tend to require high education, and education is known to be a strong correlate of all forms of political and organizational participation[6], so it is difficult to disentangle the two effects. Oberschall's claim that movement activists will come from independent occupations receives little support. Except for activists paid by movement organizations, the vast majority are employed by large, elite–controlled public or private organizations. There are only handfuls of independent professionals or small business owners among the activists.

Three–quarters of the paid movement activists are employed by independent neighborhood movement organizations. However, nearly all of these organizations are funded by some combination of government and foundation grants or contracts, so the boundary between movement–paid and government–paid activists is blurry. Many neighborhood organizations that are formally independent and private (such as neighborhood development corporations, community action agencies, and the more diversified groups of more recent origin) have achieved routinized, quasi–governmental status.

Nearly all of the paid activists have staff titles: only two are elected officers of associations. "Organizing" was mentioned as a part or all of their job description by 36%; another 16% described their job in terms related to the concept of organizing, terms such as advocacy or education. A large group, 37%, described their job as administrative or coordinative.

*Age.* Table 2 shows the distribution of activists' ages in five–year ranges defined by the year the activist became 18. Activists span the entire range of adult ages, but most come from the years of peak adult responsibility, 23 to 47. Comparing the sample to the resident adult population of the United States using standard census categories indicates that the 35–44 age group is by far the most overrepresented in the sample, and that representation in the sample has a bell–shaped distribution with those 18–21 and those over 65 most underrepresented (data not shown). Contrary to expectations established during the 1960s, this social movement is staffed not by the young, but by adults. Of course, many of these participants were young in the 1960s.

Table 2 also shows the percentage of paid activists within each age group because preliminary analysis revealed a significant deviation from linearity. Inspection of these percentages indicates that it is precisely those persons who reached maturity in the 1960s, and especially those who came of age in the latter half of the decade, who are most likely to become paid neighborhood activists. For this reason, subsequent analysis of the effect of age employs a dummy variable for membership in the 1960s cohort; those younger and those older are grouped together in the reference category.

*Table 2.* Age Distribution of Activists, and Age by Proportion Paid Activists

| Age in 1979 | Year Became 18 | n | Percent | Percent Paid |
|:---:|:---:|:---:|:---:|:---:|
| 19–22 | 1975–1978 | 9 | 5 | 33 |
| 23–27 | 1970–1974 | 19 | 11 | 42 |
| 28–32 | 1965–1969 | 29 | 17 | 69 |
| 33–37 | 1960–1964 | 26 | 16 | 58 |
| 38–42 | 1955–1959 | 22 | 13 | 36 |
| 43–47 | 1950–1954 | 20 | 12 | 25 |
| 48–52 | 1945–1949 | 9 | 5 | 44 |
| 53–57 | 1940–1944 | 8 | 5 | 25 |
| 58–62 | 1935–1939 | 10 | 6 | 30 |
| 63–67 | 1930–1934 | 7 | 4 | 0 |
| 68+ | before 1930 | 7 | 4 | 43 |
| TOTAL | | 166 | 98* | |

*Note:* *rounding error

*Neighborhood Integration.*   The means, standard deviations, and coding conventions for the extent to which the activists have significant social ties to the neighborhoods in which they reside are shown in the first section of Table 3.[7] It is difficult to interpret means of the neighborhood integration variables without a comparison group of nonactivists, but they seem to be at least as high as one would expect of comparable nonactivists.

*Political Integration.*   Two indicators assess the activist's involvement with political activities besides the neighborhood movement and are shown in the second section of Table 3. The levels of activity reported on these variables appear higher than those obtained in general population samples (e.g., Verba and Nie, 1972), indicating that these activists are quite involved in community political affairs. This is consistent with Oberschall's predictions.

*Movement Experience.*   Four indicators tap the activist's past involvement in social movements and are shown in the third section of Table 3. Again, the means of these variables indicate rather higher levels of movement experience than would be obtained in the general population.

*Movement Ideology.*   Three indicators assess the activists' adherence to movement–relevant ideologies and are shown in the fourth section of Table 3. The first assesses the person's general political orientation; the other two deal with issues directly relevant to the neighborhood movement. One question asked whether neighborhood organizations should concentrate on meeting local neighborhood needs even if they conflict with others, should concentrate on developing city–wide cooperation among neighborhood organizations, or should concentrate on linking up with a larger struggle for social justice. The first two choices were contrasted with the last. The other item derives from coding of

*Table 3.*    Means, Standard Deviations and Coding Conventions for
Independent Variables

| Variables and Coding Conventions | Mean | s.d. |
|---|---|---|
| *Neighborhood Integration* | | |
| *Kin:* Have kin in other households in neighborhood (1=yes, 0=no) | .33 | .47 |
| *Known:* Proportion of neighbors known personally (1=none, 2=handful, 3=less than half, 4=more than half, 5=nearly all) | 3.84 | 1.06 |
| *Years Lived:* Proportion of life lived in neighborhood (Years in neigh./Age) | .28 | .26 |
| *Church:* Attends church (1=yes, 0=no) | .46 | .50 |
| *Political Integration* | | |
| *Elections:* How often works in elections (1=never, 2=occasionally, 3=fairly often, 4=regularly) | 2.57 | 1.11 |
| *Political Orgs.:* Membership in a political or special issue group other than neighborhood movement group (1=yes, 0=no) | .51 | .50 |
| *Movement Experience* | | |
| *Civil Rights:* Was active in the civil rights movement (1=yes, 0=no) | .40 | .49 |
| *Anti-War:* Was active in the anti-war movement (1=yes, 0=no) | .28 | .45 |
| *Feminist:* Was active in the feminist or related movements (1=yes, 0=no) | .20 | .40 |
| *Years Active:* Proportion of adult life as neighborhood activist (Years Active/ (Age-18)) | .42 | .27 |
| *Movement Ideology* | | |
| *General Politics:* General political orientation; coded responses to an open–ended question. (4=radical, socialist, etc.; 3=liberal, progressive, etc.; 2=mixed, moderate, independent, other; 1=conservative.) | 2.75 | .94 |
| *Local Orientation:* Neighborhood movement should encourage local neighborhood needs and/or city–wide cooperation among neighborhood groups (=1) rather than treat neighborhood movement as part of larger struggle for social justice (=0). | .59 | .49 |
| *Issue Orientation:* Named one or more specific problems or issues such as housing, crime, displacement, or services as being important for movement activity (=1) rather than only abstractions such as justice or inequality (=0). | .59 | .49 |
| *Demographic Variables* | | |
| *Sex:* (1=male, 0=female) | .44 | .50 |
| *Race:* (1=minority, 0=white) | .36 | .48 |
| *College Grad:* (1=college graduate, 0=not) | .61 | .49 |
| *60s Cohort:* (1=age 28–37 in 1979, 0=other) | .33 | .47 |

open–ended responses to a question asking what issues the neighborhood movement should give first priority to. Those activists who listed any specific neighborhood–related problem were coded as having an issue orientation and contrasted with those who responded only in general abstract terms. These two items
capture the extent to which the activist is concerned about the specific issues of
the neighborhood movement as opposed to a diffuse interest in social change.[8]
The activists' general political orientations are significantly more liber-

al–to–radical than the general population. The other two items are not meaning-ful for nonactivists.

*Demographic Variables.* The last section of Table 3 shows the means and standard deviations for sex, race, years of education, and whether the person is a college graduate. The sample has only slightly more women than men, is over a third minority, and is very highly educated.

## B. Multivariate Analysis

Data to address theoretical predictions were obtained from ordinary least squares multiple regressions. The table of bivariate correlations is given in Table 4. Two strategies of analysis are reported. The first involves assessing the strength of sets of variables as predictors of paid activism; the second involves estimating the coefficients of a model predicting paid activism from move-ment–related attitudes and experiences.

Tables 5 and 6 provide data for assessing the strength of sets of variables as predictors of paid activism. Table 5 shows the $R^2$ and significance for each set of variables as predictors of paid activism. Table 6 shows the regression of paid activism on all of the independent variables. The patterns shown in these tables hold up under all other modes of analysis. The Neighborhood Integration and Political Integration variables, individually and collectively, are simply not sig-nificant predictors of paid activism. Within this sample of neighborhood activ-ists, there is no difference between paid and volunteer activists in their levels of integration with local neighborhoods and politics. Paid and volunteer activists do not differ in their orientations to issues specifically relevant to the neighborhood movement. These non–relations hold up when other variables are controlled: the few small non–zero bivariate correlations are eliminated without creating any new ones.

Since all preliminary multivariate analyses indicate that the above variables play no direct or indirect role in predicting paid activism, the causal sequence that leads to paid activism appears to involve only movement-specific experi-ences. The multiple regression analysis is presented as a path model to portray the process whereby volunteer activists become paid activists. Exogenous vari-ables are dummy variables for minority race, male, college graduate, and 60's cohort. Causal order among social movement experiences can be assumed be-cause of the chronological order in which those movements occurred in the 1960s. Years of activism is assumed to be a consequence of past political experi-ences, since its magnitude today depends upon whether the person was politi-cally involved in the past. Political attitudes are assumed to be a result of past political experiences. Being a paid activist is assumed to be a consequence of the preceeding factors. Table 7 shows the coefficients of the full model with all possible paths, and the restricted model recalculated through backwards elimina-tion to include only those coefficients for which $p < .1$. The restricted model is shown graphically in Figure 1.

*Table 4.*   Table of Bivariate Correlations. Correlation in Upper Triangle, Number of Cases in Lower Triangle

|  | (1) | (2) | (3) | (4) | (5) | (6) | (7) | (8) |
|---|---|---|---|---|---|---|---|---|
| (1) Paid Activist |  | .05 | −.13* | −.08 | −.09 | .02 | −.01 | .09 |
| (2) Kin | 166 |  | .25* | .33* | .18* | .22* | −.07 | .04 |
| (3) Known | 165 | 168 |  | .27* | .30* | .11 | −.04 | −.04 |
| (4) Years Lived | 157 | 155 | 154 |  | .08 | .36* | −.10 | .05 |
| (5) Church | 168 | 166 | 165 | 155 |  | .04 | −.08 | −.05 |
| (6) Elections | 166 | 165 | 164 | 152 | 165 |  | .22* | .35* |
| (7) Political Orgs. | 171 | 168 | 167 | 157 | 171 | 168 |  | .24* |
| (8) Civil Rights | 171 | 168 | 167 | 157 | 171 | 168 | 174 |  |
| (9) Anti–War | 171 | 168 | 167 | 157 | 171 | 168 | 174 | 174 |
| (10) Feminist | 171 | 168 | 167 | 157 | 171 | 168 | 174 | 174 |
| (11) Years Active | 154 | 151 | 150 | 151 | 152 | 149 | 154 | 154 |
| (12) Politics (Left) | 150 | 148 | 147 | 137 | 149 | 147 | 152 | 152 |
| (13) Local Orient. | 165 | 162 | 161 | 151 | 164 | 162 | 167 | 167 |
| (14) Issue Orient. | 162 | 160 | 159 | 148 | 161 | 159 | 164 | 164 |
| (15) Sex (Male) | 173 | 167 | 166 | 157 | 169 | 167 | 172 | 172 |
| (16) Race (Minority) | 172 | 167 | 166 | 157 | 168 | 166 | 171 | 171 |
| (17) College Grad | 173 | 167 | 166 | 157 | 169 | 167 | 172 | 172 |
| (18) 60s Cohort | 166 | 160 | 159 | 157 | 169 | 167 | 172 | 172 |

*Table 5.*   Variance Accounted for and Significance of Clusters of Independent Variables as Predictors of Paid Activism

| Independent Variables | $R^2$ | p |
|---|---|---|
| Political Attitudes (Leftist Politics, Local Orientation, Issue Orientation) | .052 | .031 |
|     Leftist Politics Only | .048 | .010 |
| Movement Experiences (Years of Activism, Civil Rights, Anti–War, and Feminist Movements) | .071 | .043 |
|     Years of Activism, Anti–War Only | .070 | .008 |
|     Years of Activism Only | .055 | .006 |
| Neighborhood Integration (Kin, Know Neighbors, Years Lived, Church) | .035 | .320 |
| Political Integration (Elections, Political Organizations) | .025 | .959 |
| Demographic Variables (Race, Sex, College Graduate, 60's Cohort) | .122 | .002 |
|     Race, College Grad, 60's Cohort | .121 | .001 |
|     College Grad, 60's Cohort | .109 | .000 |

*Table 4.* (continued)

|      | (9)   | (10)  | (11)  | (12)  | (13)  | (14)  | (15)  | (16)  | (17)  | (18)  |
|------|-------|-------|-------|-------|-------|-------|-------|-------|-------|-------|
| (1)  | .17*  | .02   | .23*  | .22*  | .01   | −.06  | .08   | .05   | .20*  | .30*  |
| (2)  | −.19* | −.14* | .10   | −.08  | .26*  | .15*  | .02   | .34*  | −.23* | −.05  |
| (3)  | −.24* | −.14* | .03   | −.26* | .14*  | .18*  | −.06  | .27*  | −.29* | −.24* |
| (4)  | −.21* | −.15* | .30*  | −.03  | .25*  | .28*  | .03   | .25*  | −.18* | −.10  |
| (5)  | −.17* | −.20* | −.05  | −.27* | −.10  | .17*  | .02   | .19*  | −.12  | −.26* |
| (6)  | .09   | .08   | .24*  | .03   | −.07  | .12   | .09   | .23*  | .00   | −.00  |
| (7)  | .17*  | .32*  | .21*  | .10   | −.27* | .00   | .05   | −.04  | .29*  | −.03  |
| (8)  | .33*  | .09   | .25*  | .24*  | −.17* | .04   | .17*  | .21*  | .13*  | .12   |
| (9)  |       | .20*  | .20*  | .46*  | −.27* | −.12  | .15*  | −.26* | .32*  | .22*  |
| (10) | 174   |       | .12   | .14*  | −.11  | −.06  | −.30* | −.11  | .20*  | .12   |
| (11) | 154   | 154   |       | .17*  | −.07  | .01   | .15*  | .07   | .14*  | .16*  |
| (12) | 152   | 152   | 137   |       | −.17* | −.05  | .20*  | −.12  | .24*  | .10   |
| (13) | 167   | 167   | 149   | 152   |       | −.07  | −.09  | .00   | −.10  | −.03  |
| (14) | 164   | 164   | 146   | 150   | 164   |       | .03   | .21*  | −.09  | −.06  |
| (15) | 172   | 172   | 154   | 151   | 166   | 163   |       | −.06  | .23*  | .04   |
| (16) | 171   | 171   | 154   | 150   | 165   | 162   | 173   |       | −.34* | −.02  |
| (17) | 172   | 172   | 154   | 151   | 166   | 163   | 174   | 173   |       | .21*  |
| (18) | 164   | 164   | 154   | 145   | 159   | 156   | 166   | 165   | 166   |       |

*Note:* * p < .05

*Table 6.* Regression of Paid Activism on All Independent Variables

| Independent Variable | Standardized Beta | Unstandardized | |
|---|---|---|---|
| | | B | s.e. |
| 60's Cohort | .20 | .213* | .095 |
| Sex, Male | −.03 | −.032 | .094 |
| College Graduate | .17 | .172 | .101 |
| Minority Race | .13 | .131 | .102 |
| Kin in Neighborhood | .09 | .095 | .097 |
| Know Neighbors | −.03 | −.012 | .044 |
| Years Lived in Neighborhood | −.17 | −.313 | .192 |
| Attend Church | −.01 | −.008 | .091 |
| Work in Elections | .02 | .009 | .044 |
| Political Organizations | −.10 | −.096 | .093 |
| Leftist Politics | .16 | .086 | .052 |
| Years Activist | .22 | .405* | .173 |
| Feminist Movement | −.07 | −.083 | .120 |
| Anti–War Movement | .01 | .008 | .117 |
| Civil Rights Movement | −.05 | −.052 | .099 |

*Note:*
*Coefficient twice its standard error

*Table 7.* Path Coefficients (Standardized Regression Coefficients), Significance Levels, and Coefficients of Determination for Full and Restricted Models Predicting Paid Activism

| Dependent and Independent Variables | Full | | Restricted | |
|---|---|---|---|---|
| | Beta | p | Beta | p |
| *Dependent: Paid Activist* | | | | |
| Leftist Politics | .17 | .09 | .17 | .04 |
| Years of Activism | .22 | .02 | .16 | .05 |
| Feminist Movement | −.07 | .49 | | |
| Anti–War Movement | .02 | .88 | | |
| Civil Rights Movement | −.05 | .61 | | |
| Minority Race | .13 | .18 | | |
| College Graduate | .16 | .11 | | |
| Male | −.03 | .77 | | |
| 60's Cohort | .20 | .03 | .25 | .002 |
| Coefficient of Determination (R²) | .21 | | .15 | |
| *Dependent: Leftist Politics* | | | | |
| Years of Activism | .05 | .56 | | |
| Feminist Movement | .09 | .33 | | |
| Anti–War Movement | .38 | .000 | .44 | .000 |
| Civil Rights Movement | .06 | .49 | | |
| Minority Race | .00 | .99 | | |
| College Graduate | .06 | .53 | | |
| Male | .14 | .11 | .13 | .08 |
| 60's Cohort | −.03 | .74 | | |
| Coefficient of Determination (R²) | .25 | | .23 | |
| *Dependent: Years Active* | | | | |
| Feminist Movement | .12 | .21 | .15 | .09 |
| Anti–War Movement | .09 | .36 | | |
| Civil Rights Movement | .15 | .12 | .21 | .01 |
| Minority Race | .10 | .29 | | |
| College Graduate | .05 | .58 | | |
| Male | .13 | .16 | .15 | .08 |
| 60's Cohort | .'0 | .26 | | |
| Coefficient of Determination (R²) | .12 | | .09 | |
| *Dependent: Feminist Movement* | | | | |
| Anti–War Movement | .15 | .10 | .19 | .02 |
| Civil Rights Movement | .08 | .40 | | |
| Minority Race | −.04 | .67 | | |
| College Graduate | .21 | .02 | .21 | .01 |
| Male | −.39 | .000 | −.38 | .000 |
| 60's Cohort | .04 | .60 | | |
| Coefficient of Determination (R²) | .21 | | .20 | |

*(continued)*

*Table 7.* (continued)

| Dependent and Independent Variables | Full Beta | p | Restricted Beta | p |
|---|---|---|---|---|
| *Dependent: Anti–War Movement* | | | | |
| Civil Rights Movement | .35 | .000 | .36 | .000 |
| Minority Race | −.28 | .001 | −.29 | .001 |
| College Graduate | .14 | .10 | .15 | .08 |
| Male | .04 | .60 | | |
| 60's Cohort | .13 | .10 | .14 | .06 |
| Coefficient of Determination (R²) | .28 | | .27 | |
| *Dependent: Civil Rights Movement* | | | | |
| Minority Race | .28 | .002 | .28 | .001 |
| College Graduate | .18 | .05 | .23 | .01 |
| Male | .14 | .10 | | |
| 60's Cohort | .08 | .32 | | |
| Coefficient of Determination (R²) | .11 | | .11 | |

*Note:* Correlations among exogenous variables are shown in Table 4.

*Figure 1.* Standardized path coefficients for model predicting paid activism. (Only those paths for which p < .10 are shown.) * p < .05 ** p < .01 ***p < .001

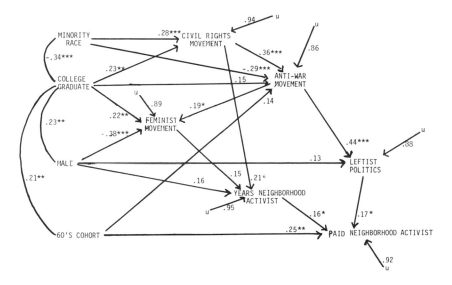

This analysis indicates that there are two routes to paid activism for this sample of activists. One comes from experience in past social movements and is mediated by acquisition of leftist political beliefs or, to a lesser extent, the proportion of adult life spent as an activist. The second source is membership in the 60's cohort, which net of political experience makes a person more likely to be a paid neighborhood activist. Although the sample is too small to allow separate analyses by race to be statistically stable, such analyses were performed on an exploratory basis and indicated that there are some differences between the races in the factors drawing them into past social movements, but only minor differences in the coefficients on the predictors of paid activism. The cohort effect net of political experience seems to be more important for whites, and the political experience effect net of cohort seems to be more important for minorities.

## VII. RESULTS OF TESTS OF PREDICTIONS

Consistent with the assumptions of the collective action/resource mobilization tradition, the majority of the activists whose occupations are detailed in Table 1 seem to have an occupational interest in the goals of the neighborhood movement. Even considering only the volunteers, these activists are certainly not a representative sample of the kinds of people who live in urban neighborhoods. Contrary to Oberschall's discussions, there is little suggestion that these activists come from occupations independent of elite control; most are employed by elite–controlled or elite–funded organizations. However, Oberschall's logic would seem to apply only to a movement facing elite opposition (which he seems to assume faces all movements). His predictions would not seem to hold for a movement with elite sponsorship. (See Marx, 1979, for more about elite sponsorship of and opposition to movements.) Another proposition implied by Oberschall, that paid activists will come disproportionately from those with blocked channels of access due to discriminatory social barriers or from those whose education or skills fit them poorly for higher–paying jobs, also has not been confirmed: paid activists have higher average levels of education than volunteers and are not significantly more likely to be members of minority groups (Table 4).

The second set of predictions involved social and organizational networks. Consistent with past research on social movement activists, the neighborhood activists in this sample appear to have rather high levels of social and political integration. However, there is no difference between paid and volunteer activists in this regard. This lack of a difference is consistent with the theory that paid activists come to their positions by way of volunteer activism, that is, they are mobilized into the movement by the same general processes and factors as volunteers are. Contrary to the implications of McCarthy and Zald's work, paid activists do not appear to be more likely than volunteers to be divorced from their constituencies, nor do they appear to have been recruited to paid activism by the lure of a job independent of ideological considerations.

The next set of predictions involved ideology and experience. Commitment models of paid activism imply that paid activists will exhibit greater ideological connection to the movement and have longer histories of movement activism than volunteers, predictions that follow necessarily from the assumption that paid activists work their ways up through the ranks of the volunteers. Even though the 1970s neighborhood movement violated the commitment theorists' assumption that paid activists are supported from internal movement sources, they nevertheless support such theorists' predictions about ideology and experience. Paid activists are more likely to have leftist political orientations and to report that they have spent greater proportions of their adult lives as "neighborhood activists" than volunteers. However, they are no different from volunteers on the indicators of specific neighborhood–movement ideology, when general political ideology is controlled. This, plus the strong correlation of leftist ideology with participation in the anti–war movement, strongly suggests that the motivation for paid neighborhood activism lies not in the neighborhood movement, but in previous social movements. The evidence is that a commitment process is involved, but not a commitment to the neighborhood movement itself. Rather, there appears to be a commitment to some larger movement or vision of a movement.

Contrary to the commitment models, the general logic of the collective action models implies that volunteers would be more motivated by purposive incentives or personal gain from the collective good than would paid activists. While many of the volunteers' occupations are consistent with the view that they are especially likely to experience pesonal gain from the goals of the neighborhood movement, there is little support for the view that volunteers are more ideologically or purposively motivated. It appears much more likely that it is the paid activists who are more ideologically motivated.

Concerning the possibility that paid activism is an economic sacrifice, it was argued that this would imply ideological differences among paid activists according to educational levels. As Table 8 shows, persons with college degrees have more leftist political orientations than persons who do not, but this difference is statistically significant for paid activists and is not for volunteers. These data are consistent with the prediction from collective action theory, but not strongly confirming.

It is very clear that the 60's cohort, persons who came of age during the 1960's, are much more likely to be paid activists than others. This finding is quite consistent with what would be predicted from the values expressed by student activists in the 1960s, and with the literature on the subsequent political involvement and occupational careers of 1960s activists. Examination of the occupations of the volunteer activists will reveal that they are also likely to have chosen careers consistent with these predictions. These data strongly indicate

*Table 8.*   Mean Leftist Politics, by Paid Activism and College Graduate

|  | Mean Leftist Politics | T-Test | | |
|---|---|---|---|---|
|  |  | *t* | *df* | *p\** |
| *Volunteer Activists* | | | | |
| Not College Graduate | 2.38 | | | |
|  | | 1.42 | 81 | .08 |
| College Graduate | 2.67 | | | |
| *Paid Activists* | | | | |
| Not College Graduate | 2.53 | | | |
|  | | 2.36 | 65 | .01 |
| College Graduate | 3.12 | | | |

*Note:* *One–tailed test of significance.

that many of the 1970s neighborhood activists are heirs of the social movements and values of the 1960s. These patterns lend support to the view that activists in the 1960s experienced commitment processes that led to permanent changes in their political and occupational behavior.

However, money to pay social movement activists also became more readily available in the 1960s. The fact that, especially for whites, there is a cohort effect net of political experience from this decade suggests that the economic factor is also significant. In assessing the economic factor, however, it is important to remember that this is a sample of activists whose political experience is substantially more extensive and whose political attitudes are substantially more leftist than the general population. There is little evidence that the net cohort effect is due to political inexperience or ideological neutrality among paid activists; rather, persons not from this cohort who are just as politically experienced and politically leftist are far less likely to be paid activists. Since occupations are usually chosen in young adulthood, it is most likely that the cohort effect is due to the availability of such occupations at the time the person is making an occupational choice.

Since both cohort and political ideology and experience have effects on paid activism net of each other, it is clear that neither a pure commitment model nor a pure collective action model adequately explains the observed data. Both processes are obviously important in creating paid activists.

## VIII. DISCUSSION

The evidence of these data is that paid neighborhood activists come from essentially the same pool as volunteers, except that they are more likely to have leftist political orientations as a result of their greater involvement in the social movements of the 1960s, have spent a somewhat greater proportion of their adult lives as neighborhood activists, and are more likely to have come of age in the 1960s. What does this mean for theories of the mobilization of activists, especially paid activists?

First, there is strong evidence that the decision to become a paid activist arises from social movement experience and commitment. The evidence strongly suggests that the values and activities of the social movements of the 1960s affected participants in ways that led them to continue lives of political activism, and led many of them to choose careers as paid activists. There is no evidence that paid activists are less socially or politically integrated than volunteer activists. The image of paid activists as being the especially committed, experienced, and ideologically motivated participants in a social movement seems justified. There is no evidence to support the idea that a salary may be an alternative or supplementary motivation for social movement activism.

Secondly, there is clear evidence that economic factors impose constraints on the limits of activist involvement. It seems fairly clear that ideological commitment alone is not sufficient to make a paid activist; there must also be the possibility of earning a livelihood in this way. In the 1960s, a generation just at the age of deciding their life's work not only encountered new values and experiences but perceived the possibility of making a career of activism in the rapidly increasing funding available for such work throughout the decade. Older generations of activists may have been just as committed (and many were also active in the 1960s social movements), but they had already chosen other careers. The 1970s generation came of age in a period of reduced activism and retrenchment in support for social movements; Table 9 shows that they are somewhat more likely to have chosen non–movement occupations than the 1960s generation did.

The responses of these activists forces us to see resources as a constraint on activism, not as a motivation for it. Neighborhood activists—regardless of their

*Table 9.* Percentage of Employed Activists in Movement and Non-movement Jobs by Age

| Age in 1979 | Percentage of Employed | | Total Number | |
|---|---|---|---|---|
| | *Movement* | *Non–Movement* | *Employed* | *Not Employed* |
| 19–22 | 60 | 40 | 5 | 4 |
| 23–27 | 53 | 47 | 15 | 4 |
| 28–37 (60s cohort) | 70 | 30 | 50 | 5 |
| 38–47 | 32 | 68 | 41 | 1 |
| 48–57 | 40 | 60 | 15 | 2 |
| 58–67 | 43 | 57 | 7 | 10 |
| 68+ | 100 | 0 | 3 | 4 |

backgrounds—speak for constituencies they are members of. But even for activists promoting causes of no immediate benefit to themselves, it seems unlikely that we will be able to say that they are activists *because* they can be paid to be activists. Rather, their desire to be social movement activists derives from fundamental beliefs and values acquired in the intense experiences of past social movements. Their beliefs and values lead them to seek ways of being able to devote full time to activism by being able to make a living doing it. They not only passively receive the benefits of increases in resources, they actively campaign for and promote resources for activism. (This is the implication of McCarthy and Zald's 1973 piece, an implication they contradicted in their 1977 work.)

To argue that paid activists are mobilized more by commitment experiences than by job opportunities is not to discount the significance of changes in job opportunities stressed by McCarthy and Zald. Job opportunities for paid activists allow activists to spend more time on activism, since they do not also have to earn a living. Job opportunities controlled by elite sponsors (as were the majority of those available in the 1960s and 1970s) raise important implications for social movements. Even though they have strong social and political ties to their communities, paid activists dependent on outsiders rather than their constituencies for their paychecks may well choose their specific actions and programs more in line with their sponsors' goals than their constituencies'. But in exploring these important issues, and other related ones, it is important to recognize that whatever the *consequences* of paid activists may be for social movement organizations in goal displacement or elite control, the *causes* of activist careers arise from commitment and ideology.

In sum, people became paid neighborhood activists through progressive social and ideological commitment constrained by the resources available to support their activism. A movement will have many paid activists when there is a conjunction of commitment experiences leading participants to dedicate themselves to the movement and resources to pay full–time activists arising at a point in activists' life cycles when they are making occupational choices.

Although this paper has compared in detail paid and volunteer activists in the neighborhood movement, its findings are significant for our more general understanding of social movement mobilization. It seems clear from the papers and discussions among participants at recent meetings that most theorists are abandoning polar contrasts between the collective behavior and resource mobilization traditions. The constructive task of building theory on the foundations of the best from both traditions seems well under way. In this context, the findings of this research call attention to several important issues.

First, the character of social movement participation is clearly affected by the presence or absence of resources. Different types of activism and activities require different amounts of resources. The occupations of the volunteers in this sample highlight the importance of discretionary time as a critical "resource." Paid activism clearly depends upon monetary resources. Material conditions clearly constrain collective action.

Secondly, mobilization for one social movement will generally be affected by past mobilizations. The history of social movements in America is replete with examples of activists from one movement becoming involved in another cause. Neither of the two main theoretical traditions in the sociological study of social movements has dealt well with continuity and historical context, or provided an adequate theoretical accounting of these phenomena. An older paper by Weiss (1963) using stimulus–response concepts may be a starting point for comparative studies of activists' shifts from movement to movement.

Thirdly, mobilization of people to activism clearly should be viewed as a process of progressive commitment, not as isolated decisions or sporadic outbursts. It is quite possible that the mobilization of activists is very different from the mobilization of occasional participants, although the implications of this possibility have rarely been explored. There is a good theoretical grounding for the study of activist mobilization since, as I discussed above, each of the two main theoretical traditions has links to the other; the combination seems likely to yield a good portrait of this process.

Finally, the work already underway to link theories of interests and decisions with theories of emotions and ideologies is clearly taking us in the proper direction toward our goal of understanding the mobilization of social movement participants.

# IX. APPENDIX

Although various writers discuss various types of paid activists or external sources of support for paid activists, no one has comprehensively treated these topics. An overview of each is provided here because these distinctions are referred to in the text, even though they are not the central topic of this paper.

## A. Sources of Support

The sources of money to pay movement activists may be grouped into three categories according to where control over the money lies: *internal, external sponsor,* and *external market.* McCarthy and Zald stressed the importance of external versus internal sources of support (1973) and discussed extensively the consequences of support from external markets (1977), but did not note important differences between external sponsors and external markets.

*Internal.* Classic political and sociological treatments of paid activists assume they are supported by contributions of money or tangible goods from a participating membership base, and this is still an important source of support for paid activists in labor unions, religious movements, and some social reform organizations. Donations may be made directly or through symbolic rituals, as when members donate goods to rummage sales whose customers are all members of the movement (John Wilson, 1973:176–182). Support is also internal when members donate labor (and sometimes materials) to produce goods or services that are sold to non–members: the money comes from outside the movement, but the profits arise from members' donations. Such sales by extremely committed movement participants can raise a great deal of money (Lofland, 1979:161). Fund–raising events such as fairs involve lower member commitment (that is, a few days a year) and are popular among community and religious organizations; the skill to put on such events is often carried by experienced volunteers from such groups into social movement organizations.

*External Sponsor.*   Although a few social movements have been sponsored by wealthy individuals (Gamson, 1975:183–4), many social movement organizations have institutional sponsors such as governments, foundations, churches, and corporations. McCarthy and Zald (1973:12–16) document increases in contributions from such institutions throughout the 1960s and argue that such support has become a dominant trend. Institutional sponsors may give money to an organization or isolated activist requesting it, or may take the initiative in employing activists to organize new movement organizations. Institutions also indirectly support social movements by paying employees who, in fact, spend their work time working for the social movement. Even when such activities are nominally "ripping off" the system, they are encouraged only in sympathetic institutions and not tolerated in others.

*External Market.*   While support from sponsors arises from decisions by small numbers of powerful persons, support from large numbers of small contributions by isolated individuals who are not active participants in the movement organization depends upon market processes. These contributions may be direct, in response to solicitations in public places, door–to–door, or through direct mail or mass media advertising; or they may be indirect, through the purchase of goods or services sold at a profit, where the labor involved has been paid a fair wage. Direct contributions are more common than the sale of goods or services because attempts by small movement organizations to make a profit fail just as do most small businesses. McCarthy and Zald (1977) devote a great deal of attention to the implications of a movement's dependence upon isolated monetary contributions (the major kind of external market), arguing that organizations with such dependence exhibit instabilities of resource flows (:1228), large advertising expenditures (:1230), dependence upon economic cycles affecting discretionary income (:1230), and recruitment of beneficiary members for strategic purposes rather than as workers (:1235).

Each of the three types of support presents different controls on paid activists. Internal support makes paid activists ultimately depend upon their membership. This, in turn, may be expected to make the activist more responsive to the desires of the membership (unless larger legal institutions make membership in the organization mandatory). Support from external sponsors makes paid activists dependent on the fairly self–conscious policy decisions of a relatively small member of elite individuals and on the allocation decisions of institutional employees. Maintenance of support from external sponsors requires the ability to impress employees who make allocation decisions and depends in good measure on shifting cultural, political, and economic trends that affect policy decisions. Support from external markets makes paid activists dependent on aggregate market forces including economic cycles, competition from other movement organizations, and shifts in public opinion, but leaves the activists free from control by specific other persons.

## B. Roles of Paid Activists

Although no single author has discussed the full range of paid movement activists, the following five roles seem to be the major types: leader, entrepreneur, staff, organizer, and institutional activist. The roles overlap somewhat, as described below, but each is an important pure type with different implications for mobilization theory.

*Leaders* arise indigenously from a movement or because of popular support from the movement's membership; they set policy and are symbolic representatives of the movement and its goals (Turner and Killian, 1972:388–405; Lang and Lang, 1961:517–524; Killian, 1964:440–443; John Wilson, 1973:194–225, 276–282; Heberle, 1951:286–290). Following Weber, many of the authors distinguish types of leaders, especially charismatic versus administrative. Leaders can, of course, be either volunteer or paid. The key distinction between a leader and the other kinds of paid activists is that a leader, by definition, has followers. That is, there are genuine participants who believe in the leader and are willing to be led by him or by her.

*Entrepreneurs* take risks to start movements. If they succeed in creating followers they turn into leaders, but some never succeed in creating followers and others never try, preferring to pursue movement goals in other ways. There is a split in the literature concerning the motivations of movement entrepreneurs. Some authors see movement entrepreneurs as seeking to make a financial profit through providing the public good to persons who are willing to pay money to have someone else incur the costs of collective action (Frohlich, et al., 1971; Schwartz and McCarthy, 1978; and, by implication McCarthy and Zald, 1973, 1977). Others, particularly James Q. Wilson (1973:196–197), believe that movement entrepreneurs are motivated by purposive incentives and are willing to forego material gain to achieve their goals, implying that many entrepreneurs are volunteer activists who gain their livelihoods in some other way than through their activism. Moe (1980) argues that some entrepreneurs are motivated by material gain and others by purposive incentives, and that they will behave differently depending on their motives.

*Staff* are hired by movement leaders or entrepreneurs (either paid or volunteer) to perform tasks oriented toward accomplishing the movement's goals. In principle, staff carry out policy set by others. Staff may include clerks, administrators, or specialists such as architects, builders, nurses, planners, social workers, and fund–raisers. The staff–leader distinction often blurs in practice as many organizations are dominated by their paid staff (James Q. Wilson, 1973:225–228). An additional confusion is that many movement entrepreneurs define the positions they create for themselves as staff; this is especially true of organizers (discussed below). True staff are likely to be hired to perform less desirable or more time–consuming tasks whenever the organization has sufficient money to do so.

*Organizers* are staff or entrepreneurs who seek specifically to increase participation in and support for a movement organization among some population of people. The large prescriptive literature on community organizing stresses that organizers should not be leaders, that is, they should play the staff role of getting things organized rather than the leader role of setting policy (e.g. Kahn, 1970; Grosser, 1968; Alinsky, 1971; and the articles in Kramer and Specht, 1974 and Ecklein and Lauffer, 1972). Even these texts stray into discussing leadership functions such as setting goals and, prescriptions notwithstanding, many organizers dominate their organizations. The classic organizer comes from outside the movement's constituency and moves on after a year or so. Labor and community organizers have long been paid, although community organizing experienced a boom in the 1960s.

*Institutional Activists* are employees of non–movement intitutions whose work includes the pursuit of movement goals. The most important group of these are government–employed activists. This group has rarely been conceptualized as a kind of paid movement activist, but the political realities of this century require just such a concept. Obviously not all employees of governments are social movement activists. But some are. Some have been elected or appointed to their positions because of the movement's activities. Some work in agencies created in response to movement agitation. Some have self-consciously sought their jobs to pursue the movement's goals by "boring from within." An institutional employee should be seen as a type of paid movement activist when major portions of his or her job further movement goals, and when he or she identifies with the movement, has social and political connections with movement members, and participates in movement activities in ways that go beyond the institutional job description. Obviously, institutional activists are supported by external institutional sponsors.

# ACKNOWLEDGMENTS

I would like to thank the Louisville Inter–Neighborhood Coalition (and especially its president, Jim Segrest) and the staff and membership of the National Association of Neighborhoods for their help and cooperation with the data collection, the Departments of Sociology of the University of Louisville and the University of Wisconsin for support and supplies; and Elizabeth Thomson, Gerald Marwell, James Fendrich and John Lemke for their comments on earlier versions of this work.

# NOTES

1.  Thirty–three or 63% of the 53 "challenging groups" in the U.S. between 1800 and 1945 that were studied by Gamson had one or more paid staff members (1975:190). Calculating from the data presented in his appendix, the following percentages in each time period had paid staff: before 1860, 25%; 1860–1879, 67%; 1880–1899, 56%; 1900–1913, 67%; 1914–1928, 71%; 1929–1945, 55%. The proportion of groups having paid staff varies with the type of group: 80% for occupational groups, 47% for reform groups, 30% for socialist groups, and 33% for right–wing groups. Other examples of paid activists in a wide variety of social movement organizations may be found in John Wilson (1973:176–191) and James Q. Wilson (1973:215–232).

2.  The question of whether there really is a "neighborhood movement" raises definitional and political questions beyond the scope of this paper. There are two key empirical problems. First, the extensive resources provided to the movement from institutional sponsors (government agencies and corporate and religious foundations), along with policies and regulations that encourage or even mandate the formation of neighborhood organizations), raise serious questions about whether this mobilization is in any sense "illegitimate" in the eyes of those in power. The second problem is whether disparate and disconnected local mobilizations over diverse issues really add up to a unified social movement. Despite the importance of these issues for interpreting the neighborhood movement, they are not germane to this paper, which focuses on the processes leading some people to become activists.

3.  Certain kinds of political and religious sects are a partial exception, in that they tend to recruit social isolates who are attracted by the close ties they can obtain within the sect to substitute for the ones they lack in the outside world (Snow et al., 1980). The movements that are the basis for this paper typically draw from a broad–based constituency and exhibit the patterns of social connections described by Oberschall.

4.  For more detailed reviews of theoretical tendencies and distinctions and of the empirical literature, see the articles by Fendrich cited in note #5, Bengston et al. (1974), Buss (1974), and Kasschau et al. (1974).

5.  This brief summary is a synthesis compiled from Fendrich (1974, 1976, 1977), Fendrich and Tarleau (1973), and Fendrich and Krauss (1978).

6.  The correlation between SES and participation in the leadership of voluntary associations is so well established in the literature that it is rarely subjected to direct test. For a major empirical report on political participation, see Verba and Nie (1972). For reviews of organizational participation, see Smith and Freedman (1972) and Smith (1975).

7.  For *known* and all other polychotomous ordinal variables listed below, analyses were performed using several different numerical coding schemes and checked with cross–tabulations; all coding schemes yielded essentially the same results so only the simplest are reported.

8.  A reviewer has critiqued this measure of localistic orientation on the grounds that leftist organizers believe that participation in activities oriented toward local issues tends over time to increase a person's vision of the need for a larger social struggle; the reviewer predicted that volunteers with longer histories of movement involvement would be more likely to believe in "larger struggle." I was aware of leftists' beliefs on this matter when I formulated the question and worded it to acknowledge that all were important, but to ask the respondent to identify priorities and say which was *most* important. I checked the reviewer's prediction, and the results will be disappointing to leftist organizers. Among volunteers, there is *no correlation* between raw years as a neighborhood activist and commitment to a "larger struggle." Raw years as an activist is highly correlated with age, and older people are more conservative, but controlling for age only further reduces this already miniscule correlation. Using the standardized variable proportion of adult life as a neighborhood activist, there is a first–order bivariate correlation for volunteers between history of activism and commitment to a larger struggle, but this correlation is entirely explained away when controls for

prior social movement experience are introduced. It is experience in the anti–war movement in particular and, to a lesser extent, experience in the civil rights movement that leads to a priority on linking the neighborhood movement to larger struggles. Being a "neighborhood activist" for a long time without being in the anti–war or civil rights movement has an extremely weak and non–significant *negative* effect on support for the "larger struggle."

# REFERENCES

Adamek, Raymond J., and Jerry M. Lewis
    1973   "Social control, violence and radicalization: The Kent State case." Social Forces 51: 342–347.
Alinsky, Saul
    1971   Rules for Radicals. New York: Random House.
Becker, Howard S.
    1960   "Notes on the concept of commitment." American Journal of Sociology 61: 32–40.
Bengtson, Vern L., Michael J. Furlong, and Robert S. Laufer
    1974   "Time, aging, and the continuity of social structure: Themes and issues in generational analysis." Journal of Social Issues 30: 1–30.
Bonacich, Phillip, Gerald H. Shure, James P. Kahan, and Robert J. Meeker
    1976   "Cooperation and group size in the n-person prisoners' dilemma." Journal of Conflict Resolution 20: 687–706.
Braungart, Richard G., and Margaret M. Braungart
    1974   "Protest attitudes and behavior among college youth: A U.S. case study." Youth and Society 6: 219–248.
    1980   "Political career patterns of radical activists in the 1960s and 1970s: Some historical comparisons." Sociological Focus 13: 237–254.
Buss, Allan R.
    1974   "Generational analysis: Description, explanation, and theory." Journal of Social Issues 30: 55–71.
Chamberlin, John
    1974   "Provision of collective goods as a function of group size." American Political Science Review 68: 707–716.
Demerath, N. J. III, Gerald Marwell, and Michael T. Aiken
    1971   Idealism: White Activists in a Black Movement. San Francisco: Jossey-Bass.
Dillick, Sidney.
    1953   Community Organization for Neighborhood Development: Past and Present. New York: William Morrow and Company and Woman's Press.
Ecklein, Joan L., and Armand A. Lauffer
    1972   Community Organizers and Social Planners. New York: Wiley.
Erlanger, Howard S.
    1977   "Social reform organizations and subsequent careers of participants: A follow-up study of early participants in the OEO Legal Services Program." American Sociological Review 42: 233–248.
Fendrich, James M.
    1974   "Activists ten years later: A test of generational unit continuty." Journal of Social Issues 30: 95–118.
    1976   "Black and white activists ten years later: Political Socialization and adult left-wing politics." Youth and Society 8: 81–104.
    1977   "Keeping the faith or pursuing the good life: A study of the consequences of participation in the civil rights movement." American Sociological Review 42: 144–157.

Fendrich James M., and Ellis S. Krauss
  1978  "Student activism and adult left-wing politics: A causal model of political socialization for black, white and Japanese students of the 1960s generation." Research in Social Movements Conflicts and Change 1: 231–255.
Fendrich, James M., and Alison T. Tarleau
  1973  "Marching to a different drummer: Occupational and political correlates of former student activists." Social Forces 52: 245–253.
Fireman, Bruce, and William A. Gamson
  1979  "Utilitarian logic in the resource mobilization perspective." In Mayer N. Zald and John D. McCarthy, (eds.), The Dynamics of Social Movements: Resource Mobilization, Social Control and Tactics. Cambridge, MA: Winthrop.
Flacks, Richard
  1967  "The liberated generation: An exploration of the roots of student protest." Journal of Social Issues 23: 7–14.
  1971  Youth and Social Change. Chicago: Markham.
Frohlich, Norman, Thomas Hunt, Joe Oppenheimer, and R. Harrison Wagner
  1975  "Individual contributions for collective goods: Alternative models." Journal of Conflict Resolution 19: 310–329.
Frohlich, Norman and Joe A. Oppenheimer
  1970  "I get by with a little help from my friends." World Politics 23: 104–120.
  1978  Modern Political Economy. Englewood Cliffs, NJ: Prentice-Hall.
Frohlich, Norman, Joe A. Oppenheimer, and Oran Young
  1971  Political Leadership and Collective Goods. Princeton: Princeton University Press.
Gamson, William A.
  1975  The Strategy of Social Protest. Homewood, Ill.: The Dorsey Press.
Gerlach, Luther P., and Virginia H. Hine
  1970  People, Power, Change: Movements of Social Transformation. Indianapolis: Bobbs-Merrill.
Greene, W.
  1970  "Where are the Savios of yesteryear?" New York Times Magazine 6: 6–10.
Grosser, Charles F.
  1968  "Staff role in neighborhood organization." Pages 133–145 in John B. Turner, Neighborhood Organization for Community Action. New York: National Association of Social Work.
Haan, Norma
  1975  "Hypothetical and actual moral reasoning in a situation of civil disobedience." Journal of Personality and Social Psychology 32: 255–270.
Heberle, Rudolf
  1951  Social Movements: An Introduction to Political Sociology. New York: Appleton-Century-Crofts.
Kahn, Si
  1970  How People Get Power: Organizing Oppressed Communities for Action. New York: McGraw-Hill.
Kasschau, Patricia L., H. Edward Ransford, and Vern L. Bengtson
  1974  "Generational consciousness and youth movement participation: Contrasts in blue collar and white collar youth." Journal of Social Issues 30: 69–94.
Killian, Lewis M.
  1964  "Social movements." In R. E. L. Faris (ed.), Handbook of Modern Sociology. Chicago: Rand McNally, 426–455.
Kornberg, Alan, and Mary L. Brehm
  1971  "Ideology, institutional identification and campus activism." Social Forces 49: 445–459.

Kornhauser, William
  1962   "Social bases of political commitment: A study of liberals and radicals." Pages 321–339
         in Arnold Rose (ed.), Human Behavior and Social Processes. Boston: Houghton Mifflin.
Kotler, Milton
  1969   Neighborhood Government: The Local Foundations of Political Life. Indianapolis: Bobbs-
         Merrill.
  1979   "A public policy for neighborhood and community organizations." Social Policy 10, (2):
         37–43.
Kramer, Ralph M., and Harry Specht (eds.)
  1974   Readings in Community Organization Practice. (Second Edition) Englewood Cliffs, NJ:
         Prentice-Hall.
Lang, Kurt, and Gladys Engel Lang
  1961   Collective Dynamics. New York: Thomas Y. Crowell Company.
Lenin, V. I.
  [1902] What Is To Be Done? Peking: Foreign Languages Press.
  1973
Lin, Nan
  [1974–5] "The McIntire march: A study of recruitment and commitment." Public Opinion Quar-
           terly 38: 562–573.
Lipset, Seymour M.
  1971   "Youth and politics." Pages 743–792 in Robert K. Merton and Robert A. Nisbet (eds.),
         Contemporary Social Problems. New York: Harcourt, Brace and World.
Lofland, John
  1977   Doomsday Cult. (Englarged Edition) New York: Irvington.
  1979   "White-hot mobilization: Strategies of a millenarian movement." In Mayer Zald and John
         McCarthy (eds.), The Dynamics of Social Movements, 157–166. Cambridge, MA:
         Winthrop.
McCarthy, John D., and Mayer N. Zald
  1973   The Trend of Social Movements in America: Professionalization and Resource Mobiliza-
         tion. Morristown, NJ: General Learning Press.
  1977   "Resource mobilization and social movements: A partial theory." American Journal of
         Sociology 82: 1212–1241.
McFalls, Joseph A., and Bernard J. Gallagher, III
  1975   "Political orientations and occupational values." Paper presented at the American So-
         ciological Association meetings, August, San Francisco.
McPhail, Clark, and David Miller
  1973   "The assembling process: A theoretical and empirical examination." American Sociologi-
         cal Review 38: 721–735.
Miadenberg, M. and P. Meyer
  1970   "The Berkeley rebels: Five years later." Paper presented at the annual meeting of the
         American Association for Public Opinion Research. Abstracted in Public Opinion Quar-
         terly 24: 477–478.
Marx, Gary T.
  1979   "External efforts to damage or facilitate social movements: Some patterns, explanations,
         outcomes, and complications." Pages 94–125 in Mayer Zald and John McCarthy (eds.),
         The Dynamics of Social Movements. Cambridge, MA: Winthrop.
Matthews, Donald, and James Prothro
  1966   Negroes and the New Southern Politics. New York: Harcourt, Brace and World.
Michels, Robert
  [1915] Political Parties. New York: Collier.
  1962

Moe, Terry M.
  1980  The Organization of Interests: Incentives and the Internal Dynamics of Political Interest
        Groups. Chicago: The University of Chicago Press.
Moynihan, Daniel P.
  1965  "The professionalization of reform." The Public Interest 1: 6–16.
  1969  Maximum Feasible Misunderstanding: Community Action in the War on Poverty. New
        York: The Free Press.
Oberschall, Anthony
  1973  Social Conflict and Social Movements. Englewood Cliffs, NJ: Prentice-Hall.
O'Brien, David J.
  1975  Neighborhood Organization and Interest-Group Processes. Princeton University Press.
Oliver, Pamela
  1980  "Rewards and punishments as selective incentives for collective action: Theoretical inves-
        tigations." American Journal of Sociology 85: 1356–1375.
Olson, Mancur, Jr.
  1965  The Logic of Collective Action. Cambridge, MA: Harvard University Press.
Perlman, Janice
  1979  "Grassroots empowerment and government response." Social Policy 10 (2): 16–21.
Rathke, Wade, Seth Borgos and Gary Delgado
  1979  "ACORN: Taking advantage of the fiscal crisis." Social Policy 10 (2): 35–36.
Schofield, Norman
  1975  "A game theoretic analysis of Olson's game of collective action." Journal of Conflict
        Resolution 19: 441–461.
Schwartz, Sanford M., and John D. McCarthy
  1978  "Marketing strategies for mass mobilization." Paper presented at the Annual Meeting of
        the Southern Sociological Society, New Orleans.
Smelser, Neil J.
  1962  Theory of Collective Behavior. New York: Free Press.
Smith, Constance and Anne Freedman
  1972  Voluntary Associations: Perspectives on the Literature. Cambridge, MA: Harvard Univer-
        sity Press.
Smith, David Horton
  1975  "Voluntary action and voluntary groups." Annual Review of Sociology 1: 247–270.
Smith, Jan
  1976  "Communities, associations, and the supply of collective goods." American Journal of
        Sociology 82: 291–308.
Snow, David A., Louis A. Zurcher, Jr., and Sheldon Ekland-Olson
  1980  "Social networks and social movements: A micro-structural approach to differential re-
        cruitment." American Sociological Review 45: 787–801.
Turner, Ralph H. and Lewis M. Killian
  1972  Collective Behavior. (Second Edition) Englewood Cliffs, NJ: Prentice-Hall.
Verba, Sidney, and Norman H. Nie
  1972  Participation in America. New York: Harper and Row.
Von Eschen, Donald, Jerome Kirk, and Maurice Pinard
  1971  "The organizational substructure of disorderly politics." Social Forces 49: 529–544.
Weiner, R. and D. Stillman
  1979  Woodstock Census: The Nationwide Survey of the Sixties Generation. New York: Viking
        Press.
Weiss, Robert F.
  1963  "Defection from social movements and subsequent recruitment to new movements."
        Sociometry 26: 1–20.

Whalen, Jack and Richard Flacks
    1980   "The Isla Vista "bank burners" ten years later: Notes on the fate of student activists."
            Sociological Focus 13: 215–236.
Wilson, James Q.
    1973   Political Organizations. New York: Basic Books.
Wilson, John
    1973   Introduction to Social Movements. New York: Basic Books.

# ON THE ROLE OF THE VANGUARD PARTY IN THE UNITED STATES:

## A CASE STUDY OF THE REVOLUTIONARY COMMUNIST PARTY AT WAIAHOLE–WAIKANE

James A. Geschwender

With the Assistance of Steven Smith

## I. INTRODUCTION

Recent years have seen a revival of interest in the concept of the vanguard party and its possible relevance to the social change process in the United States and other advanced capitalist societies. The vanguard party virtually disappeared from the American political scene in the decade following World War II. Then in the mid–to late–1970's the vanguard structure experienced a rebirth through

Research in Social Movements, Conflicts and Change, Vol. 5, pages 171–202.
Copyright © 1983 by JAI Press Inc.
All rights of reproduction in any form reserved.
ISBN: 0-89232-301-9

both the creation of new and the revitalization of old vanguardist organizations. This rebirth stimulated a debate among leftist intellectuals. One segment argued that the vanguard organization had great relevance for pre–revolutionary Russia and is probably still an appropriate structure for third world countries, but that it is both unnecessary and undesirable in contemporary United States (passing reference is often made to other advanced capitalist societies, but the primary focus of concern is the United States). Others sharply disagree and continue in their attempts to build vanguard organizations.

This paper will examine the role played by a self–designated vanguard party (the Revolutionary Communist Party) in a social movement that grew up around a struggle of a community in Hawaii (Waiahole–Waikane) to prevent itself from being evicted from its land and its homes. It is hoped that the larger debate shall be informed by what is learned from the examination of this case study. It is clear that what is essentially a theoretical debate cannot be resolved by a single case study, but implications may be derived that will suggest answers to theoretical questions. This paper will be organized into three sections. The first section will define the vanguard concept, briefly describe the evolution of the vanguard type structure in the United States, review the current debate, and relate the substance of this debate to the shaping of the concept through the writings and actions of Marx and Lenin. The second section will consist of a description of the Waiahole–Waikane community struggle and an assessment of the role of the Revolutionary Communist Party in that struggle. The third and final section will consist of an attempt to apply to the debate understandings derived from this case study.

## II. THE VANGUARD PARTY

The vanguard party is essentially a combat organization that develops within capitalist society and has as its primary task the provision of leadership and direction to the struggle to bring about a socialist transformation. Obviously the pursuit of such an objective brings the organization into direct conflict with both the state and powerful segments of the capitalist class. It is this combat role played in a hostile environment that has been responsible for the development of several of the characteristics of the vanguard party. The party has to organize itself in such a manner that it will be able to effectively pursue its primary task of bringing about the socialist transformation and at the same time protect itself against inevitable counterattacks from those whose vested interests are threatened.

Probably the most striking feature of the vanguard party structure is its demo-cratic–centralism. Issues may be freely debated, but only to the point that they are officially resolved. From that point on all debate must cease, and party members must submit themselves to internal discipline. No organized factions are permitted. The minority must subordinate itself to the will of the majority as expressed and disseminated from the central committee to the membership and from higher to lower party levels. Secrecy, a second key feature of vanguard structures, has two key functions. It helps to protect the party membership from acts of repression on the part of the state and the party's class enemies, but it also enables the party to follow a strategy that incorporates a blend of legal and extra–legal activities.

A restricted membership is the third key feature characteristic of vanguard parties. No attempt is made to attract a mass membership. Most workers are seen as having limited vision as a consequence of their day–to–day work–place experiences. Consequently they tend to see their situation in relation to a single job, a single employer, or a single industry and they tend to develop a fairly narrow economistic view of their situation. Advanced workers are those who, in the course of struggles with their employers, have come to develop a broader view. They increasingly define their situations in class terms and come to understand the class nature of the struggle. The party brings a number of advanced workers together with revolutionary theorists and creates the opportunity for the furthering of their political education. These advanced workers may then carry their enhanced theoretical understandings back to the work–place where they may help broaden the perspectives of other workers and provide leadership and direction to workers' struggles as they emerge.

It should be noted that an organization does not constitute a vanguard party simply by virtue of having all of the characteristics described above. As Mandel notes, in the last regard, it is the working class rather than revolutionary intellectuals that determines which, if any, party organization shall win designation as a vanguard:

> According to Lenin's concept of organization, there is no self–proclaimed vanguard. Rather, the vanguard must win recognition as a vanguard (i.e., the historical right to act as a vanguard) through its attempts to establish revolutionary ties with the advanced part of the class and its actual struggle. (1970:29)

## A. The Vanguard Party in the United States

Prior to World War II, the Communist Party was the largest and most significant of the vanguard–type organizations in the United States with the Socialist Workers Party as its major challenger (O'Brien, 1977–78; Judis, 1973). The position of the Communist Party was greatly eroded during and after the war, partly as a consequence of its uncritical support for the Soviet Union, and partly as a consequence of the repression of the cold war, McCarthyist period. The Socialist Workers Party also suffered greatly during this period despite its unrelenting opposition to the bureaucratic structure of the Soviet Union.

While vanguard elements were present throughout, most social protest in the decades after the war took place independent of vanguard leadership. This protest emerged initially in the form of the Civil Rights Movement, which then spawned the student and women's movements. These jointly provided the impetus for the development of the anti–war movement. This trend culminated in the emergence of the New Left, which was explicitly anti–vanguardist in conception and execution—although organized vanguard elements existed within its ranks. The New Left flourished for awhile, but then it faded into relative insignificance after the ending of the war in Vietnam. Political struggle would later re-emerge in a new form.

The period of political quiescence that followed led many people to reconsider the earlier rejection of the vanguard party. Many began to question whether it was the absence of a vanguard that allowed such a vast amount of political unrest to have been dissipated with so little objective results and so little carry over to ongoing political activity. Thus in March 1973, the *Guardian* sponsored a series of forums on the topic of building a new communist party, and the period of the seventies saw the establishment of a series of vanguard party–type organizations. Perhaps among the most prominent of these new parties that were all oriented toward Mao and China were the Revolutionary Communist Party, which grew out of the Revolutionary Union; the Communist Party (Marxist–Leninist), which developed out of the October League; the Communist Labor Party; and the Black Workers Congress, although there were a host of smaller organizations. In addition, both the Moscow–oriented Communist Party and the Socialist Workers Party experienced a substantial revival. Most of the new vanguard parties utilized a cadre structure, practiced democratic centralism, maintained secrecy, often restricting the number of public members, and attempted to spread their message through publications that endorsed all working–class struggles and attempted to link them to transitional demands.

## B. The Debate

This revival of vanguardist structures in the United States touched off a debate on the left as to the relevancy of the vanguard structure to the advanced capitalist societies and, most particularly, to contemporary United States. In the following discussion I will make reference only to the discussion as it has taken place among the socialist left and not include the positions of such old–line radicals as Saul Alinsky (1972), whose activism has always been in behalf of short–term reforms without any effort to link these reforms to an eventual socialist transformation.

A large portion of the debate begins with the assertion that Lenin had designed the vanguard party to meet a particular set of historical circumstances—the extreme autocracy and oppression of tsarist Russia—and that differing circumstances called for different forms of political organization (Glaberman, 1974; Weiner, 1977; Healey, 1975; Taft, 1975; Judis, 1973, 1974, 1975; Ackerman and Boyte, 1973, 1974; Boggs, Dancis, and Rotkin, 1975). While these critics are not in complete agreement among themselves, they do use a very similar starting point in attempting to demonstrate that Lenin's position is misrepresented by the most extreme advocates of the vanguard party. A number of statements made by Lenin are cited in support of this position—statements that suggest Lenin, in his polemical fervor, may also have misrepresented Lenin.[1]

Having established the fact that Lenin believed that organizational forms should vary according to political circumstances, the critics go on to argue that contemporary United States differs significantly from pre–revolutionary Russia and consequently requires a different style of organization. The United States is an urban society. The American working class is literate and educated. They argue that free elections exist and overt political repression is, for the most part, absent in the United States. While these critics differ in what form of organizations and activity that they do advocate, all agree that the vanguard party is unnecessary and undesirable. Kinoy (1973) adovcates participation in the electoral process with a reform–oriented party that leaves the question of socialism or capitalism to be resolved at some indefinite future time. Judis (1973; 1974) advocates the formation of a mass socialist party that participates in the electoral process openly under that banner. Ackerman and Boyte (1973; 1974) favor the formation of a broad open democratic socialist organization that builds a socialist consciousness and may eventually give rise to a socialist party, which would then take part in elections. The DeKalb New American Movement group (1974) applauded the Ackerman and Boyte commitment to democracy but also endorsed the Judis call for a socialist party now. Healey (1975; Weiner, 1977) is less clear on what she advocates but is highly critical of the amount of secrecy that existed in the Communist Party (of which she was a member) and in the new communist parties.

Healey's and others criticism of secrecy appear to be based primarily upon its presumed undemocratic character, but Oppenheimer (1969: 68–72) and, in a less explicit fashion, Gary Marx (1974) take a different tack. Secret organizations are seen as being especially vulnerable to infiltration by informants and agent provocateurs. The former weakens the organization and its associated movement by passing information on resources, strategies, and tactics to the opposition. The latter often exhibits the type of dedication and commitment that enables them to move into influential positions within the organization. Once having attained positions of responsibility, they may cause serious disruption by advocating policy alternatives that might prove damaging to the organization. The fear of infiltration may become as debilitating as actual infiltration in that morale and organizational efficiency may be disrupted by an atmosphere of mutual suspicion and distrust.

Some of the differences found among the critics in terms of programmatic suggestions (for example, those between Judis and Boyte and Ackerman) may result from differing conceptions of the state. Electoral politics are attractive to those who view the state as the primary vehicle of capitalist oppression and who feel that the state apparatus may be used by socialists to reverse that oppression. If one believes as Boyte and Ackerman do that the primary source of oppression lies elsewhere, participation in the electoral arena may be less attractive.

Glaberman supports the formation of a revolutionary socialist organization, but one which is not a vanguard party. His position is the logical outgrowth of two theoretical positions that he holds. First, in a position similar to that of Michals (1915), he believes that Lenin underestimated the inevitable conservatism of a party as a political institution—by which he really means the conservatism of the party bureaucracy (Glaberman, 1974:25–26). Second, and more importantly, Glaberman is a strong believer in spontaneity (1974:25–31). This is based upon, in part, the empirical observation that workers have spontaneously created worker's councils in the course of revolutionary activities in such diverse contests as the Paris Commune; the February 1917 revolution in Russia; Germany in 1918 and 1919; the Hungarian Revolution of 1956; and the French uprising in 1968—to which he would now add Poland in 1981. His position is also based upon the theoretical analysis of C.L.R. James (1966), who saw the distinction between party and mass as a continuation of the distinction between mental and manual labor as it exists in capitalist society.[2] The proletariat was expected to struggle against this contradiction leading to the eventual disappearance of the party, corresponding to the process leading to the withering away of the state. The theoretical position that Glaberman assumed was not one of a believer in pure spontaneity. He believed that there was still an important role to be played by a Marxist organization that could disseminate news of various forms of struggle and publish theoretical analyses linking these together, showing the relationship between them and the longer term struggle for socialism. This organization should differ from a vanguard party in its lack of bureaucracy and its willingness to lend support to workers' struggles without attempting to take them over, guide them, direct them, or even inhibit them as some vanguard organizations have done in the past. Glaberman appears to believe that it will be possible to form such an organization and for it to avoid the bureaucratic pitfalls that he feels plague vanguard parties, but he is not overly specific as just how this can be brought about.

The current advocates of the vanguard party (e.g., Mandel, 1978; Taft, 1975) tend to emphasize a number of points in addition to reaffirming their basic doubts that the mass of workers could, left to their own devices, develop a revolutionary socialist consciousness. They believe that the vanguard party is essential to bring the necessary theory to workers so that they can better understand the meaning of their experiences in a single plant, a single industry, or a single union. They do not argue against the importance of either spontaneity or disruptive tactics. But they do insist that spontaneity has its limits. It rapidly tends to become conservatized—limited to simple economic demands, perhaps buttressed by the call for moderate political reforms. They argue that a vanguard party is required to give direction, continuity, and meaning to the spontaneous and often disruptive activities of workers and that it particularly takes such an organization to give continuity to the struggle during quiescent periods exhibiting an absence of spontaneous worker activities. They also argue (citing the experience of the Black Panthers, Civil Rights and anti—war groups in the sixties) that the critics underestimate the extent of state repression of dissident political activists in the United States. The amount of oppression, legal and otherwise, that does exist fully justifies, in their minds, the resort to secrecy and requires the adoption of principles of democratic centralism.

Piven and Cloward (1977a; 1977b; 1977c; 1978) go even further than Glaberman when they argue against reliance in the change process on the use of formal organizations, *per se*. They specifically state that (1978:177) ". . . the emphasis on building mass—based bureaucratic organizations generates oligarchical tendencies, facilitates the cooptation of movement leadership by dominant groups, and . . . diminishes the use of disruptive tactics . . . in favor of an electoral strategy that wins little." They advocate the use of mass mobilization and of disruptive tactics over a reliance upon formal organization. It may not be completely fair to locate Piven and Cloward among the critics of vanguard parties inasmuch as they do not directly consider this form of organization in their writings and, as illustrated by the case study presented herein, there is nothing inherent in the vanguard structure that prohibits mass mobilization and use of disruptive tactics. Nevertheless, it is useful to remind the reader that there are leftist activist intellectuals who oppose all forms of formal organization and not simply the vanguard structure.

## C. The Writings of Marx and Lenin

Glaberman (1974:27) notes that Lenin's theory of organization was different from that of Marx. He is correct to the extent that Marx did not present a formulation of the concept of the vanguard party and that it is highly unlikely if he, in fact, even had such a concept. Nevertheless, an analysis of his writings and actions over time suggest that he came to believe in the need for working—class action coordinated by a leadership centralized through a party structure. Marx was a central figure in the Communist league, which was founded in 1847. It was a secret organization that had a central committee but, despite these features, the League in fact really comprised little more than an umbrella organization loosely linking together a number of national sections and serving primarily to coordinate debate among the various political tendencies of the day (Riazanov, n.d.:63—102).

Marx's position shifted somewhat by the time of the founding of the First International (The International Workingmen's Association) in 1864 (Riazanov, n.d.:129—198). The First International also included a number of different political tendencies, but this time Marx actively worked to make the organization more centralized. Then in 1871 a resolution was passed that, in effect, barred from the International any group that advocated an independent program. While this was primarily aimed at Bakunin and his followers it applied more generally and, if fully implemented, would have eventuated in an organization characterized by a high degree of unified action and internal discipline.

Marx also seems to have developed the belief that such centralization and discipline should also characterize the state after the working class' seizure of power. One can find throughout Marx's writings many references to the dictatorship of the proletariat that was to be established in the course of the revolutionary struggle, but which was to disappear once the revolution was made secure.[3] But he said very little to specify its characteristics prior to the Paris Commune of 1871. It is clear that Marx considered the Paris Commune to be a highly significant event that offered useful insights into the manner in which the socialist transformation would come about, and which foreshadowed the shape of the future socialist society. Nevertheless, he was critical of the Commune for its limited amount of centralized leadership, and of the Central Committee for surrendering its power to the Commune at too early a point in the struggle.[4] Engels even more strongly asserted his belief in the continued need for a centralized leadership and a party–like structure to the state after the worker seizure of power.[5]

Despite the tentative moves in this direction made by Marx and Engels, it remained for Lenin (1897; 1902; 1904; 1905a), to fully explicate the concept of the vanguard party. He laid out in broad form his theory of organization, tactics, and programs in an important series of polemics issued during the period ranging approximately from the establishment of the Russian Social Democratic Party (RSDLP) in 1898 to shortly after the Revolution of 1905. These include *Two Tactics of Scial Democracy; What Is To Be Done?;* and *One Step Forward—Two Steps Back*. Both Lenin's writings and actions indicate his belief that the revolutionary party should be organized along cadre principles. He clearly stated his belief that workers had a limited range of experiences that would inhibit them from developing a true working–class consciousness, although a few advanced workers would be able to develop a higher level of consciousness as a consequence of participation in struggle.[6] Much of his work with the RSDLP appears to be predicated upon this principle. He seemed to be striving to build a party that would include both advanced workers and revolutionary theorists, who had the time, training, and experience to enable them to take a sweeping view of history and to understand the relationship between isolated struggles against employers and the political class struggle between capital and labor. Efforts were made to develop the level of political sophistication of the advanced workers. The vast mass of workers was excluded from party membership. The RSDLP largely related to them through the advanced workers and through the tactic of the transitional demand. This tactic involves the Party recognizing all progressive movements regardless of how narrow or economistic their objectives and assuming their demands as the Party's own. During the course of the struggle for these demands, further related demands would be made that were logically related to the original demands, but which have been extended to the point where they could not be met without threatening the very foundations of capitalism. Thus workers could gain the experience of struggle—hopefully successful struggle—and have their political consciousness raised at the same time.

Lenin believed that if a Party were to carry out the pursuit of the socialist transformation in a hostile environment, it would have to practice secrecy and internal discipline. He defined democratic centralism as the subordination of the minority to the majority, of the part (for example, local committees) to the whole, lower levels to higher levels, and the membership to the Party Congress (or to the Central Committee as its voice). Organizational rules implementing these principles were hammered out in a series of Party Congress debates beginning in 1902 at the second congress of the RSDLP. Lenin, and indeed the majority, advocated increased centralization of the party and sought to make party decisions binding on all members. They insisted that all potential members apply, be screened and accepted by the Central Committee, and be incorporated into a functioning party organization immediately upon membership.

However, it is all too easy to make Lenin's position on the vanguard party into a caricature of what it really was. Lenin was highly flexible and recognized that organizational forms, strategies, and tactics all had to be adjusted to particular socio–historical conditions. He appeared to be impressed by the progressive and vigorous role played by the proletariat in the Revolution of 1905, despite the fact that the vanguard party played virtually no role in the struggle.[7] But he did not endorse pure spontaneity as he also, at least implicitly, argued that the failure of that revolution to go any further than it did might have been, in part, a consequence of the type of leadership available to workers at the time and the absence of a revolutionary vanguard that was prepared to actively intervene and give direction to the struggle.

Lenin's views on the composition of the party and the amount of internal democracy that it could practice also seemed to vary according to circumstances. The Tsar was forced by protest and strikes to grant a number of constitutional liberties in the years after 1905, which had the net impact of allowing for a wider range of activities. In this context Lenin argued for the increased use of electoral principles within the party, to bring into the Party increased numbers of advanced workers, and for the development of new legal and semi–legal party apparatus to take advantage of newly created opportunities for collective action (Lenin, 1905c; Mandel, 1970:48; Peters, 1975).[8] He also defended the need for open debate within the plenaries and the right of rank and file membership to remove party members who were derelict in carrying out the mandate of the majority.

This may be contrasted to the position that Lenin took at the Tenth Party Congress in 1921 when circumstances were quite different (Taft, 1975:94–97). The Bolshevik Party was in power. The Soviet Union had emerged from a disasterous war followed by foreign invasion. Economic recovery was slow in coming, and both workers and peasants were expressing great dissatisfaction with the leadership provided by the Party. Lenin argued very strongly for the reduction of internal democracy, the return to a more stringent enforcement of the principles of democratic centralism and the outlawing of factionalism. However, Lenin made a number of statements that indicated he was taking this position in response to external conditions and not because he believed that such practices were dictated by basic principles.[9]

Thus the political writings and practices of Marx and Lenin lend support to both sides and does little to resolve the debate over the vanguard party. It is clear that Lenin envisaged a socialist transformation brought about by a revolution led by a vanguard party. The party was expected to be secret and structured according to principles of democratic centralism. It was to be more open and internally democratic when conditions allowed and to move toward the restriction of internal democracy when required by threatening circumstances. Perhaps disagreement over the nature of the circumstances prevailing in the United States and advanced capitalist societies today are what really lie at the heart of the debate over the vanguard party. It is possible that the question should be reformulated to ask what type of organization is demanded by present circumstances. We shall not be able to answer questions so broadly shaped simply by examining the role played by one self–designated vanguard party in a single community struggle, but let us now turn to that struggle to see what, if any, light it might shed on the problem under consideration.

## III.  A CASE STUDY: THE RCP AND WAIAHOLE-WAIKANE

It would be useful to briefly trace the development of the Revolutionary Communist Party nationally and in Hawaii up to the time period covered by this analysis (O'Brien, 1977–78; Tom Peters, 1977; Gene Parker, 1979). The Revolutionary Communist Party developed out of the Revolutionary Union, which was a Maoist organization of students and former students. It began in 1968 as a study group of persons involved in community and work–place organizing in the San Francisco Bay area. The study group formally became the Bay Area Revolutionary Union (BARU) in the Spring of 1969. It played a major role in the fight against the Progressive Labor attempt to take over Students for a Democratic Society at its convention that year. BARU made contact with similarly inclined people throughout the country through its publication and distribution of the Red Papers. Groups of former students in other cities formed collectives, which were brought together in 1970 as part of a national organization—the Revolutionary Union. There was an organizational split in 1972 when a minority left to form Venceremos—a group dedicated to urban guerrilla warfare. The majority who stayed with Revolutionary Union were committed to members getting blue collar jobs and organizing at the work–place. Organizing in the working class was seen as part of a larger program of developing a foundation for a Leninist party while at the same time building a united front against American imperialism.

The Revolutionary Union was one of the groups involved in the *Guardian*-sponsored forums on building a new communist party, but it soon became clear that it would be impossible to build a single umbrella party uniting all of the new Maoist groups. Revolutionary Union continued its work–place activities throughout the early seventies and had its most notable success in building a strike support movement around the Farrah strike.

The middle–1970's was a period when Maoist groups were transforming themselves into political parties and the Revolutionary Union formed the Revolutionary Communist Party (RCP) in October 1975. RCP continued to be the largest of the Maoist organizations throughout the seventies but, consistent with its conception of a Leninist Party, it never became a mass organization. It recruited many of its members through its student affiliate, the Revolutionary Student Brigade, and has had some success in organizing at the work–place. The National United Workers Organization was founded in September 1977, with RCP members providing its central core of strength. There has subsequently been internal problems leading to another split but this will not be considered herein as it falls outside the time period under examination.

## A. The Revolutionary Communist Party in Hawaii

The Honolulu chapter of RCP was formed in October 1975, bringing together a number of political activists indigenous to Hawaii and some members of Revolutionary Union who had recently moved there (*Revolution*, March 15, 1976; February, 1977; March, 1978; Gene Parker, 1979). It was a secret organization operating according to principles of democratic centralism. To my knowledge, Gene Parker was the only public member in Hawaii during the period that I am analyzing. For this reason, I shall in this paper refer to persons close to the RCP rather than RCP members. This account of developments in Hawaii relies on discussions with friends of the RCP who prefer not to be directly cited as well as upon the sources cited above. The RCP on the mainland devoted most of its activities to work–place organizing eschewing, for the most part, community organizing. The Hawaii chapter agreed with the mainland organization as to relevant theoretical principles. However, they felt that upon close analysis, Hawaii formed a different type of situation that called for a different strategy of party building.

They thought that some of the potentially most progressive struggles currently going on in Hawaii were community struggles over the issues of land and housing—particularly struggles of various community groups to resist eviction. In each case the community groups had a working–class base even if the issues were not defined in terms of relations of production. They believed that the spontaneous dynamism of these community–based struggles would be dissipated into nothingness if they were allowed to remain as simply struggles of tenants, aided by outside supporters, for the amelioration of their problems through limited reforms. However, there was a real potential for party building if, instead, these struggles were to be carried on as united class–based movements bringing together all who have common cause in a united struggle against their common class enemies—the capitalist class. The RCP thus made an important distinction between those who are supporters of someone else's struggles and those that are allies united in a common struggle.

The RCP played a major role in building the "Stop All Evictions Coalition," which was able to attract as many as 1,500 demonstrators to one of its demonstrations. Persons close to the RCP affiliated themselves with a large number of community struggles. In the Fall of 1976 the leadership of the RCP decided to concentrate all of the Party's resources upon a single struggle—Waiahole–Waikane. There were three basic reasons for the decision: Waiahole-Waikane was beginning to move to "center stage" in the public consciousness; it appeared that it would be a long–term struggle; and it seemed that there might be a chance to win significant concessions. Thus participation in this struggle would provide RCP with a unique opportunity for political education and for party building.

## B. The Battle over Waiahole-Waikane[10]

The struggle over Waiahole–Waikane can be divided into four phases. These will be discussed in turn after a brief presentation of the socio–historical context. Waiahole and Waikane are two well watered valleys located on Oahu's windward side. Mountains separate them only at their heads so, to a certain extent, they comprise a common area. Over time, Lincoln McCandless (a member of the territorial legislature) used questionable practices to acquire a large portion of the habitable land in the valleys. Sprinkled among his holdings were a number of small, individually owned plots of land. His holdings were passed on to his children who took on the collective legal identity of the McCandless Heirs. Continued immigration to Hawaii combined with an expanded tourist industry placed intense pressure upon existing land utilization patterns in the state. Some marginal lands were taken out of sugar and pineapple production, but the greatest source of land for residential and tourist development was that which had been used to produce agricultural goods for the home market. The McCandless Heirs saw the potential for profitable development of Waiahole–Waikane and phased out long–term leases between 1956 and 1959. Thereafter, all tenants held month–to–month leases which enabled evictions after a twenty-eight day notice.

Four types of people lived in Waiahole and Waikane at the beginning of 1974: tenants who worked in the city, lived in the valleys and grew produce for their own use and/or sale; tenants who lived in the valleys and farmed commercially; tenants who lived elsewhere but leased valley land for commercial agriculture; and small landowners who generally worked in the city and used their land to grow some produce (Anderson, 1974). The residents were ethnically mixed. Almost half (46%) were pure or part–Hawaiian; 20% were Japanese–Americans; 17% were Filipino-American; 12% were haole; and five percent fell into other categories. Most persons tended to be long–term residents of the valleys. Their educational and income levels tended to be lower than those characterizing Oahu as a whole.

*Phase One.*   The first phase of the struggle was that of community mobilization. The McCandless Heirs filed a letter of intent with the State on December 1, 1973, in which they stated their intention to reclassify 1,337 acres of agricultural land in Waiahole and Waikane (752 acres as urban and 585 acres as rural). An urban classification would allow small lot residential development. Development on one acre lots was legally possible for land classified as rural. This letter was not immediately made public, but windward residents were sensitized to the possibility of such development. Kahaluu (a neighborhing valley) and Kuilima had recently experienced development activities, and windward residents had already organized themselves to oppose further development on that side of Oahu.

Outsiders in expensive cars were observed driving the dirt roads of Waiahole and Waikane in January and February 1974. This created fears and speculation regarding immanent development, which were intensified in February and March when Robert Anderson of the University of Hawaii conducted a survey of valley residents for development planners under the guise of doing objective scholarly research. Bob Nakata, director of the Key Project in Kahaluu, had as a member of the Windward Regional Council, already participated, in a Vista supported survey of agriculture in Waiahole–Waikane as part of a long–term plan for resisting further development on the windward side. Nakata had a background of community organizing and was the nephew of Sei Serikaku, one of the larger farmers in Waiahole. Nakata was made aware of events, went to Honolulu, discovered the letter of intent, and began meeting with groups of Waiahole–Waikane farmers in January and February 1974. At a very early point he brought to these meetings representatives of Life of the Land (an organization of political activists concerned with ecology among other things) and ''Tom Peters'' (a part–Hawaiian community organizer, then associated with the Ethnic Studies Program at the University of Hawaii, who had been involved in previous windward community struggles).[11] Shortly thereafter, Peters left for a trip to the Peoples Republic of China and did not play an active role until after his return in July or August.

A general meeting of Waiahole–Waikane residents was held on April 8, the Waiahole–Waikane Community Association (WWCA) was formed, a Steering Committee was elected on April 24, and Bobby Fernandez was elected president on May 6. The McCandless Heirs filed a revised rezoning request on June 30, 1974, which along with subsequent revisions described three five–year development stages that would culminate in some 6,700 housing units and over 20,000 residents. The WWCA was determined to prevent Waiahole–Waikane from being transformed into another urban Honolulu neighborhood.

This period of community mobilization was not without problems. People with diverse economic interests had to be brought together in common cause.

Race has high saliency in Hawaii and racial/ethnic differences caused some tensions that had to be overcome. Racial/ethnic and economic lines of cleavage tended to reinforce each other as most of the larger and more affluent farmers were Japanese–Americans. These cleavages were further reinforced when the larger landowners and more affluent farmers were elected to positions where they might disproportionately influence decision making. These tensions were never fully overcome, but the WWCA had a period of time to develop patterns of good working relations, build its organization, and plan a defense of the valleys without the added tensions that would have been created by an immediate crisis confrontation. Thus the WWCA had the time it required to develop in the valley residents a sense of common threat, of communal interests, of solidarity, and of mutual trust.

*Phase Two.*    The second phase began with the State Land Use Commission hearings to consider McCandless Heirs' request for land reclassification. The hearings were held on October 24, 1974, after having been postponed from October 10. The WWCA selected a strategy that emphasized environmental and life style issues. Attempts were made to elicit public support by noting that development would remove two productive valleys from agriculture increasing Hawaii's dependence upon imported food, lead to worse contamination of Kaneohe Bay, cause increased congestion on already overcrowded highways, destroy one of the few remaining natural areas on Oahu, contribute to increased air pollution, and destroy a meaningful and healthy life style for a number of persons.

This strategy was successful as far as it went. Governor George Ariyoshi expressed his desire to keep the valleys in diversified agriculture and Mayor Frank Fasi indicated his opposition to development. Twenty thousand people, including Senator Daniel Inouye, signed an anti–development petition that was presented at the hearings attended by more than 800 WWCA members and supporters who held up signs, sang, and chanted their opposition to development. On December 20, 1974, the State Land Use Commission voted seven to zero, with two abstentions, to deny the rezoning request. The McCandless Heirs had apparently anticipated this outcome. They submitted a revised proposal directly to the WWCA on October 29 in which they offered to allow an increased amount of land to remain in agriculture (mostly land not well suited for agricultural purposes), in exchange for the WWCA agreeing to cease its opposition to development. The WWCA rejected the proposal on November 4.

This victory for the WWCA did not bring the matter to a close, although things remained quiet for several months. On December 21, 1974, the McCandless Heirs assigned full ownership rights to one of their members, Mrs. Loy McCandless Marks, in exchange for some land on leeward Oahu. Nothing further happened until May 1, 1975, when all tenants received a letter from Mrs. Marks informing them that she was now the sole owner, that leases would have to be renegotiated effective June 1, and that a survey indicated the need to increase rents in accordance with increased land value and rising property taxes. On May 5, the WWCA formed a negotiating committee to handle all of the tenants' leases and on May 19, Attorney Michael Hare was given their power of attorney. It should be noted at this point that Michael Hare was a young attorney of working–class origins with a history of radical activism in Hawaii. He committed himself to the Waiahole-Waikane struggle without reservation. He continued his participation in the struggle even when it cost him his position with a prestigious law firm.

It was announced on May 22 that controversial developer Joe Pao had purchased the 2,868 acres owned by Mrs. Marks in Waiahole and Waikane. This sale was not registered and no details were released at the time. It later became clear that only a small portion of Waikane was purchased outright—the portion scheduled for development in the first five–year phase of the development plan described above. The purchase of the remainder of Waikane was contingent upon rezoning. A deposit was made and an option to buy was taken on Waiahole land. It had to be exercised prior to November 1, 1977, or the deposit would be lost. Its exercise was, presumably, dependent upon favorable reclassification. Pao stated that he would announce a new plan to keep agriculture in the valleys as soon as his request to reclassify some land urban was granted. He further stated that if his reclassification request was denied he would develop the land in large lot (two acres) residential units. On June 2 the Waikane tenants received letters from Mrs. Marks cancelling their leases effective June 1 and informing them that their new landlord, the Pao Investment Company, would contact them shortly regarding their future tenancy. On June 3 the Waiahole tenants received letters from Mrs. Marks raising their rents effective July 1 by amounts ranging from 50 to 745 percent.

The Waiahole tenants objected to the magnitude of the increases, arguing that much of the increase in land value was a result of their own efforts. In many cases they had cleared the land, built the roads, developed the water supply, constructed the sewage system, and built their own homes. Some even paid their own taxes in addition to paying rent. On July 1, 92 out of 120 lessees presented Mrs. Marks with a common check for their rent at the old rates. When this was refused they set up a trust fund under the control of their attorney, Michael Hare, into which they deposited amounts of money equal to rental at the old rates.

It was announced on June 24 that Pao had submitted a request to the City Department of Land Utilization for a subdivision of property lines to enable the construction of residential housing on two acre lots in Waikane. Pao announced on July 16 the formation of Windward Partners, and that they had arranged for adequate bank financing to develop Waiahole–Waikane. Windward Partners included both labor leaders and politicians as well as professional developers. This announcement was followed by a period of intensified maneuvering for position during which both sides put out massive amounts of propaganda in the attempt to elicit public support. Mrs. Marks attempted to destroy the unity of the Waiahole tenants by offering new one–year leases (cancellable with sixty days notice) at rents below those previously set, but above the former rates. The opportunity to farm with some degree of security led some Waiahole tenants to sign the leases that she offered, although most tenants refused.

This was followed by a period of jockeying over rents, in which Windward Partners accepted August rents from the Waikane tenants and Mrs. Marks accepted back payments of Waiahole July rents but refused checks for August. Finally in August, all Waiahole tenants who had not signed new leases received eviction notices; on August 14, Joe Pao filed an official request with the City Department of Land Utilization to develop 130 large house lots in Waikane; and Waikane tenants were given notice of eviction effective of September 30 with the end of their current leases. The WWCA announced that neither the Waiahole nor the Waikane tenants had any intention of leaving. They would remain and the valleys would remain in agriculture.

The WWCA continued to pursue the same basic strategy but with a stepped up rate of activities. There were marches, demonstrations, and picketing. A rally was held at the Waiahole elementary school on September 8, which included a potluck lunch, speeches and entertainment. The key feature was hiking and jeep tours of the valley, which were repeated on numerous occasions over the next several months. These tours were supplemented by a benefit concert held at the bandshell in Waikiki in January 1976, which presented an exhibit of the sights, sounds and feel of country living to a crowd attracted by some of the biggest names in Hawaiian folk and popular music. These tactics again appeared to be effective when on January 24, the City Department of Land Utilization denied Pao's request for large lot development of Waikane. He submitted a revised request, which was also rejected in early March. A new compromise proposal was submitted to, and rejected by, the WWCA. However, these victories again proved elusive. On April 22, 1976, Judge Arthur S. K. Fong granted a final order to Mrs. Marks to repossess the land of nine Waikane residents, and on May 5 he ordered the eviction of 79 Waiahole tenants.

*Transition between Phases.* These events led into a transition between phases two and three. The membership of the WWCA was beginning to wonder exactly what it would take to end the struggle. They organized, educated the public, gained support, won what appeared to be important victories, and yet still appeared on the verge of defeat with the setting of October 1, 1976, as the eviction date for Waiahole tenants. It seemed that everything was stacked in favor of the developer and the landlord. They had enough resources so that they could afford to have endless patience. If a particular proposal was rejected by one agency a revised version could be resubmitted, to be followed by another and another, until one finally was accepted. At the very worst, the developer and landlord might have to wait until the composition of the agencies was altered, partially through their own efforts. Recalcitrant members could be replaced by others who would be more cooperative. In other words, every Waiahole–Waikane victory could prove to be nothing more than a brief setback for the developer and the landlord while a single developer victory would spell the end for Waiahole-Waikane. Thus it is not surprising that a portion of the WWCA membership was becoming increasingly desperate, increasingly strident and increasingly attracted toward confrontation tactics.

It is at this point in the struggle that the Revolutionary Communist Party (RCP) dramatically increased its level of involvement. Some people close to the RCP, including Tom Peters, had been involved in the Waiahole–Waikane struggle from close to its inception, and they were able to convince the remainder of the RCP leadership that this was a struggle they should support because of both the importance of the struggle and the opportunity that it would provide for party building. Consequently, the RCP leadership decided in the early Fall of 1976 to make the Waiahole–Waikane fight their number one priority. They attempted to build a strong base of support for the WWCA in the community at the same time as they sought to present a class analysis to the membership of the WWCA. They were somewhat successful in both objectives. A number of support groups were developed among students, workers, GI's, the unemployed, and welfare recipients. Persons close to the RCP were at the core of each of the support groups. The presentation of the RCP line of analysis helped to stimulate the formation of a group within the WWCA which called itself "Up In Arms." This group was primarily made up of smaller landowners and tenants who were urban blue–collar workers. They accepted a class analysis and urged a strategy that would involve the seeking of allies from other groups on a class basis and that would utilize more militant confrontation tactics.

The debate within the WWCA raged during late summer and early fall of 1976, culminating in the election of the majority of the WWCA steering committee from the ranks of "Up In Arms." This change in leadership was reflected in the content of the September 25, 1976 rally at the Waiahole Waikane school. The high-light of this rally was not a tour of the valley but a mock eviction drill. After a series of speeches a siren signalled an alert and indicated the section of land "invaded" by the police. A crowd of between 600 and 1,000 people rushed to the threatened house, formed several rows of arm–linked people, and then repulsed four simulated police attacks. This was reported in the newspapers and over television, informing the entire community that evictions would not come easy.

The WWCA sought a stay of execution of the eviction orders and won a conditional stay. Judge Fong agreed to stay the evictions so that an appeal to the State Supreme Court might be pursued, but he made the stay conditional upon the WWCA turning the rental trust fund over to him and increasing payments into the fund by fifty percent. This was hotly debated within the WWCA with its first group of leaders urging compliance and the "Up In Arms" faction opposing it. Debate was long and acrimonious but the WWCA eventually voted 39 to 36 not to accept those conditions. With this vote a number of the larger landowners and more affluent farmers drifted away from the association, completing the transition to the third phase of the struggle. This vote also ultimately led to the setting of January 3, 1977 as the final eviction date for 79 Waiahole families.

*Phase Three.*   The interim period was marked by continued maneuvering for position. Windward Partners made another compromise proposal that was rejected. The WWCA held several demonstrations, the most noteworthy of which took place in front of police headquarters. Police were reminded of their class, ethnic and kinship ties to Waiahole–Waikane residents and asked not to participate in any evictions. Then on January 2, a tent city was set up in Waiahole. Each of the various support groups occupied one or more tents and erected signs identifying the tent occupants. A large number of additional people came to the valley during the day but returned to their own homes at night. The sheriff came on January 3 to serve writs of possession effective immediately. An observation team equipped with citizen band radios alerted the WWCA to the fact that he was en route so he was greeted by an arm–linked crowd of several hundred persons blocking the only road into the valley. The writs were served, accepted and burned. The sheriff left, and nothing more happened that day.

By early afternoon on Tuesday, January 4, the force at tent city had become considerably reduced. Many people had to leave to go to their jobs, meet other obligations, or simply became bored. That night, around 11:00 p.m., another alert was sounded. A large amount of police activity led the observation team to conclude that a police eviction team was en route. Within minutes a half–mile stretch of Kamehameha Highway was blockaded on either side of Waiahole. Traffic on the windward side was brought to a total stop for more than an hour. The blockade was not lifted until trusted police sources gave their word that eviction teams would not come that night. These two blockades were extremely important. Governor Ariyoshi and his aides became convinced that evictions could not take place without a major confrontation at the very least, and that there was a real possibility, if not a probability, the violence would erupt. They wished to avoid this. The Governor persuaded Mrs. Marks to postpone any further eviction attempts until March 1 to give him an opportunity to work out a peaceful solution.

The WWCA intensified its efforts to build public support during this intermission. Demonstrations and marches were held. Strong public support was exhibited on February 9 and 10 when the State Land Use Commission held hearings on the request by Windward Partners to have a portion of Waikane reclassified urban. Another benefit concert was held—this time at Waiahole—attracting a crowd of 6,000 persons and creating congested conditions that tied up traffic on the windward side for hours. Then finally on February 26, Governor George Ariyoshi made an announcement that led many WWCA members and supporters to call him the "six million dollar man." He announced that the State would purchase 600 acres of Waiahole from Mrs. Marks for $6,000,000, the land to be developed along a "village agriculture" concept. All present valley residents were promised long–term leases at low rentals. However, all of this would only be possible if Windward Partners chose not to exercise its option to purchase Waiahole.

On April 18, 1977, Joe Pao died. In August, the State Land Use Commission rejected Windward Partners' request to have Waikane reclassified urban. Windward Partners allowed the November 1 deadline to pass without exercising its option, and the State carried out its agreement to purchase the land from Mrs. Marks. It appeared once again that the WWCA had won, but the victory was not total. Nine Waikane families still faced a threat of eviction, although large–scale development of their valley now seemed to be ruled out. The State purchase of Waiahole did not include the land makai (on the oceanside) of Kamehameha Highway, and about 12 families lived there. In addition, the Governor's commitments regarding future State actions were not overly specific. Much still remained to be nailed down. Nevertheless, the third phase of the struggle appeared to have ended with a significant victory for the WWCA.

*Phase Four.* The fourth phase of the struggle has been marked by the WWCA's attempt to expand and consolidate its victory. It has not been entirely successful in this regard. The apparent victory had the ironic effect of contributing to the withering away of the WWCA's support base. Powerful financial forces in the community became concerned both over Windward Partners' economic well being and over the precedent that had been set. They exerted pressure to insure that Windward Partners did not completely lose its investment. Windward Partners applied for permission to develop a 144 lot subdivision on 391 of the 537 acres that it owned at the entrance to Waikane. This proposal was opposed by both the WWCA and the Board of Water Supply, who suggested that difficulties would result from an absence of sewage treatment facilities and a ban against ground disposal. Windward Partners was anxious to salvage something from its investment, the WWCA was concerned over the possible eviction of the Waikane tenants, and it was not overly confident regarding its ability to entirely block development in Waikane. Consequently a bargain was struck. The WWCA agreed to withdraw all opposition to Windward Partners' scaled down plan to develop 31 lots in a 90 acre agricultural subdivision of Waikane if in exchange all Waikane tenants facing eviction were granted land that would enable them to remain.

Armed with this agreement, Windward Partners was able to gain approval from the City's Land Utilization Department and the City Council. They were later able, over WWCA opposition, to gain approval of a plan for a five lot (each lot one acre in size) subdivision in Waikane Valley on the ocean side of Kamehameha Highway. Thus Windward Partners has been able to develop for sale a total of 31 lots in Waikane Valley, but all threatened tenants received land and are able to remain permanently. To this date, the State of Hawaii has not announced its plans for Waiahole. It appears to have retreated a bit from earlier assurances that all present residents would receive long–term leases at low rental rates, but it remains committed to allowing them to remain. The struggle continues with the WWCA attempting to insure that the valley will remain in agriculture and that all current residents will be issued long–term leases at fair (low) rentals. Even though we have not seen the final chapter, I believe that we may still use this struggle to analyze the role played by a vanguard party organization, the RCP, in a social movement in an advanced capitalist society.

## C. Contributions of RCP to the Waiahole–Waikane Struggle

Perhaps the most important if one of the less obvious contributions that RCP made to the WWCA in the conduct of its struggle was political education. Some members of the WWCA had been initially uncomfortable when Tom Peters and others with a radical activist reputation showed up at one of their early meetings. Their initial resistance was overcome partly because Peters was part–Hawaiian, born and raised in Windward Oahu, and because he had been active in Windward community causes. He was also accepted, in part, because he was introduced and supported by Bob Nakata. Nakata was the lay director of the Methodist sponsored Key Project in neighboring Kahaluu, a relative of a Waiahole farmer, a member of the Windward Regional Council, and was known and respected by many WWCA members. He argued that the WWCA faced a long hard fight and that the expertise of experienced community organizers like Tom Peters was essential to any chance of success.

Nakata and Peters became non–voting members of the WWCA Steering Committee. Peters contributed to discussions of strategy and tactics during which he consistently presented a class analysis relating the present conflict to other arenas of class struggle. When Michael Hare became WWCA attorney he also contributed to the presentation of a class analysis. Bob Nakata had been raised in a radical family (his father had been close to the Communist Party), and he was generally receptive to a class analysis of the situation and to the militant tactics it logically implied. Thus the more experienced activists coming to the aid of the WWCA were all inclined to think in class terms, and all believed that the cause would be lost unless a militant, mass movement could be generated on behalf of Waiahole–Waikane.

It is perhaps important at this point to illustrate concretely what a class analysis of Waiahole–Waikane would include. The major arena of contention had to do with the desire of the landlord to evict tenants from her land, so that this land could be turned into a housing development. A proper class analysis would begin by noting that the landlord did, in fact, have legal title to the land. It might be true, but it was certainly irrelevant, that Lincoln McCandless originally acquired the land by use of questionable means. His title was recognized as valid. The landlord owned the land and had the right to expect a fair return from it.

It could easily be demonstrated that the landlord was earning far less from the land by renting it to tenants than she could have earned through other uses. Furthermore, the tenants could not afford to meet any increase in rent that would enable the landlord to make the level of profits that were available through the sale of the land and reinvestment of the proceeds in other ways. The landlord had a legal right to sell her land and, under the logic of capitalism, she almost had a moral obligation to increase her rate of return. Thus any movement of the tenants to prevent eviction was forced to challenge the right of the legal owner to use her private property in a manner to maximize return on investment, and which was consistent with the public good. The building of new homes had always been viewed as being consistent with the public good. Thus the movement was required to struggle to alter the definition of the rights of private property. It is only a short step from this point to the raising of questions about the very existence of private property.

The tenants in Waiahole–Waikane and other areas facing eviction could then be brought to recognize the existence of the alliance between landlords, finance capital, and state agencies in support of profit maximization even when it caused great disruption of life style and suffering to working–class and farming communities. The long–run political implications could then be simply alluded to, while short–term implications were derived regarding the need for a class conscious, united mass movement to stop all evictions beginning with Waiahole–Waikane. Past victories of the WWCA and other peoples' movements could then be alluded to as evidence of the fact that united (class) action could ultimately overwhelm the opposition and force state agencies to act on behalf of the people's needs, although in the long run, taking over the state was preferable to coercing its agencies.

The larger farmers and landowners who formed the early leadership of the WWCA, understandably, were not receptive to this type of class analysis or to the militant tactics which it logically implied. But gradually the mounting number of apparent victories that disappeared produced a greater degree of receptivity among many of the WWCA members—especially among many of the urban workers. It is this latter group that formed the core of Up In Arms. The coincidence in timing between the rise of Up in Arms to a leadership position and the increased involvement of the RCP in Waiahole–Waikane was not accidental. Each of these developments mutually contributed to the other.

RCP played an increased role in the discussion of strategy and tactics after the accession of Up in Arms to dominance. However, after an initial period of confusion on this issue, they always played this role as non–voting participants in discussions. All freely participated in the debate, but decisions were finally made by Waiahole–Waikane residents. The new partnership jointly was responsible for the change in tactics between Phases Two and Three. There is no question that without this shift in tactics the WWCA would have lost and all tenants would have been evicted. All the sympathy with their plight, concern for the environment, and desire to have land retained in agriculture could not have countered the fact that Marks and Pao were acting well within their rights and in accordance with recent precedent. Eviction orders would ultimately have been forthcoming, and law–abiding tenants would have obeyed the orders of the sheriff. Up In Arms *may* have been formed and this line of resistance chosen even without the political education process unstintingly carried out by Peters and others close to the RCP, but there is no reason to believe that this is the case. I do not wish to imply that tenants passively accepted the political line that was being handed out to them. Quite to the contrary. Their acceptance of a class analysis of their situation was a creative act on their part and it happened precisely because the events that they were experiencing confirmed in their minds the truth of the analysis.

The acceptance of a class analysis and the selection of militant confrontation tactics would not have been sufficient to achieve victory without a broad-based support structure bringing into the movement large numbers of persons from outside the valleys. The change to more militant tactics alienated some of the middle–class supporters that had aided the movement in Phase One. The RCP worked to replace them with a larger number of allies who believed that they shared a common cause, that is, their own community or occupational struggle and the WWCA struggle to retain the land and homes of its members were both part of the same larger cause. The RCP continually provided the type of class analysis that would help individuals to develop the perception that they all presently suffered because of their class position within a capitalist society. The RCP helped to establish numerous support organizations among a wide range of constituencies. A college organization, Students United For Land and Housing, was formed at the University of Hawaii with members of the Revolutionary Student Brigade at its core. Youth United was formed for students in the high schools and junior high schools. Similar groups were formed among pineapple cannery workers, hotel and service workers, transportation workers, unemployed workers, servicemen, welfare mothers, and so on. In each case, one or more persons close to the RCP were found at the core of these organizations helping to build and direct them—and always to provide a class analysis of the current situation.

It may be argued that many of these organizations were largely paper organizations in that they had few formal members. This charge has a degree of validity. But the very organizational structure lent both respectability and strength to the overall movement. The constant citing of numerous groups supporting Waiahole–Waikane gave an impression of strength, which may have helped in their relation to outside forces. Similarly, the existence of the organizations, no matter how small in formal membership, provided a base for recruitment among the various constituencies for which they were named. The ability to pass out to cannery workers a leaflet written by cannery workers for cannery workers relating their situation to that of the Waiahole–Waikane tenants is more likely to get a cannery worker to participate in a march or a demonstration than is an identical leaflet asking for aid written by a Waiahole resident. Furthermore, the leaflet is more likely to be effective than one signed on behalf of the RCP.

The vanguard structure of the RCP creates a cadre willing to dedicate itself to an extent that can never be matched by those lacking a similar degree of ideological commitment. Its democratic centralist structure allows for a highly effective coordination of activities, and its secrecy prevents red–baiting from being effective. It is not possible for opponents to disparage a program or analysis by simply stating that its proponent is a member of the Revolutionary Communist Party if the proponent is not publicly so identified. Thus the opposition is forced to come to grips with the program or analysis itself. One should not confuse keeping secret the relationship between the RCP and individual organizer–activists with manipulation and lack of democracy. It is only the membership of a revolutionary party and its list of close associates that is kept secret, not its analysis of the situation. At all times, persons close to the RCP would relate the particular problems under discussion to their roots in the capitalist system and would disinguish between the achievement of reformist objectives through militant struggle and the ultimate necessity for a socialist transformation to solve the basic problem. They were open about their beliefs and objectives and people were free to accept or reject. Rather than being manipulative or undemocratic, keeping party affiliations secret may be the only way that a revolutionary organization can gain an open forum for its ideas.

The RCP accomplished two things in helping to build this support structure. They developed a mass of persons who would turn out on behalf of the Waiahole–Waikane cause when needed and, in so doing, they also linked the WWCA membership into other class–oriented struggles. The RCP was directly or indirectly responsible for bringing out a large portion of the people who participated in marches and demonstrations, who walked the picket lines, were part of tent city, blockaded the highway, and who ultimately helped bring about the final victory. But they were also directly or indirectly responsible for the presence of WWCA members—both as individuals and as official representatives of the WWCA—on unemployed workers picket lines, participating in the occupation of the Aloha Hotel in Chinatown to prevent the eviction of elderly and poor residents, and at numerous other demonstrations on behalf of the struggles of their allies.

Thus it can be said that the RCP helped to build a sense of class consciousness and a willingness to actively participate in the class struggle among significant elements within the WWCA and significant elements in the various support organizations. Speeches by tenants, workers, and housewives increasingly incorporated a class analysis, even if in very crude terms, as the struggle wore on. For at least a while, a broad–based class movement was being forged in Hawaii that could bring together various groups experiencing their own disparate problems, help them to interpret these common elements in class terms, and form an alliance of people ready to engage in united struggle to solve their shared problems. For this, I give the primary credit to the Revolutionary Communist Party, although their task was made easier by the involvement in the struggle of radical activists such as Bob Nakata and Michael Hare, support given by some older radicals in Hawaii, and the presence in Waiahole–Waikane of the community equivalent of advanced workers.

This group of more politically sophisticated young people was comprised of persons who were active in earlier community struggles and who had profited by the experience so gained—especially in Kalama Valley (Kent, n.d.). Kalama Valley was a valley populated by tenants engaged in agricultural pursuits that were threatened by eviction in the early 1970's so that the land could be used for a housing development. A resistance movement was formed and the valley occupied in a manner similar to the setting up of the tent city in Waiahole. A campaign of red–baiting (which involved the use of racial/ethnic stereotypes) was waged against the support movement. It had an effect. The night before the eviction was to take place the supporters voted to expel haoles (caucasians) and radicals from the valley. The eviction then proceeded and there was little effective resistance. The lesson was not lost upon the Waiahole–Waikane tenants— especially those who had been involved in Kalama. Neither race–hatred nor red–baiting was going to be allowed to destroy the Waiahole–Waikane struggle. Both came to be interpreted as weapons cynically used by capital to weaken its opposition.

## IV. THEORETICAL IMPLICATIONS

It has been demonstrated that the Revolutionary Communist Party contributed greatly to the success of the Waihole–Waikane struggle, but two questions still remain unanswered. While it seems evident that the WWCA would have failed without some form of organized support movement, we have not determined whether any organization other than a vanguard party could have accomplished the same results, nor have we determined whether the Revolutionary Communist Party through its actions in this struggle furthered its ultimate objective of bringing about a socialist transformation. The answer to these two questions may shed some light on the controversy over the role of vanguard parties in the United States and in advanced capitalist societies. Let us consider these questions one at a time.

We have argued that the democratic centralism of the Party facilitated effective coordination of activities among diverse groups. We have also argued that Party secrecy contributed to the ability of the RCP to generate increased numbers of active participants in the Waihole–Waikane defense movement as well as to help gain a more receptive hearing for the class analysis that it presented. Whether it also contributed to the security of the party depends upon the degree of state repression existing in Hawaii and the United States at the time of the struggle. We have no direct evidence on this point, although public agencies closely observed participants in the struggle. The possibility of future repression of identified members of the RCP is, I fear, all too real.

A vanguard party because of its very nature as a revolutionary party is made up of committed revolutionaries. They are people who have a wholehearted dedication to bringing about a socialist transformation, willing to take risks and to work unstintingly for their cause. It took this type of commitment to accomplish what was accomplished at Waiahole–Waikane. It is conceivable that it may have also been found among other than professional revolutionaries, but no good examples come readily to mind. It is also conceivable that the same kind of dedication may be found among those radicals who are ideologically opposed to vanguard parties (that is, the followers of C.L.R. James), but few were in evidence in Hawaii at this time and, in fact, they are a relatively rare breed anywhere. It is clear that this type of dedication would not have been forthcoming from "Alinsky-type" radical activists simply because those individuals, while highly dedicated, only come into a movement when they are well paid, and the WWCA could never have afforded them.

Thus it is conceivable, but not demonstrated, that some organization of radical activists other than the RCP might have accomplished what the RCP did at Waiahole–Waikane. It is even conceivable that a non–vanguardist mass socialist organization such as that currently being built in Hawaii around *Modern Times* might have been able to create a similar support structure that could have helped win the victory at Waiahole–Waikane, but I doubt very much if it could have developed the same kind of widespread, class–conscious movement in the community as a whole as that built by the RCP. At any rate, regardless of the logical possibilities, the fact remains that the RCP was the only organization currently existing in Hawaii that had even the remotest chance of accomplishing what they accomplished.

The second question is more difficult to answer. Winning a land struggle is not bringing about a socialist transformation. The RCP helped to develop a degree of class consciousness among the membership of the WWCA and among many workers and students who became associated with one or another of the various support organizations. Yet there is no socialist revolution in Hawaii in the immediate offing nor is there any reason to believe that the socialist transformation of America is likely to begin in Hawaii. Nevertheless, there are a number of important things that were accomplished. A large number of people came to question the sanctity of private property. They also had the experience of successful struggle against vested interests. The mystique of property and wealth was shattered. A large number of people had the experience of challenging legal authority and winning. Laws were violated, illegal actions were taken, and victory resulted. People came to realize that the law was not sacred and that mass united action, even that which involves illegal activities, can bring about desired results. Perhaps the greatest set of accomplishments of the RCP was the contribution it made to this demystification process, to the political education of large numbers of workers, to the building of class consciousness, and to the development of a legacy of struggle among the workers of Hawaii. No socialist revolution is immediately in the offing but a foundation has been laid. It may be easier to build similar movements in the future, and that may have a cumulative impact. These are not small accomplishments.

The third question is even more difficult to answer. It is very difficult to generalize from a single case study. The RCP helped the WWCA both to win its battle and create a climate of opinion that is more receptive to a socialist movement than it would have been without the active involvement of the RCP. However, the RCP has not demonstrated that it can build upon these accomplishments and sustain developments over time. It has not yet been demonstrated that the class unity displayed in the support movement can be sustained without the Waiahole–Waikane struggle as a central unifying focus. Causes and struggles may be needed to maintain unity, and they cannot be manufactured. They must develop out of natural situations to be meaningful, and they simply may not arise when needed. The real test of a vanguard organization is its ability to keep the struggle alive in the absence of an overt conflict. Thus one cannot draw any solid conclusions with regard to the final and most important problem—the role of the vanguard party in advanced capitalist societies. Still I would argue that the very significant accomplishments of the RCP in the struggle under examination suggest that we should not be too hasty in writing off the vanguard party. It may yet prove to be the most effective form of organization for the United States and for all advanced capitalist societies—especially as we enter into an era of conservatism during which spontaneous action may become increasingly rare; and the primary task of socialists may be simply keeping alive a revolutionary socialist tradition.

I would like to add one final note as I do not wish my argument to be misunderstood. I am arguing against those persons who have prematurely concluded that the vanguard party is an inappropriate structure for the United States and for all advanced capitalist societies. However, I do not claim to have demonstrated the obverse—that the vanguard party is the only appropriate structure. I simply ask that we keep this as an open question to be decided in the course of time and struggle. Nor am I arguing that the Revolutionary Communist Party is *the vanguard party* to lead the socialist transformation. I have analyzed something they did that I consider to be very important, but I share with Mandel the belief that a candidate vanguard party must earn that status by winning over the working class to its leadership. No candidate vanguard party has yet accomplished this. The Revolutionary Communist Party, one of the other self–proclaimed vanguard parties, or no such party currently in existence, may win such a designation in the future. In the end, it is the workers who will decide which, if any, vanguard will lead the socialist transformation.

# ACKNOWLEDGMENTS

This paper is the product of research supported by Grant Number 5R01MH2847902S1 from the Center for the Study of Metropolitan Problems, National Institute of Mental Health, and a Fellowship from the National Endowment for the Humanities for which I am truly grateful. I am also indebted to the Waiahole–Waikane Community Association, many of its members and its allies, for the cooperation that I received. I am also indebted to Martin Murray and Mark Selden for the critical comments that they provided to an earlier version of the first section of this paper. I have a very great debt to Steven Smith for the intellectual stimulation that he provided during our discussions and collaborations on a never completed but more comprehensive theoretical treatment of the vanguard party.

# NOTES

1. The three statements quoted below indicate that Lenin later described *What Is to Be Done?* as an extreme statement designed to meet the problems of a particular set of historical circumstances and not a prescription for all times and all places. Boyte and Ackerman (1973) and Healey (Weiner, 1977) argue that Lenin acknowledged this even within the document itself—particularly when he stated that its prescriptions would not apply to Germany where parties, unions, and free elections all existed.

"I shall now go over to the disputed passages of my pamphlet, *What Is to Be Done?*, which gave rise to so much discussion here. . . . It is obvious that here an episode in the struggle against 'economism' has been confused with a discussion of the principles of a major theoretical question. . . . We all know that the 'economists' have gone to one extreme. To straighten matters out somebody had to pull in the opposite direction—and that is what I have done . . . '' (Lenin, 1903:490–491).

"The basic mistake by those who now criticize *What Is to Be Done?* is to treat the pamphlet apart from its connection with the concrete historical situation of a definite, and now long past period in the development of our Party." (Lenin, 1907:101).

"*What Is to Be Done?* is a controversial correction of Economist distortions and it would be wrong to regard the pamphlet in any other light." (Lenin, 1907:1108).

2. Glaberman (1974:29–30) quotes James as follows:

"The development of the antagonistic elements *in* the labor movement is clear. Constantly higher stages, sharper conflicts of development between it as object and as consciousness. *Increasingly violent profound attempts by the masses to break through this.* . . . It is obvious that the conflict of the proletariat is between itself as object and itself as consciousness, its party. . . . The solution of the conflict is the fundamental abolition of this division. . . . The party as we have known it must disappear. It will disappear as the state is disappearing. The whole laboring population becomes the state. *That is the disappearance of the state.* It can have no other meaning. It withers away by *expanding* to such a degree that it is transformed into its opposite. And the party does the same. The state withers away and the party withers away. But for the proletariat the most important, the primary is the withering away of the party. For if the party does not wither away, the state never will." (emphasis added by Glaberman)

"One might raise a question as to the timing involved in James' analysis. If the state and the party wither away in parallel processes, and the withering away of the state is expected to take place after the working class has seized power, can the party be expected to wither away at any earlier time?"

3. "Every provisional political set up following a revolution requires a dictatorship and an energetic dictatorship at that. From the very beginning we blamed Camphausen for not having acted in a dictatorial manner, for not having immediately smashed up and removed the remains of the old

institutions. While thus Herr Camphausen indulged in constitutional dreaming, the defeated party strengthened its positions within the bureaucracy and in the army, and occasionally even risked an open fight'' (Marx, 1848). ''. . . And now as to myself, no credit is due me for discovering the existence of classes in modern society or the struggle between them. Long before me bourgeois historians had described the historical development of this class struggle and the bourgeois economists the economic anatomy of the classes. What I did that was new was to prove: 1) that the *existence of classes* is *only bound up with particular historical phases in the development of production,* 2) that the class struggle necessarily leads to the *dictatorship of the proletariat,* 3) that this dictatorship itself only constitutes the transition to the abolition of all classes and to a *classless society*'' (Marx, 1852, emphasis in the original).

   ''If you look at the last chapter of my *Eighteenth Brumaire,* you will find that I declare that the next attempt of the French Revolution will be no longer, as before, to transfer the bureaucratic military machine from one hand to another, but to smash it, and this is the preliminary condition for every real people's revolution on the Continent. And this is what our heroic Party comrades in Paris are attempting'' (Marx, 1871). ''The Question then arises: what transformation will the state undergo in communistic society? In other words, what social functions will remain in existence there that are analogous to present state functions? This question can only be answered scientifically, and one does not get a flea-hop nearer to the problem by a thousandfold combination of the word people with the word state. Between capitalist society and communist society lies the period of the revolutionary transformation of the one into the other. Corresponding to this is also a political transition period in which the state can be nothing but the *revolutionary dictatorship of the proletariat*'' (Marx, 1875:331, emphasis in the original).

   4. ''If they are defeated only their 'good nature' will be to blame. They should have marched at once on Versailles after first Vinoy and then the reactionary section of the Paris National Guard had themselves retreated. They missed their opportunity because of conscientious scruples. They did not want to *start a civil war,* as if that mischievous abortion Thiers had not already started the civil war with his attempt to disarm Paris! Second mistake: The Central Committee surrendered its power too soon, to make way for the Commune. Again from a too 'honourable'' scrupulosity.' However that may be, the present rising in Paris—even if it be crushed by the wolves, swine, and vile curs of the old society—is the most glorious deed of our Party since the June insurrection in Paris (Marx, 1871, emphasis in the original).

   5. ''The 'people's state' has been thrown in our faces by the anarchists to the point of disgust, although already Marx's book against Proudhon, and later the *Communist Manifesto* directly declare that with the introduction of the socialist order of society the state will dissolve of itself and disappear. As, therefore, the state is only a transitional institution which is used in the struggle in the revolution, to hold down one's adversaries by force, it is pure nonsense to talk of a free people's state. So long as the proletariat still *uses* the state, it does not use it in the interests of freedom but in order to hold down its adversaries, and as soon as it becomes possible to speak of freedom the state as such ceases to exist'' (Engels, 1875:339).

   6. ''We have said that *there could not have been* Social–Democratic consciousness among the workers. It would have to be brought to them from without. The history of all countries shows that the working class, exclusively by its own efforts, is able to develop only trade–union consciousness . . .'' (Lenin, 1902, emphasis in the original).

   7. ''One is struck by the amazingly rapid shift of the movement from the purely economic to the political ground, by the tremendous solidarity and energy displayed by hundreds of thousands of proletarians—and all this, notwithstanding the fact that conscious Social–Democratic influence is lacking or is but slightly evident. The primitive character of the socialist views held by some of the leaders of the movement and the tenacity with which some elements of the working class cling to their naive faith in the tsar enhance rather than lessen the significance of the revolutionary instinct now asserting itself among the proletariat. The political protest of the leading oppressed class and its revolutionary energy break through all obstacles, both external, in the form of police bans, and

internal, in the form of the ideological immaturity and backwardness of some of the leaders" (Lenin, 1905:92–93).

8.   Perhaps it should be noted that this "opening up" of the party had a certain degree of tentativeness to it. Conference delegates continued to use party names and the Party retained its structure of cells. Later events confirmed the wisdom of this procedure. Off duty policemen and others continued even during the "free Period of 1905–1907" to attempt to suppress the Bolsheviks through direct action, but following 1907 the government initiated a wave of terroristic repression.

9.   The following quotations are only three of many that could have been selected to illustrate Lenin's basic argument that threatening circumstances required the elimination of factionalism and the restriction of the rights of opposition but not an end to theoretical debate, and that "better times" might allow for a wider range of acceptable activities within the party:

"This undoubtedly demands of the ruling party of Communists and of leading elements of the proletariat a different attitude to the one we have time and time again displayed over the past year. It is a danger that undoubtedly calls for much greater unity and discipline; it undoubtedly requires that we should pull hard together. Otherwise we shall not cope with the dangers that have fallen to our lot. (Lenin, 1921:186). This is an extreme measure that is being adopted specially, in view of the dangerous situation." (Lenin, 1921b:258).

"Comrades this is no time to have an opposition. Either you are on this side, or on the other, but then your weapon must be a gun. This follows from the objective situation and you must not blame us for it. Comrades, let's not have an opposition just now" (Lenin, 1921c:200).

10.   I think that it would be useful to the reader if I were to describe my relationship to this struggle and my methods of research. I spent the academic year of 1976–77 in Hawaii on research. I became aware of the tenants' struggle against eviction and joined it as an active participant. I did not then intend to study or write about it because my entire past experience and understanding of society convinced me that the tenants would lose, and I felt that we had too many tales of "glorious lost causes." However, the events of January, 1977 led me to reconsider my position. From that point on I was a participant–observer. I also retrospectively analyzed the events of the past several months, researched all relevant documents, consulted journalistic accounts, and conducted a series of formal interviews and informal discussions. These latter two activities were continued on my return to Hawaii for the summers of 1978, 1979 and 1981.

Besides directly participating in the struggle, I also actively interacted with the Revolutionary Student Brigade—the student affiliate of the Revolutionary Communist Party—at the University of Hawaii. I participated in both their open meetings and their more private discussions of strategy and tactics as well as in a broader meeting with representatives from other related groups called to discuss longer range implications for future actions after the community struggle had, for all intents and purposes, been won. I was not a member of the Revolutionary Communist Party and never gave any serious thought to joining it. This is not an account of a dispassionate observer, as I strongly believed in the struggle. At the same time, I am neither a supporter nor an opponent of the Revolutionary Communist Party and have no axe to grind in this regard. This account is written by one who was passionately involved in the struggle as a "foot soldier"—not a leader—but it is, nevertheless, accurate and objective in the sense that it corresponds to historical fact.

This description of events is based upon my own observations; discussions that were less than formal interviews with numerous active participants and observers; formal interviews with several participants, including Michael Hare (1978), Calvin Hoe (1978), Bob Nakata (1978; 1979), Gene Parker (1979), and Tom Peters (1977; 1978); and accounts of events appearing in the *Honolulu Star Bulletin*, and the *Honolulu Advertiser*. Each of the persons who were formally interviewed also were provided with drafts of written accounts and interpretations of events and were asked to evaluate them for accuracy.

11.   Tom Peters is a pseudonym. I was requested not to use his real name because it was feared that revealing his identity and suggesting that he was close to the RCP might cause him to be subjected to future acts of repression.

# REFERENCES

Ackerman, Frank, and Harry Boyte
  1974  "Reply to John Judis and the DeKalb criticism." Socialist Revolution 4
        (Jan.–Mar.):113–123.
Alinsky, Saul D.
  1972  Rules for Radicals: A Pragmatic Primer for Realistic Radicals. New York: Vintage.
Anderson, Robert
  1974  "Report on Waiahole-Waikane." Unpublished.
Boggs, Carl, Bruce Dancis and Michael Rotkin
  1975  "Comments on Taft's 'the Leninist Party'." Socialist Revolution 4 (Jan.):101–106.
Boyte, Harry, and Frank Ackerman
  1973  "Revolution and democracy." Socialist Revolution 3 (July–Aug.): 7–74.
DeKalb, NAM
  1974  "Revolution and democracy: A critique." Socialist Revolution 4 (Jan.–Mar.):99–112.
Engels, Frederick
  1875  "Letter to A. Bebel, March 18–28." Pp. 336–341 in Karl Marx and Frederick Engels,
        Selected Works. New York: International.
Glaberman, Martin
  1974  "Toward an American revolutionary perspective." Insurgent Sociologist 4
        (Winter):21–35.
Hare, Michael
  1978  "Interview, June."
Healey, Dorothy
  1975  "Selections from the Australian community party: Introduction." Socialist Revolution 4
        (Jan.):57–62.
Hoe, Calvin
  1978  "Interview, June."
Honolulu Advertiser
  1975–1981
Honolulu Star Bulletin
  1975–1981
James, C. L. R.
  1966  Notes on Dialectics. Detroit: Facing Reality. (Quoted in Martin Glaberman, "Toward an
        American revolutionary perspective." Insurgent Sociologist 4 (Winter, 1974):29–30.
Judis, John
  1973  "From the New Left to a new socialist party." Socialist Revolution 3 (Nov.–Dec.):55–82.
  1974  "Response." Socialist Revolution 4 (Jan.–Mar.):123–126.
  1975  "New American movement, 1975." Socialist Revolution (Oct.–Dec.):117–142.
Kinoy, Arthur
  1973  "Article in Liberation." December 11.
Lenin, Vladimir Ilich
  [1897]  "The tasks of the Russian social democrats." Reprinted in Robert C. Tucker (ed.), The
  1975    Lenin Anthology. New York: W. W. Norton, 3–11.
  [1902]  "What is to be done? burning question of our movement." Reprinted in Robert C. Tucker
  1975    (ed.), The Lenin Anthology. New York: W. W. Norton, 12–114.
  1903    "Speech on the party programme to second congress of RSDLP, August 14." Reprinted in
          V. I. Lenin, Collected Works, Vol. 6, Moscow: Progress Publishers, 489–491.
  [1904]  "One step forward, two steps back (the crisis in our party)." Reprinted in Robert C.
  1975    Tucker (ed.), The Lenin Anthology. New York: W. W. Norton, 115–119.
  [1905a]"Two tactics of social-democracy in the democratic revolution." Reprinted in Robert C.
  1975    Tucker (ed.), The Lenin Anthology. New York: W. W. Norton, 120–147.

1905b "The St. Petersberg strike, articles written between January 23 and 30." Reprinted in V. I.
Lenin, Collected Works, Vol. 8, Moscow: Progress Publishers, 90–93.

1905c "The reorganisation of the Party." *Novaya Zhizn*. Reprinted in V. I. Lenin, Collected
Works, Vol. 10, Moscow: Progress Publishers, 29–39.

1907 "Preface to the collection Twelve Years." Reprinted in V. I. Lenin, Collected Works,
Vol. 10, Moscow: Progress Publishers, 94–113.

1921a "Report on the political work of the R.C.P.(B.), March 8." Reprinted in V. I. Lenin,
Collected Works, Vol. 32, Moscow: Progress Publishers, 170–191.

1921b "Summing up speech on party unity and the Anarcho-Syndaclist Deviation, March 6."
reprinted in V. I. Lenin, Collected Works, Vol. 32, Moscow: Progress Publishers,
257–260.

1921c "Summing up speech on the report of the central committee of the R.C.P.(B.), March 8."
Reprinted in V. I. Lenin, Collected Works, Vol. 32, Moscow: Progress Publishers,
192–208.

Mandel, Ernest
1970 "The Leninist theory of organization: Its relevance for today." International Socialist
Review 31 (Dec.):26–50.

Marx, Gary
1974 "Thoughts on a neglected category of social movement participant: The agent provocateur
and the informant." American Journal of Sociology 80 (September):402–442.

Marx, Karl
1848 "Neue Rheinsche Zeitung, September 14." Newspaper article. Reprinted in Karl Marx
and Frederick Engels: Collected Works, Vol. 7, New York: International, 430–431.

1852 "Letter to J. Weydemeyer, March 5." Reprinted in Karl Marx and Frederick Engels,
Selected Works, New York: International, 679.

1871 "Letter to L. Kugelmann, April 12." Reprinted in Karl Marx and Frederick Engels,
Selected Works, New York: International, 679–680.

1875 "Critique of the Gotha Programme." Reprinted in Karl Marx and Frederick Engels,
Selected Works, New York: International. 315–335.

Michels, Robert
[1915] Political Parties. Eden and Cedar Paul (Trans.), New York: The Free Press.
1949

Nakata, Bob
1978 "Interview, June."
1979 "Interview, May."

O'Brien, Jim
[1977] "American Leninism in the 1970's." Radical America 11–12 (Nov.–Feb.):27–63.
1978

Oppenheimer, Martin
1969 The Urban Guerrilla. Chicago: Quadrangle.

Parker, Gene
1979 "Interview, June."

Peters, J.
1975 The Communist Party: A Manual on Organization. San Francisco: Proletarian Publishers.

Peters, Tom (pseud.)
1977 "Interview, August."
1978 "Interview, May."

Piven, Frances Fox, and Richard A. Cloward
1977a "The urban crisis as an arena for class mobilization." Radical America 11
(Jan.–Feb.):9–17.

1977b Poor People's Movements. New York: Vintage.

1977c "Dilemmas of organization building." Radical America 11 (Sept.–Oct.):39–60.

1978    "Social movements and societal conditions: a response to Roach and Roach." Social
        Problems 26 (December):172–178.
*Revolution*
1976–
1978
Riazanov, D.
    n.d.   Karl Marx and Friedrich Engels. London: Martin Lawrence.
Taft, Bernie
    1975    "Selections from the Australian communist party: The Leninist party." Socialist Revolu-
            tion 4 (Jan.):85–100.
Weiner, Jon
    1977    "The communist party today and yesterday: An interview with Dorothy Healey." Radical
            America 11 (May–June):25–96.

# SELF-HELP GROUPS AS SOCIAL MOVEMENT ORGANIZATIONS: SOCIAL STRUCTURE AND SOCIAL CHANGE

David Horton Smith and Karl Pillemer

## I. OVERVIEW OF SELF-HELP GROUPS

*A. Definition*

In recent years, organizations grouped loosely under the rubric of "self–help" have come to the attention of academic and social welfare professionals. A body of literature has slowly developed on this topic. However, the term "self–help group" is used in many different senses in the research and theoretical literature.

Research in Social Movements, Conflicts and Change, Vol. 5, pages 203–233.
Copyright © 1983 by JAI Press Inc.
All rights of reproduction in any form reserved.
ISBN: 0-89232-301-9

This is at least in part due to the vast array of organizations that have at times been identified as following a self–help model. Perhaps the best–known of these are Alcoholics Anonymous (AA) and groups patterned on the AA model (e.g., Schizoprenics Anonymous, Gamblers Anonymous). A large number of medical self–help groups have been identified, which provide support to persons with heart disease (Mended Hearts), cancer (Make Today Count), and a host of other illnesses. Some writers have also used "self–help group" to refer to such large voluntary associations as the American Cancer Society, and even labor unions.

This variety of uses causes confusion and unnecessary, and even futile, debate (especially when scholars are arguing about definitions while suffering from the misunderstanding that they are arguing about empirical reality). Clearly, self–help groups (abbreviated as "SHGs") are a form of voluntary group, as defined, for instance, by Smith (1975). But not all voluntary groups are SHGs. Some would argue that SHGs are distinguished by being small; however, there is no indication of what "small" means, nor if there were such an indication would it be likely to be other than arbitrary. Yet there is *something* about small size, in our view, that characterizes most voluntary groups that we would like to define as SHGs. As we see it, this "something" is the fact that the smallest groups or units of SHGs emphasize the intrinsic value of personal, preferably face-to-face interaction among participants as an explicit or implicit goal. Such interaction is, of course, more likely to occur in substantial quantity and with significantly meaningful quality in smaller rather than larger groups.

Another characteristic that is often said to be essential to the definition of SHGs is their being structured for mutual aid. Using the term "mutual aid" in a definition of SHG has, unfortunately, a definite circularity—unless "mutual aid" is itself defined independently (i.e., without reference to self–help), and this is virtually never done. Beyond the problem of circularity or tautology in definition, there is the further problem that many kinds of voluntary groups involving mutual aid are *not* really self–help groups as the latter term is usually understood. If "mutual aid" refers to the fact that the members of a group expend substantial effort in their roles as group members trying to improve the situations and quality of life of other members (usually with a focus on some special aspect of quality of life, but not necessarily), then labor unions, employers' associations, community associations, taxpayers' associations, producer and consumer cooperatives, and many other kinds of voluntary groups with "internally focused" goals (Smith et al., 1972) are clearly mutual aid groups. In our view, SHGs have mutual aid as a necessary but *not* sufficient defining characteristic, using the definition of "mutual aid" given above to avoid circularity.

SHGs are often viewed as, by definition, therapeutic, curative, or in fact helpful to their members with regard to dealing with some major personal problem, or with regard to their quality of life more generally. The research on SHG–like groups is so scanty with regard to impact, that using some kind of positive impact on members as a defining characteristic of SHGs makes little sense. It is far more sensible, in our view, to include in the definition of SHGs that they are voluntary groups with some explicit *intent* or *goal* of being therapeutic, curative, or otherwise helpful to their members. But this is merely another way of stating that SHGs are necessarily mutual aid groups of a special kind, as noted above. Leaving aside an insistence on *actual* mutual aid or helping impact, then perhaps there is something about the kind of mutual aid that is being referred to that is important when SHGs are characterized as "therapeutic."

What is special about the mutual aid that characterizes SHGs? The notion of therapy or cure suggests that, unlike other voluntary mutual aid groups, SHGs have as participants primarily individuals who believe themselves to have some kind of immediate and personal disadvantage (relative to the rest of the members of their sociocultural reference systems), which is either believed to be remediable (at least in part) or whose effects are believed to be ameliorable through the activities of the group. This complex statement involves several distinct and important elements. Foremost is the idea that self–help groups involve mainly people who, for reasons that may be investigated empirically, define themselves as having a pressing personal problem. This problem involves a perception of relative deprivation and personal stigma by the SHG participant, compared to members of larger sociocultural systems of reference for the individual. The problem is immediate in the sense that its effects are present or potentially present for the SHG participant during the period of SHG involvement. The problem is personal in the sense that it directly affects the individual participant, whether or not any other individuals suffer from it, and in the sense that the individual may secure some relief from or amelioration of its effects again, whether or not others with the same problem obtain such positive results. As such, the problem is not essentially a collective and indivisible one (in the sense in which economists speak of "collective goods"). The problems on which SHGs focus are, by definition, not impossible to remedy (in part, at least) or if irremediable, they are not impossible to ameliorate in terms of their effects in the view of participants. This view of what we may call "alterability" of the problem is a "construction of reality" by the participants in a SHG, and may or may not correspond to the probabilities that would be assigned on the basis of scientific knowledge.

In sum, our view of SHGs is that they can most fruitfully be defined as voluntary groups jointly characterized by (a) goals that emphasize the intrinsic value of personal interaction among participants at the lowest level of group activity (e.g., local units or branches), (b) goals that emphasize mutual aid in the sense that members of the group expend substantial effort in their roles as group members trying to improve the situations and quality of life of other members, and (c) a majority of participants who believe themselves to have an alterable, pressing, personal problem (as defined above). In the briefest form, *a SHG is a*

*voluntary group valuing personal interaction and mutual aid as means of alter-
ing or ameliorating problems perceived as alterable, pressing, and personal by
most of its participants.*

Our definition has a number of virtues. Among them is the manner in which it
shows SHGs in the larger context of voluntary groups more generally and mutual
aid groups more specifically. Unlike some other definitions, it does not confuse
characteristics of voluntary groups or groups in general (e.g., the presence of a
shared sense of collective identity, or of a shared special purpose or goal) with
the distinctive characteristics of SHGs. Similarly, the definition does not beg
empirical questions about the degree of presence–absence of a number of common but not defining characteristics of SHGs. It thus permits one to investigate
the degree of formalization, anti–professional orientation, political advocacy,
emphemerality, self–reliance and numerous other SHG characteristics that are
*not* essential defining qualities of SHGS. Our definition also allows one to
consider the dynamics of transition of a voluntary group becoming a SHG or
ceasing to be a SHG over time.

## B. Distinctiveness

As defined here, SHGs are distinctive from other types of voluntary groups,
with which they are sometimes confused. Thus, SHGs are not always political
advocacy groups, although many of them engage in political advocacy at various
territorial levels. Political advocacy groups as a general type include political
parties and all manner of political pressure and protest groups, only partially
overlapping SHGs as a type of voluntary group. Some SHGs have an almost
entirely internal focus on changing their participants and actively shun political
advocacy (e.g., Alcoholics Anonymous). SHGs are not to be confused either
with other helping social service groups, even though the targets of help and
change may be similar in both instances. Traditional other helping health and
welfare service groups involve people *not* suffering from an alterable, pressing,
personal problem attempting to help those who *do* suffer from such a problem. In
SHGs, the helpers and the helpees both are current or past sufferers from the
problem in question. Further, SHGs are different from self–improvement groups
comprised of individuals who really suffer from no alterable, pressing, personal
problem, but who nonetheless seek to develop some personal quality or skill
(e.g., Great Books Discussion Groups, Toastmasters and Toastmistresses
groups). And as noted earlier, the category of mutual aid groups includes many
other kinds of groups besides SHGs, among them labor unions, professional
associations, mutual benefit associations, friendly societies, credit unions, and
so on. (Katz (1981) has distinguished SHGs from other current concepts such as
"self care," "the support system," and "social networks." Lieberman
(1975:101–102) has distinguished SHGs from other types of "healing groups,"
including group psychotherapy, the human potential movement (sensitivity training, encounter groups, and so on), and consciousness–raising groups.

## C. Typological Categories

Most attempts at developing a typology of SHGs in the past have an *ad hoc* and unsystematic quality (e.g., Katz and Bender, 1976; Bean, 1975; Levy, 1976). Our own attempt differs little from prior attempts except in being more comprehensive and in viewing as matters of degree what prior authors have viewed as qualitative differences. For us, SHGs can be most fruitfully categorized according to the extent to which they exhibit the following characteristics, each viewed as mutually compatible with the other numbered characteristics:

1. Emphasis on physical vs. intellectual vs. emotional vs. behavioral vs. relational problems as the stigmatizing condition.
2. Permanence vs. alterability of the stigmatizing condition (alterability of the condition being seen as different from alterability of one's reactions and ways of coping with the condition—the latter sense of alterability always being present for SHGs by definition) for most group members.
3. Age at acquisition of stigmatizing condition (congenital vs. acquired at some later time) for most group members.
4. Intensity of social stigma attached to condition of most group members (generally ranging from moderate to very high intensity).
5. Emphasis on self–actualization and self–change vs. acceptance of and adjustment to stigmatizing condition.
6. Emphasis on sociopolitical advocacy for societal change in treatment of people with stigmatizing condition.
7. Emphasis on a residential–communal alternative lifestyle and/or an alternative subculture supportive of stigmatized people.
8. Negative vs. neutral vs. positive relationships with relevant professionals and professional organizations.
9. Integration vs. non–integration with established treatment institutions and processes for stigmatized people for given type.
10. Inclusiveness vs. exclusiveness of group with regard to friends and relatives of stigmatized people.
11. Use of ''Anonymous'' organizational format.
12. Formalization of the group and its procedures/activities.
13. Vertical integration vs. non–integration with higher territorrial level organization (e.g., state or national level).
14. Internal democracy and participativeness of members in the policy decision–making of the group.
15. Growth stage of the group, ranging from origin period through rapid growth to stability and potential decline.
16. Independence and self–reliance of the group in terms of sources of financial and material support.

17.   Other characteristics of voluntary groups in general (cf., Smith, *et al.*, 1973).

# II. INTERNAL PROCESSES OF SHGS AND PERSONAL CHANGE

In this section, we attempt to identify the central processes that have been reported in the literature as central to SHG activity. The processes we describe are, on the whole, positive, and reflect well on SHGs. This is not so much indicative of our own perspective, as it is of the nature of the existing literature on SHGs. Case studies predominate, which are generally laudatory testimonials to the groups under study. In spite of this somewhat biased slant, it is possible to isolate certain key processes operative in SHGs.

Other attempts to isolate major processes in SHGs include that by Killilea (1976), who identified seven major characteristics of SHGs from the research literature, and Levy (1976), who found eleven central processes in qualitative study of a number of SHGs. Here, we do not attempt to replicate these earlier attempts, which seem to us rather diffuse and general. The focus of this chapter is on *change*. In a later section, we deal with SHGs and *social* change; here, we examine processes in SHGs, which contribute to change on the *personal* level, derived from a review of the major works in the field.

## A. The "Helper" Therapy Principle

This concept is perhaps the most frequently cited source of personal change in SHGs. The idea was originated by Riessman, who expounded upon it in a, by now, classic article (Riessman, 1965). In it, he notes that when a person with a problem helps another with the same problem, the former benefits as much or more than the latter. Riessman asserts: "While it may be uncertain that people receiving help are always benefitted, it seems more likely that the people *giving* help are profiting from their role" (1965: 27). Possible reasons for this beneficial effect include the rise in status associated with a helping role; increased self–confidence from being healthy enough to help another; and the self–persuasive aspects of convincing someone else to change behavior. Corroboration of Riessman's findings comes from many quarters. Ritchie (1948), in his seminal study of Alcoholics Anonymous, noted the benefits of group interaction between members who share the same problem. He found that the "twelfth step" of AA, which requires reformed alcoholics to help others, was highly therapeutic to the helper. Killilea (1976) echoed this, stating that in SHGs the target of change is also the agent of change. Silverman (1976) notes that helping interactions and networks are an integral part of human life. However, she continues:

"Help takes on a special meaning when the person helping has experienced the difficulty firsthand, and it is this experience that provides the basis for the help he now offers. In the process of helping, the helper may still be working through some of his own residual difficulties and therefore derives some help from the process of helping another'' (233).

Similar observations have been made by many others such as Ablon (1978), Dean (1971), Katz (1965), Gartner and Riessman (1980), and Withorn (1980).

Related to the helper therapy principle is the assertion that those who suffer from a given problem are especially capable to counsel others with the same problem. This has been labeled "experiential empathy" by Mantell, et al. (1976), and is echoed in virtually every major work on self help. As Silverman asserts: "The most important quality of mutual help is that it is offered by someone who is or was a fellow sufferer" (1978: 263–4). To give only two other examples, Camberg found in a detailed evaluation of cancer support groups:

"No one can better support a cancer patient through a difficult treatment than someone who has gone through the same treatment..None is better able to say that it is possible to feel feminine after a mastectomy than someone who does" (1978: 36).

Or as Dean has expressed it:

"After all, who knows better how a mental patient, alcoholic or drug addict thinks and feels than other victims of the same malady? It is this unique feature that is so conducive to the effectiveness of self-directed groups" (Dean, 1971 a: 935).

Further examples of this perspective are provided by Wechsler (1960), Petrunik (1972), Killilea (1976), and Kleeman and DePree (1976).

A third aspect of the helper therapy principle is that successfully adapted group members help others by acting as role models for them. As Silverman (1976) found, "By his very presence, a recovered patient is a living model for identification." Gartner and Riessman (1976) also hold that the provision of models of success is a key element of SHGs (see also Tracy and Gussow, 1976, and Wechsler, 1976.

### B. Cognitive Re–ordering

Under this admittedly awkward title falls the process of reinterpreting the member's problem or deviance, and casting it in to a new, more acceptable light. This is closely tied in with a raising of the self–image of members, which occurs as a part of the "re-ordering". Numerous writers have identified this process: for example, Wechsler (1976) found that Recovery, Inc. provided activities that led to an ordering of the psychological field as a means of reducing anxiety. Similarly, Levy found that many SHGs provide members with a rationale for their distress, which is accepted by members "as a framework within which they can see order and change as possibilities" (Levy, 1976: 318). An ideology can also serve this function (see Antze, 1976.)

Perhaps the best description of this process is contained in an insightful article by Trice and Roman (1970). In their study of Alcoholics Anonymous, the authors identified processes of "delabeling" and "relabeling." By promoting an "allergy concept" of alcohol addiction, which holds that alcoholics have a physiological response to alcohol that brings on the drinking problem, AA ideology diminishes the alcoholic's personal responsibility for his condition. In addition, this illness model allows for the possibility of a clear, well–defined cure.

In addition to the illness model, Alcoholics Anonymous provides a "repentant role" for alcoholics. This facilitates the relabeling of members from deviants to respectable members of society. As Trice and Roman sum up this process:

> "Alcoholics Anonymous possesses, as a consequence of the nature of the disorder of alcoholism, its uniqueness as an organization, and the existence of certain value orientations within American society, a pattern of social processing whereby a labeled deviant can become "delabeled" as a stigmatized deviant and relabeled as a former and repentant deviant" (1970: 545).

Such a reinterpretation and recasting of deviance in a more favorable light is a central process of numerous other SHGs as well.

## C. Experiential Knowledge Application

This characteristic of SHGs, which can perhaps only loosely be termed a process, appears to us to be one of the most useful concepts available for the interpretation of self–help activity. Vattano (1972) touched on this issue when he highlighted the fundamental differences between lay and professional knowledge and practice. SHGs, he noted, pay less attention to psychodynamic factors and administrative issues, focusing instead on action, and a "here–to–now" emphasis on behavior. Rather than reliance on theory or technical skill, SHGs emphasize "observable events, modeling procedures, and positive reinforcement of adaptive behavior by means of group support" (Vattano, 1972: 14).

Borkman (1976) extends this concept, and gives it its fullest expression in the literature on SHGs. She differentiates between experiential and professional knowledge. The former is "truth learned from personal experience with a phenomenon rather than truth acquired by discursive reasoning, observation, or reflection or information provided by others" (446). Experiential knowledge is closely related to experiential *expertise,* or the competence one develops through direct experience. Finally, experiential knowledge is that fostered by SHGs. Borkman contrasts experiential knowledge with professional knowledge: "In contrast to professional information, experiential knowledge is (1) problematic rather than theoretical or scientific, (2) oriented to here–and–now action rather than to the long–term development and systematic accumulation of knowledge, and (3) holistic and total rather than segmented" (449).

Borkman then uses this concept to interpret SHG activity. She views SHG structure as a vehicle for the sharing of experiential knowledge. SHGs allow for the pooling of the experiences of a variety of people; this permits individuals to compare their situations with those of others. In addition, inapplicable knowledge can be rejected by the group. Borkman notes that in more established groups, a codified format, or model exists for the sharing of experiential knowledge; the "twelve steps" of Alcoholics Anonymous provide an example of this.

The development and sharing, or application of experiential knowledge, then, has been identified as a major process in SHGs. Pillemer (1981) has described a variant of this process; the role of a SHG as a forum for the development of lay "theories" regarding the nature and cause of the condition. Pillemer notes that this process of developing alternative theories that augment, and in some cases replace, professional knowledge can invest the person's situation with a greater degree of meaning. This in turn may lead to a heightened sense of control over the problematic condition.

## D. Sharing Information and Advice

Another internal process mentioned by almost every writer on SHGs is the sharing of information, advice, and coping strategies. Killilea (1976: 72) states, "Information, including both technical and anticipatory guidance on expectable problems and phases or transitions, is an important element in almost all mutual help organizations." This can take the form, as in Alcoholics Anonymous, of "a candid sharing of experiences—of emotional reactions to and practical strategies for coping with the common problems" (Ablon, 1978: 38). It can be as specific as advice on how to deal with prostheses, and suggestions as to how to tailor such assisting devices to individual needs (Tracy and Gussow, 1976). Additional examples of the importance of information–sharing in SHGs can be found in Borman (1976), Katz (1979), Camberg (1978), Gartner and Riessmann (1976), Kleeman and Depree (1976), Ascheim, et al. (1978) and Levy (1976).

## E. Acceptance and Support

SHGs are frequently held to be "safe" or "sheltered" environments where deviance is accepted, and relatively unconditional social support offered. The SHGs in which this aspect has been most carefully analyzed have been groups for the mentally ill. Wechsler (1960), in an early study of ex–mental patient organizations, found that these groups provided opportunities for ex–patients to meet with others who accept them, regardless of the stigma attached to mental illness. In such organizations, a milieu relatively free from stress is created, which allows members to develop relationships more easily than elsewhere, and to test new, more adaptive behavior patterns.

Similarly, Landy and Singer (1961) characterize the ex–mental patient club as a place to escape from family and society, and to socialize without ordinary pressure. The club accepts the member's inability or refusal to work, and his or her economic dependence or lack of resources. In general, if offers its members freedom from social ranking. Evidence from other groups such as those for cancer patients (Camberg, 1978) and Al–Anon (Ablon, 1978) show the presence of similar processes.

## F. Learning New Behaviors and Attitudes

Closely related to the previous process is that of learning new, more adaptive behaviors. According to some observers, it is precisely the accepting environment fostered in SHGs that allows for the testing of new ways of interacting and relating to others. Levy (1976) claims that in SHGs, one can observe the "development of an alternative culture and social structure within which members can develop new definitions of their personal identities and new norms upon which they base their self–esteem" (Levy, 1976: 319–320). Katz states that taking a SHG as a new reference group "facilitates the taking of first steps toward changing self perception and anxiety" (Katz and Bender, 1976).

A number of mechanisms have been identified that encourage behavioral change in SHGs, beyond the secure environment. Dean (1971a) reports that group members in Recovery, Inc. compete with one another to see who can improve more quickly. SHGs also provide activities and opportunities for leadership. Weiss, in a study of Parents without Partners, notes, "Both men and women sometimes found that contribution to the organization through service in administrative or planning roles supported their own sense of worth" (Weiss, 1976: 180). Tracy and Gussow (1976) maintain that many SHG participants involve themselves so heavily in acceptable activities related to the condition they they become "career patients." They claim that this can be an extremely successful adaptation.

The learning of new behaviors is extremely important in times of critical role transition (Silverman, 1976). Groups like Recovery, Inc. have claimed to help smooth the transition from mental hospital to society (Dean, 1971b). Often, SHGs involve persons who have just undergone an abrupt change in status, such as widowhood or the discovery that one has cancer. Assistance in adaptation to a new physical condition or social role can, according to these reports, be mediated and facilitated by SHGs.

## G. Opportunity for Self–Revelation

A frequently cited process that transpires in SHGs is self–revelation and open discussion of one's problems. Alcoholics Anonymous, as well as other groups organized along "Anonymous" lines, emphasize a form of ritualized confession, symbolized perhaps by the standard AA self–introduction: "My name is _____, and I am an alcoholic." Mowrer (1974), in his discussion of Integrity Groups, stresses this confessional aspect as the major reason for their effectiveness. The cathartic value of the confessional aspect of SHGs has also been observed in Recovery, Inc. groups by Dean (1971a), in groups for women undergoing the stress of moving (Kaplan, 1978), and in cancer support groups (Camberg, 1978).

An extremely important result of this sharing of personal experiences and feelings is a process of SHGs mentioned repeatedly in the literature: the reduction of the sense of isolation of members. SHG participants have often felt themselves to be entirely alone with their problem and find that hearing others in the group report struggling with identical fears and emotions is something of a liberating experience. As Borman, et al. (1981: 32) write in reference to epilepsy SHGs:

"The importance of universality and acceptance, of being part of a group of others who share your condition and understand what you are experiencing seems to be central. You are not isolated and alone, but in the same boat with others like yourself."

Levy (1976: 319) describes this process as working through operation of social comparison and consensual validation. Others describe it more simply as the relief experienced by discovering that one "is not the only one in the world who has this problem" (Silverman, 1976: 238). Further examples of this process can be found in Weiss (1976), Henry (1978), Ablon (1978), Silverman (1978).

## H. Other Processes

A number of other processes are discussed in the literature, but are not emphasized to the degree the foregoing processes were. We touch on them only briefly here. First, it has been held that SHG participation can improve family or other relationships. As Kleeman and DePree (1970) note, SHGs provide a means for renormalization, and enable members to manage better lives with others. Another process characteristic observed in SHGs is informal social interaction outside of the group. Weiss (1976) found this to occur in Parents Without Partners. In her study of a women's group, Kaplan (1978) writes that members formed lasting friendships that were carried on outside of the group. Borman, et. al. (1981) note in a similar vein that the trip to a nearby restaurant for informal socialization after an epilepsy SHG meeting served an extremely important function for members.

A different aspect of SHGs is the use by some of a special technique or therapeutic method. Re–evaluation Counseling is a good example of this type of group. Developed by Harvey Jackins, these groups train participants to use a special terminology to analyze feelings and behaviors (e.g., psychological discomfort is referred to as "distress"). Weekly small groups reinforce the Re–evaluation Counseling philosophy. Synanon (Holzinger, 1965; Ofshe, 1974), Recovery, Inc. (Dean, 1971a), Integrity Groups (Mowrer, 1976), and Alcoholics Anonymous (Trice and Roman, 1970) all provide additional examples of groups that rely on a special technique.

Finally, some SHGs exhibit concern with larger social goals and engage in political activity to achieve those goals. We will defer a discussion of this aspect of SHGs until the following section. Here, we have focused on internal processes of SHGs, those which attempt to bring about positive behavioral, or attitudinal changes in members. In the remainder of this paper, we look at their social movement and social change potential.

## III.  SELF HELP GROUPS AND SOCIAL MOVEMENT
## ORGANIZATIONS

The title of this chapter states a major thesis of the authors regarding SHGs, namely that they are generally social movement organizations (SMOs). SMOs are groups, usually voluntary groups, that can be viewed as part of or as having the quality of a social movement. Social movements have in turn been defined in a variety of ways. Drawing on common elements of prior definitions and trying to be as parsimonious as possible, we define a social movement as a set of isolated individuals, informal communication networks, informal groups, and formal groups all working for some kind of significant change in a sociocultural system (that is, in a society's social structure or culture). The term "movement" in "social movement" refers to this working for social change, however modest or extreme. To determine whether or not a particular person, network, or group is part of a social movement, one must examine the extent to which that entity is working for significant change in its sociocultural system. It is *not* required that the process of working for systemic change be a conscious one on the part of the entities involved, although awareness of being part of a movement is a common occurrence with most SMOs.

### A.  The Local Level

There are several senses in which local SHGs may be seen generally as SMOs. Explicit in the definition of SHGs is the "therapeutic" use of personal interaction as a means of altering or ameliorating certain kinds of personal problems of participants. In modern society, with highly professionalized and bureaucratized help delivery systems in the areas of health and social welfare, the very notion of self–help involves a challenge to the system and an attempt to bring about a kind of systemic change. Crucial to this particular challenge is the general assumption (implicit or explicit) by SHGs that the companionship and sharing of experiences with fellow sufferers from a given personal problem are not merely important but essential ingredients of successful coping with the life stress and strain associated with a stigmatizing condition. Further, SHGs generally operate on the assumption that such successful coping is inherently more likely to occur if, in addition to any other aid received, the stigmatized participant receives mutual aid of an instrumental sort motivated by a combination of shared experience of suffering and altruism toward fellow suffers. It is in this sense that SHGs are mutual support groups as well as mutual aid groups. Thus, the very definition of SHGs, in our view, marks them as a kind of social change–seeking group, given the nature of modern society.

Another kind of social change that SHGs strive to bring about, in addition to challenging professional and bureaucratic help delivery systems, is a change in the usual informal support systems that are available to people with stigmatizing problems in modern society. SHGs provide a special or auxiliary informal social support system for those suffering from stigmatizing conditions of all sorts. This informal support may supplement significant existing informal support, or it may substitute for generally lacking social support. Either way, SHGs are working to make a change in how people with stigmatizing conditions are treated by other people in society. SHGs are providing for their members and participants a special form of companionship of fellow sufferers, whose common experience and personal reassurance regarding individual worth makes all the difference.

Besides the two foregoing senses in which SHGs are seeking sociocultural system change for members and potential members, SHGs also differ among themselves in having varying degrees of social movement/social change orientation. Here the typological categories noted earlier in this chapter become relevant to delineating which types of SHGs are more likely to be strong or extreme in their social movement orientation, and which SHGs are likely to be only moderate or even weak in such orientation. Specifically, SHGs are likely to be strong in social movement orientation where they emphasize sociopolitical advocacy for societal change in treatment of people with the stigmatizing condition; where they emphasize a residential–communal alternative lifestyle and/or an alternative subculture supportive of stigmatized people; where they have negative relationships with relevant professionals and professional organizations; where they are not integrated with established treatment institutions; where they have greater internal democracy and participativeness of members in the policy decision-making of the group; and where they are more independent and self reliant in terms of sources of financial and material support as groups. At present, the foregoing series of propositions can be viewed as working hypotheses, based on case study materials and impressions, that should be put to systematic test in future comparative research with samples of SHGs of various types. Such research may show others of the typological characteristics mentioned earlier also to be relevant to determining the degree of social movement orientation of a SHG. At the same time that research may indicate variations in the degree of relationship with social movement orientation and in the nature of interrelationships for the characteristics just noted.

Although our principal thesis is that SHGs as small, local groups are generally social movement organizations (SMOs), it is interesting to speculate on the extent to which national organizations with SHGs as local chapters have social movement characteristics. It is our impression that the degree of social movement orientation at the national versus local level is variable rather than consistent. Some SHGs that are very much social movement oriented at the local level lose much of that orientation at the national level, where accommodation to the larger sociocultural system plays a dominant role. On the other hand, there are national organizations with highly change-oriented leaders that are far more social movement oriented than their local SHGs. And there are, of course, national organizations that reflect rather accurately the level of social movement orientation of their local SHGs. It would be interesting to know what factors, besides national leadership characteristics, account for these variations.

## B. The National Level

Another level at which it is useful to consider the degree of social movement orientation of SHGs is among groups concerned with different stigmatizing conditions. To what extent is there a general self help movement, of which various local and national groups are a part? The United States and Great Britain seem to be the most well developed in terms of SHGs, although SHGs are present in significant numbers in West Germany, the Netherlands, and in other advanced industrial and post–industrial nations (cf., Smith and Katz, 1982; Robinson and Henry, 1978; Moeller, 1978; Lieberman and Borman, 1979; Gartner and Riessman, 1977; Katz and Bender, 1976; Van Harberden and Lafaille, 1978). Some kinds of SHGs have been around for a very long time; Sagarin (1969:34) described the Washingtonians as a group very much like Alcoholics Anonymous that sprang up in the middle of the last century in the United States. Nonetheless, these older SHG examples either died out, or did not spark, or become part of a social movement. Alcoholics Anonymous (1957) was probably the first of the still existing SHGs, by our definition, started in the 1930s. Yet only in the 1960s and 1970s have SHGs really burgeoned in their growth in the United States and elsewhere (see Katz, 1981, and the sources cited earlier in this paragraph).

Toch (1965:71) was one of the first to view SHGs both individually as SMOs and collectively as a social movement (or movements) "which collectively promote individual change." Many subsequent authors have referred to self help as a social movement (e.g., Dumont, 1974; Tracy and Gussow, 1976; Vattano, 1972; Killilea, 1976; Katz and Bender, 1976: Chapter 3). A common theme that runs through the work of several authors here is the view of the self–help movement as a movement of client power, or consumer initiated services (e.g., Vattano, 1972; Tracy and Gussow, 1976). Others see the distinctive characteristic of self–help as a social movement more in terms of self–care, especially self–care and self–reliance in *health* matters (Levin, Katz, and Holst, 1979: Chapter 4).

A third major theme that comes out, perhaps most frequently, in characterizing the self–help movement is its anti–professional and anti-institutional stance (e.g., Gartner and Riessman, 1977:152; Katz and Bender, 1976:28). There is a great deal of discussion in the literature regarding the appropriate relationship of the self–help movement and SHGs to professionals and established helping institutions. At one extreme we find Rosen (1976) referring to "non–prescription therapies" like SHGs that need "regulation" by professionals, if only to "save" SHGs from governmental regulation in behalf of consumer protection. In the middle, as moderates, we find authors like Silverman (1975) who argue that we need to examine new roles for professionals in relation to SHGs, traditional professional roles, with the control and intellectual elitism they entail, being inadequate. And at the other extreme we find authors like Righton (1976) who make a strong case for keeping professionals and institutions away from the treatment of the stigmatized because professionals are no different from the average person in being unable to control feelings of revulsion regarding the condition, especially when the stigma of the condition is great. Such discussion notwithstanding, we agree with Gartner and Riessman (1977:152) that "whether directly concerned with major societal transformation or not, the thrust of the movement is critical of much of human service practice, professional behavior, and institutional arrangements."

The structure of the self–help movement is at present rather amorphous, according to most of the evidence. Many SHGs are unaffiliated with larger national or regional organizations, or even with local human service institutions or organizations. Those SHGs that have national coordinating secretariats generally have little to do with each other, except in occasional and informal ways. The closest thing to national coordination of SHGs in the Unites States is the National Self–Help Clearinghouse, operated by the Graduate School and University Center of the City University of New York. Gartner and Riessman, the founders and directors of this Clearinghouse, have recently expanded on their 1977 listing of national SHGs in the United States by publishing a separate directory called *HELP* (1979). Similar directories have been published by various agencies covering a particular state (e.g., Blue Cross and Blue Shield, 1974), a county, or metropolitan area (cf., Gartner, 1981:7). But the coordination given by such directories and by the Clearinghouse is essentially informational, not organizational. And to the best of our knowledge, there has not been a single study that has explored in detail the network of interorganizational relationships of national or even local SHGs. This clearly is an area needing much research attention.

The self–help movement is clearly at a rather early stage in its life cycle, undergoing rapid growth in groups and participants but lacking coalescence and coherence organizationally. Nonetheless, this movement satisfies readily the five criteria that Gerlach and Hine (1970:xvii) identify as essential to a social movement: First, the self–help movement is segmented, polycephalous (multiply–led), decentralized, and composed of units that are connected in a network fashion by "various personal, structural, and ideological ties." Second, the self–help movement depends heavily on *"face–to–face recruitment* by committed individuals using their own pre–existing, significant social relationships." Third, the self–help movement involves *"personal commitment* generated by an act or an experience which separates the convert in some significant way from the established order (or his previous place in it), identifies him with a new set of values, and commits him to changed patterns of behavior." Fourth, the self–help movement, usually at the local SHG level, provides *"an ideology* which codifies values and goals, (gives) a conceptual framework by which all experiences or events relative to these goals may be interpreted, motivates and provides a rationale for envisioned unification of a segmented network of groups." And finally, the self–help movement can be characterized by "*real or perceived opposition* from society at large or from that segment of the established order within which the movement has arisen"—the professional human service establishment in this instance.

## C. Origin Dynamics

One final general question we may put in this section is how one can explain the origins and recent rapid development of the self–help movement and individual SHGs and their memberships. In particular, one may ask about how general theories of SMO, or social movement origins, seem to fit the self-help movement. Smelser's (1962) value–added theory is perhaps the most widely known and used model. Emphasizing societal disorganization or breakdown and strain as the underlying dynamic, this theory seems to fit the self-help movement fairly well. We draw on Marx and Wood's (1975:410–411) statement of the theory: *First,* the period of general social ferment that was the 1960s made for structural conduciveness (permissive social arrangements) for the self–help movement to arise. *Second,* there was structural strain for a wide variety of stigmatized individuals in society, many of whom were subject to relative deprivation in seeing other disadvantaged groups in society moving toward important social change goals, while they themselves were receiving little or no attention. *Third,* there was the growth and spread of generalized beliefs that identified as the source of strain, prejudice on the part of the entire public toward stigmatized individuals and lack of adequate and appropriate treatment by professionals and human service institutions. Further, these beliefs attributed ignorance and incompetence to professionals and service institutions, and they specified self–help and mutual aid by fellow stigma sufferers as the appropriate responses of potential participants.

A *fourth* element of Smelser's theory is precipating factors that give the generalized beliefs concrete meaning. Here there are a variety of examples of life events and social situations that have precipitated different SHGs. *Fifth,* mobilization of participants for action has been present as stigmatized individuals have come in contact with SHG organizers and active members and have been recruited into active membership themselves. *Sixth,* social control mechanisms in society have been ineffective generally in preventing, interrupting, or otherwise inhibiting the cumulative effect of the other five factors for the self–help movement, even though some very highly stigmatized conditions and individuals have been involved. This *laissez faire* attitude of societal regulatory agencies and the public in general has been part of the aftermath of both the 1960s ferment and the Watergate scandal and attendant revelations of government interference with voluntary groups in the 1960s and early 1970s. In sum, all six of Smelser's conditions or determinants favored the rise of the self–help movement in the past two decades, with special emphasis on the 1970s as a period of greatest growth.

The self–help movement has clearly been a norm–oriented rather than a value oriented social movement in Smelser's terms, as would be expected in our highly differentiated society. A norm–oriented movement is also to be expected given the rather narrowly defined beliefs about needed change that this movement has espoused and the corresponding toleration by authorities and the public. The self–help movement really has not tried to nor succeeded in rocking very many boats. The professions and social service institutions that have been challenged by the movement have not so much been actively attacked as passively withdrawn from by participants in the self–help movement. And at the same time, there have been many forms of cooperation, increasingly in recent years, between SHGs and helping professionals and institutions. Where earlier there was fairly systematic hostility on both sides, now there is in many instances active collaboration and a tendency to seek out long term accommodation. All of this has helped to mute the criticisms and attacks that the helping professions might otherwise be mounting against the self–help movement, perhaps with the backing of the government and regulatory institutions of society.

There are many other theories dealing with the dynamics of social movements in the literature. However, the principal alternative theory, articulated by various scholars, may be referred to as the ''power–incentives-resource mobilization theory''—the label including the three major variants of the theory. According to Tilly (1969), studying collective violence, the presence of discontents is less important in the generation of collective action than is the presence of power struggles. Although this perspective may well apply to SMOs that engage in collective protests, the case study literature does not suggest power struggles to be very important factors in the dynamics of SHGs. However, this may be a result of the failure of scholars of SHGs to be interested in power struggles and hence to write about or inquire into them. In part, this latter situation may arise from the tendency for scholars to write about SHGs from either a laudatory or a condemnatory perspective, too rarely from an objective point of view.

Olson's (1965) theory of collective action emphasizes the importance of selective material incentives if individuals are to participate in or even to join voluntary groups. It applies only partially to the situation of SHGs. Where it would argue that mere solidary (fellowship, companionship) incentives are too weak to generate group commitment in most instances, with purposive (goal attainment) and especially material incentives generally necessary, SHGs tend to generate very substantial commitment to the group largely from solidary incentives, with some admixture of purposive incentives, and very little in the way of material incentives in most cases. Yet the theory is applicable in the sense that the solidary and purposive incentives that are offered to SHG participants are clearly *selective* incentives that one can enjoy only as a member of the group, by and large.

McCarthy and Zald (1973) represent the resource mobilization approach, which is related to the two foregoing theories. From this perspective, SMOs succeed or fail, grow or decline according to the resource access they have. One important kind of resource, for instance, is the availability of career professionals who will serve as "social movement entrepreneurs" in starting and leading SMOs and larger social movements. The self–help movement has had relatively few such social movement "career professionals," being instead largely a grassroots and even anti–professional movement. In some cases SHGs have been formed by human service professionals, or guided and helped by them, but on the whole the resource mobilization approach seems to have only limited applicability to understanding the self–help movement. Once again, this may be in part a result of insufficient attention to resource mobilization by scholars studying SHGs, a matter that future research should remedy.

To sum up, Smelser's strain theory seems to apply to the self–help movement and SHG origins better than the power–incentives–resource mobilization approaches, insofar as the extant literature gives us basis for judgment. This conclusion must be tempered by the further statement that the evidence is far from complete with regard to the power–incentives–resource mobilization theories. Moreover, there have been useful attempts to blend the two general approaches (Korpi, 1974; Marx and Wood, 1975), for they are not necessarily mutually exclusive.

## IV. SELF–HELP AND SOCIAL CHANGE

In an earlier section, we discussed certain internal characteristics of SHGs and identified processes that have been alleged to bring about personal change in participants. It has been argued that another dimension of self–help activity exists: This is the existence of goals and activities that attempt to bring about change in the larger society. This issue has been the topic of considerable controversy in the literature on SHGs.

In particular, a debate of sorts has been carried on between writers who hold that self–help activity *inherently* involves a political challenge to the existing power structure, and those who argue that SHGs focus almost exclusively on changing individual behavior. The former assert that the "non-professional" character of self–help threatens professional hegemony, and that SHGs often develop far–reaching goals for improving the social conditions of their members. The latter claim that SHGs may stifle desires for fundamental social change by focusing exclusively upon the problems of the individual. As Gartner has written, SHGs "may blame the victim and fail to deal with larger structural issues" (Gartner and Riessman, 1976: 3).

A major proponent of the view that SHGs are by their very nature catalysts of social change is Vattano. He asserts that SHGs are part of a "general cultural revolution," and are "directed at achieving new freedom and well–being for man" (Vattano, 1972: 9). He states: "People are responding to contemporary social conditions with a new activism. Their actions are transforming society by changing many of its basic institutions, and are posing a new challenge to the helping professions in health and welfare programs. *The challenge is particularly evident in the emergence of self-help groups''* (1972: 7; emphasis added).

In this view, SHGs are placed firmly in the forefront of social change. Hurvitz (1976) offers an opposing viewpoint in his discussion of ''Peer Self–Help Psychotherapy Groups'' (PSHGPs). These are formed to aid members in overcoming psychological and emotional problems; Recovery, Inc. and Alcoholics Anonymous are examples of such groups. Hurvitz argues that a social change focus has not developed in PSHPGs. This is due to the religious roots of these groups, in conjunction with American individualist ideology and a ''psychologistic'' view of human nature that prevailed at the time many were formed.

Hurvitz claims that as a result of these factors, PSHPGs adopted a psychological explanation of behavior, rather than a social one. The former blames emotional distress on the failure of the individual; the latter places responsibility on social structure and culture. A function of the psychological orientation is to conceive change as ''offered to—or imposed upon—people to secure their conformity with the prevailing values and goals of their society'' (1976:290). The result of this, Hurvitz observes, is a lack of interest on the part of PSHPGs in social change.

The contrast between these two perspectives is exemplified by an interchange that appeared on the pages of *Social Science and Medicine.* While the specific case under discussion was self–help health groups, the issues are applicable to the range of SHGs. In that journal, Victor and Ruth Sidel (1977) presented a critique of SHGs in the health care field. They argued that SHGs focus on individual deviance, thereby placing the burden of change on the individual, rather than on society to change the conditions that create a deviant response. They assert as well that medical SHGs may actually perpetuate inequities in the health care system, by relieving pressure on the state to provide needed services (1977: 417). Katz (1979) responded to this argument by asserting the opposite: SHGs, he claimed, are intensely involved in social change. ''Far from reducing pressures for preventive services, one could cite many U.S. examples of ways in which self–help groups have tipped public policy towards prevention'' (491). As evidence, he points to the research and legislative activities of certain large voluntary organizations. In short, Katz maintains that SHGs are already heavily involved in social change activities.

This is only one example of what has become a fairly widespread controversy (for other examples, see Borman, 1974; and Gartner and Riessman, 1976). Upon close examination, two elements become apparent here. First, in large part the debate is caused by differences in the definition of SHG. Second, it is clear from the literature that SHGs are *heterogeneous,* and vary a great deal in terms of their involvement in social change activities; hence our inclusion of this dimension in the list of major SHG typological characteristcs.

As regards the first point, the Sidel-Katz interchange shows clearly some of the common misunderstandings that cloud discussions of the self–help movement. At issue is the question of what can accurately be called a "self–help group." It seems likely that the Sidels are considering groups that are most commonly thought to embody self–help principles, such as Alcoholics Anonymous, Mended Hearts and Make Today Count. Katz, on the other hand, makes reference also to national voluntary associations, which, while perhaps started by persons afflicted with a medical problem, have evolved into bureaucratic social service agencies, at least at the national level.

Katz cites as examples of SHGs such established organizations as the National Hemophilia Foundation and the United Cerebral Palsy Associations of America. It is questionable whether such agencies are true SHGs in any sense of the word, depending on the precise nature of their local units. For example, does the United Cerebral Palsy Association, with a board of directors made up largely of the able–bodied, and annual expenditures of over $3.5 million (UPCA Annual Report, 1978), really fit even Katz's own definition of SHGs: "In our view, face–to–face interaction is a key defining characteristic of self–help groups. By these criteria, bureaucratization is the enemy of the self–help organization" (Katz and Bender, 1976: 10)? A distinction between these two conceptualizations of SHGs and the matter of local versus national groups must be kept clearly in mind if the problem of the relation of self–help and social change is to be resolved.

Further, as noted above, these two perspectives can largely be reconciled with the simple recognition of the heterogeneity of SHGs. SHGs develop in different contexts, serve different populations, employ varying styles of leadership, have differing financial resources, and so forth. Some begin with a social change focus; others may develop it over time; while still others may lose this focus. For some it is present only at the local level; others have it only at the national level; and still others have it at both levels. This heterogeneous nature of SHGs is reflected in some of the typologies that have been developed to classify them. Tracy and Gussow (1976) created a two–part typology: one type provides services, while the other concentrates on lobbying and educational campaigns. Silverman (1978) classifies SHGs into four categories, one of which is "*political action,* which involves changing laws and *changing public attitudes* toward the common shared condition" (Silverman, 1978: 260–1; emphasis in original). Sagarin (1969) similarly distinguishes between SHGs that reform the deviant, and those that attempt to reform society and change its norms.

Clearly, there is little support in the literature of either sweepingly positive or negative statements regarding the social change potential or self–help groups. A number of authors, however, have approached this issue in a somewhat different way. They hold that while a SHG may at one point in its existence concentrate on individual problems, it is likely to develop social change goals over time. Spiegel (1976), for example, studied three SHGs (for burn victims, drug abusers, and homosexuals) and found that "in all three cases as the organizations developed, they seemed to grow in the direction of political activism" (1976: 151). Back and Taylor (1976) employ Blumer's series of five stages in the growth of a social movement to explain self–help group activity. They detail an evolution from dissatisfaction with professionally provided services to engaging in social action to achieve the group's goals.

As Pillemer (1980) has noted, case studies of SHGs indicate that such a progression is by no means inevitable; rather, the static nature of many groups is repeatedly demonstrated. Our review of the literature encountered no longitudinal studies of SHGs; however, a comparison between separate studies carried out at different points in a group's history is illuminating. Oscar Ritchie's study of Alcoholics Anonymous (Ritchie, 1948) shows an organization nearly identical to that described by Trice and Roman (1970) two decades later. Wechsler's (1960) study of Recovery, Inc. does not lead one to believe that much change had occurred by the time Dean (1971a, 1971b) wrote about that organization over ten years later. As we asserted above, the, the issue is not whether SHGs are inherently agents of social change. Instead, the questions should be phrased as: What structural or environmental factors help determine a SHGs orientation towards social change? Under what circumstances do groups that began with a focus solely on individual change develop social change goals over time? What circumstances lead to a loss of social change orientation? And what determines the similarity–difference in social change orientation at local versus national levels?

Before proceeding with these questions, however, another issue must be addressed. If some SHGs do indeed focus upon social change, what are the specific conditions they attempt to alter? From our review of the literature on SHGs, we have identified a number of social problems to which change–oriented SHGs respond. First, it is widely accepted that SHGs are a response to the breakdown of "traditional" informal support systems. In the absence of strong family ties and meaningful community relationships, people turn to groups for assistance and social support. This view is often expressed in the general literature on voluntary associations (cf. Goldhammer, 1964; Gans, 1975), and it is applicable to SHGs. It is also held that groups arise in order to pressure for social and medical services (Katz, 1979). Society is viewed as unable to care for all in need of services; this triggers the self–help response. As Katz and Bender maintain: "When society does not help suffering people, they seek solace from others with the same complaint, even though there may be little else in common" (Katz and Bender, 1976: 31). They continue: "Implicit in every self–help group, then, including those focused on individual adaptation, is a criticism of lacks or failures of the larger society" (231).

Another aspect of modern society more often held responsible for SHG formation than general social conditions is the nature of professionally provided services. Some have identified the inevitable gaps in professional service provision as areas where SHGs spring up (Dumont, 1974; Borman, 1976). Others go beyond this, asserting that the negative, ineffective nature of professional care drives people to SHGs. Such groups, they assert, work directly or indirectly to change those conditions.

In a recent edition of the *Self–Help Reporter* (Gartner, 1980), this issue was treated in some detail. It was argued that services are too big, inaccessible, bureaucratic, and distant from consumers. They are also overly costly, but often ineffective. Many human service interventions are not oriented towards basic cure or prevention; instead, they are mere "patch–ups." Finally, human service workers are "affected by a deep malaise—feeling burned out, cynical, and defeated by the rigidity of bureaucratic forces" (Gartner, 1980). SHGs can arise, it is asserted, to alter and alleviate these conditions.

Finally, SHGs can attempt to change societal attitudes that stigmatize persons with the problem, and which foster occupational and social discrimination against them. SHGs may carry out informational programs, provide speakers to schools, and encourage well–known sufferers from the condition to publicly identify themselves with the group. SHGs may inform members of their rights to employment, housing, or insurance, and promote legislation to overcome discrimination.

In the remainder of this section, we attempt to identify certain factors that may influence whether a SHG pursues social change or focuses solely on individual behavior and adaptation. First, however, a point of clarification is necessary. As we have repeatedly noted, in this discussion we will remain within the bounds of our own definition of SHGs. We include therefore only groups that have at least some emphasis on the therapeutic value of small group, personal (face–to–face or phone–to–phone) interaction, and omit other mutual aid and "movement" organizations such as welfare rights groups.

Having stated above that SHGs vary in their concern with social change, we will consider certain factors that may help determine the extent to which a group begins with, or develops, social change goals. The four elements we consider here are: 1) relationships with professionals; 2) leadership; 3) ideology; and 4) transitory versus enduring nature of the condition or problem. We advance these factors very tentatively, and with the knowledge that research is needed to determine empirically whether these, or others, are the major factors. We are also cognizant of the fact that these four variables may interact, and must be considered to operate in conjunction with one another.

## A. Relationships with Professionals

SHG professional relations have been widely discussed in the literature; in fact, explicating this issue has become something of an obsession to professionals involved in self–help. An entire book has been largely devoted to discussing ways in which professionals can collaborate with groups (Silverman, 1980), and virtually every major article in the field at least makes mention of the problem.

Some writers, as we noted above, have emphasized the conflict that exists between the self–help ideal and professionally provided services. Greer (1976:4) sums up this point well:

> "As professional delivery and control of services have come to reflect and reinforce a service system (and larger social system) predicated on unequal dependent, exploitative relationships, the self–help modality expresses and offers the promise of a quite contrary style of human relations. At root, self–help challenges and considerably modifies, the traditional professional role."

Other writers, such as Jertson (1975), have construed this point to imply that professional involvement may contaminate SHGs. Jertson asks: "Will professional involvement contribute to the loss of that one value uniquely cherished by the self–help group: the perceived ability to help itself, including the organization and recruitment of its own members" (145)? Similarly, Gartner and Riessman (1977) raise the question of whether the populist character of the self–help movement will be compromised by becoming an adjunct to professional services.

Interestingly, only a few writers have identified ties to the professional community as a factor in the attitude a group takes towards social change. Henry (1978) has been most explicit regarding this, claiming that close ties to the professional world are an inhibiting factor in the development of a social change focus. He notes that many SHGs have been established by professionals, and thereby, "influenced into adopting prevailing social attitudes" of acceptance of professional dominance (1978: 656). Other groups, he claims, have professionals working behind the scenes. SHGs are often forced to have these ties, Henry asserts, in order to acquire adequate financial support and to insure a steady stream of referrals.

Withorn (1980) goes beyond this, and suggests that social change goals may be incompatible with ties to professionals. She writes: "The more critical the groups become of the quality of professional care . . . the more they are resisted by doctors and professional workers" (1980: 23). From Withorn's and Henry's work, it can be inferred that most SHGs do attempt to challenge the dominant social order in some way, but are forced to reach some accommodation with the professional world if they are to survive. The degree to which a group must compromise its social change stance may be in part influenced by the other factors we will discuss here, and by the amount of supportive professionals they can attract without changing their position.

In summary, the literature on SHGs provides some evidence that groups that exhibit strong ties to professionals are more likely to focus on individual change, and less on institutional or societal change. Groups like the Mental Patient Liberation Front, which strenuously rejects all professionals, tend to promote social change (Ginsberg, 1974). Others with strong professional links, such as Alcoholics Anonymous or Recovery, Inc., do not.

## B. Leadership

Considerable anecdotal and case study evidence exists that identifies the style of leadership as an important variable in determining the effectiveness of a SHG. Borkman (in Ascheim, et al., 1978: 13) has found: "Our group was friendly to newcomers. We shared our problems openly and enjoyed each other's company. But reliance on one or two members was our downfall." Hamilton (1980) studied three Parents Anonymous chapers, and found that the major reason for the decline of these groups was autocratic leadership style on the part of the founders. This leadership made membership participation impossible. Smith (1982) has described in detail the way in which poor leadership in a group for men in divorce made that group's attempts at social change ineffective. Although evidence is somewhat sketchy, we include leadership pattern as a key variable in whether a SHG becomes involved in social change activities.

## C. Ideology

The individual primarily responsible for raising the issue of the ideology of a SHG is Antze (1976). Antze stresses this aspect, and details a "persuasive process" by which members are brought to accept a certain body of teachings. These teachings are not treated by the participants as an abstract set of beliefs, but rather as a "living reality that is reconfirmed in each day's experience" (Antze, 1976: 325). This ideology can determine the developmental path a group takes in regard to social change orientation.

Antze's discussion of Alcoholics Anonymous provides a good example of the way in which a SHG's ideology can affect its development of social change goals. He notes that the ideology facilitates individual change, and can alter those personality traits that led the person to alcoholism. In his account, Antze makes it clear that no aspect of AA's teachings calls for change at the societal level; rather, change in the individual is exclusively recommended. Similarly, as we have noted above, Hurvitz (1976) emphasizes the ideological context of psychologically–oriented SHGs as a prime factor in their lack of interest in social change.

Numerous variations in a group's ideology can be advanced as determinants of a social change focus; we propose only one here, which seems to us to be particularly promising. This is the strictness of a group's ideology. The ideologies of SHGs can be placed on a continuum ranging from a structured, well–developed ideology, often contained in a "bible," to a loose, more diffuse ideology that leaves room for development and growth. Recovery, Inc., Alcoholics Anonymous, and Take Off Pounds Sensibly are examples of the former; the women's self–help health movement and the Mental Patient Liberation Front are examples of the latter. Katz and Bender posed the question: "Does tightness of structure and enforced belief contribute to stability and maintenance of membership? (1976: 121). To this one could add: Does it also contribute to the development of social change goals, or inhibit them, as we suggest?

## D. Transitory versus Enduring Condition

This variable has surfaced only rarely in the literature on SHGs. Katz (1981) is among the few who identify it as an important item for study. In the light of our reading of the literature, as well as our own research experience, this appears to be a promising characteristic for future exploration. In particular, some limited evidence suggests that permanency of condition may be related to social change goals. Smith (1982), for example, has noted that the transitory status of being in divorce was not conducive to the effective carrying out of social change activities. A more enduring condition, however (e.g., a disability, one's gender, homosexuality) may give one the incentive to attempt institutional change, for otherwise, no permanent solution is possible. This, clearly, is an issue for further empirical investigation.

From the foregoing discussion, a model to explain the extent of a focus on social change versus individual change, or adaptation, could be constructed. Based upon the admittedly insufficient evidence we have presented above, the model could be developed along the lines of that presented in Figure 1. If each continuum in that figure is taken as a research hypothesis, this could provide part of a program for research.

*Figure 1.* Determinants of Extent of Social Change Orientation of SHGs

Individual Focus                                                           Social Change Focus

1. Strong ties to professionals————————————Antagonistic to professionals
2. Authoritarian leadership ————————————Egalitarian, rotating leadership
3. Developed, formal ideology————————————Loose, informal ideology
4. Transitory problem ————————————————————Enduring problem

# V. CONCLUSIONS

There are two types of conclusions that the present chapter leads us toward: some generalizations about self–help groups and some areas of needed future research. Treating the two types in order, the first generalization we must make is that the terms "self–help group," "mutual help group," "mutual aid group" and related terms are not used with precision in most of the literature. In the first section of this chapter we have tried to clarify and explicate the terms self–help group (SHG) and mutual aid group, showing that SHGs properly understood are one type of mutual aid group but not the only type. The members of SHGs value personal interaction and mutual aid as a means of altering or ameliorating some pressing, alterable (at least in effects), personal problem—a stigmatizing condition. It is important to distinguish "true" SHGs, so defined, from other mutual aid, and from social service and political advocacy groups more generally.

A second substantive generalization we make is that SHGs are indeed social movement organizations because SHGs generally seek change in both the informal social support system of stigmatized individuals and in the relationship of such individuals to the relevant human service professionals and institutions. Third, SHGs are groups that try to bring about personal change by means of a variety of processes, such change ranging from adaptation to the enduring presence of a stigmatizing condition, on the one hand, to strenuous efforts to change the stigmatizing condition, on the other hand. Fourth, the socio-political change orientation of SHGs is a matter of degree, and the extent of such change orientation is a result of the effects of such SHG structural–functional factors as relationships with professionals, ideology, leadership, and the probable time span of the stigmatizing condition of most members.

Moving on to the second type of conclusions, we may first remark generally that the SHG literature is in a state of rapid growth, but its quality is far lower than its quantity. The bulk of the literature consists of simple, descriptive case studies, with little or no attempt at quantification and still less attempt to test hypotheses about relationships using quantitative data. There is a dearth of comparative studies as well. It is desirable that various types of SHGs (in case studies) be compared in a systematic qualitative analysis even if no quantative comparison is possible. It is fair to say that most of the researchers in the field of SHG study seem essentially oblivious of the large extant literatures on social movements (e.g., Marx and Wood, 1975), and voluntary action more broadly (e.g., Smith, 1975). The SHG research literature would be markedly improved in quality if its authors took the time to do more preparatory reading of relevant literature in these related fields. Finally, the SHG literature is notable for its general lack of longitudinal research, which makes causal generalizations very difficult, if not impossible to draw.

Our present literature review leads us also to some more specific suggestions for needed future research. A few of these areas that need much more research effort are answers to the following questions: What is the patterning of typological characteristics in a random sample of a population of SHGs from a defined territorial area? What are the determinants of the prevalence and incidence of SHGs in different territorial areas? What are the cross cultural variations in typological patterns and incidence–prevalence determinants for SHGs? To what extent do the various major theories of social movement origins and development apply to SHGs of various types, particularly the theories taking the power-incentives–resource mobilization approaches? What is the set of personal change processes at work in SHGs of various types, and does this pattern vary systematically with typological characteristics of SHGs? How much actual change, along what personal dimensions, tends to take place as a result of these processes, and to what extent is apparent change the result of selection effects? What is the full range of factors affecting the social change orientation of a SHG and how do these factors arise and operate together? How much sociopolitical change can actually be attributed to the activities of various kinds of SHGs? What is the role of the life cycle stage of a SHG or the larger self–help movement in all of the foregoing questions? And how do various specific SHGs and SHG types relate to each other, if at all, in networks of various types (i.e., with various types of flows and linkages)? Answering such questions as these in future years should make SHG research an active and exciting field of study of social movements, conflict and change.

# REFERENCES

Ablon, J.
  1978  "Al-Anon family groups." American Journal of Psychotherapy 28 (1): 30–45.
Alcoholics Anonymous
  1957  Alcoholics Anonymous Comes of Age: A Brief History of AA. New York: Alcoholics Anonymous Publishing.
Antze, P.
  1976  "The role of ideologies in peer psychotherapy organizations: Some theoretical considerations and three case studies." Journal of Applied Behavioral Science 12 (3): 323–46.
Ascheim, B., E. Horman, T. Queisser, and P. Silverman
  1978  Development of Special Mental Health Technical Assistance Materials for Self–Help Groups in Particular Populations. Cambridge, MA: American Institutes for Research in the Behavioral Sciences.
Back, K., and R. Taylor
  1976  "Self–Help groups: Tool or symbol?" Journal of Applied Behavioral Science 12 (3): 295–309.
Bean, Margaret
  1975  "Alcoholics Anonymous. Part II." Psychiatric Annals 5 (3): 7–57.
Blue Cross and Blue Shield
  1974  Directory of Mutual Help Organizations in Massachusetts. Boston: Blue Cross, Blue Shield.
Borkman, T.
  1976  "Experiential knowledge: A new concept for the analysis of self–help groups." Social Service Review (September): 445–456.
Borman, L.
  1974  Explorations in Self–Help and Mutual Aid. Evanston, Ill.: Center for Urban Affairs, Northwestern University.
  1976  "Self–jelp and the professional." Social Policy 7 (2): 47.
Borman, L., J. Davies, and D. Droge
  1980  "Self–help groups for persons with epilepsy." In B. Hermann (ed.), A Multidisciplinary Handbook of Epilepsy. Springfield, Ill.: Charles Thomas, Inc.
Camberg, L.
  1978  Cancer Support Group: Pilot Project Evaluation Report. Boston: Sidney Farber Cancer Institute.
Dean, S.
  1969  "Recovery, inc.: Giving psychiatry an assist." Medical Economics (September 2): 150.
  1971a  "The role of self-conducted group therapy in psycho-rehabilitation: A look at Recovery, inc." American Journal of Psychiatry 127 (7): 934–937.
  1971b  "Self–Help group therapy: Mental patients rediscover will power." International Journal of Social Psychiatry 17: 72–78.

Dumont, Matthew P.
    1974  "Self–Help treatment programs." American Journal of Psychiatry 131(6): 631–635.
Gans, Herbert
    1975  "The Levittowners." In P. Rose (ed.), Seeing Ourselves, New York: Knopf, 185–202.
Gartner, A., and F. Riessman
    1975  Self–Help and Health: A Report. New York: New Careers Training Laboratory.
Gartner, Alan, and Frank Riessman
    1977  Self–Help in the Human Services. San Francisco: Jossey-Bass.
    1979  HELP: A Working Guide to Self–Help Groups. New York: New Viewpoints.
    1980  "Lots of helping hands." New York Times, February 18.
Gartner, Audrey
    1980  Self–Help Reporter 4 (2): 1–2.
    1981  Self–Help Reporter 5 (3): 1–8.
Gerlach, Luther, and Virginia Hine
    1970  People, Power, Change: Movements of Social Transformation. Indianapolis: Bobbs-Merrill.
Ginsberg, L.
    1974  "The mental patients liberation movement." Social Work 19 (1): 3–4, 103.
Goldhammer, H.
    1964  "Some factors affecting participation in voluntary associations." In E. W. Burgess and D. Bogue (eds.), Contributions to Urban Sociology. Chicago: U. of Chicago Press.
Greer, C.
    1976  "A cautionary note." Social Policy 7 (2): 2.
Hamilton, A.
    1980  An Exploratory Study of Therapeutic Self–Help Child Abuse Groups. D. S. W. Thesis, U.C.L.A. School of Social Welfare.
Henry, S.
    1978  "The dangers of self–help groups." New Society 22: 654–656.
Holzinger, A.
    1965  "Synanon through the eyes of a visiting psychologist." Quarterly Journal of Studies in Alcohol 26: 304–339.
Hurvitz, N.
    1976  "The origins of the peer self–help psychotherapy group movement." Journal of Applied Behavioral Science 12 (3): 363–380.
Jertson, H.
    1975  "Self–help groups." Social Work 20 (2): 144–145.
Kaplan, M.
    1978  "Women and the stress of moving." Social Casework (July): 434–436.
Katz, A.
    1965  "Application of self–help concepts in current social welfare." Social Work 10 (3): 68–74.
    1979  "Self–help heath groups: Some clarifications." Social Science and Medicine 13A: 491–494.
Katz, Alfred
    1981  "Self–help health groups: Some clarifications." Social Science and Medicine 13A: 491–94.
Katz, Alfred, and Eugene Bender
    1976  The Strength in Us: Self–Help Groups in the Modern World. New York: Franklin-Watts.
Killilea, Marie
    1976  "Mutual help organizations: Interpretations in the literature." In G. Caplan and M. Killilea (eds.), Support Systems and Mutual Help: Miltidisciplinary Explorations. New York: Grune and Stratton, 34–62.

Kleeman, M., and DePree, J.
1976   "Self–help groups and their effectiveness as agents for chronic illness care: The case of kidney transplant patients." In Gartner, A. and Riessman, F. (eds.), Self–Help and Health: A Report. New York: New Careers Training Laboratory, 69–76.

Korpi, W.
1974   "Conflict, power and relative deprivation." American Political Science Review 68: 1569–1578.

Landy, D. and Singer, S.
1961   "The social organization and culture of a club for former mental patients. Human Relations 14 (1): 34–41.

Levin, L., A. Katz, and E. Holst
1979   Self–Care: Lay Initiatives in Health. Second Edition. New York: Prodist.

Levy, L.
1976   "Self–help groups: Types and psychological processes. Journal of Applied Behavioral Science 12 (3): 455–465.

Lieberman, Morton
1975   "Group therapies." In G. Usdin (ed.), Overview of the Psychotherapies. New York: Brunner-Mazel: 92–117.

Lieberman, Morton, and Leonard Borman
1979   Self–Help Groups for Coping with Crisis. San Francisco: Jossey-Bass.

Lieberman, M., and Gourash, N.
1979   "Effects of change groups on the elderly." In Lieberman, M., and L. Borman (eds.), Self–Help Groups for Coping with Crisis. San Francisco: Jossey Bass, 387–405.

McCarthy, John D., and Mayer N. Zald
1973   The Trends of Social Movements in America: Professionalization and Resource Mobilization. Morristown, NJ: General Learning Press.

Mantell, J., E. Alexander, and M. Kleiman
1976   "Social work and self–help groups." Health and Social Work 1 (1): 86–100.

Marx, Gary, and James L. Wood
1975   "Strands of theory and research in collective behavior." Annual Review of Sociology 1: 363–428.

Mowrer, O.
1974   "Small groups movement in historical perspective." In L. Borman (ed.), Explorations in Self–Help and Mutual Aid. Evanston, Ill.: Center for Urban Affairs, Northwestern University, 22–44.

Moeller, M.
1978   Selbsthilfegruppen. Hamburg: Rohwolt.

Ofshe, R.
1974   "Social structure and social control in synanon." Journal of Voluntary Action Research 3 (3–4): 67–76.

Olson, Mancur
1965   The Logic of Collective Action. Cambridge, MA: Harvard University Press.

Petrunik, M.
1972   "Seeing the light: A study of conversion to Alcoholics Anonymous." Journal of Voluntary Action Research 1 (4): 30–38.

Pillemer, K.
1980   "The self–help movement: A political challenge?" Presented at the Conference on the Clinical Application of the Social Sciences to Health, Urbana, Ill.
1981   "Group interaction and adaptation to a chronic condition." Presented at the Annual Meeting of the American Sociological Association, Toronto.

Riessman, F.
    1965    "The 'helper' therapy principle." Social Work 10 (2): 27–32.
Righton, Peter
    1976    "Sexual minorities and social work." Health and Social Service Journal 86: 392–393.
Ritchie, O.
    1948    "A sociohistorical survey of Alcoholics Anonymous." Quarterly Journal of Studies in
            Alcohol 9: 119–156.
Robinson, David, and Stuart Henry
    1977    Self–Help and Health. London: Martin Robertson.
Rosen, Gerald M.
    1976    "The development and use of nonprescription behavior therapies." American Psychologist
            31 (2): 139–141.
Sagarin, Edward
    1969    Odd Man In: Societies of Deviants in America. New York: Quadrangle Books.
Sidel, V., and R. Sidel
    1977    "Primary health care in relation to socio-political structure." Social Science and Medicine
            11: 415–419.
Silverman, P.
    1976    "Mutual help." In R. Hirschowitz and B. Levy (eds.), The Changing Mental Health
            Scene. New York: Spectrum, 233–244.
    1978    "Mutual help: An alternate network." In Women in Midlife: Secrity and Fulfillment (Part
            I). Select Committee on Aging, U.S. House of Representatives: 256–269.
    1980    Mutual Help Groups: Organization and Development. Beverly Hills, CA: Sage
            Publications.
Silverman, Phyllis R.
    1975    "Are we really 'already doing it'?" Archives of the Foundation of Thanatology 5 (1): 52.
Smelser, Neil J.
*    1962    Theory of Collective Behavior. New York: Free Press of Glencoe.
Smith, D.
    1982    "Sources of ineffectiveness in self–help groups: The example of a self–help group for men
            in divorce." In D. Smith and A. Katz (eds.), Self–Help Groups and Voluntary Action:
            Some International Perspectives. New York: Irvington Publishers.
Smith, David Horton
    1975    "Voluntary action and voluntary groups." Annual Review of Sociology 1: 247–270.
Smith, David Horton, Richard D. Reddy, and Burt R. Baldwin
    1972    "Types of voluntary action: A definitional essay." In D. H. Smith et al. (eds.), Voluntary
            Action Research 1972. Lexington, MA: Lexington Books, D. C. Heath, 159–195.
Smith, David Horton, Mary Seguin, and Marjorie Collins
    1973    "Dimensions and categories of voluntary organizations/NGOs." Journal of Voluntary
            Action Research 2 (2): 116–120.
Smith, David Horton, and Alfred H. Katz
    1982    Self–Help Groups and Voluntary Action: Some International Perspectives. New York:
            Irvington Publishers.
Spiegel, D.
    1976    "Going public and self–help." In G. Caplan and M. Killilea (eds.), Support Systems and
            Mutual Help. New York: Grune and Stratton, 135–154.
Tilly, Charles
    1969    "Collective violence in European perspective." In H. G. Davis and T. R. Gurr (eds.), The
            History of Violence in America. New York: Praeger, 4–45.
Toch, Hans
    1965    The Social Psychology of Social Movements. Indianapolis: Bobbs-Merrill.

Tracy, G., and Z. Gussow
   1976   "Self–help health groups: A grassroots response to the need for services." Journal of
          Applied Behavioral Science 12 (3): 381–396.
Trice, H., and P. Roman
   1970   "Delabeling, relabeling, and Alcoholics Anonymous." Social Problems 17 (4): 538–546.
United Cerebral Palsy Associations, Inc.
   1978   Annual Report.
Van Harberden, P., and R. Lafaille
   1978   Zelf-hulp. The Hague: VUGA.
Vattano, A. J.
   1972   "Power to the people: Self–help groups." Social Work 17 (4): 7–15.
Wechsler, H.
   1960   "The expatient organization: A survey." Journal of Social Issues 16 (2): 47–53.
   1976   "The self–help organization in the mental health field: Recovery, inc., a case study." In
          G. Caplan and M. Killilea (eds.), Support Systems and Mutual Help. New York: Grune
          and Stratton: 187–212.
Weiss, R.
   1976   "The contributions of an organization of single parents to the well-being of its members."
          In G. Caplan and M. Killilea (eds.), Support Systems and Mutual Help. New York: Grune
          and Stratton: 177–185.
Withorn, A.
   1980   "Helping ourselves: The limits and potential of self–help." Social Policy 11 (3): 20–28.

# SOCIAL CHANGE AND THE PARTICIPATION OF WOMEN IN THE AMERICAN MILITARY

Mady Wechsler Segal and David R. Segal

## I. INTRODUCTION

The representation of women in the United States armed forces has increased from less than 2 percent of the force in 1971 to approximately 8 percent in 1981. Early in the Carter administration, it had been projected to reach 12 percent by the mid–1980s. However, opposition to this goal within the defense establishment became apparent in the late 1970s, and decisions were made during the first

Research in Social Movements, Conflicts and Change, Vol. 5, pages 235–258.
Copyright © 1983 by JAI Press Inc.
All rights of reproduction in any form reserved.
ISBN: 0-89232-301-9

year of the Reagan administration to postpone further increases until the impact of greater representation of females among our military personnel could be more systematically assessed. It is our thesis that policies regarding the utilization of women in the American armed forces have resulted primarily from changes in America's domestic situation, and reflect a national ambivalence regarding appropriate roles for women. We do not mean to suggest that the United States has been unique in experiencing the phenomena we shall describe below. Indeed, in some instances they are common, at least among the industrial nations of the West. In other cases, it is anticipated that they will become common, although they have not yet become widespread. The important point is that no other nation, either friendly or potentially belligerent, has responded to these phenomena by increasing its dependence upon female military personnel to the extent that the United States has.

The first set of factors affecting the increased utilization of women reflects changes in the nature of the military institution. These include: changes in military technology that make warfare more capital intensive and permit a reduction in the size of basic weapon systems; a change in the definition of military mission that has deemphasized the concept of wartime mobilization and emphasized in its place the existence of a force–in–being to fulfill deterrence and constabulary functions even in peacetime; and a change in our philosophy of military manpower management related to the conversion from a military force based upon a mixture of conscription and voluntarism to an all–volunteer armed force.

The second set of factors is demographic, and reflects the bursting of the baby–boom bubble in the late 1950s. The birth dearth of the 1960s, responsive in part to ecological concerns regarding population growth, will yield increasingly small groups of young men of traditional age–eligibility for military service. If we assume a force–in–being of constant or increasing size, means must be found to expand the pool of people available for military service.

The third set of factors reflects changing roles of women in the United States, including increased participation in the labor force, and broader citizenship participation generally. As military service in the United States has come to be increasingly defined as simply another form of employment in the era of the all–volunteer force, increased representation of women in the military can be seen as an outgrowth of their greater labor force participation. Beyond this, given the traditional association of the ''right to fight'' with other kinds of citizenship rights and obligations, the increased utilization of women in the military can be seen as a demand for, and manifestation of, advances made in the ongoing citizenship revolution. Fluctuations in policies regarding the utilization of women in the military can likewise be seen as a lack of national consensus on the extension of full citizenship to women. This lack is reflected as well in the failure to ratify the Equal Rights Amendment.

# II. THE CHANGING NATURE OF MILITARY ORGANIZATION

## A. Technological Change

The military institution has changed historically, both as a function of general technological development, and as a function of changing technologies of warfare in particular. Although conflict between political units has been an ever present characteristic of human society (Andreski, 1968), the emergence of large standing armed forces, as opposed to armies composed of agricultural workers mobilized to fight wars when they were not engaged in harvesting or sowing, was dependent on the ability of a social unit to produce the economic resources necessary to maintain large numbers of people outside the domestic productive economy. In the pre–industrial world, this economic base was provided by the armed force itself, through conquest and expansion. To the extent that an army could conquer and occupy new territory, and gain control of new resources, it could be supported. Where they did not fulfill this function, armies were composed of people who played productive roles in the civilian economy, as farmers, hunters, and so on, and played warrior or military roles only periodically.

Modern economic systems, by contrast, are able to produce a sufficient surplus to maintain professional soldiers even when they are not engaged in imperial conquest. The return to such an investment of societal resources is low, however, relative to other potential uses. Thus, at least through the first part of the twentieth century, the industrial nations of the West utilized a mobilization model of military manpower, maintaining relatively small nuclei of military organizations in peacetime, and expanding the force in times of conflict by taking large numbers of people out of civilian roles, and making soldiers of them. This was accomplished largely through conscription.

The mobilization model assumed that in the event of war, the states involved would have time to raise, train, and field their fighting forces, and that the peacetime nucleus could fill the organizational and training functions, as well as necessary defensive functions, until the newly mobilized force was ready to take the field. Technological changes in the mid–twentieth century, however, deprived nations of the luxuries of time and distance from the battlefield that the mobilization model assumed. The advent of air power and, more recently, nuclear technology decreased the time needed and increased the distance possible for the use of weapon systems. This put at risk concentrations of civilian populations at great distance from the battlefield, and blurred the distinctions between military and civilian, combatant and noncombatant, through the socialization of danger (Lasswell, 1941). The technologies themselves blurred the military and civilian sector distinction as military forces came increasingly to depend on material and organizational technologies found in the civilian sector. The great majority of military personnel through the American Civil War were infantry-men, and their basic tools were rifles and bayonets. The industrial revolution imposed increasing occupational specialization on the armed forces, first in the navy, as steam power replaced the sail, and ultimately in the other services as well, as they became increasingly dependent upon vehicular transport, electronics, and increasingly sophisticated weapon systems (Wool, 1968). If the exclusion of women from the armed forces in the early years was justified by the rigors of infantry combat, that justification became less applicable as increasingly larger proportions of military personnel found themselves in transportation, communications, electronics, supply, and other technical and administrative specialties frequently performed by women in the civilian labor force, rather than in combat specialties.

Another component of technological change was miniaturization: the ability to package increasingly powerful mechanical devices in increasingly smaller units. In the civilian sector, this trend has been most obvious with regard to computational machinery, and this is manifested in the armed forces as well, which are no less dependent than any large civilian organization on computers. In the military, it extends to basic field equipment as well. Infantry rifles and radio equipment, for example, have historically been heavy items. Indeed, in the Vietnam War, the size of our basic infantry weapon, the M–14 rifle, was a disadvantage. It was difficult for our South Vietnamese allies to use because they are smaller in stature, on the average, than American soldiers. The solution to this problem was the development of the smaller and lighter M–16 rifle, a weapon that could more easily be used by South Vietnamese men and, if necessary, by American women, who are also, on the average, smaller in stature than the average American male soldier.

## B. Definition of Military Mission

The increasing power of military technology, and the waning of the era of military imperialism in the West, made the mobilization model increasingly inappropriate. Not only did nations find themselves deprived of the lead time required for mobilization for large–scale wars, but as it became obvious that in a confrontation between major powers victory would be Pyrrhic, the military mission came increasingly to be defined in terms of constabulary, or peacekeeping, rather than war–fighting operations (e.g., Janowitz, 1960: 418–441; Janowitz, 1974: 471–508; Moskos, 1976). The distinction between peacetime and wartime became less relevant for military organization, and the need to maintain a large standing force became obvious as the deterrence concept and the need to respond rapidly should deterrence fail, assumed primacy. The mass force, based upon the mobilization model, declined after World War II. With the emergence of a "new long term trend . . . toward smaller, fully professional, and more fully alerted and self–contained military forces; the direction was away from a mobilization force to a military force 'in being'" (Janowitz, 1975: 121). The mission of armed forces oriented "not to wage war but to preserve the peace" (the motto of the United States Army War College since early in the twentieth century) was reflected in the attitudes of Army personnel who were surveyed in 1978 regarding the kinds of armed conflicts in which the United States might be involved during the next decade. Over 80 percent of officers and enlisted men thought it likely that the United States would be involved in peacekeeping operations. By contrast, less than 65 percent expected that we would be involved in guerilla wars or limited conventional wars, and even fewer expected that we would be engaged in large–scale conventional wars, or either tactical or strategic nuclear conflicts (Segal, 1981). The change in mission definition, away from overt conflict and toward constabulary, police–type operations, suggests a structure amenable to increased female participation, parallel to the trend in civilian peace– keeping forces in America.

## C. Tools of Manpower Management

The basis of the mobilization model is the process of conscription, which brings people into the armed forces not with the intention of making career soldiers of them, but rather as exacting a citizenship obligation in support of national security, which is assumed to be a public good. The process of conscription has appeared most legitimate in wartime, in the face of an apparent threat to national security. However, as the military mission has deemphasized war–fighting and stressed instead deterrence and constabulary operations, the external threat has been less apparent, the military mission more ambiguous, and the conscription process more difficult to justify. Indeed, Van Doorn (1975) and others have noted a general trend away from military conscription in the industrialized nations of the West, as an element of the decline of the mass army. The transition from a force combining conscription with voluntarism (in which some voluntarism was conscription–motivated) to an all–volunteer force (which some have characterized as a system of economic conscription) occurred in the United States in 1973.

The change from conscription to an all–volunteer force was part of a broader redefinition of the nature of military service in America. In a presentation focusing on enlisted personnel, at the 1973 meetings of the American Sociological Association, Charles Moskos noted, almost in passing, an "organizational shift from a predominantly institutional format (i.e., legitimized by normative values) to one more resembling that of an occupation (i.e., akin to civilian marketplace standards)" (Mokos, 1973a). By 1976, Moskos had identified the definition of military service as a calling, as the individual orientation associated with the institutional format; and the definition of service as a job, as the individual orientation associated with the occupational format (Moskos, 1978). Policymakers in the United States have been greatly influenced by Moskos' conceptualization, and behave as though a choice must be made between these definitions. At least as far as the recruitment of personnel is concerned, they have emphasized the similarities between military service and civilian employment. Econometric assumptions of military service made by President Nixon's Commission on an All–Volunteer Force (1970), and by military recruiting strategies that have tried to compete with civilian employers for high quality personnel, have emphasized the least traditionally military characteristics of service, and have emphasized pecuniary rewards and skill training, rather than symbolic and solidary incentives. This has brought into the armed services young people who in fact think of their service as a job, and tend not to think of war–fighting as a part of that job (Gottlieb, 1980). The progressive redefinition of military service in terms of civilian labor force processes, coupled with an emphasis on affirmative action employment programs within the entire federal government structure, in turn, had implications for the perceptions by groups discriminated against in the private sector of the civilian labor force, notably racial and ethnic minorities and women, regarding employment opportunities in the military.

It is important to recall that the demise of military conscription in the United States, and the adoption of an all–volunteer force, was in part a response to pressures from the anti–Vietnam War movement in the United States. The military draft, never very popular in America, came under increasing criticism during the Vietnam War in the 1960s (Bachman, Blair, and Segal, 1977: 9–15). By 1966, there were student demonstrations against the draft and its inequities. On July 1 of that year, President Johnson appointed a national advisory commission on Selective Service (the Marshall Commission), to consider the past, present, and prospective functioning of the selective service (and other systems of national service) in the light of such factors as fairness to all citizens, military manpower requirements, and budgetary and administrative considerations.

The existing draft that the Marshall Commission had to evaluate was not an equitable one. Indeed, during the post–Korean War period, with decreased manpower needs, the Selective Service System had found it increasingly difficult to find criteria for not drafting large categories of young men, which was necessary to justify the selections that were made. Deferments on the basis of age, education, occupation, and parenthood made the draft appear increasingly inequitable. In 1963, as the post–World War II baby boom began to come of military age eligibility, the Selective Service began to defer all married men.

In part on the basis of the work of the Marshall Commission, President Johnson included a number of reforms of the Selective Service System in his March 1967 request to the Congress for a four year extension of his power to induct men into the armed forces. In his message to the Congress, the President stated a personal preference for an all–volunteer military, but he felt that an all–volunteer force could not be expanded rapidly enough to meet a sudden challenge, and that it would be very expensive.

The unpopularity of the Vietnam War increased, as did the visibility of the peace movement and demonstrations on campuses and in Washington. There was also increasing hostility to the draft itself, as draft calls increased to fill the ranks of the American Army in Vietnam. During the 1968 presidential campaign, Richard Nixon promised to end the draft once the Vietnam War was over. Within three months of his inauguration, Nixon had appointed the President's Commission on an All–Volunteer Armed Force (The Gates Commission), which was charged with the development of "a comprehensive plan for eliminating conscription. . . ." The Gates Commission report emphasized the disadvantages of conscription, and proposed an all–volunteer force as being more consistent with our basic national values. The President accepted the major conclusions of the Commission and, in a message to Congress in April 1970, stated his objective to reduce draft calls to zero, an objective that he repeated in a message to the Congress in January 1971.

Public opposition to the Vietnam War, and perceptions that the draft discriminated against blacks and the poor, continued to erode public support for military conscription (Segal and Blair, 1976:7). Steps taken in the late 1960s and in 1970 to reduce the inequities of conscription were not sufficient to turn the tide of public opinion. In 1971, the Selective Service law expired, but was extended for two years by the Congress. However, draft calls remained low. In January 1973, six months earlier than required by Congress, Secretary of Defense Melvin Laird announced the end of peacetime conscription.

## III. The Changing Demographic Context

The changes in the nature of military organization, military mission, and, perhaps most importantly, military manpower policies, discussed above, have taken place in the context of fluctuating demographic patterns. Indeed, it is possible that the very size of the post–World War II baby–boom, leading to a very small percentage of those liable to conscription cohorts, in fact being drafted, contributed materially to the perceived inequity of the draft, and to its eventual demise.

Prior to World War II, the birth rates in most industrial nations of the West reached their nadirs during the depression of the 1930s. However, they rose during the 1940s and 1950s, and indeed, while they declined again starting in the late 1950s, they remained above the depression level until the early 1970s. The average number of births per woman in the United States had fallen to about 2.2 during the depression. It reached a zenith of 3.3 in the late 1950s, and subsequently has returned to the lower level.

The growth of the population during the 1940s and 1950s, influenced both by high birth rates and by large numbers of young women, is the period referred to as the "baby boom," and produced the cohorts that were to come of military age eligibility between the late 1950s and the late 1970s, during most of which time the United States had a system of military conscription. As noted above, the presence of large numbers of young men in the draft pool in these baby boom cohorts, of whom only a relatively small proportion were actually drafted, increased the apparent inequity of the draft. In the last years of conscription, attempts were made to remove systematic deferment patterns, which had become exemption patterns, from the selection process, and to increase the randomness of selections through the use of the draft lottery. Randomness, however, is not equivalent to equity, and it is our feeling that the size of the cohorts, and hence the selection ratio, were more important contributors to the unpopularity of the draft than was the method of selection employed.

The fertility decline since the late 1950s reflected the fact that people delayed their marriages longer than they had in the 1940s and early 1950s. In addition, they delayed the births of their first children longer, and spaced their children more widely. In part, this reflects the widespread adoption of new and more effective methods of contraception in the 1960s and 1970s, allowing parents to exert some choice in family size. Preferences for smaller families, in turn, may reflect to some extent a general ecological concern with the consequences of population growth (Wrong; 1977:70).

Whatever the reason for declining fertility, it has implications for military personnel policy. The number of 18–21 year old males in the American population peaked in 1978. This is the last baby–boom cohort. The decline from 1978 to 1982 has been modest: less than 1 percent per year. The major effect of the birth dearth of the 1960s will be observed between 1983 and 1987, when the decline in group size will increase to 2.5 percent per year. By 1990, the number of 17–21 year old American males will be 17 percent below the 1978 level of 10,800,000 young men.

Faced with declining cohort size, a number of options are available to policy makers, short of returning to a system of military conscription. One is to reduce the size of the force. The size of our armed forces was indeed reduced in the wake of the Vietnam War, but the Reagan administration has indicated that it will seek to increase the size of our armed forces, even given the smaller personnel pool. A second option is to reduce the minimum standards for volunteers, and accept declines in quality to get the needed quantity of personnel. This was in fact done during the 1970s, but raised major questions about the combat effectiveness of the force (Moskos, 1980). A third option is to decrease the emphasis on youth in the armed forces, and accept larger numbers of older people for service (Binkin and Kyriakopoulos, 1979). The services have tried to avoid this option, but in 1981, the Army decided that it would emphasize the retention of people already in the service, rather than the recruitment of new personnel in meeting its manpower needs. This of course will produce a force that is not only older, but also has a different mix of short–term citizen soldiers and long–term careerists. A fourth option is to make greater use of new sources of manpower, including women.

## IV. CHANGES IN WOMEN'S ROLES
## IN THE UNITED STATES

*A. The Citizenship Revolution*

Changes in the roles of women in the armed forces, and in the labor force more generally, can be seen as a reflection of an ongoing transformation of Western societies, which "have steadily moved to a condition in which the rights of citizenship are universal" (Bendix, 1964: 3). In the nations of Western Europe, the most dramatic manifestation of this citizenship revolution has been the extension of citizenship to the lower classes. New middle–class and working–class groups also had to be progressively incorporated into the citizenry of the United States. However, the absence of a long history of repressive class politics in this country relative to Europe made the ascriptive elements of citizenship extension in this country more pronounced (see, for example, Dahl, 1961).

Marshall (1950) has noted the importance of military service as an obligation of citizenship, and Janowitz has analyzed the central role played by military institutions in the evolution of parliamentary democracy, and of military service as a component of citizenship. "From World War I onward, citizen military service had been seen as a device by which excluded segments of society could achieve political legitimacy and rights" (Janowitz, 1975: 77–78).

In twentieth–century America, this relationship between military service and citizenship has been most dramatic with regard to the racial integration of the armed forces. Through the World War II period, the incorporation of blacks into the civilian citizenry was only minimally effective, and blacks in the military served in segregated units, under a quota, for the most part limited to non–combat jobs, and with an infinitesimally small likelihood of being commissioned as an officer. On the eve of Pearl Harbor, there were only five black officers in the Army, and three of these were chaplains (Moskos, 1973b: 96).

During World War II, with the exception of a short period of integration under battle conditions in the Ardennes, blacks continued to serve in segregated units, performing primarily quartermaster, construction, and transportation functions. Even the black combat units that did exist were used largely as a source of unskilled labor. The demand for recognition of the "right to fight" became a major slogan of black organizations that wanted the willingness of the black community to fulfill citizenship obligations demonstrated. However, an Army board in 1945 recommended the continuation of racial segregation and the quota system, as well as the use of blacks exclusively in support rather than combat functions. It was not until 1950, under the direction of President Truman's 1948 executive order to desegregate the armed forces and most importantly the manpower requirements of the Korean War, that segregation, the quota, and the combat exclusion truly disappeared. The racial integration of the armed forces during the Korean War preceded the gains achieved by the civil rights movement toward racial integration and equality in American civilian institutions. The integration of blacks into the armed forces anticipated the issues raised with regard to integrating women by three decades (Segal, Kinzer and Woelfel, 1977).

The relationship between military service and political citizenship was more recently demonstrated in the case of young adults. One of the themes of the movement against the Vietnam War was that young men between the ages of eighteen and twenty–one, who were liable to military conscription, were not eligible to vote. They were, therefore, not able to participate in the political processes that selected the members of the executive and legislative branches of the federal government who determined American military policy, including policies regarding the waging of war. The contribution of the anti–war movement to the end of conscription was preceded by its contribution to the passage in 1971 of the twenty-sixth amendment to the United States Constitution, which lowered the age of political majority to eighteen, allowing those liable to military conscription to participate in the electoral process. The unfortunate lesson of the Korean and Vietnam Wars with regard to the extension of citizenship rights to blacks and to young adults may be that the military serves as a vehicle for the citizenship revolution primarily during times of war.

The social strains reflecting the extension of equality to women, in both civilian and military institutions in America, can be seen as the current phase of the citizenship revolution. The major barrier to women's participation in the armed forces has been the constellation of cultural values about appropriate roles for women. Such values have had two interrelated thrusts. First, women have been seen as psychologically different from men. The stereotypical feminine personality traits include warmth, nurturance, submissiveness, dependency, passivity, and lack of aggressiveness: characteristics that are not highly valued in the military. Second, the belief in psychological differences between males and females has reinforced cultural acceptance of a division of labor based on gender. The world of work has been viewed as a man's world; woman's world has revolved around the family. The culturally ideal role for women has been that of the full–time wife and mother. These cultural values are in a state of transition, as they are being affected by changes in women's actual participation in family and work roles.

## B. Changing Family Patterns and Women's Labor Force Participation

Women's participation in the labor force is dependent upon the degree to which they are free from family responsibilities, their motivation to be employed, and the availability of jobs. Trends in family patterns in the United States show women marrying later, married women having fewer children, more women choosing not to have children, and more female–headed families (Current Population Reports, 1975; U.S. Department of Labor, 1969). These changes, as well as increased longevity, have contributed to the housewife role becoming a less exclusive role for women. Women are spending considerably less of their adult lives preoccupied with raising children and running households. This enables them to be available to participate in the labor force for a greater proportion of their lives.

The motivation of women to be employed has been increasing as a result of both financial and ideological factors. The greater number of female–headed families means that more women are responsible for the financial support of their families. The high rates of inflation in the 1970s and early 1980s have created pressure on the married woman to work outside the home in order to help maintain her family's standard of living. These financial pressures have occurred at a time when the women's movement for equality has encouraged women to recognize and express desires to work as a means of personal fulfillment, power, and financial independence.

The women's movement has also affected the availability of jobs to women and the attractiveness of those jobs. Affirmative action programs have increased job opportunities for women. Legislation, court actions, and private sector policies have helped to decrease wage discrimination against women, relative to men in the same jobs. Liberalized maternity leave policies and the increased availability of child care facilities have enabled women to more effectively combine work and family roles.

All of these trends have contributed to a virtual revolution in the proportion of women in the labor force. The labor force participation rates of women have increased continuously since 1920, and increases since 1950 have been dramatic. By 1980, 51 percent of all American women were in the labor force. The percentage varies by age, marital status, and number and ages of children, but is at least 50 percent in each category of women under 55 years of age, except those with at least one child under 6 years old. Even among women with preschool children, the percent in the labor foce has increased sharply: to 47 percent by 1980 (Bureau of Labor Statistics, 1980).

It has become increasingly common for American women to work outside the home for all or most of their adult lives. The most common family pattern in the United States today consists of a husband and wife and children, with both parents in the labor force. In 1980, of married women (husband present) with children 6 to 17 years old, 62 percent were in the labor force (Bureau of Labor Statistics, 1980).

Despite the increased labor force participation of women, they are still concentrated in relatively few occupations: clerical work, service work, retail sales, teaching, and nursing. These occupations account for more than two–thirds of employed women (U.S. Census Bureau, 1979). In addition, the average income of full–time workers is substantially lower for women than men. This difference persists when we control for the effects of age, education, marital status, and occupational prestige (Featherman and Hauser, 1976; McLaughlin, 1978; Suter and Miller, 1973; Treiman and Terrell, 1975). Employed married women also spend more time on household tasks (including child care) than their husbands and make more career sacrifices for their families than men do (Duncan, Schuman, and Duncan, 1973; Frieze et al., 1978).

## C. Women in Predominantly Male Spheres

Most roles culturally defined as appropriate for women, both family roles and work roles, are "characterized by their supportive, enabling, facilitating, and vicarious features" (Lipman–Blumen and Tickamyer, 1975: 309). These features are absent from predominantly male arenas, including not only the military, but also mathematics, science, corporate management, police work, and sports. These fields have been traditionally socially defined as male domains; girls and women have been socialized to avoid participation in these fields. Achievement in these arenas has been seen as unfeminine and inappropriate for females.

During the past two decades, there has been a great deal of social change in the actual and normatively expected roles for American women, including greater recognition of girls' and women's abilities in male–dominated areas. As stereotypes and norms are altered and the expectations communicated to girls change, we can expect more girls to pursue study and careers in previously male fields. If this happens, there would be an increase in the number of women who desire to enter the military and who have the requisite abilities to perform in military jobs. At the present time, however, the socialization experiences of the cohorts already of military age act to minimize aspirations for military service among women, and accentuate resistance among men to the notion of women in the military. While movement of females into male dominated areas is slow, and not inevitable, there are nonetheless some indications that it is occurring.

For example, there is evidence of much greater female participation and success in sports (Leonard, 1980; Sprint, 1980). The number of girls participating in high school interscholastic sports programs increased by over 600 percent from 1970 to 1978 (Leonard, 1980: 201). This dramatic increase is largely attributable to recent legislation requiring schools to provide sports programs for female students and to equalize salaries for male and female coaches. From 1978 to 1980, the number of girls in high school athletic programs fell by about 10 percent, but the number of boys in such programs fell by about 16 percent (National Federation of State High School Associations, 1980).

Another traditionally male arena, police work, shows an increase in the number of women, and their work now includes patrol duties (Bloch and Anderson, 1974; Greenwald, Connolly, and Bloch, 1974; Martin, 1980). The performance of American policewomen in situations of potential and actual physical violence may be particularly important in changing attitudes toward and policies affecting women's participation in the military, given the assumption, noted earlier, that service in the modern military may be more like police work than like traditional military operations.

## D. Women in the United States Military: Public Opinion and Public Policy

Before World War II, with some minor exceptions, women in the United States military served only as nurses. These nurses were under a separate command structure from regular military personnel. During World War II, each of the services established a women's unit, distinct from the nurse corps and also distinct from the rest of the force, with a separate command structure. (For a thorough history of women's participation through World War II, see Treadwell, 1954.) Only recently have the women's branches been integrated with the men's armed services: in 1978, Congress passed legislation abolishing the Women's Army Corps as a separate unit.

The number of women in the military has varied greatly, while the percentage has always been small. The largest number and concentration of women in the United States military, until recently, occurred in 1945, when approximately 265,000 women constituted 2.2 percent of the force of over 12 million (Goldman, 1973: 895). Legislation passed in 1947 and 1948 placed severe limitations on the numbers and functions of military women (see Binkin and Bach, 1977: 10–12). A ceiling of 2 percent was placed on the percentage of enlisted personnel who could be female, and female officers (not counting nurses) could number at most 10 percent of enlisted women. In the 1950s, the number of military women varied between approximately 22,000 in 1950 (1.5 percent) and approximately 35,000 in 1955 (1.3 percent). In 1967, the 2 percent limitation was removed, but by 1971 women still constituted less than 2 percent of the military (about 42,800).

The minimal participation of women in the military from the 1940s through the 1960s reflects American public opinion of that era, which is a crucial constraint on policy, and an important indicator of the degree of movement toward equality between men and women. Table 1 presents a series of questions regarding service by women included over the years in national surveys of between 1500 and 1600 persons. Responses to these questions manifest some interesting and fairly regular patterns. In November 1940, prior to American involvement in World War II, only minorities of both men and women were favorable toward drafting women for non–combat jobs, even where the question did not specify that they might be drafted to do those jobs within the military. Women, however, were somewhat more favorable than men. It should be noted that America's first "peacetime" draft had been established just two months earlier. Some of the opposition to drafting women may well reflect general opposition to this draft

In December 1941, with the recent bombing of Pearl Harbor and America's entry into the war, pro–involvement sentiment soared, with almost two–thirds of

*Table 1.*   American Public Opinion Toward the Military Service
of Women Over Time

| | | Percent Favorable | |
| Date | Question Wording | Male | Female |
|---|---|---|---|
| Nov. 1940 | "Would you be in favor of starting now to draft American women between the ages of 21 and 35 to train them for jobs in war time?" | 38.0 | 47.5 |
| Dec. 1941 | (Same as Nov. 1940) | 64.0 | 72.7 |
| July 1943 | "Would you be in favor of drafting single women between the ages of 21 and 35 to serve in the WACS, WAVES, or other similar branches of the armed services?" | 43.9 | 51.1 |
| Nov. 1943 | "The army can either draft 300,000 single women aged 21–35 for the WACS for non–fighting jobs, or it can draft the same number of married men with families for the same work. Which plan do you favor?" (Percent for drafting women) | 74.0 | 81.3 |
| April 1944 | "Do you think that single women between the ages of 21 and 30 should be drafted for service in the WACS, to take over non–fighting jobs of young Army men to release them for active combat?" | 43.9 | 51.7 |
| July 1947 | "During the last war, women served in the armed forces as members of the WACS, WAVES, Spars, and Marine Women's Reserve. In peacetime, do you think there should be units in the armed forces in which young women could enlist?" | 53.4 | 57.1 |
| July 1950 | "Do you think that single women between the ages of 21 and 30 should be drafted now for non–fighting jobs in the Army, Navy, and Air Force?" | 31.9 | 34.1 |
| Dec. 1951 | "Many typing and clerical jobs in the armed forces are now filled by service men. Would you favor or oppose having Congress pass a law now to draft young, single women to do such jobs?" | 38.2 | 38.5 |
| March 1979 | "If a draft were to become necessary, should young women be required to participate as well as young men?" | 48.0 | 38.0 |
| Feb. 1980 | "Would you favor or oppose the registration of the names of all young men so that in the event of an emergency the time needed to call up men for a draft would be reduced?" | 85.0 | 81.0 |
| | "Would you favor or oppose the registration of the names of all young women under these circumstances?" | 59.0 | 52.0 |
| | "Do you think we should return to the military draft at this time or not?" | 66.0 | 53.0 |
| | "If a draft were to become necessary, should young women be required to participate as well as young men, or not?" | 58.0 | 45.0 |

*Source:* Roper Center for Public Opinion Research

the men, and almost three–quarters of the women, favoring the drafting of women. By July 1943, however, a question specifying service in women's branches found only slightly more men and women favorable to a women's draft than had been the case in November 1940.

Protection of women has been a major theme in definitions of the role of the military, and these data reflect the theme. An interesting variation of the question casts the issue in a somewhat different light. The most commonly asked questions suggested the alternatives of drafting women or not drafting women. However, in November 1943, an opinion poll suggested the alternatives of drafting single women or drafting ''married men with families.'' Although the jobs would be non–combat in either case, maintenance of the family unit won out over protection of women. Almost three–quarters of the men, and over 80 percent of the women, felt that single women should be drafted first. When, in April 1944, the more common question was asked, however, the figures were virtually identical to those observed in July 1943.

Post–war sentiment toward voluntary service by women in peacetime, interestingly, saw majorities of both men and women favoring the existence of units in which women could enlist. The July 1947 question, however, is not directly comparable to questions regarding the drafting of women.

The responses to questions asked during the Korean War reflect attitudes on the part of men that were more opposed to women being drafted than was the case during World War II. Interestingly, while women remain slightly more favorable toward such service than men, the gender differential that existed through the World War II period decreased somewhat after that war. It should again be noted that responses to the July 1950 question, like the November 1940 question, also reflect opposition to the draft, in general.

From 1971 to 1980, the number and percent of women in the United States military has increased dramatically. Table 2 shows the number of enlisted women, and their percent of the total enlisted force, for selected years during this period. At the end of fiscal year 1971, there were about 30,000 enlisted women

*Table 2.*   Enlisted Women in the United States Military, 1971 to 1980

| Date | Number of Active Duty Enlisted Women (in thousands) | Enlisted Women as Percent of Enlisted Total |
|---|---|---|
| end FY 1971 | 30 | 1.3 |
| end FY 1973 | 43 | 2.2 |
| end FY 1976 | 95 | 5.3 |
| end FY 1977 | 104 | 5.8 |
| end FY 1978 | 117 | 6.6 |
| end FY 1979 | 131 | 7.5 |
| 31 Dec. 1980 | 151 | 8.6 |

and 13,000 officers, together constituting 1.6 percent of the total active duty military personnel. By the end of 1980, there were about 151,000 enlisted women (8.6 percent of enlisted strength) and 22,000 female officers (7.9 percent of all active duty officers), for a total of 173,000 women in uniform (8.5 percent of the total armed forces).

The variety of jobs performed by military women parallels the pattern of their numbers. That is, during peacetime, women have played only "traditionally" female roles in the military. During World War II, while "the vast majority were employed in health care, administration, and communications, women demonstrated their competences in virtually every occupation outside of direct combat—they were employed as airplane mechanics, parachute riggers, gunnery instructors, air traffic controllers, naval air navigators, and the like" (Binkin and Bach, 1977:7). Thus, although women were still concentrated in a few job classifications, the pressures of wartime necessity opened other jobs to them. The end of World War II saw a return to limitations on women's military jobs.

In addition to the recent increase in the number and percent of female enlistees, the past ten years have witnessed an increase in the number of job specialties open to women. Currently, only the combat specialities are closed to women. When many of the traditionally all–male jobs were open to new recruits, the women were not signing up in great numbers for these jobs. However, there are limits on the numbers of new recruits needed for the military positions women usually hold (administrative and medical specialties). Once the traditional female specialties were filled, women desiring to enlist began to accept "nontraditional" jobs, such as those in communications, supply, and equipment repair. In 1972, the percentage of enlisted women in the nontraditional jobs was less than 10 percent. By 1976, this figure had climbed to 40 percent (Binkin and Bach, 1977:17); by 1979, it was 46 percent. By the end of 1980, 55 percent of enlisted women were in traditionally all–male specialties.

The groundwork for the increases in the 1970s in the numbers and roles of women in the United States armed forces was laid in early 1973. At the start of the all–volunteer period, the number of male enlistees was falling short of the goals set by the military in order to maintain an effective active duty force. In addition, those who were attempting to enlist were coming increasingly from what the military considers "low quality" personnel: those who had not graduated from high school and those in the lower categories on the aptitude tests used by the services. The services were aware that while they were lowering enlistment standards for men, they were turning away women who wanted to enlist, despite the fact that these women were high school graduates and scored in the upper categories on the mental tests. This was because the armed forces had separate goals for the number of new enlisted men and women. At the same time, it was anticipated that the Equal Rights Amendment, which had been passed by Congress in 1972, would be ratified by the States. Military leaders and civilian policy makers within the defense establishment recognized that such ratification would make their extant policies regarding the enlistment and assignment of women unconstitutional. Many leaders were concerned that such an event might cause a tremendous upheaval if they had to create equality in their policies all at once. This concern led to a desire to make changes gradually. These pressures directly contributed to the policy of increasing women's participation in the military, the first step of which was to substantially increase the quotas for female enlistments. The number of women officers was then increased and women were admitted to the service academies for the first time in 1976.

The recent changes in the number and roles of women in the military also reflect shifts in American public opinion, both with regard to military service generally, and with regard to the role of women in the military in particular. With regard to the draft, in March 1977, four years into the all–volunteer force era, public opinion polls showed only 36 percent of the American people in favor of reinstituting the draft. During Jimmy Carter's presidency, there was widespread debate on the success of the all–volunteer force. Although the administration's position was that the all–volunteer force was working, and a draft was not necessary, by the spring of 1979, 45 percent of the population felt that a draft should be reinstated; and by February 1980, 59 percent favored a draft. More importantly, as shown in Table 1, in March 1979 almost half the men felt that if there were a draft, women should be required to participate. Women were less favorable to female inclusion than were men: a major reversal of past patterns. In 1980, even larger percentages favored the participation of women in a draft, but the difference between men and women increased. Perhaps most interesting, among those men who felt that women should be included in a draft, 46 percent felt that women should be eligible for combat roles in 1979, and 51 percent in 1980. The percentage was slightly lower among women favoring drafting women (42 percent in 1979 and 45 percent in 1980).

Current laws and policies regarding the positions that may be held by women vary among the different services. In all services, women are permitted to hold all jobs that do not involve direct combat. Women are permitted to and do serve in combat support and combat service support specialities, which may involve service in a combat environment.

In the Navy and the Marine Corps, until recently, women were restricted from serving aboard most ships by 10 U.S.C. 6015 (1976), which stated in part: ". . . women may not be assigned to duty in aircraft that are engaged in combat missions nor may they be assigned to duty on vessels of the Navy other than hospital ships and transports." The effect of this statute was to bar women from service aboard ships (since the Navy currently has no hospital ships or transports). In Owens v. Brown, Judge John J. Sirica ruled that the Navy could not use this statute as the sole basis for excluding women from duty aboard ship. In 1978, Congress passed a modification of this law, to permit women to serve on hospital and transport ships and other such vessels not expected to be assigned combat missions and to serve up to six months temporary duty on other Navy vessels. The Navy is "beginning to assign women to permanent duty on some ships. Women on temporary duty assigned to combat ships do not replace men. In case a vessel, with women on board, is assigned to a combat mission, every effort would be made to disembark the women but not in such a way as to interfere with the accomplishment of the mission. In the Navy, women still may not serve on vessels or aircraft engaged in combat missions" (Department of Defense, 1978: 76). Women in the Air Force are similarly prohibited (by U.S.C. 8549) from serving on aircraft engaged in a combat mission.

The Army has no statutory prohibition against women in combat. The current Army policy states: "Women are authorized to serve in any officer or enlisted specialty, except some selected specialties, in any organizational level and in any unit of the Army except infantry, armor, cannon field artillery, combat engineer, and low altitude air defense artillery units of battalion/squadron or smaller size." (HQ DA message, DAPE-MPE-C5, Washington, D.C., R082058z, 8 Sept 77.) There may be concern among some policy makers in the Army that the current Army policy of assigning women to combat support and combat service support specialties, which would be likely to involve them in combat in the event of war, is a violation of Congressional intent, given the statutory restrictions on the other services.

The Subcommittee on Military Personnel of the House Armed Services Committee held hearings in November 1979 on the utilization of women in the military. Included in their public hearings was consideration of the repeal of sections 6015 and 8549 of Title 10, which are the only laws prohibiting American women from serving in combat. While such repeal is not immediately forthcoming, it is noteworthy that the Department of Defense was in favor of such repeal at that time. Even if these legal restrictions were removed, it is still likely that Department of Defense policy would restrict the combat role of women, at least in the immediate future. It seems that the United States military services would like the option of assigning women to combat roles, and they might do so on a very limited basis, with extensive study and evaluation of the performance of women in these roles.

In February 1980, with Americans held hostage in Iran and Soviet troops in Afghanistan, President Carter called for the military registration of all American males and females born in 1960 or 1961. The debate over such registration centered around two major issues. First, there was (and still is) disagreement both in Congress and the general public as to whether such registration and a possible return to military conscription is necessary or desirable. Shortly after the President's announcement that he would seek funds to register men, and authority to register women, public opinion polls showed 59 percent of the population in favor of reinstitution of the draft and 36 percent opposed. Second, the proposed registration of women for the draft created a public discussion laden with emotion.

Debate over the registration of women has linked it to the ratification of the

Equal Rights Amendment (E.R.A.) by those on both sides of the E.R.A. issue. Some feminists argue that women should not agree to military registration until ratification of the E.R.A., while those opposed to the E.R.A. point to the drafting of women and the possible use of women in combat as examples of the dire consequences of equal rights. Despite such objections by these spokespersons, national surveys conducted in early February 1980 show majorities of both males (59 percent) and females (52 percent) favoring the registration of women (see Table 1). As shown in the last entry in Table 1, 58 percent of the men and 45 percent of the women surveyed felt that women should be included in a draft.

The draft registration bill enacted by Congress in 1980 excluded women, and was declared unconstitutional by a federal district court in Philadelphia as a violation of the equal protection guarantees of the Fifth Amendment. That ruling was overturned by the Supreme Court in June 1981 (Rostker v. Goldberg), with the Court basing its decision primarily on its interpretation of Congress' prerogatives on military matters.

The issue of the military registration of women initially created some highly unusual political coalitions and produced ambivalence and lack of consensus in many women's rights organizations. In addition to the argument advanced by some spokespersons (and voiced during television "woman on the street" interviews) that women should not be required to register for the draft before passage of the E.R.A., such organizations traditionally have been anti–war and anti–military, or at least anti–draft. Nevertheless, *amicus curiae* briefs for the Rostker v. Goldberg case opposing the exclusion of women from draft registration were prepared by the Women's Equity Action League and the National Organization for Women (the latter after much internal debate).

Through the end of 1980, the military planned to continue to increase the numbers of women to about 254,000 (223,700 enlisted and 30,600 officers) by 1985, with women constituting about 12 percent of active duty personnel. At the beginning of 1981, the Reagan administration announced that it would reexamine those goals, and keep the number of women at the 1980 levels for the present time. The basis of this "pause" in the increasing utilization of women is stated to be a concern about problems encountered with integrating women into the services and anticipation that such problems would be exacerbated by increasing female representation, especially in combat support units. These problems include the following: lost duty time of pregnant women and consequent shortages of personnel in their units; lack of acceptance and sexual harassment of women by men; physical strength limitations of women; and high rates of attrition of women from traditionally male specialities. Increasing enlistment of women would require recruiting more women for traditionally male jobs. It would also involve accepting more women without high school degrees and with lower aptitude levels, who have higher rates of attrition and disciplinary problems in the military.

The pause affected the services in very different ways. The Army stopped recruiting women in mid–1981 for the rest of the fiscal year. The Marine Corps, which expanded programs for women during the 1970s, "refined" these programs going into the 1980s, closing some specialities and some units to women. The Navy has been assigning more women to sea duty, and still projects a slight increase by 1985. The Air Force was already 11 percent female in 1981, with women serving in all officer career fields and all but four enlisted career fields, and 30 percent of the women serving in traditionally male specialties.

# V. CONCLUSION

As part of the traditional gender–based definitions of social roles, the participation of women in military forces has historically been limited except under the most extreme circumstances. The number of women allowed to serve has been kept low except during periods of wartime mobilization as through the World War II period, when their service was in an auxiliary capacity. In time of peace, the women who did serve filled traditionally female roles, such as nurses and clerks. During wartime mobilization, the women were allowed to move into traditionally male roles, and this was as true in civilian factories as in the armed forces. They were, however, excluded from combat jobs, and with the end of hostilities once more moved into the traditionally female areas. Indeed, the only historical evidence we have of the participation of women in combat specialties occurs in instances of extreme and immediate threat to territorial integrity. This is most likely in guerrilla warfare, as in the case of Israel prior to independence, and the Balkan states during World War II. Even in these instances, women seem to have been quickly relegated to more traditional roles. The only modern example of female participation in conventional combat formations was in the Soviet Union during World War II. Here, there was an immediate and great threat to territorial integrity, manpower resources were exhausted, and the use of womanpower was seen as a last resort.

The utilization of women in the United States armed forces during the 1970s can be seen as a divergence from historical precedent. In a peacetime period, quotas for women were raised but not eliminated. Women were admitted to all traditionally male specialties except those defined as direct combat. Gender segregation of the armed forces was reduced through the elimination of the women's branches, which at the same time deprived women in the services of advocacy at a high level in the organizational structure. Women were admitted to the service academies. And the issues of drafting women and the utilization of women in combat became matters of public debate.

These changes must be seen against a backdrop of dramatic social change in the United States during the 1960s and 1970s. Social movements opposed to the war in Viet Nam, and those pressing for more equitable treatment of disadvantaged groups, contributed to an end to the war; the demise of military conscription; and broadened citizenship rights for youth, for racial and ethnic minorities, and for women.

These changes were reflected institutionally, in part, in the racial integration of schools; in the extension of civil rights in the polity; in changing definitions of appropriate roles for women in the labor force, the family, and in sports; in the passage by the Congress of the Equal Rights Amendment; and in the redefinition of military service to a form of labor force participation. They were expedited by technological changes, both with regard to contraception, and with regard to the machinery used by the labor force, including military equipment.

Going into the decade of the 1980s, the engine of social change appears to have slowed. The facts that the E.R.A. has not yet been ratified by the states, and that Ronald Reagan succeeded Jimmy Carter in the presidency, manifest a conservative mood in the country. With regard to military manpower, this has been reflected in the exclusion of women from draft registration, and a levelling of the proportion of women in the armed services.

The effects of technology and of public opinion are, in part, in opposition to each other with regard to the utilization of women in the military. Where the material technology of a service is similar to technologies found in the civilian labor force, and particularly where that technology substitutes capital intensive automated conflict for more traditional mass face–to–face battle, acceptance of women is higher. Thus, women have been integrated most fully into the high technology Air Force. The Navy, with a considerably more traditional structure but a high technology base, still projects increases in female utilization. The acceptability of women in these traditionally male roles, however, is limited to those roles that have counterparts in the civilian labor force, into which women are also moving. Public opinion has not gone the next step and defined as acceptable women serving in the traditionally male ground combat specialties that do not have counterparts in the civilian labor force. Thus, the greatest restrictions to expansion are found in the Army and the Marine Corps. During the 1970s, the Marines began to assign women to duty as embassy security guards when that role appeared to primarily have a police function. They ceased to make such assignments when the problems of defending besieged embassies made the role more similar to that of a combat soldier.

This is not to say that the pendulum will necessarily swing all the way back in a traditional direction. Changes in the direction of gender equality in the military have been made that will be very difficult to reverse. Even the reinstitution of a male only draft, for example, will not justify the exclusion of women serving as volunteers, or indeed attending the service academies.

At the same time, it is important not to overstate the magnitude of the changes that have taken place. At the peak of enthusiasm about women in the services, in the late 1970s, they remained a small proportion of the force; they were excluded from combat roles; and they in fact preferred traditionally female jobs. Despite the fact that some women did enter, and continue to enter, traditionally male jobs, both in the civilian labor force and in the military, the number doing so remains small. Furthermore, such women experience serious problems on the job, including lack of acceptance by the men, intense performance pressures, social isolation, and sexual harassment (Kanter, 1977; Mackinnon, 1979; Martin, 1980; Meyer and Lee, 1978). It appears that the degree of change in social attitudes has not been sufficient to allow full integration in traditionally male arenas, including the military. The experience of the armed services during the decade of the 1970s may well indicate that they have reached a threshold beyond which they cannot advance unless there is further social change in women's roles and in men's attitudes in American society, or unless definitions of citizen rights and obligations are once more changed to meet the mobilization requirements of a war. In the short run, it must be recognized that the expansion of women's roles in the armed forces in the 1970s has already served to reinforce equalitarian sex role attitudes in the civilian sector. If the military continues to expand women's participation, or even maintains it at present levels, it will in the process be serving as a critical agent for future social change.

# ACKNOWLEDGMENTS

When this paper was written, Mady Wechsler Segal was serving as a Research Sociologist in the Department of Military Psychiatry, Walter Reed Army Institute of Research. The opinions or assertions contained herein are the private views of the authors and are not to be construed as official or as reflecting the views of the Department of the Army or the Department of Defense.

# REFERENCES

Andreski, Stanislav
   1968   Military Organization and Society. Berkeley: University of California Press.
Bachman, Jerald, John D. Blair, and David R. Segal
   1977   The All-Volunteer Force. Ann Arbor: University of Michigan Press.
Bendix, Reinhard
   1964   Nation-Building and Citizenship. New York: Wiley.
Binkin, Martin and Shirley J. Bach
   1977   Women and the Military. Washington: Brookings Institution.
Binkin, Martin and Irene Kyriakopoulos
   1979   Youth or Experience? Washington: Brookings Institution.
Bloch, Peter B. and Deborah Anderson
   1974   Policewomen on Patrol: Final Report. Washington: Police Foundation.
Bureau of Labor Statistics
   1980   "Marital and family characteristics of workers, March 1980." News Release USDL 80-767.
Current Population Reports
   1975   "Estimates of the population of the United States and components of change: 1974 (with annual data from 1930)." Population Estimates and Projections Series P-25, No. 545. Washington: U.S. Government Printing Office.
Dahl, Robert A.
   1961   Who Governs? New Haven: Yale University Press.
Department of Defense
   1978   America's Volunteers. Washington: Office of the Assistant Secretary of Defense for Manpower, Reserve Affairs, and Logistics.

Duncan, Otis Dudley, Howard Schuman, and Beverly Duncan
  1973   Social Change in a Metropolitan Community. New York: Russell Sage Foundation.
Featherman, David L. and Robert M. Hauser
  1976   "Sexual inequalities and socioeconomic achievement in the United States, 1962–1973."
         American Sociological Review 41:462–83.
Frieze, Irene H., et al.
  1978   Women and Sex Roles: A Social Psychological Perspective. New York: W. W. Norton &
         Co.
Goldman, Nancy
  1973   "The changing role of women in the military." American Journal of Sociology
         79:892–911.
Gottlieb, David
  1980   Babes in Arms. Beverly Hills: Sage.
Greenwald, Judith, Harriet Connolly, and Peter Bloch
  1974   New York City Policewomen on Patrol. Washington: Police Foundation.
Janowitz, Morris
  1960   The Professional Soldier. Glencoe: Free Press.
  1974   "Toward a redefinition of military strategy in international relations." World Politics
         26:471–508.
  1975   Military Conflict. Beverly Hills: Sage.
Kanter, Rosabeth Moss
  1977   "Some effects of proportions on group life: Skewed sex ratios and responses to token
         women." American Journal of Sociology 82:965–90.
Lasswell, Harold D.
  1941   "The garrison state." American Journal of Sociology 46:455–68.
Leonard, Wilbert M., II
  1980   A Sociological Perspective of Sport. Minneapolis: Burgess.
Lipmen-Blumen, Jean and Ann R. Tickamyer
  1975   "Sex roles in transition: A ten-year perspective." Pp. 297–337 in Alex Inkeles, James
         Coleman, and Neil Smelser (eds.), Annual Review of Sociology, Volume 1. Palo Alto:
         Annual Reviews Inc.
MacKinnon, Catherine
  1979   Sexual Harassment of Working Women. New Haven: Yale University Press.
Marshall, T. H.
  1950   Citizenship and Social Class. Cambridge: Cambridge University Press.
Martin, Susan Ehrlich
  1980   Breaking and Entering: Policewomen on Patrol. Berkeley: University of California Press.
McLaughlin, Steven D.
  1978   "Occupational sex identification and the assessment of male and female earnings in-
         equality." American Sociological Review 43:909–21.
Meyer, Herbert H. and Mary Dean Lee
  1978   Women in Traditionally Male Jobs: The Experience of Ten Public Utility Companies.
         Washington: U.S. Department of Labor.
Moskos, Charles C.
  1973a  "Studies on the American soldier." Paper presented at the annual meeting of the American
         Sociological Association, New York, August.
  1973b  "The American dilemma in uniform." Annals of the American Academy of Political and
         Social Science 406:94–106.
  1976   Peace Soldiers. Chicago: University of Chicago Press.
  1978   "The military: Occupation, profession, or calling?" Pp. 199–206 in F. G. Margiotta (ed.),
         The Changing World of the American Military. Boulder: Westview Press.
  1980   "Saving the all-volunteer force." The Public Interest 61:74–89.

National Federation of State High School Associations
   1980   High School Sports Survey, Dec. 30.
Segal, David R., Nora Scott Kinzer, and John C. Woelfel
   1977   "The concept of citizenship and attitudes toward women in combat." Sex Roles
          3:469–477.
Segal, David R.
   1981   "Sociopolitical attitudes of the American enlisted soldier." Paper presented at the sym-
          posium on civic education, The University of Chicago, October 15–17.
Segal, David R. and John D. Blair
   1976   "Public confidence in the U.S. military." Armed Forces and Society 3:3–11.
SPRINT
   1980   Statistics from the SPRINT Files Showing Evidence of Growth in the Participation of
          Women in Sport. Washington: Women's Equity Action League Educational and Legal
          Defense Fund.
Suter, Larry E. and Herman P. Miller
   1973   "Income differences between men and career women." American Journal of Sociology
          78:962–74.
Treadwell, Mattie
   1954   The Women's Army Corps. Washington: Office of the Chief of Military History.
U.S. Census Bureau
   1979   Population Profiles of the United States, 1979.
U.S. Department of Labor
   1969   Handbook of Women Workers. Women's Bureau Bulletin No. 294. Washington: U.S.
          Government Printing Office.
Van Doorn, Jacques
   1975   "The decline of the mass army in the west." Armed Forces and Society 1:147–57.
Wool, Harold
   1968   The Military Specialist. Baltimore: Johns Hopkins University Press.
Wrong, Dennis H.
   1977   Population and Society. New York: Random House.

# ETATIZATION:

## ITS CONCEPT AND VARIETIES

Szymon Chodak

Our times have been described in many ways, for example, as an era of corporate capitalist and socialist societies, or as an age of post–industrial societies. I would like to view it as the age of etatization, that is, of the emergence, under different programs, of societal systems highly controlled and regulated by the state.

The world, of course, continues to be divided into capitalist and communist societies, into industrialized and economically developed North and newly inde-pendent and developing South. Yet everywhere, in all present–day societies, regardless of the ideology they claim to practice, the peculiarity of its economic condition or the degree of technological and economic development, the state is attaining an unprecedented control over all aspects of the life of individuals. Early in the nineteenth century, Alexis de Tocqueville wrote:

> I seek to trace the novel features under which despotism may appear in the world. The first thing that strikes the observation is an innumerable multitude of men all equal and alike, incessantly endeavouring to procure the petty and paltry pleasures with which they glut their

Research in Social Movements, Conflicts and Change, Vol. 5, pages 259–294.
Copyright © 1983 by JAI Press Inc.
All rights of reproduction in any form reserved.
ISBN: 0-89232-301-9

lives. . . . Above this race of men stands an immense and tutelary power, which takes upon itself alone to secure their gratifications, and to watch over their fate. That power is absolute, minute, regular, provident and mild . . . It provides for their security, foresees and supplies their necessities, facilitates their pleasures, manages their principal concerns, directs their industry, regulates the descent of property, and subdivides their inheritance—what remains, but to spare them all the care of thinking and all the trouble of living? . . . It covers the surface of society with a network of small complicated rules, minute and uniform through which the most original minds and most energetic characters cannot penetrate, to rise above the crowd (Tocqueville 1972: Vo. II, 380–82).

Of all visions of the future, this one seems to have described most accurately the features of our contemporary situation.

De Tocqueville, however, failed to anticipate certain aspects of our conditions. Although guided and supervised by the omnipotent and omnipresent tutelar governments that are periodically elected by the people, our societies are split by conflicts of interest in which we not only confront each other but which we experience as an internal struggle, a struggle between our many selves and our own conflicting interests. The societies of which we are part are ridden with crime and violence, which no power seems to be able to control. In spite of the regulation and organization provided from above and below to sustain what is deemed to be order and social justice, the social environment in which we endure is rapidly changing into a vast anarchy; it is under state control, but lacks any moral authority. In spite, or perhaps because of all scientific management, the natural environment on which we must depend is rapidly changing into a poisoned desert as a result of excessive technological development. We are reaching the point where more and more of the resources we depend on will be exhausted. Tocqueville did not foresee that as the state grew bigger and bigger, becoming to all appearances omnipotent, it would also become more inept, ineffectual and incapable of handling the affairs of its citizens and of providing them with the necessities, security and mundane pleasures that they now claim to be their entitlements. He also did not expect the ''Man of the Future'' to rise in rebellion against tutelary authority and its bureaucratic control and imposition as we see happening today.

Analysing the trends of development before and during World War II in Germany, America, and Russia before and during the 1905 and 1917 revolutions, Max Weber envisioned an outcome of societal development that was similar to de Tocqueville's vision. In earlier writings, Weber had viewed capitalism as a process of growing rationality. He later discovered that capitalist rationality required development of bureaucratic hierarchies. He saw them mushrooming throughout various segments of the new capitalist economy and pervading society from the top via the imposition of numerous governmental, civilian, and military administrations, and growing from the bottom as scaffolds of democracy. ''The future belongs to the bureaucratization,'' wrote Weber repeatedly at that time. Socialism and Communism, he predicted, would develop into just another form of domineering bureaucratization. Thus he envisioned the emergence of a gigantic structure informed by a compulsive association of consumers, organized and manipulated by the state, which was to absorb self-imposing corporations, mandatory professionalization, imperative unions, and every other type of compulsive organization that could be invented and developed into one huge gigantic structure of *Verstaatlichung und Verstadtlichung* of society—what we call at present—etatization (Weber, 1971: 63. See also Gerth and Mills, 1958: 17–18). It was imminent and what was worse, Weber did not have much to offer to either prevent it or to solve it.

In the thirties, Adolf Berle and Gardiner Means, James Burnham and a few other less influential writers, analysing economic development in the United States and comparing it with the development in Nazi Germany and Stalinist Soviet Union, introduced the theory of the managerial society. They believed that the increase in concentration of capital under the control of large financing corporations, the growing dispersion of stockholding, changes in the structure of private property and in the administration of business, such as an increasing trend for managers to administer both large private corporations and the state, were bound to produce a new socio–economic structure that would be neither capitalist, nor socialist, but managerial. They wrote that capitalists, as a class, were becoming redundant. In the future, they predicted, managers and experts will acquire an even greater say in the decision–making processes and will eventually become the ruling elite of society.

Although these writers made many keen observations on capitalist development, they exaggerated the degree of power attained by managers and underestimated the resilience of the capitalist hold over the economy. Capitalism demonstrates an ability to exist and to grow under changing conditions in which the state takes over many new regulatory functions and the managerial elite becomes a new class with its own value system, status hierarchy, interests, and norms. What is more important, Burnham predicted that most capitalists will withdraw from active involvement in decision-making, and even from the management of their own financial affairs, to live leisurely lives without working. He failed to anticipate that many of the wealthy capitalists would not only involve themselves in leisurely activities, but would obtain expertise, education and without giving up their capitalist positions, would assume other managerial posts as top executives, politicians, bankers, and even champions of the causes of the poor and of the underdeveloped countries.

What has actually emerged in Western Europe and North America is a society that is becoming increasingly etatized but, at the same time, one in which capitalists play an important role by financing both the private as well as the public corporate sector; a society in which capitalists become managers and where managers evolve into capitalists; a society with an economy that is comprised of both private capitalist and state owned industries operating under state supervision. We are still in the transmutative stage; a stage where the old of the capitalist system and the new of an emerging civilization of etatized societies appear simultaneously, and seem to be inseparably intertwined. That is why some observers, discussing such processes, are able to attribute greater significance to aspects of the past that still remain. Others, on the other hand, see the emerging new as being of greater importance and of demonstrating its potential to overwhelm the past.

The interest in this essay is not in the state in the role of a Leviathan, as perceived by Hobbes, or in the State as the actuality of the ethical idea and the end–result of development, as Hegel visualized it; it is not in the state as an apparatus of class domination, as viewed by Marx, nor in the state in any other classical interpretation. *Its interest is not in the state* as a systemic or static establishment as it is frequently portrayed in political science theories. Although these perspectives are legitimate and instrumental in the understanding of many important aspects of social activity, this essay, is interested in something different—*in the view of the process of etatization as a manifestation of societal development.* The following explanation can be offered as to why this approach was chosen: It is known that institutions, established to the service associations, in some conditions develop their own existence independent of their mother–association; and even come eventually, to dominate the structure that brought them into existence. This is what now seems to be occurring. The state is an institution that was established to serve the ruling class, or according to a different interpretation, the entire society. Although it still performs its many traditional functions, the state is evolving towards a new type of existence. It is in the process of superceding society.

This paper is an excerpt of a larger manuscript on the subject of etatization that is being prepared for publication. As such, its scope will be somewhat limited. I would like to introduce the concept of etatization by outlining some of its most important aspects, and then focus the discussion on a general analysis of the current civilizational transmutation processes that cause the generation of etatization in Western capitalist societies.

# I. ETATIZATION: ITS PRINCIPAL CHARACTERISTICS

Most of the classic works in sociology are concerned with various aspects of the transmutation of precapitalist societies into industrialized and capitalist ones. Marx and Engels discussed this topic particularly in the *Communist Manifesto*. Of the other, more strictly sociological works that usually discuss only certain selected aspects of the actual processes of change engendered by the development of capitalism, I would like to mention a few. Toennies was particularly alarmed by the declining role of the *Gemeinschaft* type of "sociation," as exemplified by kinship, neighborhood, community, friendship, and the spreading of *Gesellschaft* type of "sociations." Durkheim described the process as a transmutation of "mechanic solidarity," which prevails in aggregates of analogous social units within previous structures, into new, more complex associational structures comprised of "organic solidarity." Cooley was concerned that transmutation evident within American and other societies results in a decline in the role of primary groups and an increasing one of secondary groups. Max Weber discussed the change in value orientation caused by the Protestant Ethic and other aspects, the specific conditions in the European city and other factors, which together generated the transmutation into capitalism. These processes are still occurring. At the same time, however, one can also observe the new transmutation that is engendering etatized societies.

Four principal features can be outlined to characterize etatized societies and to distinguish them from social orders of the past:

a. The concept of "etatization" derived from the French word *etat*—state. The derivation from the French has been developed in order to avoid the confusion that may occur as a result of the many connotations of the English equivalent. The obvious was said already: etatized societies are societies that are highly controlled and regulated by the state. Early in the century, most analysts, discussing the role of the state shared the view that the state performs two principal functions. The external function was defined as the protection of the nation against any foreign encroachment. The internal function was said to consist of the maintenance of law and order. Lenin and other Marxist writers differed from academic theoreticians in their evaluation of these functions. Academic theoreticians believed that these functions were conducted for the benefit of the entire society. Lenin, especially in *The State and Revolution,* referring to Marx and Engels, claimed that the state exists only where there are class antagonisms and class struggle. In these conditions, he wrote, the state constitutes "an instrument for the exploitation of the oppressed class." Although this difference in opinion persists and has a bearing on the ways etatization is being evaluated, it cannot be discussed here. What is important to point out is that, at present, the state performs many new functions. Neville Abraham, for instance, in analysing the functions of government in regard to what he calls big business in Britain, uses the term "The New Disorder," and lists the following roles of government in contemporary society:

> As a *regulator* the government's aim is to apply rules so that companies, trade unions and others conduct themselves without too much damage to the interests of their customers . . . As a *communicator* the government is a major publisher of statistics . . . As a *protector* of people, the government prescribes what is permissible across a wide field . . . As a *peacemaker,* the state can provide money, facilities, and staff . . . As a *major buyer,* sometimes even monopoly purchaser . . . the state has an enormous leverage.

He also lists other functions of the contemporary government, such as *entrepreneur, shareholder, employer, planner,* and *manager* (Abraham, 1974: 23–27).

Similar lists of functions of the contemporary state were set down in other literature as well.

b.   Weber's definition of the "modern state" is widely accepted. He defined it as a "system of order" that exercises binding authority and monopoly of legitimate use of coercion within a territory under its jurisdiction (Weber, 1978: 56). When applied to post—modern conditions, this definition must be extended. In the etatized society, the state exercises not only the right of monopoly of coercion to maintain law and order but acquires new monopolistic rights to regulate and manage the economy of the nation, to own large sections or nearly all of it, to exclusively control the education of new generations, to determine the principal direction of societal and cultural developments. As in the instance of monopoly of coercion, which produced a wide gamut of differing systems, from democracies to extreme forms of authoritarian rule, one can expect the etatized societies to differ in the ways of their exercise of other monopolistic functions; in economic management and social direction particularly.

c.   In a society in which all the above—listed functions are implemented by the state, the individual can exist by himself or herself outside any primary group or secondary association, as well as outside any particular class; relations need only be with the state. To put it in terms of another, general sociological theory: as the society becomes increasingly etatized, the individual can live and satisfy his or her needs, not only with no significant involvement in the primordial, primary, *Gemeinschaft* type of associations, to use Toennies' categories but without any significant involvement in *Gesellschaft* type of associations as well, or acceptance of class belonging. To exist, he or she needs only the state, which provides substitutions for all natural as well as secondary institutions and supervises any contractual relationship. More recently, Louis Kriesberg, discussing some aspects of this process, pointed out that the hierarchical orders of macro—structures are increasing at the expense of "the non—hierarchical and local aspects of social life: the family, the small—scale household production, and the solidarity based upon networks of kin and upon small villages" (Kriesberg, 1975: 10).

It must be asserted with all due circumspection that the individual *can,* but does not *have to,* live solely in relation to, and as a dependent on the state in the role of a foster parent who takes care of everything.

There is another aspect of this growing condition that is important as well. Although the state relieves citizens from their tedious, tiresome, and costly obligations and duties in regard to their children, spouses, relatives, community members, associates, and fellow citizens, and provides them with opportunities to enjoy individual freedoms, never before have so many felt, for so many different reasons, as alienated and forsaken as they do now that they are unburdened of these duties and are living under an equalized and depersonalized guardianship. Escapism as life attitude is common in these conditions. Manifestations of it appear in the widespread use of hallucinogenic drugs, popularity of religious and semi—religious cults, in the heightened interest in the supernatural as well as growing political apathy.

d.   Etatization represents a new stage in societal development. Invariably, it generates centralization, which is then institutionalized in order to regulate the increase in centrifugation, which, in turn, is caused by growing differentiation and specialization. Both processes occur simultaneously. Institutions, agencies, industries and sectors of activity become increasingly interdependent. Any work stoppage or major accident, any error in a decision that affects one area may seriously affect even distantly related groups. Specialization and differentiation multiply the divergency of interests and, therefore, of conflicts. The state is expected to regulate both the increasing interdependence and the growing differentiations. In these conditions, a highly complex social stratification emerges.

Whereas one's position within the social strata still tends to be assessed by one's manifestations of wealth and power, another criterion is acquiring importance. An individual is evaluated according to his or her job within a given organization and of the organization's place within the more general network of the national structure.[1] Although apparently related to occupational role and class, job–holding represents, rather, a different criterion. Its value lies not only in how much money it generates, the kind of activity it requires and the scope of power it may represent, but also in its links with the etatized structure, the kind of information access it provides, the scope of social and private contacts it offers; in sum, the value of the privileges and entitlements it brings.

Because of the increase of employment in bureaucracies, the decline of the percentage of the self–employed, as well as employment of 65–75 percent of the labor force in tertiary industries, the division demarcating the social strata tend to be blurred. On the one hand, rather than viewing it as a strict hierarchy in which everyone is placed in distinct castes and social classes—as was apparent at the earlier stages of capitalist development—the social stratification is being perceived more as a ladder to be climbed, using the proper tactics and connections. On the other, as a result of greater equalization, it is a system of much tougher individual competition, and even more so between gigantic bureaucracies, gigantic administrations and gigantic unions.

*The Soviet Union* and other societies under communist rule are, evidently, most etatized of all. Here, etatization was imposed *from above,* on the Party's command, ostensibly, to build socialism. Under this system of etatization, the entire land, all natural resources, and most of the residential buildings are owned by the state. The exception is Poland, where most of the land under cultivation is still owned by individual peasants. The state in communist countries is practically the sole employer of the entire labor force. The economy is administered by state agencies implementing plans and targets set by the government. Both the achievements and the failures of the systems of these countries are produced by etatization: achievements, such as the ability to rapidly concentrate enormous resources and manpower in order to implement certain selected objectives; and failures, such as increasingly stagnant centralized systems, constant shortages of commodities (especially of food), of which the bureaucratized system of agriculture is unable to produce enough, and a widespread underground economy that flourishes because of the legal economy's inability to provide for the needs of the population. Correct decisions in such a centralized system bear tremendous achievements. Mistakes, however, produce devastating and costly disasters that affect millions of people. Conscious of this stifling situation, the state is cautious of changes and restrains any private initiatives, whether in the sphere of economics, technological innovation, or culture.

In *Western Europe and Canada,* etatization is growing as a result of several factors: (a) Societal development, that is, growth of interdependency between increasingly specialized and differentiated agencies and institutions of society that all require regulations and must be balanced. Writers who earlier discussed these developments assumed that differentiated activities would require increasing integration. They did not foresee that such an integration would be transformed into etatization (Durkheim, 1949: 61–69, 109–131; Smelser, 1968: 125–146; Chodak, 1973: 67–76); (b) Evolution of the capitalist economy into a two sector, mixed economy of private and state owned enterprises. An eventual shift to an economy that is under state management and in which the constantly growing nationalized economy attains prevalence. Selected instances of development will be further characterized; (c) To some extent, these societies etatize because of demands from below that require the governments to solve social problems and to provide the population with more social security; (d) A number of other processes related to technological development, changes in the value orientation of society and property relations constitute other factors of this development.

As a result of these processes, in the West and particularly within the last two decades, the state has assumed the numerous, previously mentioned functions. Employing fiscal and monetary policies and regulations, the state determines how the entire national income will be utilized, what portion thereof will be consumed by individuals, how much of it will be spent on public services, and how much of it will be reinvested to generate development. The state has made itself responsible for the organization of the essential services on which everybody depends today. It has emerged as the sole provider of large sections of the population. Thirty to fifty percent of the labor force in Western nations is currently employed by different levels of state administration or in state–owned industries. Many are dependent on transfers of payment from the government as the principal source of their livelihood.

Although some of the above listed processes have taken place in *the United States,* in many respects development in that country proceeded differently. Except for space exploration, communication services, and a few relatively insignificant entrepreneurial activities, the United States government does not own industries. President Carter's decision to establish a state–owned synthetic fuel industry would have been the first major venture taken in a direction in which all other Western nations are far advanced. But his plan was not implemented. To be sure, the central government in the United States does own large areas of land, but most of it is not exploited for productive purposes. Some services, particularly by ones like universal medicare have not been established in the United States. President Reagan's policies can be viewed as an attempt to arrest and reverse the advancement of etatization. One can envision, however, at least in theory, another process of etatization that may occur in this land. Etatization, as was pointed out, consists of increase in state monopoly. Unregulated capitalism inevitably breeds corporate monopolies. They emerge as a result of mergers and of the subordination of small companies to a few big ones. One can envision, therefore, a type of development where corporate monopolies will not only have a strong influence on political decision-making but will actually be involved in forming governments. Some writers claim that this is already happening.

In *Japan,* presently the most capitalist of all nations, the employers and the family of an individual are expected to play the principal role of social security agencies. Taxes are relatively low. Yet, in spite of the striving to leave everything that could be left to private initiative, the state involved itself in many new functions. It is currently spending close to 30 percent of the Gross National Product, much of it on research and development and other preparatory work needed for new industries. In the past it created conditions for development of the steel, petrochemical and auto industries. At present, it is supporting the new knowledge–intensive industries that employ computerization, photo technology, electronics, and industrial robots.

Many *Third World Nations* can be described as being involved in the establishment of underdeveloped etatization; underdeveloped because it does not involve most of the inhabitants and, apart from schools, consists of few social services. The state frequently restricts other forces from engaging in capital formation and industrial development. The state provides the vehicles of modernization and for economic growth.

The way in which etatization is introduced and how it operates differs thus from country to country. This essay, will focus on the transmutative processes that generate etatization in Western societies.

One can analyse the growing transmutation of capitalist societies into etatized ones by employing a quantitative and/or qualitative approach. For a *quantitative study* of the processes of etatization, the data pertaining to certain indicative elements are of particular importance:[2]

a.  Figures on the percentage of the Gross National Product appropriated by the state through taxation or directly, by profit–making from nationalized industries;

b.  Figures on government expenditure, subdivided into external and domestic, or according to budgetary division and in relation to national income (e.g. Nutter, 1978),

c.  Figures on the percentage of the labor force directly employed by differ-
    ent levels of governments and in the state industry. Figures on the per-
    centage of population dependent on transfers of payment from the govern-
    ment or other income generated by governmental agencies;
d.  Figures on the size of state owned industries: estimates of assets involved,
    employment as part of total employment in society, generated profit and
    other related data;
e.  Figures on the size of services provided by the state.

A *qualitative analysis* of the transmutative processes that generate etatized
societies requires the consideration of a number of ongoing processes:

a.  Changes in social structure, economy, and administration of society
    caused by technological development and their impact on etatization;
b.  Changes in the organization and structure of the economy;
c.  Changes in the structure of ownership and property relations;
d.  Changes in societal values and life styles;
e.  Development of social problems, control and alleviation of which re-
    quires intensive state involvement and, therefore, generates etatization as
    well as social problems engendered by etatization;
f.  Emergence of new social stratifications as a result of the above–listed
processes;
g.  Formation of new structures of conflicts in society.

Only some of these process will be characterized in the following parts of this
essay.

## II. CONFLICT IN ETATIZED SOCIETY

The importance of conflict analyses for the understanding of societal development is obvious. Louis Kriesberg draws our attention to the fact that "many
persons believe that conflict properly institutionalized is an effective vehicle for
discovering truth, for attaining justice and for the long run benefit of society as a
whole" (Kriesberg, 1973: 3). At each different stage of societal development,
there arise conflicts over specific issues. By distinguishing these different issues,
one can effectively differentiate one stage of societal development from another.

What are the principal conflicts of capitalist society, those that distinguish it
from earlier stages of development? Karl Marx believed that the principal conflict of capitalist society, the one that determined its entire character, arose from
the discrepancy between the pace of development of material forces of production and the pace of change of relations of production. He asserted that this
conflict is engendered by the existence of private property, and particularly by
the private ownership of means of production. In the sphere of social interaction,

this conflict takes shape as class struggle. Neither Weber, nor the functionalists, whose theories are usually contrasted with those of Marx, denied that property relations constitute one of the principal factors of the socio–economic structure. For Weber, Marx's scheme was too simple to explain the nature of capitalist society. He believed that scarcity of wealth, power and prestige, and differences in interest that are manifest in attitudes and political orientations, generate a more complex structure of conflict. For Weber, therefore, the most important hierarchies of social stratification were class—and he distinguished a property and acquisitive class structure—and status. He also believed that the conflict inherent in bureaucratic structures is of equal, if not greater, importance, as ownership of means of production in determining the nature of capitalism. Functionalists defined class not in relation to ownership of means of production but in relation to many factors, such as residence, education, occupation, and so on. For them, class was both an objective and a subjective construct. They claimed that classes complement one another regardless of conflict. Other theorists, for instance, Pareto, Mosca and Michels, were more interested in a different aspect; in the inevitability, in any society, of the existence of an elite and an oligarchy, and they discussed the conflict resulting from this situation.

I recall these assertions of major sociological theories in order to point out that definitions of capitalist relations inevitably contain a reference to private ownership, by capitalists, of the main means of production as being at least one of its principal components. Regardless of what it is called, capitalism without private ownership of means of production, which determines the character of other relations, is no longer capitalism. Other conflicts that exist in capitalist relations are not always necessary conditions for capitalist relations. These include conflicts such as the one between the elite and the masses that is universal, or the ones that occasionally emerge in ethnic and majority–minority relations. The latter arise from situations where there is a struggle for democracy and freedom, where there is a divergency of life styles between different groups, for example, religious or ideological affiliations, which are peculiar to specific situations. These types of conflicts may or may not occur at the capitalist stage of development just as they may or may not occur at any other stage of development. Each stage of societal development is marked by different sets of conflicts. The analysis of the characteristics of the capitalist stage must include an analysis of the conflicts brought about by the existence of private ownership of means of production. To the extent that etatized society continues to be capitalist, it can be seen as having retained conflicts typical of a capitalist structure. But the point I am trying to make in this paper is that etatized societies represent a new stage of societal development. This claim has merit only if a new, significantly different set of conflicts than those attributed to capitalist conditions can be distinguished. I believe that such a difference is already evident and that it will become more so with the advancement of etatization.

Whereas some issues that cause conflict in capitalist societies continue to endure, one can list a number of new, significantly different issues that have recently emerged. To some extent they pertain to property relations, but now there is more concern about control. In the past, the issue was: Who get's what out of the capitalist ownership of the means of production? Now the issue is: Who get's what out of the state ownership of the means of production, out of state control of the economy and state distribution of the national income? It must be emphasized that this is not yet the over riding conflict, but the shift towards it is evident enough to merit attention. The new issues, resulting from concerns with control, are not universal enough to be equated with the ever–existing divisions into ruling elites and masses. They are not as peculiar to specific conditions, or temporary enough to be endemic only to the capitalist structure. I am speaking about a new set of conflicts, all engendered by the new structure of controls; conflicts that are evidently inherent in the social organization and in the emerging value system. Such conflicts are generated by etatization.

What then are the principal conflicts of etatized society? A three point answer will be offered to this question.

A. *Point One:* Principal Issues of Conflict in Etatized Society. The list of principal issues can be made up as follows:

1.   Sphere of state, corporate business and individual ownership; what should be owned by whom and who should control it under the new conditions.

2.   What kind of use of public property should be made by individuals occupying the controlling positions in society. The right and the ability of the public to determine what kinds of uses are made of public wealth and the right of individuals to an adequate share of the national product. In other words, who should get what or be entitled to get what, in conditions where a large part of the means of production, and of many facilities maintained for consumption, is owned by the state or constitutes part of the economy that is controlled and directed by the state.

3.   To what degree the state should be allowed to dominate, control and interfere in the lives of individuals who are transformed, in one way or another, into its dependents. The individual is no longer a member of a tribe, extended family, or a tight community network as he once was. He is no longer a royal subject, free to exist and to prosper at the king's pleasure. He is no longer just a citizen with rights guaranteed by law. His new status is citizen—dependent with entitlements guaranteed by the state. He is allowed to grumble, but he had better remember that the bread, the butter and the paychecks he receives, the school he attends, the hospital he may need, the road on which he may walk, and the grave he will eventually lie in, are mostly the property of the beloved state .How much control should then be given to the state?

4.   Who is allowed access to sources of information? Because of technological development, the etatized society is also developing into an information society. Because of this situation, what one gets in the form of entitlements or

rewards for work is to a great extent dependent on what one knows and what one is allowed to learn and to know. The basis of this conflict is, therefore, the issue of who gets access to the sources of this information, which is essential for the exercise of control and for the receipt of an adequate share of the rewards.

5.  What share of the Gross National Product ought to be allocated for investments, and what share ought to be allocated for consumption? In a regular capitalist society, where only a negligible part of the national asset is owned or controlled by the state, this issue does not exist; it is, rather, resolved naturally in the market place. Under the new conditions, the interests of various sections of the public and those of the bureaucracies who decide such matters, must inevitably differ. The public debates that are now taking place in all Western societies are manifestations of the conflicts that are emerging. These debates are about whether to strive for economic growth, to maintain a zero–sum economy, or to reduce the level of growth below the standards that have been attained in order to spend more on solving social problems and on combatting poverty. In more truly capitalist societies, the public did not really concern itself with state budgets: now it must concern itself with such problems.

B. *Point Two:* New Income Structure as the Cause of Conflict.

Until fairly recently people derived their incomes from wages, salaries, royalties, and other payments for professional activities; and from profits, interest and dividends. Although these forms of income still exist, a new income structure is developing simultaneously.

1.  A portion of income is now being received in the form of entitlements. These occur in transfers of payment from the government, and in services such as public education and, in some countries, universal medical services and consumer and environmental protection; or in kind, in the form of food stamps, subsidized housing for the needy, and so on. One can say that, in principle, these incomes are being distributed equally.

2.  The second kind, that is, remuneration for work, plus fringe benefits, profits and interest, is, evidently, differentiated as it was in the past.

3.  On top of these two forms of income, certain individuals derive substantial benefits, mostly in kind but also indirectly, in the form of pecuniary benefits, or privileges and "connections" that their top executive positions in the governmental or corporate administration allow them. In the past, only a very small number of officials enjoyed such privileges. At present, such benefits constitute the spoil of the vast "new class" and the personnel that serve them.

The size of the incomes to be derived in each of these three forms is bound to be an issue of continuing controversy in an etatized society. The first or the third can be increased at the expense of the second. The Scandinavian nations increased the first category of income at the expense of the second kind. The Soviet Union significantly reduced the entire volume of the income of its citizens in

order to spend more on industrialization and armaments. They also augmented
the third category of income at the expense of the first and second categories.

*C. Point Three:* Lines of Divisions Generated by Conflicts.

The etatized society is highly divided by conflicts, both along the horizontal
and vertical axes. The issues listed above and the causes of conflict are only a
reflection of the divergency of interests emerging in the new social stratification.
This new structure will not be protrayed in this paper. I would like, however, to
point out that etatized societies are comprised of highly competitive hierarchical
orders of functionaries. The general contours of this stratification can be projected from the list of conflicts current in etatized societies.

The etatized society is more than ever profoundly divided along the vertical
lines as well. At least in the West, the political, economic and cultural structures
of society are developing increasingly separate segments with distinctive value
orientations. Some of the conflicts engendered in this process are considered in
the final part of this paper. ''The Changing Value Orientation in Contemporary
Society.''

# III. THE CHANGING CHARACTER OF SOCIETAL AND ECONOMIC STRUCTURES

The most consequential and irreversible metamorphosis of Western capitalism
into etatized society has occurred in the last decade as a result of either economic
evolution of the development of institutions whose functions were intended to
increase social and political security in society.

Of the many aspects of advancing etatization, five processes are particularly
evident in transmutative changes occurring in the economic organization of
society:

a.   The mixed capitalist economy, brought about into existence after World
War II as a result of the adoption of a Keynesian economic philosophy, and
manifesting itself most strongly in state involvement in the general management
of the economy and the establishment of many nationalized industries, has now
evolved towards a stage where it is changing into a state–dominated, mixed
economy.

b.   In the United States and Japan the government owns few industries. In
Europe and Canada, however, the state–sector is growing at a faster rate than is
the private sector in all aspects except in profit made by the invested capital. The
key industries, that is, coal, steel, transportation and utilities, were usually
nationalized first. Some principal manufacturing industries are acquired by the
state next.[3] The retail business is usually left to the private entrepreneurs. In
some instances, as in Italy, state–owned businesses have subcontractors from the
private sector. In most European nations, the value of the output of the private
sector still exceeds that of the state sector, but the growth of the latter is advanc-

ing more rapidly with new nationalizations and with the establishment of new state–owned businesses. What is even more important is that the state sector in many European nations employs a constantly increasing number of employees at a time when the number of those who obtain a living as employees or who are self–employed in the private sector is shrinking. Thus the role of the state–owned sector, in relation to the private one, is constantly increasing.

c.   As a result of a number of processes, the notion of property has changed significantly. Property ownership rights are being increasingly restricted by the state and by other public rights. In various ways, the state determines the uses which can be made of property in general and of profit, generating property, in particular. Today, ownership entitles one to only certain, strictly defined uses. This change is an important factor in the emergence of new social relations.

d.   Overlapping corporate and state oligopolies in economic activity and cliques controlling information attain a dominant position in society. The principal choices and opportunities made available to individuals are determined by bureaucracies of state and corporate oligopolies, and by monopolistic cliques in the sphere of culture.

e.   With the growing dependency of individuals on services and opportunities provided by the state, the quality of services and the real value of gratifications tends to decline. Unable to deliver all it promised, the state resorts to inflationary practices, paying citizens with less valuable currency, and providing medical, educational, informational and other services of lesser quality and reliability.

f.   The extended family, which used to provide its members with care and assistance in need, is disappearing. The nuclear family fulfills fewer and fewer functions. The state, in its tutelary role, is providing the individuals with some elementary necessities and services. It advises them what to eat, how to work and relax, what rights they have. The state and not society takes over the functions of primary groups. It cannot, however, supply the warmth and love, which those groups can provide and which are needed as much as material conditions are needed for one's well-being. While taking over some functions performed by the family in the past, the state remains an alien, ruling power imposed on society from above. To some, it is nothing but an administration of a vast national prison with cages in cages.

As a member and dependent of the state–family one is entitled to a share of the national pie, not because he or she works but because of belonging. As a citizen one has the right to participate in elections and to require police protection against unlawful encroachments of others. Of course, one has also duties: the main—payment of taxes. As a prisoner of the system, one can do nothing about decisions of authorities except to wage riots or try to escape. The state's economic functions are determined by this situation. It nationalizes industries and redistributes the national income, in a vain attempt, to keep all members of the family happy.

The Nazi and Fascist governments nationalized some of their country's industries. After World War II, Italy's new governments, and to a lesser extent Germany's, took over these industries. Certain industries, particularly in France, were nationalized in retribution for the owners' cooperation with the Nazis. The British government nationalized the coal industry in order to save both the owners and the miners' jobs as well as to keep the entire economy in balance at a time when the market for coal was shrinking.

Another reason why West European governments got involved in general management of their economy and in establishing state–owned sectors is to sustain the welfare system and in order to run a balanced development as advocated by Keynesian economists. The metamorphosis, from strictly capitalist to a predominantly capitalist, mixed economy, and from a two-sector economy to one with a dominating state sector, advanced differently in each of the European nations. I would like to discuss some examples of these differences.

*In Great Britain,* this process was furthered mainly through nationalization. The utilities and, as was mentioned, the coal industry were the first to be nationalized immediately after the Second World War. Then came the nationalization of the steel industry, of some ship–building firms, and of other branches of industry. These processes paralleled the development of the welfare state and a general and considerable improvement of the working conditions in Britain. The power of the unions increased tremendously, enabling them to exert great pressure on national decision-making. For the first time, the workers and the public servants became involved in strike action, confronting the state as employer. Recently Margaret Thatcher and her conservative associates decided to seriously reverse this situation. They intended to denationalize certain industries, to reduce the power of the union, and to curtail inflation by refusing to accept new demands on the part of the workers and state employees for higher wages or for any other costly improvements. The new, more radically leftist, Labor Party intends to nationalize even more industries and to widen the social programs, thereby substantially reducing the private sector. The emerging Social Democratic Party would like to follow the middle road in order to retain the *status quo.*

The main objective for nationalizing industries in Britain has been a social one; to provide employment and relatively cheap services to the population. But the programs were costly. The government had to pay huge compensations to former owners. Nationalized industries were modernized at a cost unacceptable to privately owned corporations. Yet, even with these improvements, the British industries have a much lower rate of productivity than other large European nations. The quality of British products has declined, and with the rising demands of the workers, frequent strikes and other related problems, Britain is losing many of its markets. It is finding it increasingly difficult to come up with enough revenue to maintain costly public services, keep unemployment low, and to meet other national objectives. Unemployment is high in Britain; at present it is 12 percent. Without the public policies aimed at keeping it low, it would have been much higher. Many nationalized industries operate at a loss. Although it is believed that the large state sector is causing, or is strongly contributing to inflation, declining productivity and deteriorating standards of living, state involvement is preferred by many to the even greater unemployment and decrease of welfare services that might ensue without it. The discovery of oil in the North Sea has somewhat alleviated the situation, but it is not enough to solve the problem. Should Britain decide to nationalize more of her profitable private industries in order to harness larger funds for immediate needs, it would, of course, have to expect more severe economic problems in the future. If it does not do it, it can soon expect more labor unrest.

*France's* objectives in becoming involved with the management of her economy have been primarily nationalistic. France is a country with a long tradition of *dirigisme,* initiated by Colbert, and of state–induced industrialization, pursued under Louis–Napoleon. After the Second World War, France embarked upon a policy of industrial reconstruction, at first under the so–called Monnet plan, and then under other schemes. The main intention was to foster her economic potential and international political and economic positions. In De Gaulle's time these goals were promoted with singular forcefulness. France was to become the Third Force or third power after the United States and the Soviet Union. After the war, Renault and a number of smaller industries were nationalized in retribution for their collaboration with the Germans. Yet, at the time, France did not set out on the path of widespread nationalization. Instead, large private and state–owned industries were supported by the government in any way possible. The idea was to establish a number of French industrial world leaders by promoting highly innovative and original products and, consequently, to enhance France' economic potential and influence. The state fostered centralization and concentration, thereby stimulating the activities of huge financial and industrial corporations. In subsequent national plans, the state set objectives deemed to be in the national interest. Private as well as state–owned corporations were induced to implement these plans. The vast, private sector of small industries catering to the needs of French and worldwide consumers was not only deprived of support and state protection but was heavily taxed to obtain revenues for defense and public services. The large state and private corporations were freed from many taxes and were given subsidies as well as governmental contracts. The objectives set by de Gaulle and his successors have been largely attained. France has developed a very modern industry. It has become the largest—after the United States and the Soviet Union—seller of armaments in the world. It is a major supplier of nuclear reactors and derives a large part of its electrical energy from nuclear stations. Yet, it simultaneously evolved into a condition that Michael Crozier and other experts characterized as a "stalled society." (Crozier, 1970; Cohen 1977; Hoffman et al, 1963).

A huge bureaucracy, recruited predominantly from a few privileged colleges, took on the administration of the economy and society. Especially under the presidency of de Gaulle and Giscard, all important decisions affecting society were made within intimate circles close to the president and his associates. The political system of the presidency developed into quite an authoritarian regime, disregarding public opinion. This nation not only pursued an international policy that tried to subordinate world economic and political interests to its own needs, but it got involved in expensive, prestigious defense research and development programs, consuming vast sums of available funds. Whereas, in some instances, such ambitious undertakings were successful, in others they ended in failure (for example, Concorde, the French competition with other huge electronic firms) or could have been achieved, at less cost, in cooperation with other nations. The small business sector, suffering under stringent bureaucratic controls, mounting taxes, and the high cost of fuel, is shrinking. The public services, especially the educational and university systems, once reputed to be among the best in the world, lack funds and facilities and have deteriorated to a level below that of most Western European nations. France is experiencing a terrible shortage of housing. After a decade of relatively low unemployment when France imported a large labor force from neighbouring Arab countries, the unemployment now has begun to increase rapidly. Conflicts are growing between the natives and the imported workers who are blamed for anything that goes wrong in daily life. Although France is one example of a country that became etatized to attain the nationalistic objectives of the right, she experiences social and organizational problems similar to those of other etatized nations that followed the path of the left. Fed up with a stagnating situation, with the prospect of greater state control under the power of the right, and fearing the prospect of an etatized society under the communists, the French elected the socialist Mitterand to the presidency in the last election as well as a largely socialist parliament.

Mitterand sees no other solution to France's growing stagnation than the nationalization of new industries, expansion of the public sector, and, therefore, evolution into a more advanced stage of etatization. The last Eight French Plan, proclaimed in October 1980 under President Giscard was aimed at (1) Bringing French research to the level of the most advanced countries; (2) Reducing France's dependence on energy and raw materials; (3) Facilitating the lives of large families; (4) Improving job training to help the unemployed; (5) Developing competitive industries with the help of high–technology techniques; (6) Expanding France's agricultural and food potential; (7) Giving priority to social protection; (8) Managing the country's natural patrimony prudently; (9) Restoring living conditions in suburbs and in the centre of old cities; (10) Opening up regions that are still isolated, like Britanny, the Massif Central and the South West; (11) Accelerating the economic development of French overseas departments and territories and (12) Augmenting the French presence in the world (by making an effort to spread French culture and techniques) (*Le Monde,* October 3, 1980). Under Giscard, both the private and public industries would have been encouraged to act commensurate with these priorities. Under the new regime, some changes can be expected in this program.

After his Spring 1981 election victory, President François Mitterand proclaimed that, although he stands neither for communism nor for social democracy, he will go "much further" than the Swedish and West German social democrats. Faced with the chronic problem of inflation, expected to rise to 18.5 percent, and an unemployment of close to 2 million, Mitterand, unlike Reagan, decided to fight unemployment first. Substantial social reforms were undertaken simultaneously. The minimum wage was raised by 10 percent. Many of the unemployed were given jobs in the public sector and in state owned industries. It is expected that these policies will cause a substantial decline in productivity and cause an increase in the 1981 fiscal deficit up to FFR. 95 billion (U.S. $15.6 billion), 50 percent more than the deficit under Giscard's regime. The government is considering a pilot collectivisation scheme in agriculture. A new social and economic plan, setting a much wider variety of economic and social targets, is in the making. The government plans to plan more in the future. A wide nationalization policy, involving 12 key industrial groups, was announced as well. Five industrial groups, including ITT France, a unit of the International Telephone and Telegraph Corporation, CII—Honeywell Bull, the computer industry, a pharamaceutical concern, of which 58 percent is owned by Hoechst A. G. of West Germany, and 36 banks be nationalized first. The government announced its intention to gradually take over the Societé Marcel Dessault Breguet Aviation, the principal aviation industry, as well as the Matra group, one of France's high–technology companies. Lavish compensations were promised to owners. Other socialist reforms were introduced as well. A wealth tax of 0.5 to 1.5 percent was introduced on citizens' assets, totalling more than FFR. 3 million (U.S. $500,000). Gold transactions were put under state control. France is moving in an opposite economic direction to the United States. It would be interesting to compare the results of the policies of these two nations after some time. I devoted more attention to France for another reason, as well. This country is, at present, the pace setter of etatization in Western Europe. By electing Papandreou and his Socialist Party's government, Greece has chosen to follow the same path as France.

*In Italy,* the process of etatization advanced in yet a different way. Leaving the existing structure of society intact, the Christian Democrats, in power for thirty-five years, developed entirely new branches of industries—petrochemical, energy, shipbuilding, communication, and so on—all under state boards. Many of the state–owned industries subcontracted small, private firms for production of technological components and equipment, for maintenance and repair, and for other services required by the larger state–owned corporations. Every third employee in Italy works for some level of government state–owned industry; many more work for private subcontractors whose only customer is the state. In no other country has the fusion of the state and private sector become so close as in this country. Such a system has created a great deal of corruption. Italy also has the largest underground economy of all Western societies. According to various accounts, 25 to 40 percent of all incomes are generated in the underground economy and, therefore, escape taxation altogether. Big scandals, implicating leading Italian politicians in kickbacks, corruption and other white collar crime, have become daily events in this society.

*The German government,* on the other hand, did not develop state–owned industries. Instead, it stimulated consumption by creating a highly absorbent market. The results of this policy became known as the German miracle. While endorsing competition and assisting declining industries, the Federal Ministry of Economics, the Federal Cartel Office and other state agencies took particular care to promote industrial mergers and to support the concentration of capital. They established a number of large cartels that dominated the internal market and developed into highly competitive, multinational corporations. At the same time, the government made great efforts to obtain a substantial share of the corporate stocks issued by "commanding" industries. In its dual capacity as government of the country and a principal or major stockholder, the state regulates and molds the economic structure and development of society.

In the sixties and seventies, West Germany's economy was strong and growing. All recent press reports from West Germany contain, however, a different message: "West Germany is in trouble," and the trouble is both economic and political. The economy, which in the seventies, in spite of the affect of high oil prices, managed to expand at an average of 3.5 percent annually, is now in recession; according to some estimates it will produce no growth in 1981, according to others—it will produce less growth than a year before. Unemployment is rising. At present, 1,300,000—6 percent of the labor force—are out of jobs; the highest percentage since 1954. "In 1970, labor costs in U.S. manufacturing, including fringe benefits, topped Germany's by 68 percent. Today, one survey pegs costs in Germany at about 25 percent higher than in America." (*U.S. News and World Report,* January 19, 1981). The once famous German efficiency, discipline, and productivity is deteriorating. Absenteeism at work is high. The bureaucracy is infecund. The *Chicago Tribune,* in one of its June 1981 issues, reported: "In the Federal Republic, 2.3 million officials are regulating the lives of 61.5 million citizens and they are doing it with a Teutonic penchant for perfection that stifles private initiative and frustrates many people." It also points out that state bureaucrats make up 3.7 percent of the population, the highest in Western Europe, and that they are well paid, too. The cost of social security is enormous. In 1960, Germany spent DM 63 billion of social programs. In 1980, such programs cost DM 450 billion. In 1980, five times as much as in 1960 was paid on family subsidies alone. Thirty percent of the national output is currently outgoing on welfare benefits. West Germany has, however, a relatively low rate of inflation, currently about 6 percent annually. The government is in the red. It already spent all substantial savings accumulated in the past. Since 1975, state deficits are growing bigger each year. The ruling Social Democratic Party is practically split. The left wing opposes the strengthening of NATO and the deployment of new United States missiles on German soil. A new ecologists' protest party, the *Greens,* which recently organized mass protests against the development of nuclear reactors is gaining strength. West Germany must face the alternative: it has to take either Reagan's or Mitterand's road.

*Sweden* is the country in which Western style etatization has so far attained the highest degree of development. For thirty–five years, under the Social Democratic government, this country attained a relatively high standard of prosperity. It was regarded as the model socialist society, providing its citizens with necessities and more, from the cradle to the grave. The government employed a steeply progressive tax system to pay for the universal welfare system and numerous equalization programs. Late in the seventies, and especially around 1980, the well–off were paying as much as 80 percent of their income to taxes. In 1979, the tax revenue constituted 53 percent of total output of goods and services. At present, Swedes pay an average of 55 percent of their income to taxes. In 1979, the average Swede paid $6,475, more than twice that of their counterparts in North America (in the U.S. $3,015). In 1981, out of a 4.3 million labor force, 444,000 individuals worked for the federal government, mostly in bureaucratic positions. Sweden has developed a huge deficit. This year alone, it is expected to be $14 billion (55 billion kronen). The foreign debt, this year, equals 10 percent of the Gross Domestic Product. As it has done in previous years the government will seek loans from foreign banks. In spite of the appearance of general well–being, an absence of poverty, and the existence of a welfare system and social security that relieves citizens of basic economic uncertainties, Swedes experience many social problems. Evidence points to the fact that Swedes experience the highest degree of alienation of all Europeans. The number of suicides, traditionally high in this society, is actually increasing. Alcoholism is common. Many individuals suffer from psychological breakdowns. It also has the highest percentage of single parent families in Europe, both because of the high divorce rate and the large number of children born to unmarried women. The Swedes see their prosperity deteriorating. They generally feel that high marginal tax rates are badly affecting entrepreneurial incentives and are causing the decline of productivity. They acknowledge that something drastic must be done in order to cut the overspending and to solve "the long-range problem." They cannot agree as to how to do that. Besides, it is easier to do nothing about it.

One can continue by discussing the predicaments of Canada, Denmark, Austria, and other nations, each promoting a different form of etatization but all having similar problems.

According to the August 11, 1981 edition of *Fortune* magazine, 53 or approximately 11 percent of the 500 largest industrial corporations outside the United States and the communist–ruled countries were state–owned. This figure is low because many of the 500 corporations are Japanese, which, although operating under a strong system of patronage, are still privately owned. The magazine does not analyse separately the performance of the state–owned and privately owned sectors. Literature and relevant statistics on the subject are still scant. According to the special survey in the December 30th, 1978 issue of *The Economist,* the state owned at least 19 of Europe's largest industrial corporations. At present, this figure is higher. Investment in government–owned enterprises accounts for more than 30 percent of all investments in Sweden, 56 percent in Austria, 42 percent in Italy, 22 percent in Britain; it is now close to 25 or more percent in Canada. If one were to include the post and telecommunication services, electricity plants, railways and airways that are owned by the state virtually everywhere as well as government owned banks, insurance companies and other types of financial and development corporations, the size of the public sector would appear even bigger. The scope of state ownership is well illustrated in the attached chart adopted from *The Economist* and the *Harvard Business Review* (Walters and Monsen, 1979). This chart demonstrates that key industries, that is, telecommunications, energy generating plants, coal and steel industries, transportation and airlines as well as large sections of the auto industry in most of the capitalist nations in the world are already state–owned. The privately owned industries, operating as a rule in more profitable fields of business, are becoming increasingly dependent on the performance of the state–owned sector.

Another set of figures stresses the more poignant side of current changes. In 1979, out of the 15 biggest money losers of the 500 largest industrial corporations, 11 were state–owned. Of the 67 money losers of the 500 corporations listed in 1981 at least 17 were state–owned. Even state–owned oil corporations such as Italy's ENI. France's *Elf Aquitaine, Petroleos de Venezuela, Empresa Colombiana de Petróleos, Petroleo Brasilero* and *Petroleos Mexicanos* in some years, were operating at a loss. As analysts point out, state–owned corporations have no fear of loss, do not pay dividends and do not have to earn profits since their deficits are covered by governments that, in turn, operate with vast cumulating deficits (Walters and Monsen, 1978, 1979). True, some of the major private corporations, such as Chrysler, Ford Motor, General Motors, British Steel, B.L., Montedison have become big money losers, too. They survive only thanks to the assistance of the state.

In view of the growing role of state–owned industries in Western Europe and differences as a result in the organization of the economy in the United States and the rest of the Western nations, it would be more proper to distinguish three types of national systems, instead of the usual capitalist systems and those under Communist party rule: (a) Nations with capitalist economies, principally the United States and Japan; (b) Nations with two–sector economies in which the state sector attains increasing prevalence, that is, all Western Europe, Canada, some countries in Latin America and Asia; (c) Communist industrialized nations.

The situation in the United States can be distinguished from others by certain new features. Whereas many theoreticians believe that the American state has managed to infilitrate the private corporations, the agencies of private corpora-

*Figure 1.* Scope of State Ownership in Principal Countries under Non-Communist Government

| | Posts | Tele-communications | Electricity | Gas | Oil production | Coal | Railways | Airlines | Motor industry | Steel | Shipbuilding |
|---|---|---|---|---|---|---|---|---|---|---|---|
| Australia | | | | | | | | | | | NA |
| Austria | | | | | | | | | | | NA |
| Belgium | | | | | NA | | | | | | |
| Brazil | | | | | | | | | | | |
| Britain | | | | | | | | | | | |
| Canada | | | | | | | | | | | |
| France | | | | | NA. | | | | | | |
| West Germany | | | | | | | | | | | |
| Holland | | | | | NA | NA | | | | | |
| India | | | | | | | | | | | |
| Italy | | | | | NA | NA | | | | | |
| Japan | | | | | NA | | | | | | |
| Mexico | | | | | | | | | | | |
| South Korea | | | | | MA | | | | | | |
| Spain | | | | | MA | | | | | | |
| Sweden | | | | | NA | NA | | | | | |
| Switzerland | | | | | NA | NA | | | | | NA |
| United States | | | | | | | | | | | |

Privately owned: all or nearly all — Publicly owned: all or nearly all — 75% — 50% — 25% — NA not applicable or negligible

Reprinted with permission from *The Economist* (London), December 30, 1978. The Chart was reprinted in an article by K. D. Walters and J. M. Monsen in *Harvard Business Review,* March–April 1979. Here, it is introduced with some alterations reflecting recent change (Britain, Canada). The nuclear industry, mostly state-owned, electronics, petrochemicals, banking, insurance, investment and other financial business, in which the state is strongly involved in some countries, are not accounted for here.

tions have, conversely, acquired profound influence over the national government apparatus. Hence, the state is becoming increasingly fused with the corporations. Selvyn Miller writes, "the trend is toward the fusion of economic power (the super corporations) and political power (the Positive State), both aided by the 'knowledge industry'; the consequence is the creation of the 'technocorporate' state" (Miller 1976: 113; Fusfeld, 1973). The state subsidizes certain industries. It is the most important, and sometimes the sole client of other industries. The most consequential interference of the United States government in the economic sphere, both in production and in consumption was and, to a lesser extent, still is enacted by means of fiscal and monetary policies as well as extensive federal controls and regulations. The scope and impact of regulatory activities was so vast and so consequential that some writers, Louis Kohlmeier, Jr., for instance, began to refer to regulatory agencies as the fourth branch of government, becoming nearly as powerful as the executive, legislative, and judiciary branches. The only problem was that this type of regulation was not reflected in the Constitution and could hardly be regarded as entirely legitimate (Kohlmeier, Jr. 1976; also Lipset and Schneider, 1979; Wilson, 1980). Although the United States government owns only a few industries, in 1979 it was employing close to 29 percent of the labor force in the vast federal and state bureaucracies; West Germany or France with a relatively large state–owned sector, employs approximately the same percentage of its labor force. Already restricted by President Carter's administration and the Congress, regulatory activities were subsequently even more drastically curtailed by President Reagan. All his fiscal, budgetary and monetary policies as well as the restriction of regulatory activities are aimed at arresting etatization and preserving free enterprise capitalism in America. Margaret Thatcher's attempt to do this in England failed or was stalemated. The rest of Western Europe, especially France under Socialist rule, is introducing more state capitalism and etatization. Will the United States alone be able to advance differently than the rest of the West?

## IV. THE CHANGING VALUE ORIENTATION IN CONTEMPORARY SOCIETY

Contemporary social scientists characterize society as being comprised of several principal spheres of activity and, correspondingly, of several overlapping and co–existing orders of interaction. Charles Wright Mills, for instance, distinguished five institutional orders: the political, the economic, the military, the kinship, and the religious (Gerth & Mills, 1953). In *The Power Elite,* he described the power elite of society as comprising the higher circles of three of these orders: the corporate chieftains, the warlords, and the political directorate. Talcott Parsons and other functionalists characterized society as consisting of four essential systems; the economy, the polity, institutions that preserve established patterns, that is, culture, and what in some works was described as household, and in others as subsystems of intergrative and socializing institutions.

At this point, I am not concerned with the merit or lack of merit of any of these theories. I feel it is necessary to refer to them in order to point out that the importance attributed to interdependencies between institutionalized orders, or realms of social action, is not simply a convenient analytical device or theoretical construct. They are important because they are valid reflections of the actual processes, of growing articulation and of differentiation and separation of spheres of social action within the overall structure. Politics, economy, "expressive symbolism" or culture, forms of private and public relations within primary and secondary groups, and religion—in traditional societies representing only different aspects of the individual and general social action—have become, and are becoming, increasingly differentiated; at the same time, they are more interdependent, more centrally regulated than ever.

These seemingly dry and speculative theories help us to understand and interpret the phenomena and predicaments of our time. Reading recent writings of scholars such as Daniel Bell, Christopher Lasch, Richard Sennett, Alex Inkeles, Jacques Ellul, Raymond Aron, and others who discuss the causes and nature of changing value orientation in Western society as well as the vast, popular literature that attempts to establish the relationship between changes in value orientation and etatization, one inevitably returns to the issues developed in those aforementioned classical works. Does the value orientation in Western society change because of new habits, beliefs, norms, or patterns of behaviour that emerge independently of technological and economic processes? Does it change as the result of the growing interference of the state in social activities? What is the principal direction and nature of these changes? Does this process consist, at present, primarily of an emerging narcissistic value orientation that is embraced by a large part of the younger generations, which is the impression one gets when reading these acclaimed works? The answers are complex. Most recently, Daniel Bell, analysing the problems of contemporary America and the Western world portrayed society as being comprised essentially of three principal realms of politics, economics, and culture. He tells us that, during the last decade or so, these realms have become differentiated to such a degree that they began to develop fairly autonomous existences. In fact, each of these realms now promotes a different value orientation.

These processes, in his opinion, not only engendered cultural contradictions and discrepancies within the social structure but also stagnation of economic development, growing ineptitude of political institutions despite their growing role, various forms of cultural narcissism and other afflictions that beset us today. To reiterate, Bell believes that, at present, each of the principal realms of social action is developing independently and asserting different demands on society. To quote, "one can see . . . that there are different 'rhythms' of social change and that there are no simple, determinate relations among the three realms. The nature of change in the techno–economic order is linear in that the principles of utility and efficiency provide clear rules for innovation, displacement, and substitution. A machine or process that is more efficient or more productive replaces one that is less efficient. This is one meaning of progress. But in culture there is always a *ricorso,* a return to the concerns and questions that are the existential agonies of human beings.'' Thus, he asserts, the new in culture does not replace the old. It is added to the eternally cherished and valued civilizational treasury in which new and old co–exist. A few pages later, discussing the relevance of these ideas to current developments, he says, ''the principles of the economic realm and those of the culture (and one may assume those of the political realm as well, S.C.) lead people in contrary directions'' (Bell 1976: 12–15). In his book, Bell goes on to discuss the multitude of contradictions faced and the conflicts experienced by society.

If Bell is correct, one could conceive of an even more consequence–laden outcome of his assumptions. Instead of one dominant elite, contemporary Western and particularly American society must now operate under the guidance of a minimum of three dominant elites, each representing different value orientations. It is not entirely clear whether Bell thinks that this is a new phenomenon or one that existed in the past as well. I am inclined to interpret his view as the former. One must ponder then whether this new contradiction in values, norms, interests, modes of action emerges and is superimposed upon the persisting old class and party divisions, or if it reduces the previous conflicts and schisms. Furthermore, there is good reason to believe that it is not only individuals who experience this situation as a form of cultural contradiction but that in contemporary society itself there exist three different and competing forces. As a matter of fact, the current division, most articulated in the United States but present also in other Western societies, of *conservatives* asserting the primacy of values engendered in the realm of economic, particularly corporate, activities; *liberal democrats,* promoting the idea of distributive justice, to be implemented through controls and regulations, thus etatization; and finally, *radical liberals,* representing primarily the cultural establishment of the universities and mass media, seems to confirm this outlook. Although each of these forces has, at present, a separate party in the United States representing its value orientation, the notion ''party'' should be applied, in this case, in its looser sense. What one must assume, therefore, is that there is a culture of economics and a politics of economics, which do not constitute the culture of culture and the politics of politics, and so on. Even this sounds paradoxical, but it does, nevertheless, reflect the current reality.

Three party divisions of this kind seem to exist, albeit in a more blurred combination, in other Western nations as well. In Canada and Great Britain, the three party divisions originated and developed differently than in the United States, but today they seem to represent a similar constellation of forces. In France, Germany, and the rest of Europe, where etatization is more advanced and the political elite is more entrenched in positions of control, this three–partite division is less pronounced.

The West used to have one dominant value orientation. This is evident when one considers the process of value orientation change that occurred during the twentieth century. Now it seems to have three value orientations competing for prevalence. Whether this is a temporary situation, typical for transition, or a more continuous change is still difficult to predict. Let us first recall how the value orientation changed since the beginning of this century. One can distinguish several periods in this process. Each can be well delineated by references to important sociological works portraying the dominant value orientation in the West at a given time. Although controversial to this day, Weber's *The Protestant Ethic,* is a most penetrating interpretation of the motivations and modes of behavior of the individuals who determined the character of western societies at the turn of the century. Whether or not Weber was entirely correct in his analysis of this value system is not essential for our purpose. Other writers characterized that system, more generally, as the bourgeois mentality of the late Victorian age; of *la belle epoque* in France. According to this literature, men of this time were trying to master their own desires and to impose their will on nature and on others. They admired conquerors and builders of both business and political empires alike. They believed in the virtue of work as a sacred duty to be performed not only to attain wealth, but to please God. "Fun," today's preoccupation, was then considered a very improper experience, if not a sin. David Riesman, in *The Lonely Crowd,* looked at society at a time when the situation was changing, employed the concept of inner–directed value orientation as distinguished from emerging, other–directed value orientation of the middle of the twentieth century, and particularly of the post–World War II period. He tells us that, instead of family, church and community—school, mass media and clubs of peers began to determine the norms and dominant life styles of these people. Instead of emulation of seniors and ancestors, the new generation emulated their successful peers. In their private as well as public lives, these people were obsessed with the desire to "keep up with the Joneses." Success was measured by wealth and ostentation consumption. During the fifties, such people were praised as Prometheans, possessed with the worthy urges to create, to innovate, to acquire, and most of all, to achieve (see McClelland, 1961; Rosen et al, 1969).

Toward the end of the sixties and in the beginning of the seventies, the achievement–striving value orientation and the whole morality and life style associated with it was rejected as a vainglorious obsession of the Mammon worshippers by a large section of the younger generation. It was written then that this unbridled striving engendered countless calamities in both industrialized and underdeveloped societies. Different forces, those who opposed the war in Vietnam, those who were concerned about the rights of minorities, women, poverty in the slums (in spite of proclaimed war against it), the environmentalist, the counter–culture movement, all arose in rebellion against the "society as it is" and the military–industrial complex said to run it. A variety of single issue movements emerged, each attempting to promote solutions to separate causes. It was said that the West was experiencing many revolutions of which the political and cultural were most imporatnt. The rebellion of the sixties and early seventies has failed however. It failed because the advocates of the new morality had no powerful substitute for the order that existed. It failed because many of those who developed an abhorrence of bourgeois society turned to various forms of escapism, to drugs, cults, sects, or adopted the life of drifters. There was a disillusionment with socialist practices in the Soviet Union, China, Cambodia, and elsewhere in the world. The revolt was not successful in attracting the support of the working class in the United States and in Western Europe. A community structure, similar to the one of the past and which some critics of the existing society wanted to restore, turned out to be a utopia. The search for the true, spiritual quality of life failed or could not be developed on a large scale. Instead of greater harmony, tenser and more competitive conditions emerged. Some writers expressed the opinion that, although overtly atipodean to those of the dominant bourgeois culture, the ideals of the rebellion were not only derived from the parents' civilizational norms and values but became eventually assimilated by them (Apter 1974: Klein, 1972). This is only partially true. The rebellion induced several processes of change, the most important being in the sphere of the value orientation of society. Although it failed to develop any enthusiasm, grand ideals and visions that could urge the masses to pursue a better future, it significantly undermined among a large part of Western society, especially among the young, the confidence in the values of Western democracy, and the hope that, with development and growth, the most painful predicaments of humanity would be eliminated. Visions of gloom and doom, despair and hopelessness spread. Social scientists used all their powers of persuasion to demonstrate the imminence of economic and social disasters, to which "the long–term solution requires nothing less than the gradual abandonment of the lethal techniques, the uncongenial life ways, and the dangerous mentality of industrial civilization itself" (Heilbroner, 1974: 138). Some called for the immediate halt of industrial development and even of production. Others advocated the transformation of the social structure of the world into one comprised of units modeled upon the ancient Greek polis (Ibid: 135; Manicas, 1974: 257). The fact that the polis was sustained by slave labor did not bother these thinkers. The state was to disappear in the long run. For the immediate needs, however, an "increase of centralized power and the encouragement of national rather than communal attitudes," was advocated; hence etatization.

In the sociological literature of the seventies, one can find two principal portraits of new, post–rebellion value orientations that were said to have emerged in Western societies. The first was mostly derived from surveys and polls. It portrays, as Daniel Yankelovich described under a corresponding title, a new morality of people who strive to be decent but to have a good life as well, or as a postmaterialistic morality, as characterized by Ronald Inglehart in his work on changes in West European values (Yankelovich, 1974; also Chamberlain, 1977; Inglehart, 1977; also March, 1975). The second is reminiscent of earlier analyses by Spengler and Pitirim Sorokin. It portrays a narcissistic, or decadent and nihilistic life attitude adopted by large sections of Western society, particularly by the more educated (Lasch, 1979; Sennet, 1976; Bell, 1978; Ellul, 1978; Revel, 1977; Johnson, 1977). It seems, however, that we can actually discern at least three differing value orientations that divide Western societies from top to bottom, across classes and other sectional divisions: (a) the post–materialistic new morality, promulgated mostly by those whose fate is linked with the progress of etatization; (b) the newly reborn conservative morality, advocated by many groups, but especially by those sections of middle classes whose fate is linked with the corporate establishment; and (c) the cultural radicalism, represented especially by members of the cultural establishment but supported by some of the poorer sections of the population.

One can delineate these by employing different criteria. As above, they can be viewed as representing three differentiated establishments of the corporate world, the polity, and the realm of culture. They can be characterized as representing the traditional achievement striving syndrome; the new morality and equity ethos; and thirdly, a fringe of what is still left of the counter culture, groups with radical leftist approaches or with escapist tendencies. They can be seen as an outgrowth of three calls of the French revolution, *liberté, égalité, fraternité:* with conservatives most cherishing *liberté* and of all freedoms attributing the greatest importance to the freedom of making money; liberals and liberal democrats attributing the greatest importance to *égalité*, economic equality particularly and interpreting the other two calls as derivatives of the new equity; and of others acting as a wide *fraternité* of groups, which feel alienated by both the capitalist and the new etatized society.[4] These and other perspectives that can be applied, do not coincide but allow to see the new situation from different sides.

*The post–materialistic new morality* is, in fact, full of conflicting ideals. Surveys have shown that modern men and women who advocate this morality—often those who already belong to the new salariat or plan to join it after they complete their studies—are greatly concerned about social problems, poverty in industrialized and underdeveloped nations, the deteriorating environment, and overpopulation. They feel that everyone should be entitled to equal life chances, but offer rather confused answers when asked how to provide such equal chances in conditions where opportunities are becoming scarce. They care most about matters pertaining to their own jobs. They would like to have a stronger voice in a less impersonal society and they believe that more meaningful ideas are needed. They are for more freedom and for non–interference in the personal lives of others. They distrust politicians and grumble against bureaucracies, but see no other solution than acceptance of greater state control and redistribution of benefits and entitlements by it. They differ on what is most important, what the state should first do, but generally see no other way to future development than through enlargement of the functions of the state. And because of this, they support the idea of progressive taxation, of nationalization of industries, and of wage and price control as fair or necessary costs of social balance:

Different kinds of people, searching for an alternative to the present, and especially those who value things as they once were, *call themselves or are called conservatives:* religious fundamentalists, extreme rightists, large sections of the middle class that oppose what they see as excessive taxation and unnecessary regulations; people who resent permissiveness, or who, for religious or other reasons oppose abortion; those who are against quotas in education or employment; libertarians who believe in free enterprise; disenchanted Marxists, those who believe the West must maintain a tough stand against the Soviets; and advocates of monetary and supply side economic theories. Thus, as present, conservatism constitutes, in a narrow sense and in a broader sense, as an ideology and a value orientation.

As an ideology it calls for less government, the preservation of capitalism, a stronger defensive posture against communism and a return to traditions. As a value orientation, contemporary conservatism differs from earlier ideologies and represents the shared concern of these and other groups in society. During the mid-fifties, Clinton Rossiter wrote, "government in the Conservative view, is something like fire. Under control, it is the most useful of servants; out of control, it is a ravaging tyrant. The danger of its getting out of control is no argument against its extended and generous use" (Rossiter 1962: 34). Those who adhere to conservative values in the eighties believe that government has too much power, exercises too many functions, and collects too many taxes. They see it as the cause of many ills in society, particularly of inflation, bureaucratic waste, and parasitism. They want the government to collect fewer taxes, provide less services, and thus make the individual more responsible for his or her own affairs. In fact, they accept more government because of defense needs and because they cannot arrest the advance of etatization.

Another value dear to conservatives is respect for traditions: traditional institutions, family, and patriotism.

Another important conservative tenet is that owning property is a natural human right and should not be restricted by the state. Ardent defenders of free enterprise and free initiatives, these people view capitalism as not only the most free but also as the most moral society known in the history of mankind. Only in this society can anyone with initiative and aspirations, who understands the mechanisms of the free market and is willing to take risks and dares, achieve success and find self-fulfillment. Since they advocate unrestrained capitalist growth, conservatives fail to see that such development breeds oligopolies, which then not only restrict the free market, subordinate and swallow large areas of free enterprise, but eventually, under the umbrella of a non–intervening state, impose monopolistic controls over all aspects of life in society endangering the existence of the competitive market and freedom, in which the conservatives defended in the first place.

I hate to pin on labels on people or movements. I do not know how to call the third orientation. Some describe it as *cultural radicalism,* others as narcissism, still others as rejectionism. Many of the individuals who express the attitude of this group claim to belong to the New Left. Some Marxists dissociate themselves from belonging to it; others claim to represent it. On the whole, such people are concerned about the evils and injustices in society. They blame and reject the system that generates social problems, and which does not eliminate deprivation and inequality. Some among them believe that socialism, of course of a different brand than in the Soviet Union or Cambodia, would bring the remedies. Others, propagate the zero–growth society with a developed system of welfare, public services, and distributive justice. They detest the state and bureaucracy, but since it is the only practical way to institute a society more to their liking, they endorse programs of etatization. Their ideal is usually some kind of unattainable utopia. Failing in their social experiment, they lapse into nihilism, extreme radicalism, the search for the understanding of the self; narcissism. Not all leftist radicals and rejectionists become narcissistic. Most, however, view narcissism as a form of alienation generated by capitalism. Others regard it as an ostensible form of protest, despair about the human predicament. The narcissists themselves, who are primarily concerned with the understanding of their own selves and with pleasure–seeking, view the world as a hostile surrounding, blame it for their alienation and, therefore, tend to lean toward some kind of radicalism or isolationism.

The conservatives claim to know the causes of the problems of contemporary society. In their opinion, it is not scarcity of resources or change in the social structure but rather the welfare system and, in fact, redistributive policies practiced by liberals and democrats that are to blame. These, in their opinion, reduce economic growth and cause the deterioration of the general standard of living, the decline of productivity, and the growing budgetary deficits. They blame the liberals for bringing about conditions that allow widespread permissiveness that is now weakening the family and general morality, and allow criminals to be protected by the law more than are their victims. They wish to restore a purer, free market economy. To this end, they (in the United States and Britain) engaged in supply side economics, and monetary policies, and a reduction in spending on welfare, Margaret Thatcher introduced denationalization of the oil industry. So far, they have not succeeded in remedying the situation.

Democrats in the United States and social democrats and socialists in Europe, reluctant to blame capitalism for all contemporary evil as the more radical leftists do, are inevitably tactiturn and impervious concerning the causes of the current situation. They claim to know the remedies that would work, or at least keep the system afloat. In France they promote further nationalization of industries, in Sweden they maintain high progressive taxation. Everywhere they stand for policies that will reduce unemployment and render greater assistance to poorer sections of the population, regardless of deficits or other consequences of such policies.

The radical leftists groups tell us that they know both the cause and the remedy. The cause is obviously capitalism. (e.g. Castells, 1980). The remedy consists in rapid nationalization of all industries, the establishment of a planned economy, and turning away from private to more collectivistic forms of consumption whenever possible. They believe that this does not have to be done as it was in the Soviet Union or other communist nations.

These cannot be regarded as merely ideological differences. The three groups represent different moralities, cognitive orientations, and values.

No other issues are more divisive today than those pertaining to etatization and the role of the state in the society. As they encounter concrete problems, some people shift from one value orientation to another. Increasingly, however, large sections of the population are adhering to one of the principal value orientations. In the United States large sections of the middle and working classes, dissatisfied with the etatist practices and radical rhetoric as well as with the accusation of American involvement in all kinds of wrongdoings, are endorsing the conservative programs of the Republicans. Yet substantial groups of the poor, of ethnic minorities, and the cultural establishment fear conservative policies and reject their value orientation. As a result, American society—and a similar situation seems to be developing in Britain as well—is, evidently, involved in a class conflict situation. This is not a Marxist text book conflict, however, with workers struggling against capitalists; in this class conflict the main issue is the role of the state in society. Classes whose livelihood already depends upon salaries, transfers of payments, and other benefits from the state raise demands to foster the welfare system and etatization, regardless of the dislike of bureaucracy. Classes that do not have much to gain from growing state control and redistribution of wealth, vehemently oppose state expansion and reduction of the free market system. But the real danger to the individual comes from monopolies that restrict freedom of initiative, either intellectually or in the free market. Etatization generates state oligopoly, and capitalist development generates the domination of corporate monopolies. A widespread organized opposition to both types of monopolies that seems to be necessary to defend the autonomy of the individual is, however, absent. One more point has to be made.

As was said, current societal development is generating growing interdependence, but also separation of spheres of economy, politics, and culture and increasingly distinctive value orientations. Certain groups in the United States and in other Western societies can be classified as liberal etatists, conservative, rejectionist cultural radicals, and narcissist. Yet in daily practice the lines of such division are quite blurred. Many of the individuals are motivated by a mixture of all three of these value orientations. They have become extremely egotistic and even narcissistic in certain regard. Yet they also expect the state to resolve their problems, and especially to relieve them from making decisions and choices when too many options are available; they even expect the state to reduce the omnipresence of the state itself. In still other striving, they would like to simultaneously restore many features of the traditional ways of life. Some long for a return to community but do not wish to give up any freedom acquired outside community controls. Others would like to preserve capitalism but, of course, without poverty, unemployment, and excessive competition. They want to have freedom to choose but do not want to be bothered with the constant necessity of making choices. They are sincerely concerned with the fate of the deprived and express support for equity, but even more are concerned with their own selves. In this situation it is extremely difficult to delineate exactly how the society is divided. The divisions are evident but also are in constant flux.

De Tocqueville, Max Weber, and other writers viewed the tendency that I described as etatization as a drive toward civilizational abyss. Contemporary writers see it as a growing calamity; according to some, it is engendered by monopoly capitalism, according to others—by state–loving liberals. It can be viewed as a genie released from a bottle over which no one has control. Whichever way one looks at it, we cannot expect the state to wither away or not even to dismantle itself. No one seems to know the word of command that will force the genie back into the bottle. This essay, therefore, has sought to discuss etatization not as a social problem, which government can resolve and not as an adequate solution to social problems, which society cannot resolve on grass–root levels but as a process of societal development.

# NOTES

1.  Richard P. Coleman and Leen Rainwater, discussing current changes in the "social standing" in America, write that respondents to their surveys "constantly coupled an occupational characterization with either an amount of money or a qualifier like 'successful,' 'average,' or 'successful business people,' 'college graduates in management doing fairly well,' and 'doctors and lawyers making lots of dough'" (Coleman and Rainwater, 1978: 49). They point out that the concept class has many faces in practice. It is interesting to note that according to their analysis, schooling amounted to a total of 58 percent of the variance, the effect of job holding for 19 percent, and income for the remaining 23 percent of the variance in social standing (Ibid.: 283). They report that family background has to be regarded as having a considerable influence on standard deviation of their scheme. They also refer to the importance of "connections" in attainment of a desirable social standing (Ibid.: 52).

2.  For an example employing a different set of quantitative indicators, see Meltzer and Richard, 1978.

3.  The role of the Multi–national Enterprise, which some theorists perceive as practically existing outside any state jurisdiction and control, is not discussed here. It seems that Mark Casson and

Peter J. Buckley are quite right in arguing that the MNE, in fact, does not represent a new phenomenon at all. It was preceded by the British and Dutch chartered companies in a similar role. The contemporary MNE engage, however, in certain new forms of activities such as dissemination of expertise and, in some instances, compete with emerging industries of host countries affecting their chances to grow (Casson, 1979; Buckley and Casson, 1976). Since they are strongly protected by their governments (The U.S., France, Japan, etc.), the MNE are, in fact, quite national. The interpenetration of national economies resulting from their operations, for instance, between the U.S. and Japan, the U.S. and Germany, France and Sweden is new. State–owned MNE, e.g., the French Renault, the Soviet trade abroad, constitute a novelty. As a result of this, host countries dealing with MNE, have, in fact, to face agencies of a foreign state when dealing with such corporations and not just with huge businesses with headquarters elsewhere.

4.   At this point, I would like to thank Professor Alex Inkeles, who called my attention to the fact that the critical turning point of the developments discussed here may well have been in the American and French revolutions.

# REFERENCES

Abraham, Neville
   1974   Big Business and Government. London: Macmillan.
Apter, David E.
   1974   "The epitaph for the revolutions that failed." *Deadelus*.
Bell, Daniel
   1978   The Cultural Contradictions of Capitalism. New York: Basic Books.
Berle Adolf A., and Gardiner C. Means
   1968   The Modern Corporation and Private Property. New York: Harcourt, Brace & World.
Buckley, Peter J., and Mark Casson
   1976   The Future of the Multinational Enterprise. London: The Macmillan Press.
Burnham, James
   1962   The Managerial Revolution. Harmondsworth, Middlesex: Penguin.
Casson, Mark
   1979   Alternative To The Multinational Enterprise. New York: Holmes & Meier.
Castells, Manuel
   1980   The Economic Crisis And American Society. Princeton, N.J.: Princeton University Press.
Chamberlain, Neil W.
   1977   Remaking American Values. New York: Basic Books.
Chodak, Szymon
   1978   Societal Development. Five Approaches with Conclusions From Comparative Analysis.
          New York: Oxford U.P.
Cohen, Stephen
   1977   Modern Capitalist Planning: The French Model. Cambridge, MA: Harvard U.P.
Coleman, Richard P., and Lee Rainwater with Kent A. McClelland
   1978   Social Standing in America. New Dimensions of Class. New York: Basic Books.
Crozier, Michael
   1970   The Stalled Society. New York: Viking.
Durkheim, Emile
   1979   The Division of Labor in Society. George Simpson (trans.), Clencos. Ill.: The Free Press.
Ellman, Michael
   1971   Soviet Planning Today: Proposals for an Optimally Functioning Economic System.
          Cambridge U.P.

Ellul, Jacques
 1964 The Technological Society. John Wilkinson (trans.), New York: Knopf.
 1978 The Betrayal of the West. Matthew J. O'Connell (trans.), New York: The Seabury Press.
Fedorenko, N. P.
 1968 O Razrabotke systemy optimalnogo funkcionirovanya ekonomiki. Moscow: Gos Izdat.
Fusfeld, Daniel R.
 1972 "The rise of the corporate state in America." *Journal of Economic Issues.* 6(1).
Gerth, H. H., and C. Wright Mills
 1958 From Max Weber: Essays in Sociology. New York: Oxford U.P.
Hardt, John P. et al.
 1967 Mathematics and Computers in Soviet Economic Planning. New Haven, CT: Yale U.P.
Heilbroner, Robert L.
 1974 An Inquiry into the Human Prospect. New York: W. W. Norton.
Hoffmann, Stanley, Chas. P. Kindleberger, Laurence Wylie, and Jessie R. Pitts
 1963 In Search of France. Cambridge, MA: Harvard U.P.
Inglehart, Ronald
 1977 The Silent Revolution. Changing Values and Political Styles Among Western Publics.
  Princeton, NJ: Princeton U.P.
Inkeles, Alex
 1975 "The emerging social structure of the world." World Politics 27 (4).
Johnson, Paul
 1977 Enemies of Society. New York: Atheneum.
Klein, Norman
 1972 "Cultural hegemony and the counter culture." in Dell Hymes (ed.), Reinventing An-
  thropology. New York: Pantgeon.
Kohlmeier, Jr. Louis
 1976 The Regulators. New York: Harper and Row.
Kriesberg, Louis
 1973 The Sociology of Social Conflicts. Englewood Cliffs, NJ: Prentice-Hall.
 1975 "Conceptual issues in analyzing world conflicts." Paper Presented at the A.S.A. Annual
  Meeting.
Lasch, Christopher
 1979 The Culture of Narcissism. American Life in An Age of Diminishing Expectations. New
  York: Warner Books.
Lipset, Seymour Martin and William Schneider
 1979 "The public view of regulation." Public Opinion 2 (1): Jan/Feb.
Manicas, Peter T.
 1974 The Death of the State. New York: Putnam's Sons.
March, A.
 1975 "The silent revolution: Value priorities and the quality of life in Britain." American
  Political Science Review 69(1).
McClelland, David C.
 1961 The Achieving Society. Princeton: D. Van Nostrand.
Meltzer, Allan H., and Scott F. Richard
 1978 "Why government grows (and grows) in a Democracy." The Public Interest (52): Winter.
Miller, Arthur Selvyn
 1976 The Modern Corporate State: Private Governments and the American Constitution. West-
  port, CT: Greenwood Press.
Mills, C. Wright, and Hans Gerth
 1953 Character and Social Structure. New York: Harcourt, Brace & World, Inc.

Nelson, Benjamin
  1968   "Scholastic rationales of 'conscience,' early modern crisis of credibility and the scientific-technological revolutions of the 17th and 20th centuries." Journal for Scientific Study of Religion. (2).
Nutter, G. Warren
  1978   Growth of Government in the West. Washington, DC: American Enterprise Institute.
Revel, Jean-François
  1977   The Totalitarian Temptation. New York: Doubleday & Co.
Riesman, David, Nathan Glazer, and Reuel Denney
  1955   The Lonely Crowd: A Study of the Changing American Character. Garden City, NY: Doubleday.
Rosen, Bernard C., Harry J. Crockett, Jr., and Clyde Z Nunn
  1969   Achievement in American Society. Cambridge, MA: Schenkman.
Rositer, Clinton
  1962   Conservatism in America: The Thankless Persuasion. New York: Knopf.
Sennett, Richard
  1974   The Fall of Public Man. On the Social Psychology of Capitalism. New York: Vintage Books.
Smelser, Neil J.
  1968   Essays in Sociological Explanation. Englewood Cliffs, NJ: Prentice-Hall.
  1972   Soviet Economic Reform: Progress and Problems (No author or editor. Transl. L. Lempert). Moscow: Progress Publ.
Tocqueville, Alexis De
  1972   Democracy in America. New York: Schocken Books.
Weber, Max
  1971   Gesammelte Politische Schriften. J. Winckelmann (ed.), Tubingen:Mohr.
  1978   Economy and Society. 1 and 2, Guenther Roth and Claus Wittich (eds.), Berkeley: University of California Press.
Walters, Kenneth D., and R. Joseph Monsen
  1979   "State-owned business abroad: New competitive threat." Harvard Business Review, March–April.
Wilson, James Q. (ed.)
  1980   The Politics of Regulation. New York: Basic Books.
Yankelovitch, Daniel
  1974   The New Morality. A Profile of American Youth in the '70's. New York: McGraw-Hill.
Znasz li ten kraj? Dokumenty.
  1970   Paris. Instytut Literacki Kultura.

# MILITARY ORIGINS OF THIRD WORLD DICTATORSHIP AND DEMOCRACY

Irving Louis Horowitz

An unusual consensus seems to be forming, from both Left and Right sources, that a swing to fascism is taking place in the Third World. Different scholars locate different sources of such fascism. For someone like Walter Laqueur such an embryonic movement is endemic to the authoritarian rulerships currently extant (Laqueur, 1976, 1980); whereas for others like Noam Chomsky, the source of such fascism is in the dependence of so much of the Third World upon imperialist powers (Chomsky, 1979). The purpose of this chapter is to dispute the assumption itself, whatever its ideological source, and assert that, to the contrary, the motion of these new nations, once their military origins are fully understood, is toward a broad-based democratization along the lines that C. B. Macpherson enunciated: the increase of intraparty party participation; the break-up of social rank and class privilege; and increased mobilization and participation

Research in Social Movements, Conflicts and Change, Vol. 5, pages 295–307.
Copyright © 1983 by JAI Press Inc.
All rights of reproduction in any form reserved.
ISBN: 0-89232-301-9

of the citizenry (Macpherson, 1966). Admittedly, this definitional framework is not perfect, and, indeed, serious questions can be raised about it concerning the distributive concept of democracy. Still, this framework does make possible a discussion of Third World militarism without leaping to the most extreme and mannered conclusions—conclusions that foreclose prematurely and needlessly on the democratic option.

Democracy is an important political issue in the late twentieth century. In part this is so because every other political concept has experienced intellectual exhaustion (or the exhaustion of intellectuals) and in part because the issue of democracy, whatever we mean by the term, has been linked to human-rights concerns in general. Democracy has a compelling force; the drive toward democracy characterizes the entire sweep of the twentieth century. Every major political movement, if it has survived, has evolved toward egalitarianism. Women's movements, racial movements, youth movements, age movements, are all raising questions about egalitarianism. At the same time, questions of liberty have become a central issue. The linchpin of all these issues is not whether these groups are committed to communism, capitalism, or social welfare, but how each addresses the question of egalitarian and libertarian persuasions.

For many years those concerned with social and political development suffered from an artificial reification: assuming that a society had to surrender democracy in order to develop. Developmentalists were bewitched by the Stalinist notion that to have growth a society had to yield personal liberty. The Third World began to rebel against an inherited European ideology that stated that in order to develop, a country must perforce accept the worst dictatorial excesses.

If we labor under the Stalinist notion that development occurs only at the price of democracy, that a society cannot have growth without the sacrifice of large numbers of people to the demons of development, then all is lost. The intellectuals will have lost the battle for the masses on whose behalf they presume to be speaking.

At the outset of the post–colonial epoch, the First World and the Second World were both suspicious of the Third World ideologically as well as functionally; culturally as well as economically. The modernization model—Rostow in economics, Rostow and Hatch, (1972), and Lipset (1968) in sociology, Lerner (1958) in political theory, Schramm (1948, 1964) in Communications—denied the possibility of "thirdness" per se. The assumption was that the automobile or television was the new absolute measuring–rod of our time. Production measured not only by material goods but by the rapidity of cultural transformation, shifts of knowledge, transfer of technology, and speed of transportation and communication became the touchstone of development. Indeed, the modernization argument stated unless the Third World recognized these changes they would never be on the high road to modernization.

The Soviet response to the "thirdness" of the Third World was to proclaim that these newly emerging nations were really on the historical road to socialism.

The USSR supports liberation movements and anti–colonialist movements because they are preconditions to this predetermined outcome. The Soviets attempted to educate Third World people to understand that their national liberation phase was a *rite de passage* toward the growth of a socialist republic. The rather tawdry model became East Europe. These countries presumably trumpeted their transformation from people's democratic movements to socialist societies. The Soviet/East European approach ultimately denied the notion of "thirdness"—if necessary by force of arms.

If the Third World has a uniqueness, an authenticity, a validity unto itself, conceptually and theoretically, then the question becomes: How do the West and the East cope with its special reality? Can the United States move beyond the modernization thesis; can the Soviet Union get beyond the socialization thesis? The assumption that there are only two world views, two world systems, two world powers, and that a country must move from one to the other, has become a dangerous illusion. The United States needs the Third World as an ally and as a recognizable entity, and the Soviet Union and its socialist satellites must also strive to have that world as an ally.

The distinct disadvantage, historically and ideologically, of Western social and political theory is that it must overcome a history of chauvinism, racism, and colonialism. Yet, it is more feasible for the First World to make that assessment than it is for the Second World. This is so because the Second World cannot easily accept the idea of a third way, without the destruction or dismemberment of its fundamental commitment to Marxian theory. The West, by virtue of not having such a solidified theory, by having strategic and policy options that make possible harmonious relationships between the First World and the Third World, can be more flexible as sources of wealth shift. The cataclysmic idea of the "decline of the West" presupposes a zero–sum game that the Third World has increasingly moved away from.

The nature of this interaction between First and Third Worlds, in relation to any given nation or region, is difficult to describe. The role of the United States could become more modest and less bellicose as the impact of Western technology expands and as mixed economies in relatively open societies grow. Development in major Third World countries like Nigeria, Brazil, and China moves along an axis that grants the possibility of democracy and development. Such a pattern of democratization, even if incomplete in form, would spare the Third World an inevitable nightmare of either Hitlerism or Stalinism.

A critical task of the Third World is to show how the military origins of its systems can still yield democratic form. To be sure, this remarkable transition from uninviting military beginnings to as yet elemental democratic forms has become the central Third World task in the final decades of the twentieth century. This combination of process and policy is one that the United States and the West can only reinforce, not determine or deter. The increase of Soviet aggression in portions of the Middle East and Africa is a response to the fact that the

Third World has by now moved beyond either communism or capitalism into a notion of democratic forms and modes that permit development to take place, and at the same time maintain traditional values.

Development without democracy still dominates Third World processes. For example, despite the intonations of Chile's enemies, the reduction of inflation, elimination of worker absenteeism, and sharp rise in industrial output are impressive. There are limits to what the military can do vis–a–vis social classes. Certainly redistribution of power or property has not occurred in Chile; concentration of wealth has occurred. Chile is an example of a type of free–market Stalinism, characterized by political repression, increased fiscal disparities, and reduced consumer spending: the military functions as a surrogate class—a repressive caste rather than a true class.

In Brazil there has been a succession of military rulers since the 1964 revolution. The direction has not been toward democratization, but there has evolved a realization of the finite limits of military rule. All ministerial portfolios except the presidency are now civilian in character. The economic ministry operates under the most stringent, balanced economic norms, present inflationary spiral notwithstanding. Brazilian concerns have shifted from raw growth to income redistribution. Present trends indicate a tremendous shift toward a social welfare emphasis, and toward redistribution of resources. Redistribution certainly is not the same as democracy; but it does presume social equity as a goal.

Argentina has been an extraordinary case since the turn of the century. It is a rare, early example of economic devolution rather than evolution. At the present time Argentina has entered a protracted process in which economic and political processes are being normalized, but not without great difficulties. The problem, however, is one of legitimacy: Argentina's military has denied in practice what it asserts in principle—the need for civilian government in a free market economy. Having achieved such a high degree of control, institutionalized throughout the century, it is reticent about, some might say incapable of, yielding power. The Argentine military, unlike most other militaries, has developed a powerful network of administrative, bureaucratic, and economic substructures. As a result, its capacity to yield power is limited by the wider interests to which it has become beholden. One might ask if this is characteristic of military regimes which inhibit the democratization process. The answer, in part at least, involves an appreciation of Argentine political history, a history that witnesses a swing not simply away from militarism but toward constitutional dictatorship (Panaia and Lesser, 1973). This pendulum–like motion from military to civilian forms of repressive regimes is precisely what may enable Argentina to function as an exception to the general democratization process of the Third World.

Political developments in Peru, a nation similar to Argentina in its military antecedents, have been at considerable variance in democratic outcomes. Its military came to power in the late 1960s through what appeared to be a typical coup led by Juan Velasco Alvarado. This in turn provided the basis for national consolidation, expropriation of key foreign holdings, and administrative rationality. But once the new government got beyond the expropriating of land and its redistribution, the more complex issues of foreign debt, high inflation, and equally high unemployment became tasks more easily performed by civilian regimes. What followed was a transitional military regime led by Francisco Morales Bermudez, who paved the way for a reestablishment of multiple party forms and electoral norms.

The stunning reemergence to power of Fernando Belaunde Terry in 1980 is a reflection of an effort to solve serious internal economic problems and also an expression of long–term political trends, in which the militarization process serves to institutionalize the specifically Third World characteristics of a nation. This process then stamps the country in a fundamentally military way, as indeed the economy stamps the First World and the polity the Second World. It is significant, for example, that the new Peruvian leader expected to have very fruitful relations with the armed forces and was interested in establishing a "broadly based government of national concord." If this is a pattern rather than an aberration, the military origin of many Third World systems, at least present–day systems, does not preclude the formation of democratic regimes; it is an evolutionary process of considerable significance not only for the structure of the Third World but for the tranquility of international relations as a whole.

The transition from dictatorship to democracy in the Third World is mediated by the military, one might even say presided over by them, in great measure because no other social or economic force is prepared to take similar steps. It is hence not so much a matter of "democracy from above" (since the military in a nation like Egypt is quite broad–based) as civilianization through elite mechanisms having broad popular support. Egypt, from Nasser through Sadat, was essentially ruled by military figures (although Sadat in his last years tended to minimize his past participation in the officer corps itself, a significant symbolic act of personal civilianization), who viewed the developmental tasks as essential and central to Egyptian maturity. In short, it was the demand for development, for the massification of the Egyptian revolution, and not simply decision–making from the top down that helps to explain the movement, however haltingly, toward democracy and certainly toward civilization.

While it is difficult to discuss outcomes of those nations newly liberated from colonial conditions, the situation is less problematic with respect to such older nations as Mexico and Turkey. Each has been a prototypical example of the long–term trend toward secularization and civilianization. Just as the twentieth century witnessed a compelling division of labor, so too has it displayed similar sorts of specialization in the political realm. Complex societies display a similar need for managerialism as a bureaucratic style, and this style comes fully equipped with its own forms of rules and regulations—precisely what civilian administrative bodies do better than military leaders. As consensus displaced command in the running of societies such as Mexico and Turkey, the old style military rule, however motivated they might have been by developmental considerations, slowly, often grudgingly, yield to civilian forms of rule and quasi–democratic norms of political relations. This has been the pattern of Peru in Latin America, Nigeria in Africa, and Malaysia in Asia. This transition from military to civilian structures, while by no means uniform in rapidity or even direction, represents an evolutionary process of considerable significance, impacting international relations no less than the internal organization of Third World nation–states.

It might well be that the capacity of a military regime to function as a handmaiden to the democratization process rests on the balance of economic and political forces in a country at the time of independence. The transition from militarization to civilianization is undoubtedly made simpler by the relatively backward state of class forces in conjunction with the concentration of party forces. In that sense, trends in Africa and the Middle East are probably more conducive to this democratization process than they are in places in Latin America, where political independence took place early, although economic dependence continued over long stretches of time. A good example of the African path to democracy is Nigeria, which (after its civil war in the 1960s over Biafran independence and Ibo separatism) has emerged as perhaps the most important country in black Africa, and where a powerful military rule has made possible normalization of the economy. Party processes and elections have become regularized and the fissures and separations of earlier periods are in the process of being healed (Herskovits, 1979/80).

The costs of military rule are for the time being seriously compared with the benefits of civilian rule. This reestimation will not be uniform or smooth. Civilian rule does not necessarily mean democratic decision–making. Civilianization is a political process in which the decision–making apparatus is normalized, and in which a linkage to democratic forces is at least possible. Democratization cuts across many ideological barriers; it includes countries as diverse as China, Nigeria, Korea, and Brazil. The process is necessarily going to be different in each country, involving electoral reform in some countries and mass uprisings in others. It is a phenomenon that allows us to characterize the Third World as a structural entity with a unique identity. The Third World does not exist in hothouse isolation from other areas; but it does nonetheless have its own agenda as well as its own evolution. Both the First and Second World approaches are characterized by a tension between the ideology of modernization on the one hand and ideology of forced industrialization on the other. These approaches assume a teleology, a sense of purpose, alien to the evolutionary processes as such. The Third World is a third structure. The term ''non–alignment'' conveys a false impression of a Third World located somewhere in limbo, but this is inexact. The Third World is not on a road to anything; it *is* a road. Therefore, the relationships between the three worlds, their quite real contradictions, stem from their relative autonomy. These connections are as important as the relationship of nations to each other.

It is a curious truth that, although many early revolutionary stages in Third World liberation were organized by military personnel, they took quite for granted the fact that in subsequent stages civilian authority, or at least a broader base of political power, would prevail. The penetration of Western technical and intellectual innovations into the systems of work and thought of the armed forces had the effect of broadening their scope and vision. Hence, Kemal Ataturk could speak of the military as "guardians of Turkey's ideals" and not simply a praetorian guard (Karpat, 1959; Ahmad, 1969). Likewise, Gamal Abdel Nasser, in speaking of the Egyptian Revolution of 1952, saw the military intervention as a mechanism by which the people of Egypt would "think of governing themselves and having the final word on their destiny" (Nasser, 1955; Rejwan, 1974). The movement toward civilianization, if not necessarily democratization, in both of these pivotal countries is indicative of how seriously the military took as their mission the transformation of the national culture and not just the passing of political authority.

The armed forces, performing as they often do as representatives of the national interest as a whole, have a unique advantage over interest groupings: they are not compelled to perform as representatives of Left, Right, or Center. As such, they are not perceived as part of factional disputes. In those cases where the military itself is aligned with well–articulated trends in the political process, such lofty remoteness is not possible; but in such situations its historic role in the Third World as arbiter of the political and bureaucratic forces within each nation is either obviated or superfluous. The precise tactics to be employed become a source of military frustration. Moshe Lissak, in summarizing the situation in Burma, indicated that military failure stemmed from the over-politicization of the society at large, whereas in Thailand tendencies to fail in its nationalizing mission stemmed from a strictly non–political model of power (Lissak, 1976). Negotiating the orders of power is thus the main task of a Third World military. The problem is that even in those instances, as in the Middle East, where the military is recognized as a focus of solidarity of the embodiment of sacred symbols of society, its high status does not necessarily carry over into the political capacity to negotiate, bargain, broker, or appease a wide array of social issues, that is, problems of racial and ethnic differentiation, or class and economic advantages (Be'eri, 1970). These notorious historical weaknesses are at least as important in propelling civilianizing trends in the Third World as the more abstract, and vague, ideological dispositions spoken of earlier.

The bourgeoisie in Third World countries realize that the military possesses a certain fear of multinationalism. Although marginal segments of the national bourgeoisie are linked with the Left, key sectors of national bourgeoisie power have been internationalized. Economic determinism, however, leads us to a blind spot. That an economic class has a relationship with a military regime does not signify the economy is the base and the military is the superstructure. Throughout the sophisticated sectors of the Third World the military informed the middle classes of their responsibilities if they expected to continue to have rights. Paying taxes, investing nationally, and sharing equitably created a new sociopolitical reality, a result of military guidance through uncharted political waters.

This emergence of a bureaucratic–authoritarian state does not discount the economic factor in Third World development, but asserts that this state rests upon an uneasy equilibrium between military and political economic forces. It would be a dangerous falsification to think that the Brazilian military coup of 1964 was made in the name of class restoration. The bourgeoisie in Brazil under the military lost that possibility; the popular classes never had the capacity to achieve such an end. Social classes, above and below, make arrangements with the military in order to survive as a class, not to seize power. The ratio of power between the military and the economy is different in the Third World from that in mature industrialized societies. This ratio gives character and body to the Third World in contrast with the American or European model of economic base and political superstructure. In the Third World the military has an autonomous role. Its power is linked directly to science and industry on the technical side and to the swollen federal bureaucracy on the civilian side.

The military origins of the Third World do not determine the limits of its democratic prospects. This should come as no surprise; the aristocratic origin of the federalists did not decide or determine the limits of American democracy. The military origins of Brazilian, Nigerian, or Egyptian revolutions no more define the limits of these nations' polity than did the military origins of the Mexican, Cuban, or Chinese revolutions in an earlier age. Militarism only defines a necessary phase that allows for ensuing struggles between democratization and authoritarianism within the Third World. To deny the realities of military power is to dismiss the fact that the Third World has its own integrity—one that cannot be reduced to a West European nineteenth–century model.

Wright Mills' belief that there are three large–scale factors that have primary importance—the political, the economic, and the military—and that these cannot a priori be reduced to each other, is a central element in any serious theory of international stratification (Mills, 1963). The location of these factors determines the mix. What does this Millsian paradigm look like if we take an international view of political, economic, and military factors, and try to look at the history of the First World, the Second World, and the Third World in terms of the way in which political, economic, and military factors assert their priority at different times?

The First World is characterized by an economic system called capitalism, which came into being long before its political forms took shape in the nineteenth century. The structure of mass politics emerged in modern England in terms of the Reform Acts of 1832 and 1867. These measures gave political shape to the economic system of capitalism by extending the franchise. But the capitalist economy had evolved and was institutionalized between 164- and 1688. Even the French Revolution assumed a democratic political form at the end of the eighteenth century, although the breakup of the landed gentry in France took place in the early years of that century. The Russian Revolution—the socialist revolution—reversed this causal process. The Soviet Union announced a new economy with a political upheaval. The political vanguard party came into being prior to the economic system called socialism. There was no long precedent to the foundation of the communist bloc. The consolidation of the communist system was a precondition to initiating plans to reach socialist objectives and goals.

The causal relationship between the economy and the polity was largely reversed in the Second World. The Third World transformed the relationship in a different way. Theories have been constructed that abandon the class model itself. In Cuba the theory was called the *foco;* change was said to be based on a focus, or locus of power, on centrality of power in groups—groups that presume all kinds of networks that have little to do with a mass or class base. The Chinese Revolution was likewise a model military revolution. In Cuba and China the military was drawn from new strata, unlike the old military of Argentina and Brazil. But new militaries acted like old militaries after they assumed power. A third model, the Nigerian civil war between rival military camps, was resolved by one military faction's victory over another military faction. We should recognize the unique role that the military has played in the Third World and that this factor defines the character of state power there. The relationship of political, economic, and military formations defines the character of state power. We cannot determine a priori whether economic power is more important than political or military power. We can, however, chart the expansion of the last at the expense of the former two.

The epoch when the Third World military is propped up by external forces has passed, in fact, if not in theory. The military, when it is propped up, is propped up internally by segments of older classes fearing disenfranchisement from multinationals. Even small powers resist United States encroachments. United States denial of military aid because of the repressive, dictatorial, reactionary nature of select Third World regimes has been met with stiff, usually effective, resistance. Private sector support is usually adequate to purchase military hardware on the increasingly active world arms market.

The critical factor is not the source of aid but the character of the military as a class. What are its strengths? What are its weaknesses? From whence does it derive its power? These are extremely complex questions. At one level the military caste is organically rooted to the portion of the industrial–technological complex that creates the means of destruction. The military class is unique in its relationship to the technological structure. The technological order is the command sector that tells the scientific order how to proceed. The relationship of the military to the technological order is the decisive pivot at the level of advanced weaponry. At the level of social formation and social forces, the military derives from a plurality of classes. The specific character of the military sector as such is shaped by World War III industries. The military is in these businesses; but here we should avoid excessive reductionism. While it is true that the military is linked to business, these are oftentimes failing businesses like Lockheed and Chrysler. That is to say, military systems are characterized not necessarily by their entrepreneurial skills but often by their indifference to entrepreneurial preparedness. NASA has a budget of $6 billion annually, in part because private enterprise has failed to cope with the advanced level of investment such space technology requires. Military classes function best when the state monopolizes industrial infrastructures. Otto Nathan (1944), and John Kenneth Galbraith (1967) have each offered a prototype of how the modern business economy is determined by the political process. The military is not necessarily interested in profitability—or even in entrepreneurship. The weaknesses of those particular kinds of military–oriented and technology–oriented "businesses" should not be overlooked. On the other hand, military regimes have the capacity to rationalize national economies in ways not easily open to democratic–civilian governments.

The class composition of this military caste does not cut a wide swathe, or have a deep base. Because it is an elite, because it has a narrow base, it cannot sustain legitimacy and is devoid of a system of legitimacy. The imposition of force necessitates the rotation of power, thus creating illegitimacy. The transition to legitimate regimes in the Third World can be institutionalized only by broad masses and broad participation, either by mass action or voter participation. Because the military's base is narrow, it often accepts limits to its own authority, and assumes a need to share in the conduct of power and the transformation of industry.

The relative strength of the military vis–a–vis the political or economic sectors of society is an empirical question, not a matter of including the military as part of the social formation. One cannot legislate a priori what variables are decisive. The military has the guns; social formations do not. With the exception of the police, which is a unique armed segment within the Third World, the military has a monopoly on weaponry, and hence a monopoly on state power. This is not always true to the same extent; what might be true in Guyana may not be true in its next–door neighbor, Venezuela. But we cannot simply say that any given variable is fundamental, and any other is derivative. The alpha and omega of any serious analysis of the democratic process is that the form of democracy does not have to be based on the Westminster model. The civil origins of a society no more contribute to militarism (that is, fascist systems) than the military origins of a society condemn such a society to dictatorship (that is, African one–party systems).

There is a rationality to the world military that is similar to the rationality of world economy that some speak about. One need not deny the world historic character of economies, or the world historic character of the polity, in order to assert the world historic character of the military. It is a mistake to think that because social systems differ, as in, say, Cuba or Paraguay, when they have the red bandana flying it necessarily means different things. We do not know how different the Communist Party is from the Colorado Party. That is an empirical question. The differences are no more sharply etched than the similiarities. As long as that is true we must look at the military as a unitary phenomenon acting for itself, not simply as a national phenomenon, or a transitional phenomenon, acting on behalf of others. It is dangerous to think in terms of heroic types, or models that dissolve at the point of discovery. We have to look beyond abstract models, to the flag, to the uniform, to the insignia, to the meaning of these symbols. Only by doing so can a sense of the military presence in Third World affairs be understood as the central dynamic it has become.

Although the military is important to the First World and the Second World, it is the bourgeoisie—the middle class—that defines the First World, and the political sector—the Communist Party, the apparatus and the bureaucracy—that defines the Second World. The role of the military has increased in both of those worlds, especially in sophisticated technological hardware. It might very well be that military determinism will not occur in older societies; but the role of the armed forces has certainly increased. What is unique about the Third World military is not merely the hardware component but the social origins of the military and how these regimes come into existence. Historically, the difference is in the character of the social system, defined and determined by the state. The military classes are crucial to the Third World as the economic classes are to the First World and the political classes to the Second World. However, the class origins or composition of the military condition do not uniquely determine the democratic prospects of developing areas.

Juan Linz (1973) expresses the larger political context in which military regimes operate. After pointing out that politics is a question not simply of policies and administration but of appealing to politically interested segments of a society, Linz notes that "large segments of society, still believe, rightly or wrongly, in the desirability of an open, competitive, democratic political system or in the desirability of an ideologically driven, possibly totalitarian society whose elites provide some sense of historical mission to the nation, and thereby satisfy some of the more politically involved citizens." In this setting an authoritarian regime has serious weaknesses. Ultimately, all authoritarian regimes face this legitimacy pull toward the polyarchical model, with political freedom for relatively full participation, or toward the committed, ideological single–party model. The lesson is clear: while one cannot predetermine dictatorial or democratic outcomes, neither should one prejudge the possibility of outcomes simply on the basis of the military origins of many Third World revolutions.[1]

# NOTE

1. This essay carries forward arguments initially presented in *Three Worlds of Development: The Theory and Practice of International Stratification.* (New York and London: Oxford University Press, 1972, second, revised edition). The chapter therein on "The Organization and Ideology of

Militarism,'' pp. 341–376, reviews the "classical" literature on the subject of Militarism, Dictatorship and Democracy, and hence I felt it to be red-ndant to recite that literature for yet another time. I mention this because the efforts of such scholars as Morris Janowitz, Samuel P. Huntington, John J. Johnson, Edwin Lieuwen, Lucien Pye—among others—deserve the most careful reconsideration in the light of the thesis herein offered in my paper.

# REFERENCES

Ahmad, Feroz
  1969   The Young Turks. London: Oxford University Press.
Be'eri, Eliezar
  1970   Army Officers in Arab Politics and Society. New York: Praeger/Holt, Rinehart & Winston: 351–59.
Chomsky, Noam
  1979   The Washington Connection and Third World Fascism: The Political Economy of Human Rights. Boston: South End Press.
Galbraith, John Kenneth
  1967   The New Industrial State. Boston: Houghton Mifflin, 304–23.
Herskovits, Jean
  1980   Democracy in Nigeria. Foreign Affairs 58, 2 (Winter): 314–35.
Karpat, Kemal
  1959   Turkey's Politics: The Transition to a Multi-Party System. Princeton: Princeton University Press.
Laqueur, Walter
  1976   "Fascism: The second coming." Commentary 61, 2 (February: 61–62.
  1980   The Political Psychology of Appeasement. New Brunswick, NJ: Transaction Books, 189–210.
Lerner, Daniel
  1958   The Passing of Traditional Society: Modernizing the Middle East. Glencoe, Ill.: The Free Press.
Linz, Juan J.
  1973   "The future of an authoritarian situation or the institutionalization of an authoritarian regime: The case of Brazil." In Alfred Stepan (ed.), Authoritarian Brazil: New Haven: Yale University Press, 251.
Lipset, Seymour Martin
  1968   Revolution and Counterrevolution: Change and Persistence in Social Structures. New York: Basic Books.
Lissak, Moshe
  1976   Military Roles in Modernization. Beverly Hills and London: Sage Publications, 247–48.
Macpherson, C. B.
  1966   The Real World of Democracy. London: Oxford University Press, 24–34.
Mills, C. Wright
  1963   Power, Politics and People. Irving Louis Horowitz (ed.), New York: Oxford University Press, 23–38, 110–39, 305–23.
Nasser, Gamal Abdel
  1955   Egypt's Liberation: Philosophy of the Revolution. Washington, D.C.: Public Affairs Press, 24–40.
Nathan, Otto
  1944   The Nazi Economic System: Germany's Mobilization for War. Durham NC: Duke University Press, 365–77.

Panaia, Marta and Ricardo Lesser
  1973  "Las estrategias militares frente al proceso de industrializacion (1942–1947)." Estudios Sobre Los Origenes Del Peronismo /2. Buenos Aires: Siglo XXI Argentina Editores, 83–164.
Rejwan, Nissim
  1974  Nasserist Ideology: Its Exponents and Critics. New York: John Wiley & Sons, and New Brunswick, N.J.: Transaction Books.
Rostow, W. W. and Richard W. Hatch
  1955  An American Policy in Asia. Cambridge, MA: MIT Press, and New York: Wiley.
  1972  The Diffusion of Power: An Essay in Recent History. New York: Macmillan.
Schramm, Wilber L.
  1948  Communication in Modern Society. Urbana: University of Illinois Press.
  1964  Mass Media and National Development: The Role of Information in the Developing Countries. Stanford: Standford University Press.

# AUTHOR INDEX

# SUBJECT INDEX

Indices prepared by Cheryl L. Carpenter